MW01293869

Flying the Hump to China— The Early Days

The humble beginning of the first airlift

Flying the Hump to China— The Early Days

The humble beginning of the first airlift

Memoirs of a WWII Pilot in the China-Burma India Theater

Starting the Airlift to China

The Early Days — 1942-43

By James Paul Segel

Former Major, United States Army Air Corps

Copyright © 2017 J.P. Segel
Reg. Writers Guild #81370
James P. Segel
All rights reserved. No part of this book may be used or reproduced by any means, graphic, electronic or mechanical, including photocopying, recording, taping or by any information storage retrieval systems without the written permission of the author, except in the case of brief quotations embodied in critical articles or reviews.

Richard Segel
462 Blue Lake Trail
Lafayette, CO 80026
rmsnewtown@comcast.net

Available from Amazon.com and other retail outlets

My story is dedicated to over 1600
air crew who were lost on the
"Aluminum Trail", and who will
never be able to tell their own stories.

"If China goes under, how many divisions of Japanese troops will be freed
to take India, which is as ripe as a plumb for the picking — and move
straight into the Middle East in a giant pincer movement." (1942)

—President Franklin Delano Roosevelt

"I gather that the air ferry route to China is seriously in danger.
The only way we can get certain supplies into China is by air
... I want you to explore every possibility, both as to airplanes
and routes. It is essential that our route be kept open, no matter
how difficult." (Memo to General Arnold, May 6, 1942)

—President Franklin Delano Roosevelt

"Never in the field of human conflict was so much
owed by so many to so few." (1940)

—Winston Churchill

"The China Air Task Force had to fight, scream, and scrape for
every man, plane, spark plug, and gallon of gas. The CATF
... was facing death from acute starvation." (1943)

—General Claire L. Chennault

"Stories of the past tell us where we are heading."

—Anonymous

i

PREFACE

Night descends on our westward bound flight. From sixteen thousand feet I see the deep gorges of the Himalayas turn from green to jet black as the sun drops below the mountain peaks. The last gleam of sunlight leaves us, and suddenly we are flying in a black void. We are as detached from all human contact as though we are on another planet.

Only the low growl of our engines reminds us that we are earthbound creatures as we drum our lonely way in darkness. Then light comes from the east as the moon rises and lights up the snow-topped ridges. It is a rare cloudless night, and we are suspended in an ocean of sky with stars making countless pinpoints of light around us.

We cannot allow our thoughts to stray, for our airplane requires constant vigilance, and we listen to every sound. I depend on a small needle suspended in our compass to guide us to a destination somewhere ahead. We must find a poorly lighted field that is shrouded in darkness before we can make a safe landing.

* * * * * *

Sitting in the cockpit of the C-47 was like a homecoming to me. I reached for the well-worn knobs on the control pedestal - first the white propeller controls, then the throttles, then I checked the mixture settings. I studied the instrument panel, the artificial horizon, noted the flight instruments for compass heading and altitude, then switched my attention to the engines, setting power at 2100 RPM and 27 inches manifold pressure. I listened to the throb of the twin Pratt & Whitney R-1830's, as I adjusted RPM's to synchronize the props.

But it was just in my imagination that I felt the vibration and the feel of the wheel, for I was sitting on the ground in a retired United Airlines DC-3 at the Air Museum at the Santa Monica, California, airport. This airport is the former home of the great Douglas Aircraft Company where this airplane had been born, rolled out of its hangar into the light of day, and finally taken flight over half a century ago.

It may be true for some that "you can't go home again," but in that left cockpit seat I was turning back the pages of the calendar, and recalling the time of my youth. Once again I was at the controls of one of these wonderful flying machines that had taken me to the other side of the world, through many adventures, and safely back home.

As the years peeled away, I was a 22-year old pilot, winging my way across vast expanses of mountains, jungles, oceans, and deserts. I was a second lieutenant, wearing wings of the Army Air Corps, heading for a lifetime of experiences condensed into a few short years. In this assignment I would find high adventure in China and India, meet national leaders, some heroes, and some people of very questionable motives. I would witness the saving of a great nation, and other events in Asia that affected the outcome of World War II and today's world.

There were times when I feared for my life, expecting death at any moment, and worried about the safety of people in my charge. Other times I found humor and pride and loneliness, and a whole gamut of other emotions that every young warrior finds when he is thrust into the turmoil of war.

I would drastically change, from a carefree young man whose main interest in life was flying airplanes, into a qualified military officer, shouldering responsibilities far beyond my years.

The DC-3 airplane was my magic carpet, taking me back to that other time. Join me on this eventful trip.

The Flight of No Return
by Sunny Young

A streak of silver in the sky... the engines roar... propellers try...
To lift the giant screaming plane... above the mountains drenched with rain..
Black ominous clouds and gale winds blow... amid the ice and swirling snow..
As plane and crew, with every breath... tries to win a fight with death...
To climb above the snow capped peak... a place not far for the very weak...
The plane is in a mighty grip... the crew can hear the metal rip...
As suction lifts them like a kite... above the peaks into the night...
Then, just as quickly dropped like snow... into the jutting rocks below...
Time has run out for plotted goals... a cry aloud, "God save our souls"!...
A crash like thunder, a flash of light... then silence in the blackened night...
Crumpled engines, wings and tail... help pave the "Hump's" Aluminum Trail...
A dog tag here... a jacket there, a picture worn by love and care...
A parachute unopened lay... no time to jump, no time to pray...
In this far, forgotten place, of jungles, mountains, rocks and space...
The wreckage lay like broken toys... discarded by mischievous boys...
And boys they were of tender years... and families weep in silent tears...
To know the sacrifice they made... the part their gift for freedom played...
Lieutenants, Captains, Sergeants too... Privates, maintenance, or crew...
Whatever rank, whatever job... they did their best with each heart throb...
Some gave their lives to save a friend... a brother to the very end...
They gave their lives, so we might live... what more can any person give.

From the book, "The Aluminum Trail" by Chic Marrs Quinn

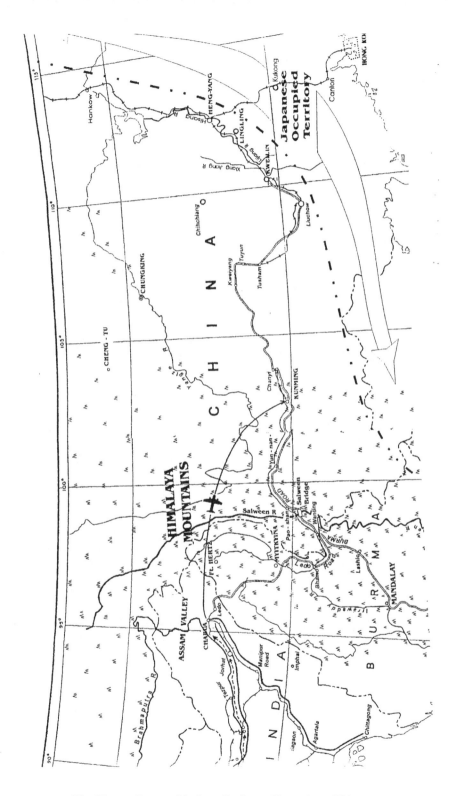

The Hump Route: Chabua, India to Kunming, China

CONTENTS

THEMES

For some time I have been urging family members and friends to write their personal histories. Many, like myself, have expressed regret that their forebears did not recount their early days, their migration to this country, and their new lives here. Their histories would be fascinating to read, and their absence makes us realize how our stories will be prized by our future generations.

I was inspired to write mine when a friend passed away, without leaving a record of his early days. He was a member of the famed Lincoln Brigade that fought against Franco in the 1936 Spanish Civil War, and had some marvelous stories to tell. I realized how every man's life story deserves recording, and how wartime events are especially meaningful, and keenly read. So I started to write.

* * * * * *

Every day since time began, somewhere in the world, men have been fighting a war. My original theme was to describe how young men, caught in the crucible of war, mature rapidly under pressure. My World War II experiences as a pilot flying for General Chennault in China and on the Hump airlift in the China-Burma-India Theater quickly changed me from a carefree, fun-loving young man. I grew up in a hurry when I faced terrifying experiences, watched comrades die, and faced death myself Like other young men, I had felt that I was indestructible, and that bad things were what happened to other people. But after facing many hazards I found that I was not a superman. Harrowing events turned my hair gray and I felt lucky to survive.

Taking command of an airplane, facing emergencies for which I was poorly prepared, and assuming the responsibility for survival of cargo, crew, and passengers, matured me beyond my years. Time has not dimmed my memory, and after all these years I still recall frightening events, and lost friends.

A second theme for my book emerged from my research. I learned of situations facing our commanders that were not evident to us on the front line. Our generals wrote personal memoirs that revealed that great dissension existed among them. These were professional soldiers, trained to the highest standards, and they held the power of life or death over us, but their personal animosities against each other may have severely interfered with their performance.

I developed ambivalent feelings about our leaders. On the one hand I greatly admired their knowledge and skills, which qualified them to lead our armed forces. On the other hand, I was disillusioned to learn that they were not the perfect officers that we assumed them to be.

A third theme explores the almost unthinkable, as it questions whether providing aid to China may have been an error in judgment. Generalissimo Chiang Kai-shek proved to be a despotic tyrant, whose principal goals were to retain total control over his tottering empire and accumulate wealth. He was more intent on outwitting his Chinese Communist opposition than defeating the Japanese enemy, and cared little about the welfare of his people or of the Allied troops sent to support him. He persuaded our leaders to aid his country, at a cost of many of our men. He was guilty of fraud and deceit yet he blatantly accused the United States of failing to meet our obligations to him. What did we ultimately accomplish in supporting him?

A fourth theme appeared when I researched the Burma campaign. The decision to push the Japanese out of that country resulted in the longest single campaign of the war, lasting almost four years. It was a vicious and terrifying event, with many fighting men losing their lives in horrifying ways. History shows that nothing important was gained by the Allies' hard-won victory, and that freeing Burma was a pointless military exercise, a deplorable waste.

This is the history of my war, but I did not imagine these themes when I first started to write. I simply wanted to tell of my life, about my eagerness to enroll as a cadet in the Army Air Corps, and about my willingness to volunteer for other duties in spite of that old military maxim to "Keep your mouth shut, and don't volunteer for anything." My study of the war in the China-Burma-India Theater is fascinating and will never end, as it reveals to me as much about the nature of man as it does about battles.

Section I

THE MISSION

♫ *"Off We Go, Into the Wide Blue Yonder..."* ♫

Chapter 1
ADVENTURE - LOW LEVEL

The first radio call from Lingling tower was, "Bandit over you at high altitude, very high." The next message, less than a minute later, was very different, and it got my adrenaline flowing. "Bandit now over you at low altitude flying southwest. Better return to Hengyang base." This was bad news. It meant that an enemy fighter had spotted me and was intent on scoring on a C-47 cargo plane, and I was the intended victim.

It was a beautiful July flying day, near Lingling in central China, not a cloud in the sky, with light winds and smooth air, and at 1500 feet altitude my twin Pratt and Whitney engines were running sweetly, sounding like music in my ears. That cloudless sky was not the best flying condition for us, for we were within 200 miles of Japanese forward bases, and a cloud could be a convenient place to hide if enemy fighters showed up.

I was flying our C-47, named "Ferdinand," on a cargo run from Kunming to the main eastern base at Kweilin, with stops at Hengyang and Lingling. These were the forward bases of the Flying Tigers, now being taken over by the China Air Task Force (CATF), a new Army Air Corps operation. "Ferdinand" was the only airplane carrying vital supplies from the Hump terminal at Kunming to these fighter bases and we called our operation the "China Express!" Our cargo included aviation gas, .50 caliber ammunition, and airplane parts, all essential to operating the P-40's that were maintaining mastery of the China skies. We also had mail and groceries, important morale and health boosters for men in need of adequate food and word from home. Our C-47 was unarmed, but the efficient aircraft warning net established by the Chinese under direction of General Chennault, gave us up-to-the-minute information on every airplane aloft in the area. We always had ample warning of any intruders, so there were no surprise visits.

I called Lingling radio. "China Express northeast of Lingling, ETA ten minutes."

"Roger, Express," was the reply from the low-power radio, which had recently been scavenged from a wrecked P-40, and placed in a camouflaged mud hut next to the runway. "Hope you got mail and beer on board." Lingling was a small, makeshift base, with a short runway, manned by a lonely group of hard working fighters whose only outside contact was our China Express.

I was about to give him the good news that I had mail bags and some clinking bottles on board, but I was interrupted by another call from Lingling. This time there was some concern in his voice as he reported, "Bandit over you at high altitude, very high," a report that got my sudden interest. This was normally no great threat even though my C-47 was much slower than any enemy airplane. The Japanese often sent lone airplanes on high altitude reconnaissance flights over our bases. They would fly at 20,000 feet, keeping them safe from interception, for by the time one of our P-40's climbed that high, the intruders would be long gone.

The next message, less than a minute later, was very different, and it got my adrenaline flowing. "Bandit is now over you at low altitude, flying southwest. Better return to Hengyang base." This meant that I had an enemy fighter keeping close company, for I was also heading southwest. He probably spotted me from his high position, and hoped to score a kill on a cargo plane. He was a daring pilot, coming this low close to one of our own fighter bases but I wasn't about to award him a medal for bravery. With chills down my back, I decided to make a dash for Lingling, which was much closer than Hengyang. I poured on power and shoved the wheel forward, heading for the treetops, hoping my camouflage paint would make me less visible to this lone ranger.

I was so close to Lingling that I could have seen the runway if I hadn't been down so low, dodging trees and hills in my attempt to escape. I yelled at my copilot, "Do you see the son-of-a-bitch?" I got a badly frightened look in return. Then I yelled into the mike without ceremony, "Get somebody up here to get this guy off my ass, if you want your mail and beer!"

This was my first trip as first pilot on "Ferdinand," and the ancient Chinese toast that says, "May you live in exciting times" was coming true for me. I had flown as copilot for three months with former airline pilot Curt Caton, bringing our C-47 from Florida to India, and now into the China area. The night before this Express trip, Curt suffered a devastating malaria attack that totally disabled him at our hostel in Kunming. He told Kunming Operations that he was turning the airplane over to me, advising them, "Jim knows the way better than I do." They assigned a copilot to me, a Lieutenant Biggins, one of the idle P-40 pilots who were sitting around with no airplanes to fly, and who was desperate to put in some flying time. He had never been in a multi-engine airplane, and told me later that he expected a dull cargo trip, but he was very surprised to find more excitement than he wanted. Biggins, crew chief Saylor, and I had climbed aboard at 7:00 A.M., crawling over the mountain of cargo to reach the cockpit, and took off for Kweilin, planning stops at Hengyang and Lingling, and feeling like Santa on his sleigh loaded with gifts.

Back to my first meeting with the enemy. By now, I was down so low I was almost scraping the leaves off the trees, zigging and zagging, egged on by the fear of a fighter on our tail with a 20 millimeter cannon and machine guns ready to blow us out of the skies. Just how close is that eager beaver, who is trying to get a medal today? Sweat was pouring off me, and Biggins was cussing his bad luck to be in an unarmed transport instead of a P-40 on his virgin encounter with the enemy. I stayed as low as I dared go, continually swerving, at one time almost digging a wing tip into the ground when I thought I heard the rattle of bullets in the cabin. I hoped the noise was just some loose cargo shifting around, until Saylor ran up to the cockpit, and yelled, "They're shooting at us!" I expected to hear the shattering sound of bullets punching holes in the front end of Ferdinand, and, more important, in myself and my crew members, if I didn't use violent evasive action. I zigged more wildly than before, and picked up the mike again, yelling, "Where is everybody?" I was desperate for some word.

There was a short delay, and suddenly a voice boomed in my headset, saying, "It's OK, Jim, you can come up now. He's gone home. " And just ahead of us at about 500 feet was a P-40 circling lazily around. It was Bob Neale, squadron commander, giving me top cover. What a beautiful sight! I fell in love with that ugly grinning shark's mouth, and never forgot it.

That evening, Bob told me that the Japanese pilot was right on my tail, but scared off by the time Bob reached me. I never did see the intruder, who probably realized he was at great risk this close to our fighters at Lingling, and left in a hurry to avoid Bob's threat. I thanked Bob for the rescue, and he laughed and said in his slow, droll way. "Heck, we sure wanted that mail and that beer." Bob was a relaxed kind of guy, formerly a Flying Tiger squadron commander, and newly commissioned major in the Air Corps, and seemed to think today's chase was just a normal event. Not so for me.

That evening we had several things to celebrate. This was July 3, 1942, and the next day was Independence Day, and the final day of the American Volunteer Group as an official organization. Bob Neale was celebrating his 18th victory, and I was happy to celebrate my expert dodging that I claimed had saved us from disaster. That was something to celebrate, as we counted about 15 bullet holes in the tail, but none vital. I proposed that we mount machine guns to fire out of our cabin windows, but the suggestion got turned down. Bob and his fighter pilots laughed and said, "Leave the fighting to us," a job they did very well.

Chapter 2
THE MISSION

In wartime, a soldier has little control over his life. A whirlpool of major events taking place in China, on the other side of the world, in early 1942, moved me about like a pawn in a chess game.

As a second-lieutenant pilot in the Ferry Command, I was assigned in April of 1942, to the project labeled the American Military Mission to China (AMMISCA). The project was being formed at Morrison Field, West Palm Beach, Florida, with India as its destination.

I arrived at Morrison in April, flying a utility airplane I was delivering to the base commander. I found the field a whirlwind of activity with confusion everywhere. New men arrived daily, some of them looking uncomfortable in starchy new uniforms. They wandered haphazardly around the air base on foot or on bicycles, or in vehicles if they had rank, looking for their assigned units. Construction crews littered the field with stacks of building materials as new buildings sprang up, creating a big air base out of barren land. Aircraft of all types were parked at random in every open spot.

Morrison was the jumping-off point for aircraft heading south across the Caribbean to Brazil where they would make final preparations for crossing the Atlantic. The city of Natal, in Brazil, is the most eastern point of land in South America, and was the springboard for the long over-water stretch to Africa. Each day, airplanes departed for mysterious destinations in Africa, Asia, and other points, to fight in a war that was erupting like a volcano, spewing men and materiel in all directions.

In a remote corner of the huge field sat a group of 15 Douglas C-47 cargo planes, looking like they wished to stay unnoticed in the hurly-burly of activity. Heavy bombers were the aircraft that attracted attention to as they trundled by with heavy machine guns pointing skyward, while our cargo fleet remained almost unnoticed.

The C-47's were the first group of aircraft of the AMMISCA project, a semi-secret group destined to fly 12,000 miles to the furthest point in India, the Assam Valley. There, against the towering Himalaya Mountains, they would establish a vitally needed airlift that would fly cargo from India to the besieged nation of China.

My orders assigning me to the AMMISCA group deliberately omitted the destination, as military security kept this a secret until just before departure. All aircraft preparing to leave the States maintained close security for fear that sabotage or other interference might jeopardize their safety or disclose major movements.

The military C-47 was not very impressive to the casual onlooker. Its dull camouflage paint hid the shiny airliner that its civilian sister DC-3 had made into the glamorous queen of the air, flown by every major airline in the world. But to us, the sleek lines of a well-proportioned airplane and the knowledge that we were flying the finest Douglas airplane ever built made us proud of our birds. There was much going on here, as crew members scurried about on various errands, each man with checklists of things to do. Crews met with other crews alongside their aircraft and compared notes, each contributing information on where to find some missing item in the great confusion of a fast growing air base

We were now at war, and everyone had many questions. We assumed that "someone up there knows what he's doing," because we certainly didn't. But we were young and full of vim and vitality, and looked forward to the mission. We had no fears for the future, as we felt invincible. "Bad things are what happen to the other guy."

This was the start of a great journey for a 22-year old second lieutenant who boasted 400 hours of flying time and was ready for any adventure. Fortunately, I flew as copilot for a highly experienced former airline captain, Curt Caton, a pilot far wiser than I, whose skill and good judgment kept us going when things got dangerous. To Curt I give my most sincere thanks, for from him I learned piloting skills that kept me alive throughout my Army Air Force tour of duty. We traveled to far-off places that were all new names to us, and met people who were as strange to us as men from another planet. We faced risky and exciting situations that I will recount in the following pages.

* * * * * *

It is very important to relate the history behind the project, as every event and every decision by a national leader had a direct effect on me and my crews. It might mean whether we lived or died.

There was great fear in the White House in 1941 that China was lost. The Japanese had advanced into the coastal cities, and were battering the defenseless Chinese on the ground and in the air. The only opposition was a rag-tag Chinese

Air Force made up of obsolete aircraft, some dating back nearly to World War I, flown by poorly trained pilots.

President Roosevelt and Winston Churchill gave the war in Europe top priority, with the war against Japan in the Pacific next on the list. Last in importance was the effort to aid China, and the president's top commanders advised him that China had so little military value that supporting it was a waste of precious resources needed elsewhere.

Roosevelt disagreed with this. He reasoned that an active Chinese army could keep Japanese forces of over a million men and a large air force very busy. If China were to collapse, this large army would be turned loose to invade Australia, India, and other areas. Australians confessed to having nightmares of large Japanese fleets just over the horizon ready to pounce on them, just as residents of California lived in fear of an enemy invasion. Burma was already under attack, and it was likely that India was next.

Chiang Kai-shek, the premier of China, pleaded for aid, and President Roosevelt responded in mid-1941 with a Lend-Lease program that provided 100 Curtiss-Wright P-40 fighters for the Chinese Air Force under command of General Claire Lee Chennault. FDR authorized release of U.S. military pilots from the services to fly these aircraft when they volunteered to join the American Volunteer Group (AVG), which later became known as the "Flying Tigers. " The entire operation was wrapped in secrecy as we were not at war with Japan, and the President did not wish to aggravate our relationship with that country. This secrecy was difficult to maintain, and the Japanese were aware that we were supporting China with aircraft. They did not consider this very threatening as they were already in possession of the important areas of the Chinese mainland. The spectacular success of the AVG was a great surprise to the Japanese. The AVG story will be told in detail.

When Pearl Harbor thrust us into war against Japan, Roosevelt made further moves to support Chiang. He established the AMMISCA project to create an airlift from India to Kunming, China, to replace the Burma Road. Military supplies had been flowing northward from the port of Rangoon to Kunming on the Road, but Japanese forces closed this route when they captured southern Burma in late 1941. This left the Chinese army almost helpless, so badly equipped that they had less than one rifle for every three soldiers, and very little ammunition. There were reports that some troops were equipped only with swords, and some soldiers had only wooden clubs as their weapons.

Our tiny group of C-47's was directed to undertake the vast job of supplying the Chinese army. We paved the way, first flying our cargo airplanes the long route from the States to India without losing a single airplane, a record that I attribute to the excellence of our first pilots, all airline veterans.

I flew over 50 round trips across the Hump, as we called the Himalaya Mountain range, facing the worst weather and the worst terrain in the world. This man-eating mission destroyed more than 500 airplanes and crews, with many never being found in the endless masses of snow-covered towering peaks and inaccessible terrain. Especially frightening was the utter silence when an airplane disappeared. It would leave India on the Hump run and just never reach its destination, with no communication of any kind to advise us of trouble.

We were very discouraged by the lack of attention our mission received in the early days. We suffered acute shortages of replacement aircraft and parts and such vital supplies as adequate radio equipment. If an airplane was forced down, its crew faced terrifying enemies in the massive jungle, teeming with vicious animals, insects, and diseases that left us little hope for survival in that wilderness.

We made ourselves heard by loud complaints, by bitching about our shortages, bad food, terrible living quarters, and lack of support. We bitched about lack of fighter protection on the Hump, and about lack of defense against bombing raids that periodically hit Our Assam bases. There were many days when our small unit in India wanted to quit. Our losses weighed heavily, and were doubly troubling as no one back in New Delhi or in Washington seemed to care enough to help. But the lives of our people across the Hump were hanging on a thread, depending on us. We buckled down to the job and kept going, moving cargo every day to the best of our ability.

* * * * * *

In June, 1942, I went on a special one day mission to deliver critically needed supplies to General Chennault's China forces in Kweilin. Once there, we found an acute need for our airplane to circulate among the Flying Tiger bases delivering supplies, and we attached ourselves to that group, without the formality of written orders. We spent several months living and flying with the Tigers and their successors, the China Air Task Force, and established the "China Express," the one-airplane airlift that carried men and supplies to the Tiger combat bases in eastern China. We flew General Chennault and other military VIP's to various points in China, and became a very vital unit in defense of free China.

This was an exciting and engrossing time, and I was part of an operation that few military men ever witness. In a military airplane, as an Air Corps pilot, I flew for a private mercenary army. I learned how a small, highly trained group, operating independently and free from the burden of military regulation and formality, can outfight a much larger military force, and do so at a fraction of the cost. This image has remained with me all these years. To this day, the very mention of "Flying Tigers" produces a picture of flying excellence and efficiency, and is a reminder of a group of fearless pilots who beat an enemy that outnumbered them ten-to-one, and changed the concept of fighter operations.

The American Volunteer Group taught a vital lesson, when it proved beyond a doubt that fighter aircraft could defeat massed bomber attacks. Unfortunately, Eighth Air Force commanders in Europe paid no attention to this lesson until they suffered devastating losses of B-17's and B-24's from German fighter action, whereupon they provided long range fighter escorts. The AVG also proved that a small group of determined fighters with good management could outfight much larger numbers of opponents by using smart strategy.

The war in the China-Burma-India (CBI) Theater taught other important lessons. The Hump airlift proved that air supply could keep a campaign alive when ground transport was cut off, a lesson that led to the successful Berlin airlift a few years later.

There are many CBI stories to tell and to this day the Hump Pilots Association holds annual conventions where gray-haired veterans of this mission swap stories and reminisce about long lost friends. The Flying Tigers also meet periodically to talk of their days of glory.

The history of the CBI Theater reads like a novel, with political and military intrigue, victories and defeats, and a final rescue by the cavalry.

Chapter 3
EARLY DAYS

Some famous fliers tell how they made their very first flight by a giant leap from a barn roof, wearing homemade wings. After they crashed, some of those amateur aviators went back to the drawing board to build better wings, while others put off their flying ambitions until some later date.

I had no barn roof. We lived in an apartment in the heart of Boston, Massachusetts.

My first introduction to flying took place when Charles Lindbergh came to Boston on his tour of the country after his solo crossing of the Atlantic Ocean in 1928. I was eight years old, and not quite sure of just how large the Atlantic Ocean was. But "Lucky Lindy" was a great celebrity, and I persuaded my mother to take me downtown to the Boston Common to join the crowds welcoming the hero.

The crowd was dense and I couldn't see the bandstand, so I squirmed my way through all those long legs as only a small kid can do, and got close to the bandstand. Then I realized I had lost touch with my mother, and was surrounded by a sea of strange faces.

Another lost kid had already been escorted to the bandstand to meet Lindbergh. Lindy made a "lost parents" announcement, which got the crowd laughing, and the parents were quickly found, brought to the bandstand, and introduced to the hero. That family now had a very special event to record for their family history. My fate was not as glamorous.

I was turned over to a burly policeman who gruffly said, "Stay with me, kid," and I did just that until my frantic mother appeared.

Fifteen years later, on Memorial Day, I was much changed, when as a 23-year-old Air Force captain, I was introduced by Boston's Mayor Hannon on that very same bandstand, and gave a speech to a large audience. It was 1943, and I was on leave after my overseas tour of duty. I talked about the war in the China-Burma-India Theater to a public that was trying to adjust to many wartime difficulties, and was eager to hear about their young men and the hardships facing them. I told about our life in that war zone, and was careful to leave out the unpleasant parts. I felt the best morale builder was to remind them that what the boys missed most was their family, and to send lots of letters. I got a laugh when I warned the girls to avoid any "Dear John" letters, to save them for when their heroes returned home.

Flying in an airplane was far from my parents' mind. Both of their families had traveled by steerage in smelly, crowded ships, in their migration to the United States from Russia in the early 1900's. They struggled to blend in and see that their children received the best education possible. My father, Samuel, was a clothing salesman who traveled New England selling coats to stores. He met my mother, Florence, a gorgeous young woman, in her father's kosher restaurant in Boston, and eventually asked for her hand in marriage. Not only was she beautiful, but she could cook.

My father worked hard, but our family finances fluctuated with the times. Mother was a great manager, and even when our finances were almost zero, she managed to feed her family of four, and see to it that the rent for our low cost basement apartment in Roxbury, a suburb of Boston, got paid. Wages were very low, but a nickel could buy a loaf of bread or pay for carfare, and 12 cents bought a sandwich in the local deli. We had no car and I recall that the most vivid daydream in my youth was to someday drive up to our apartment in a shiny new car and take my family for a ride. Life was that simple in those days.

Our apartment house on Maple Street was surrounded by more prosperous neighbors, one of them the Bernstein family whose prodigy son, Leonard, became one of the music geniuses of the century. Our gang might be playing stickball in the street or stairball on the apartment house steps and we would yell out to Lenny, two stories up, "Come on down and play, we're short a guy." His reply was invariably, "Can't, gotta practice."

And shortly after we would hear the vibrant tones of a classical piano piece that he constantly practiced which still rings in my ears. I identified it years later as a Rachmaninoff prelude, and whenever I hear it, I am taken back to those days on Maple Street. We kids would shake our heads and say, "Boy, is he wasting his time!"

Lenny Bernstein kept somewhat apart from the rest of the kids, not very athletic, and seldom joining us in street games. He knew that his special talent made him different, and this was further shown when he entered Boston Latin High School, known as a prep school for Harvard. Most of us attended the local Roxbury Memorial High School.

In the 1930's the Boston school system had standards that look very antiquated today. Female teachers had to be unmarried, and grade school teachers wore ankle-length black dresses. The boys' and girls' high schools were separate, and I am sure that this barrier to casual social mixing led to shy and uneasy relations between boys and girls.

Military drill was a required high school course in the 1930's. I can still picture pompous, pot-bellied Captain Kelly, our drill instructor, in immaculate uniform, conducting close-order drill. "Squads Right!", followed by "Squads Left!", along with the manual-of-arms, was taught for three years, two sessions a week. I later learned that what we spent three years learning took only two days of instruction in an army boot camp. Drill was conducted in the gymnasium, which was actually a covered-over swimming pool. Athletic classes would have been far more beneficial for us than the military drill, but the shadow of World War I still hung over the nation and the conservative Boston school board refused to change. Each year there was a military parade in downtown Boston, with high school students in uniform carrying mock rifles. The uniforms closely resembled World War I outfits, and families were hard pressed to pay for them in those depression days. There was a brisk business in buying and selling used uniforms before parade time.

My very first career choice as I grew up was to be a "Lucky Lindy" and fly across oceans. Every young boy had this dream, but dreams change often as we grow older. For a short time, I became interested in a sailor's career. The father of my friend Ralph owned a large Army-Navy store in Charlestown, home of the Navy Yard, and on our visits to the store we browsed through the strange-looking clothing and equipment used by sailors.

The thrill of strange shores and distant places filled that store, and we could almost smell the sea. We visited the nearby Navy Yard and spent time aboard the historic war ship, "Old Ironsides." This is the famous USS Constitution, the oldest commissioned warship in the world, launched in 1789, and a thrilling experience for every American to visit. Boston was a major seaport with an active navy base, and I was captivated by all types of boats and ships, It was normal for youngsters to dream of building a boat some day and sailing away, and the prospect of the life of a sailor made it my career choice for a time. It was a prophecy that would be fulfilled much later in life, when I became involved in the yacht business, and spent much time on the water.

Most young boys are interested in mechanical gadgets, and I dismantled the usual assortment of alarm clocks and other devices when they failed to work. Working on cars was fun when I visited my cousin Bernie in the town of Quincy, where his family owned a large automobile junk yard with hundreds of wrecked cars. I was very envious of Bernie, who at my age, only 13, had a wide choice of cars to drive over the bumpy dirt roads of their acreage. He would proudly drive me around in his favorite car, a topless Packard touring sedan, a car that would be a collector's joy today. We had great times getting greasy working on the innards of various cars, and at that time, I decided that auto mechanics would be my future career.

My future plans swung back to flying when I visited East Boston Airport in 1935 with a group of teenagers. The shiny new Douglas DC~3 airliners just coming into use were a far cry from the "Spirit of St. Louis" of Lindbergh fame. They were flown by a special breed of aviators, the airline captains, who had reached the highest level of flying and were considered the "Princes of the Sky." The public adored them as they would the captain of the Queen Mary, and the kids held them in awe. The wonder of flying one of these wonderful airplanes became a special dream, and I said that 'maybe someday' I might do that. And I did.

* * * * * *

High school graduation in the deep depression year of 1936 meant finding a job, and attending night college. I had achieved "A" grades in mathematics and science subjects and had a dream of entering Massachusetts Institute of Technology in Cambridge, but the tuition fee of $500 per year for that distinguished university was out of sight, and no scholarships turned up. Needing to work days, I chose evening school at Northeastern University School of Law. Some friends entering law school persuaded me that evening law school was a better choice than an evening engineering college. They reasoned that the practice of law depended greatly on personal ability, regardless of the college. On the other hand, an engineering degree from an evening college was considered second rate, compared to the education provided at MIT, which "was the number one college of choice".

It was difficult for young men to cope with career problems in those hard times. We lacked adequate counseling, yet we had to make choices that would affect our adult lives in an unknown future. I recall being envious of my older sister. Young women of those times had a single goal: to meet "Mr. Right" and settle down to raise a family. And that is what she did, becoming a proper housewife and joining her husband in his business for many years.

My college years were turbulent. My job kept me working 60-hour weeks, and I spent evenings at law school or studying at home. My precious Sunday off found me hunched over my law books, reading cases and writing brief analyses. This is called the casebook method of studying law. It was a harsh schedule and after two years, my grades started to deteriorate, and I was burned out. I felt that I had chosen badly, so I explored the new program offered at the Lowell Institute evening school at MIT,that led to a Certificate in Electrical Engineering I knew that my parents would not be very happy if I quit law school. Their son's education was very important to them, and they considered the legal profession one of great prestige. A lawyer in the family was something they could be very proud of, and they did not understand the field of engineering.

My older sister, Irene, supported me. She was in favor of my following my choice of career, rather than continuing in a field that had become a boring grind to this 18-year old. I made the decision to change, and never regretted the choice.

I applied for admission at the Lowell Institute offices at MIT, and spent a day browsing through the labs and classrooms. I wanted to reassure myself that the big change I was about to make was the right move. Just being on the grounds of MIT was a thrill. It was inspiring to visit famous buildings that had a history of research and invention. I was breathing an atmosphere where great advances in science had taken place. The college was staffed with wonderful professors who had helped create modern technology.

After signing up for admission, with classes just about to start, I was very distressed to find that I did not pass the entrance exams in mathematics. In the two years since high school, I had forgotten much algebra and trigonometry. The math professor saw an eager young man who wanted something very badly, and I was most gratified when he agreed to my entering his class on a trial basis for three months. I worked furiously and passed all the quarterly examinations.

Classes at Lowell Institute were a breath of fresh air, after the tedium of law class lectures. The instructors were most articulate and helpful, who left no questions unanswered, and I had no doubt in my mind that I was receiving the very best technical education. I felt that this was the greatest college in the world, and where I really belonged.

* * * * * *

All my classes were in the evening,and I worked long hours daytimes. But I found time on Sundays to follow a new interest - sailing. The MIT sailing club started me on a lifetime hobby that became a business for me many years later.

Sailing was the greatest way to relax for this hard-studying, hard-working young man who found the thrill of silent movement over the water an unbeatable sensation. A puff of wind to set me off, and my magic carpet would take me anywhere in the world, or at least anywhere on the Charles River Basin. It was a time to forget studies and other worldly cares and to concentrate on this wonderful way to enjoy the beauties of nature. There were other joys when the Charles River Shell hosted the Boston Symphony Pops Orchestra evening concerts. Then, I would anchor my Tech sailing dinghy nearby, and enjoy the wonderful music, the gentle rocking of the boat, and the warmth of a lovely companion snuggled up in a blanket with me, under a star-filled heaven.

Sailing had its technical side, and I had my first taste of aerodynamics, learning how a sail resembles an airplane wing and creates lift. I was fascinated by a study of this ancient skill, where the force of nature, the wind, had provided a means of travel for more than 5000 years of recorded history. Many airplane pilots are devoted to the art of sailing at slow speed as a change from flying the skies at jet speeds. In later years, I sailed boats wherever I could find one, an Arab dhow at Karachi, four-masted schooners in the Caribbean, and on a variety of other vessels. It is a joyful sport.

* * * * * *

On the work front, there had been problems in the depression year of 1936. Graduation from Roxbury Memorial High School at the age of 16 pushed me out into the working world, with few jobs available. Those high school graduates who could not afford college were flooding employment agencies looking for work that did not exist. I vividly recall the frustrating daily trips to the agencies, where there might be a few openings posted for bricklayers, plumbers, other skilled tradesmen, but not for unskilled youths just emerging into the workplace.

My first job in a small neighborhood grocery store paid one-dollar a day. After one week I quit and went job hunting seriously. I was starting evening school that fall, and needed the $120 per semester tuition money. In addition, I was helping out at home, where money was very tight.

A full time job turned up that fall working in the paint department of a large retail hardware store. Most jobs were obtained by personal connections, and in this case the owner of the store was a family acquaintance. It paid only 20 cents per hour, but I was lucky to have it. The work was mostly manual labor, carrying cases of paint up and downstairs, as the store was housed in an ancient building that had four floors but no freight elevator. Hours were from 7:30 A.M. to 6:30 P.M., with one-half hour off for lunch. We worked six days a week, netting me about $12.50 weekly wages. That was typical of depression era work conditions. The work had one unanticipated advantage; it kept me in excellent physical condition

The walk from the hardware store, located in Boston's South End, to Northeastern University Law School, next door to Symphony Hall, took 30 minutes. Classes started at 7:00 P.M., so I left work approximately 30 minutes early on school nights. This gave me time to gulp down a 15 cent hamburger and milk at the White Tower. The assistant manager of the store dutifully marked down my departure time, and I was docked for the 30 minutes two times per week. This totaled one hour, reducing my pay check by 20 cents.

The Christmas season improved things, as I worked at assembling bicycles and tricycles.

Being adept with tools made me a whirlwind assembler, and I was able to set a fast pace that impressed the management. I was rewarded with a Christmas present - a pay raise of ten-percent, to 22 cents per hour.

There was other work that helped me build muscles. The store manager often called me in to help unload freight cars full of 100-pound sacks of bone-meal fertilizer, which had a distinctive pungent odor that clung to my clothes no matter how hard I brushed them. I had no advance notice, and no opportunity to change into other work clothes. If I went to a class that night, I sat well away from other students, who avoided me like the plague.

A major improvement came when the shipping manager learned that I had a driver's license, and he promptly put me to work driving one of the delivery trucks whenever a regular driver failed to show. His department benefited as they paid me only one-half the drivers' normal salary. I enjoyed this driving two or three days a week, as it got me away from boring store work and sent me all over the big city

I received a bitter lesson in management technique on this job, for I witnessed some very harsh treatment of employees by a ruthless business owner. The founder of the business was a fine gentleman of the old school, who started a tiny business and built it to a very successful group of three stores. We all liked the old fellow, who was retired, but came in occasionally to chat with us.

His son, the heir to the business, was an entirely different cut of person. He was born with the proverbial silver spoon, attended an Ivy League college, but his college major must have been, "Damn the employees!" He took over the business and ran it with an iron hand, exercising vicious authority without any regard for the help. Our wages were the lowest possible, which kept married men impoverished, and he ruthlessly fired experienced men when he could hire new ones for less money.

A number of employees ate brown-bag lunches in a small secluded stockroom that was close to the office of the owner. At lunch one day, I learned the meaning of the expression "slum lord." He owned a number of low-rent apartment buildings in the adjacent South End of Boston, and often gave instructions to his property manager on the phone in a shout, loud enough for us to overhear him from our lunch hideaway. One day we were electrified to hear him instruct his manager to, "Raise the rents and if they can't afford it, put them out on the streets!" This was a real shocker, and we shook our heads in amazement. This was a real live Mr. Scrooge, directly out of Dickens.

This accidental eavesdropping exposed the true nature of the owner. When he fired another batch of older employees for no reason except to replace them with cheaper help, the employees held a secret meeting with a union organizer. We decided to form a union, and go out on strike against this intolerable owner. Unions were new in 1937, and there was great concern about the outcome of a strike. The employees were mostly family men, just barely scraping by on starvation wages, and the union executive convinced them that a strike would bring beneficial results. Off we went to form a picket line, in the very worst of economic times.

I found the strike very stimulating. At the age of 17, I was a first-year student in law school, experiencing an exciting event, walking a picket line, involved in one of the few strikes of the depression years. My youthful voice called out at the front entrance of the store, "Trading here is taking food out of the mouths of our hungry children!" "We work for starvation wages! This store is unfair to hard-working employees " Customers stayed away, perhaps from fear of crossing a picket line or out of sympathy for the strikers. After a week of no business, a miracle took place. We proudly emerged with a victory, when the owner agreed to a union contract that called for reasonable wages. I was upgraded to the heavenly salary of $20.00 per week and was in seventh heaven. What a success! I was rich!

This state of euphoria did not last for long. The owner apparently had other plans, a way to outwit us. A loophole in the union contract stated that if the company closed any one of the three stores, it could layoff any personnel it wished. Within a few weeks, it announced the going-out-of-business sale of their Summer Street store in downtown Boston. Shortly after that all the strikers were laid off, including me. The remaining employees were given an ultimatum - either cancel the union contract and go back to the original wage scale, or get fired. They stayed on at the low wage, and the newly laid-off employees scrambled to find any kind of work to support their families. The owner gloated. I look back with regrets for the family men who lost their jobs, and realize how difficult a time it was for them. At my age, it was only another adventure in life, soon to be followed by other important events.

That failure of management to show any regard for the welfare of their employees is one of the most appalling that I have personally witnessed. It made an indelible impression on me, leaving me especially sensitive to the needs of personnel. Yet, this terrible treatment was not so unusual in those days of economic hardship. Whoever among us yearns for the 'good old days' should read history.

We like to think that modern management is more enlightened, but there is ample evidence that today, many top executives are little concerned over the needs of employees. I learned some years later that one organization that cares a great deal is the military. Military policy instructs commanders to take care of the troops first, before seeking safety or comfort for themselves. The extreme example of that is when an aircraft commander remains at the controls of a stricken aircraft until he is sure that his crew has bailed out before following them, often running out of time and sacrificing his own life,.

After that humble ending to my job in the hardware store, I found work in a grocery market, and managed the years at evening college very well. On graduation at Lowell Institute in June, 1940, I started a serious search for technical employment, meanwhile spending weekends that summer learning to fly in the Civilian Pilot Training Program. The CPTP opened new doors to me as I found myself moving directly into flying, and soon found work in the field of aviation.

Chapter 4
CUB PILOT

The 60 horsepower Lycoming engine in my Piper Cub is humming along like a buzz saw on my solo cross country flight from Norwood Airport to Dedham, Massachusetts, and other places. This is the final test for my private pilot license, the last of my 35 hours.

I love this Piper Cub. It looks flimsy as a kite with its fabric covered surfaces, frail looking wing struts, and baby-carriage size landing gear. Don't let the looks fool you. This is a very tough airplane. It holds up very nicely with the slamming and banging and general hard use of student flying. It can also perform acrobatics such as snap rolls, loops, spins, and other maneuvers. Even simulated forced landings are fun, when the instructor cuts the throttle, and you must find a landing spot to glide into among the rolling fields of New England countryside.

In wartime the Cub, renamed the L-4 liaison airplane, proved to be one of the hardiest of all of our utility aircraft, performing almost impossible missions. It spotted for artillery, hauled critical supplies, and carried VIP's like General Eisenhower. It could land on a bumpy field barely big enough to turn a truck around, and take off with a wounded man in a stretched out cabin layout, straining hard with its 65 horsepower engine. Some became tank busters, outfitted with six rocket tubes under the wings. Each rocket held enough explosive charge to blow up a Tiger tank unless the tank gunner fired first. That was a very dangerous business.

Amazingly, in this little Piper Cub I feel solid as a rock, even though I have always had queasy feelings, when standing on the edge of a roof or other high place. I especially like the two-piece entry hatch; one piece hangs up, and the other one flips down. This allows you to actually lean out and wave to people, like pretty girls.

It is the summer of 1940, and I am part of the Civilian Pilot Training Program (CPTP), which an agency in Washington, D.C., started, to build up the number of young men involved in flying. It is open to men of college age, and when I learned of it I rushed to Northeastern University across town to enroll. I expected to find a mob scene, but, amazingly, I was the only one there that day and it turned out that there were many vacancies in the program.

I always wanted to fly. As a depression kid, in a family with very low income, it was just out of the question. This didn't stop me from admiring the Douglas airliners that flew into East Boston airport (later Logan Field), and wondering just how one got to be a pilot. It seemed like an impossible dream at age 15.

The CPTP program was like a miracle that just fell into my lap. It provided 35 hours in the Cub, gaining me a private pilot license, and there were advanced courses to follow in larger airplanes.

I can still remember the excitement of my very first flight in an airplane in July of 1940. The Cub bumped along the dirt field and finally became airborne. I was absolutely thrilled at the sight of trees whizzing by, watching the earth fall away, and having a birds eye view of the local area suddenly opening up before my startled eyes.

I had learned to sail a year before at the MIT sailing club on the Charles River, and I loved the wonderful experience of silently gliding across the water, moved by the force of the wind, able to control direction and even sail against the wind.

The thrill of flying topped sailing. I have always had nighttime dreams of flying by the strength of my own arms, as Deadalus and Icarus of the famous Greek fable, and here I was, learning the art of flight, fulfilling my dream.

I could not believe that I was expected to master this complicated skill and solo in eight hours. After the first few hours it fell into place, and after eight hours I was all charged up for my solo. That first flight was far easier than I had thought. I did one circle of the field with the instructor on board, and then he climbed out of the airplane and said," Just go ahead and do what you've been doing right along." I did it without a hitch. It was even better than I expected; the airplane was lighter without his 200 pounds, and just floated off the ground like a bird. I was serenely carefree and in my glory felt that I could float all day. That was a wonderful day, indeed.

Now, on my final flight, a solo cross-country, I am carefully checking all the landmarks, like railroads, signs on water towers, and highways, on my way to the airport at Dedham. I will land and check in at the airport office, and then take off again for the return to Norwood by another route over other landmarks. My 35 hours of flying time will be complete, and I will qualify for my private pilot license.

But this will not be the end of my flying time at Norwood. On Saturdays and Sundays I become a salesman, working my way up and down the flight line selling rides for $2 in a four-place Stinson to visitors to the little country field. My arrangement is that I get paid in flying time instead of the commission. Most people are afraid of flying, so this is a real challenge and a lesson in creative marketing. I talk about flying with such enthusiasm that I have people lined up all day. This early experience of selling a new idea to skeptical people played a big part in my life.

Yesterday I fell in love — with an airplane. I spotted a gorgeous red biplane coming in over the trees to land at our airport. As it taxied in I could see it was different from any other airplane I had ever seen. It was the famous four-place Staggerwing Beechcraft, designed with the upper wing set behind the lower one.

The young pilot emerged from the cabin, tied the airplane down securely, and left in a waiting car. I walked around that beauty several times, just not able to get enough of it. I caressed the shining propeller, admired the spotless radial engine, the polished shiny fire- engine colored fuselage and wings, and enjoyed a romantic image of actually owning it. But I had just bought a used 1930 Model A Ford sedan for $40 and was broke.

I have always admired this glorious airplane, and learned later that there were only about 200 Staggerwings built. Those remaining are among the greatest of the classics, and are kept in first-class condition by their proud owners. They have been exhibited at the Smithsonian Air and Space Museum in Washington, D.C. .. I consider them to be the most beautiful of the biplanes.

I looked forward to taking the CPTP advance course in a Waco biplane the following summer, but other events soon steered me in another direction.

* * * * * *

After completing the certificate course in electrical engineering at MIT's Lowell Institute, I was in need of a job, It opened up at the Pratt and Whitney airplane engine factory in East Hartford, Connecticut in that fall of 1940.

I was delighted to find work in the aviation industry; and enjoyed all the smells and sounds of the factory where the finest radial engines in the world were built. Most military aircraft used air-cooled radial design engines, which were extremely durable despite their many parts and ungainly looks. They did not require liquid coolant, which was a vulnerable feature with in-line engines such as the Allison. One bullet in the cooling system of an in-line model meant loss of coolant and freezing up of the engine.

My first job was setting up engine parts kits for the assembly department. In 1940 there was no assembly line system to build these high quality airplane engines. One team assembled the entire engine very carefully from parts kits that

I supplied in large trays. Great care was taken in quality control. If I found minor flaws such as scratches on oil tubes, or other questionable marks on parts, I would drop them in the reclaim bin for later inspection. The work varied from day to day. One day the team might be assembling an R-685 Wasp, and the next day a big 14-cylinder R-1830.

This was quite an education for me, as most of my flying in later years was behind Pratt and Whitney engines and I knew these engines intimately. I developed a great affection for them. Although I don't consider myself a superstitious person, I felt that they actually knew me and would never let me down. It must have been a mutual love affair for in thousands of hours behind the R-1830. 1200 HP model, and the bigger R-2800, 2000 HP engine, I never had an engine failure, and hardly ever had a rough running engine. Who says an inanimate object can't love you!

The company was falling behind in deliveries, so a new system was being designed to put engine production on an assembly line basis. I applied almost daily for a position in planning this change, which might lead to a supervisory job for me, and I started wearing a necktie to work and even carried a slide rule around in my shirt pocket hoping to impress the management.

Life in Hartford, Connecticut, was good. I loved the job and the weekly payroll. I shared a room in a lovely private residence with a former school friend, costing us $12 each per week, and we enjoyed a very active social life. There were several colleges nearby just loaded with co-eds, and our $75 weekly paychecks went a long way, with gasoline at six gallons for $1, and the usual cost of a date about $3. My four-door sedan Model A Ford was a blessing for double dating although it had its problems, like a leaky radiator, which lost all the anti-freeze I put in. I could not afford to replace the radiator, so I switched to plain water and drained it each night to keep it from freezing up in the frigid winter weather.

One day fate sat on my shoulder and nudged me over to the east side of the factory to find some missing engine parts. I was drawn to the large windows overlooking the factory airport. An airplane landed and taxied in to the parking ramp, and I recall every detail very vividly, even though it was over a half-century ago. It was a military airplane that I later identified at an AT -6 advanced trainer. The young Army Air Corps pilot slid back the hatch, climbed out on the wing, reached in for his hat, and strode proudly into the operations office. He wore big sunglasses, and a leather flight jacket with Air Corps wings insignia on the left breast, and was the target of many eyes, especially mine. This young man was sitting on top of the world.

As I gazed out, a most amazing thing happened to me, as though a loud bell went off in my head. What on earth was I doing in a plant assembling engines when I could be flying again? Everyone knew about the Flying Cadets, and I suddenly realized that was what I wanted to be! There was absolutely no question in my mind from that very moment, nor could later discussions with my parents dissuade me from joining the Air Corps. I knew that I belonged there. Besides, the draft board was bringing men into the services very rapidly, and some day my number might be drawn and place me in the infantry. Several friends had already been inducted, and everyone felt the threat. Some younger workers at our factory had been called up, so it was apparent that working in the aviation industry did not justify deferment.

Events moved pretty fast after that. I failed the first physical due to a lack of eye muscle flexibility that reduced depth perception. This was corrected by a unique device - a stereo viewer that had two rotating discs, one for each eye, that were individually controllable. I looked into the viewer, a long box, partitioned down the middle, with each eye focussing on its respective disc. The optometrist applying the therapy changed the radius of disc rotation for each eye separately, causing the eye muscles to flex accordingly. One eye might be rotating in a wide circle while the other circled in a small radius. This created great muscle flexibility, allowing excellent depth perception. I asked as a joke if he could rotate the discs in opposite directions and teach my eyes to roll in opposing circles, but the machine was not designed to do this. After three sessions I was able to cross my eyes readily, and had achieved better than 20/20 vision.

I passed the next physical exam and was sworn in as a Flying Cadet in the U.S. Army Air Corps in March of 1941. My orders directed me to report to Darr Aero Tech, in Albany, Georgia, on May 1st, as a member of cadet Class 41-1.

Two things enter my mind as I write this. One is the awesome speed with which a young person's life can change. The transition from one life style to another overnight is very difficult for a mature person to absorb, but for a 21 year old, it is no shock at all. Our mental attitude at that age allows major transitions in life to be accepted readily, with little loss of sleep. It may well be that in our youth we cannot imagine the dangers that lie ahead.

The other thought is political. There were obvious signs of an impending war and I was involved in many. I received pilot training in the Civilian Pilot Training Program, paid for by Uncle Sam. I worked in the aircraft engine industry that was fast expanding.

There was a nationwide draft into the armed services, and my personal choice was into a select service that was also going through frantic expansion. If we were undergoing such a rapid growth of military power in 1940 and 1941, making ready for a coming war, how could we be caught at Pearl Harbor with all our defenses down?

This question has been asked many times. Looking back after many decades, I never cease to be amazed at the egotistical attitude of so many military leaders. There are self- styled experts who believe their professional training makes them infallible. Many times I have repeated the comment, "There goes another 'General Yesterday:" to describe one who wears blinders, and fights the last war. My admiration is for those who accept new ideas and forge ahead.

New Cadets: "Suck that gut in."

Chapter 5
FLYING CADET

"You're in the army now" chant my buddies as I pack up my Model A Ford for the trip from Boston to Darr Aero Tech primary flying school in Georgia. It is May of 1941, and they all live in the shadow of the draft. I detect a feeling of envy that I had bit the bullet and volunteered for a very select branch of the service, and had passed the physical.

I have no big concern about being in the army. At the age of 17 I spent a summer month at Reserve Officers Training Camp (ROTC) at Casco Bay in Portland, Maine, where I was introduced to the life of soldiering.

There was military discipline there but it was not exceedingly harsh, although the voice of our top sergeant sure was. This sergeant was the perfect example of the tough noncom drill instructor (DI) who knew everything, let nothing get by him, and whose very presence put fear into us. Every morning at 5:45 sharp he burst into our barracks like a cyclone, blowing his shrill whistle, and in the loudest bellow I had ever heard chased us into our clothes and outdoors in 5 minutes. We shivered in the early morning chill, but after a few minutes of violent calisthenics, we were warm as toast, and ready to follow up with a prodigious breakfast.

Those ROTC days were filled with drills, marches, rifle practice, and lots of physical exercise. The DI's rode us hard but they were very aware of our youth and the need to keep our interest high enough to bring us back the next year for more officer training. Their bark was worse than their bite, and we learned a lot.

I was not greatly interested in a military life, but I realize that the 30 days spent there made a very big change in my life. It took a non-athletic pudgy kid, trimmed him down to a lean physique, and turned him into an aggressive volleyball player and good swimmer. Best of all was the confidence gained from scoring in the top level of rifle marksmanship, which brought an invitation to participate in ROTC national rifle competition.

Another 3 years of ROTC would have earned me a reserve commission in what was still called the cavalry, but now, as a Flying Cadet, I am on my way to becoming an officer and pilot in the Army Air Corps, and absolutely nothing can beat that. I am 21 years old, and looking forward to the biggest adventure in my life. I am sure that great things are waiting for me.

Driving to Georgia is a new adventure as I have never been south of New York City. I bought a new tire, packed my bag, and left with the blessings and tears of my family who just couldn't understand why anyone would want to fly an army airplane.

My Model A purrs along at 40 MPH into the Deep South that is very different from the New England countryside around Boston. There are very few cars on the road, and I can leisurely examine the quiet countryside. Just rural folks are awed by their first glimpse of the Big City, I gawk at the new sights, the countless magnolia trees, sleepy little towns on dusty roads, scattered pockets of poverty, and occasional glimpses of stately old mansions that remind me of Tara in "Gone With the Wind." I get the impression that our country is a very large one indeed and full of very nice people who lead a more leisurely life than I am used to.

A salesman friend, who has traveled the south, told me that guest homes are good clean places to stay overnight, and he is more than right. I find them very homey and low priced, and when the host families learn that I am a new Flying Cadet they could not be more hospitable. They welcome me into their family circle, have me join them for dinner and breakfast at no extra fee, and then wish me Godspeed when I leave. This is the warm, cordial southern hospitality I had heard about, and it is really true.

The roads are two-lane, with such light traffic that driving through the south is like a Sunday drive in lovely spring weather. I drive into Georgia with a smile on my face.

When I finally arrive at Albany, a middle-sized town in southern Georgia, I look for the police station for directions to Darr Aero Tech, and am welcomed most cordially by the local police chief. On the way I stop at the Globe Department Store to buy a pair of swim trunks that I forgot to pack. Later, I will meet the Globe family and be welcomed into their home and enjoy their hospitality.

* * * * * *

Darr is 3 miles south of town, and my introduction is very messy. I arrive early and find that the parking lot for the few cadet-owned cars is a field of mud across the road from the main gate. I pick my way carefully through the mud, and am told to stand by at the gate until the bus arrives.

Darr has recently been opened as a contract flying school providing primary flight training to Army Air Corp cadets. Two Air Corps officers oversee the school, but ground school and flight instruction is all done by civilians. Its newness shows in the modem buildings and hangers and a paved flying field, but the surrounding grounds are open fields that become muddy bogs after a rain. We call it the mud hole of the south.

As I watch, a bus pulls up to the main gate, opens up its door, and unloads a group of new cadets. I join the line, and so begins my army career.

The moment the new cadet walks through the gate of the military school, he starts to change. Watch the change take place right in front of you.

First, look at that line of sloppy looking civilians. See how they slouch, how they shuffle as they walk, how they stand in a ragged line when asked to line up. Then watch the upper class men, nattily dressed in tans, descend on the sloppy group.

Listen to these uppers address the new men like they were less than human. Listen to loud commands that straighten out the line, order the men to assume a "brace"; criticize each one for some fault, and keep this up until the new people start to shape up.

Listen to them explain a "brace".

"PUT THOSE SHOULDERS BACK, MISTER!" "SUCK IN YOUR GUT, MISTER!" "TUCK YOUR CHIN IN AND STAND AT ATTENTION, MISTER!"

That's what a brace is, and it will be standard posture from now on.

I have joined the group right up front. Having had some experience in the ROTC, I stand in the brace position right off, and even smile to show my spirit of cooperation. That's a big mistake. I am immediately ordered, "WIPE THAT SMILE OFF YOUR FACE, MISTER!" I had forgotten; smiles are not permitted.

We are now lined up and marched into registration, and then issued bedding and uniforms. We really are a motley, raggedy looking bunch, dressed in all kinds of ways, and with varying lengths of hair. The upperclassmen are very happy to order us around, handing out the same treatment they had received five weeks before. They are going to keep it up for five weeks, until they move into their next stage of training called "Basic", and our class becomes the upperclassmen at Darr, ready to lord it over a new bunch of cadets.

This disciplining by the upper class is a pain, but it has a definite place in military training. Turning high-spirited new cadets into Air Force officers in 30 weeks is a major undertaking that requires lots of instruction and close supervision. It takes many instructors to do the job, and they are present in the form of upperclassmen, who are eager to pitch in with their own new-found know-how.

They are on constant alert for infractions of the rules and will award "gigs", or punishments, readily, usually right on the spot. These can take the form of 20 pushups, jogging twice around the compound, called "tours", or some other unpleasant form of physical punishment.

The gigs are tough enough to remind us of many rules - stay in a brace and say the right words when addressed, keep neat, make up our bunks with the top blanket stretched taut enough to bounce a quarter on it, keep lockers clean as a pin, roll our socks tightly, etc., etc.. The weekly white glove barracks inspection produces plenty of gigs for dust found on window ledges, shoes that didn't gleam with polish, or other sloppiness.

The uniforms we are issued become the laugh of the new cadets. Due to shortages, we receive one pair of mechanics coveralls each week. Period. These are worn for every activity except calisthenics for which we wear our own shorts and tee shirts, or whatever we brought with us. For weekends off the base, we can wear our civvies, as it is peacetime.

Back to the coveralls. These are long sleeved, and made of a very stiff fabric, which softens when soaked in sweat. That happens early in the day due to the high humidity of southern Georgia in the spring. When they dry out, they become stiff again.

The ultimate disgrace is the odor in the barracks. We joke about putting our coveralls against the wall where they could practically stand by themselves when they dried out and stiffen up. We hope that the breezes flowing through our barracks will reduce the offensive odors by morning reveille, so we can put them on again.

That and the perpetual disciplining are really our only complaints. Under the critical eye of the uppers we march everywhere and observe all the customs in military fashion. This especially includes careful table manners at meal times. We certainly need that, as there are cadets here from every walk of life, and some of them have never been exposed to good table manners.

Seating arrangements at the long mess hall tables are a problem. No matter where you sit, you are in a bad spot. The end men have to wait patiently for the platters to be passed to them. The middle men have to do the passing, and are often so busy at this that they are constantly in motion, finding it hard to complete a bite. Each table has an upper class cadet to supervise, who keeps an eagle eye on every move. Heaven help an offender who grabs, or reaches too far, or raises his voice in frustration. The food is good, and we would all gain weight except for the rigorous physical routine.

Hazing does take place. It is formally described as putting someone to work at humiliating or embarrassing situations by having him do menial or foolish tasks. There are always a few uppers who use excessive hazing to take revenge on what they suffered when they were lowers, but most uppers are intent on doing their job of passing along the knowledge they have gained in their previous five weeks. Cadets regard any gigs they receive as hazing, but to be fair, most gigs are deserved. I have received a few, which I deserved, and I learned to straighten out my act to avoid more.

"Fall in for the flight line!" Finally we hear that exciting order which gives us a great lift; as that's why we are here. Today is our first visit to meet our instructors, and get acquainted with the airplanes. We are thrilled with anticipation as we march down to the hanger line on winged feet, eager to get into a cockpit and actually fly the primary trainer. Sorry, no flying today. We get lots of ground instruction on safety, and then crowd around the airplanes for close examination.

Our trainer is the Stearman PT-17, the favorite of the Army and Navy, and for good reasons. It is an open cockpit biplane powered with a 220 HP radial engine, and is built sturdy enough to handle the unusual stresses that it will suffer in the hands of student pilots. It is a business-like airplane with lots of struts and guy wires, but to us, it's a thing of great beauty. It is not fast, cruising at less than 100 MPH, but it has wonderful flying characteristics of great stability, plenty of advance warning of a stall, and ability to do all kinds of acrobatic maneuvers. On the negative side, the narrow spaced landing gear makes it easy to ground loop on landing, requiring careful attention. It is also quite uncomfortable with its drafty open cockpit offering no protection from cold and rain. It has no radio and has poor communication between front and rear cockpits. There has a bare minimum of instruments, with no airspeed indicator, so you judge your speed by the sound of the slipstream in the wire rigging.

The PT is a big jump from a Cub, and will be a challenge to fly with the same precision that I developed with the smaller airplane. I develop an instant affection for this wonderful airplane, and can see myself with helmet and goggles, white scarf flying, soaring into the sun, just like in a Hollywood movie. I recall, as I write this, that I loved every airplane I ever flew, even the ones that tried to kill me.

My instructor is a great young guy named Sheffy, who enjoys his work and becomes quite friendly. Our instructors are civilians, and generally take a dim view of serious military discipline, and we are able to relax a bit in their presence, but careful not to take advantage of this. Their word is law on the flight line, and we hang on their every instruction.

Sheffy has four students, and I am the only one with previous flying experience, so he takes me up first to see what I know. On that first flight, Sheffy does the takeoff and shortly after, motions to me to take the stick. This is the first time in a year that I have flown, and I am rusty and feel awkward. He motions for me to do some turns, checks my rudder-aileron coordination, which I am careful to accentuate, and then turns me loose for steep turns. I would love to do something more exciting, like a snap roll, but I follow instructions carefully.

Sheffy lands the airplane very neatly, and we chat a bit. He criticizes my coordination, which I think he does to keep me from getting too cocky, and then says the magic words, "You're gonna do fine," then goes about the business of breaking in some new students. In later sessions, he drills me at length on precision flying, but when things get a little boring we get into acrobatics - rolls, loops, and spins - which are all part of the program. Sheffy shows me the maneuvers, and then I try to outdo him. We get into a kind of competition, and end up having a great time of it. The Stearman can handle it very well, and I can't get enough flying. My greatest glory is inverted flight, hanging from the safety harness until the engine conks out from fuel starvation, then rolling out to restart the engine by the wind milling prop, then rolling inverted again.

Ground school turns out to be a snap, as I have been through it before, and I am called on to help some of the other cadets with a few of the subjects. The big fear of all cadets is the "washing machine". Washing out of flight training is a fate considered worse than hanging by the thumbs, and is usually caused by poor dexterity or lack of inherent flying ability," which labels the cadet as unsuitable pilot material. He will be transferred to navigator or bombardier school, where he achieves the same rank of second lieutenant as a pilot, but can never be an aircraft commander. Pilots reign supreme. A cadet can also wash out for disciplinary or other reasons, which can cause discharge from the Air Corps and place him back in the hands of his draft board, but these cases are rare. Washing out of pilot training is very depressing to a young man who considers himself pretty special since he has been selected as a Flying Cadet. Many do not take it very well, and carry their resentment to the other schools.

Cadets have time off starting Saturday afternoon if they don't have tours to walk. Our social life downtown revolves around the newly opened Cadet Club, located in the basement of the Albany Hotel, complete with a well-stocked jukebox. It is where a number of young ladies congregate to meet the cadets, and I meet some lovelies, including one very special one named Margie. I love to dance, and the jitterbugging of the day is enough to draw Margie and me together to enjoy Glenn Miller and Benny Goodman dance tunes till closing time.

We have a date every Saturday night, so I load up my Model A with roommates for a rip- roaring ride into town, at a very respectable 30 miles per hour. We are careful not to intimidate the local authorities by any kind of out-of-line behavior. A bad report could end our flying career, just as it is getting started.

On Sundays, I am invited to join Margie's family, the owners of the Globe Department Store, in their sprawling home on the outskirts of town. This magnificent antebellum mansion nestles in a great grove of magnolia trees, and gives off a wonderful air of relaxed calm and quiet. Aunts, uncles, and cousins who flock in from various parts of the south for long visits occupy its many rooms. Their Sunday dinner is a lavish but homey event with huge amounts of food eaten casually, as members of the family run in and out of the house intent on their various sports and other activities. It is a wonderful display of a loving family and their warmth has an intoxicating effect on me, as I am accepted so graciously into their midst. Two girl cousins are engaged to servicemen, and they ask me loads of questions about the services, and never stop talking about the next time the boys are on leave. They look at me with a big unspoken question about my relationship to their little cousin, Margie.

Meanwhile, back at Darr, the weeks whiz by at high speed. I feel right at home in the Stearman after soloing in the minimum eight hours. I love acrobatics and develop such a closeness to the performance of the airplane that I think I can do anything. I spend a lot of my solo time hanging upside down from my safety belt, and doing spins, and, on one occasion, almost make my own hole in the ground. We are careful to note that in a spin the altimeter lags, and does not follow you down as fast as you are actually descending. You can get a false reading, thinking you have more altitude than you actually have.

One time, I was cockily showing off to some young lady acquaintances gathered by the river for a picnic. I pulled up into a stall and started my spin, holding it a tad longer than caution dictates. By the time I pulled out, I was just barely above the high trees lining the river bank. The girls told me later that I really had them scared, but I nonchalantly, in the best John Wayne manner, brushed it off with,

"Oh, I was perfectly in control". Actually, it scared me, too.

After five weeks go by, our upper class moves to another school, and we graduate from lower to upper class. A new group of cadets disgorges itself from the buses as did our class five weeks ago, and our group, now in suntan uniforms with ties, lords it over the new men. I am very restrained in my disciplining of the new men as I am not an admirer of the hazing that goes on, and I prefer to spend my time in mastering aerodynamic studies, which I had started a year before at MIT.'s special classes. This is much more interesting to me than mothering a new group of cadets, and I earn a reputation for studiousness.

Our ten weeks go by like lightning. They have seen an incredible change in the lives of a group of bright young men who have been molded into responsible soldiers, with military bearing and alertness. They exude confidence, aware that they are mastering a special skill that is the most highly valued in the armed forces. About 40 of the original cadet corps have washed out, but the remainder moves up to the next flight level, called "Basic".

After a few days with time off, I report to Augusta Field in Augusta, Georgia, for 10 weeks of more advanced instruction that will mean more powerful airplanes and more demanding skills to learn.

BASIC & ADVANCED.

The 3 levels of flight instruction are Primary, Basic, and Advanced The contract school at Augusta teaches Basic with civilian instructors. We fly Vultee BT-13 low wing monoplanes that resemble the tactical airplanes we anticipate flying in the near future. These all-aluminum beauties look like high performance airplanes to us, just fresh from Stearman biplanes, but we soon learn that they have their quirks.

The big 450 horsepower engines are very loud, and cause so much vibration that they have earned the nickname of "Vultee Vibrators." The BT has a two-speed propeller, wing flaps, and a much higher landing speed than previous planes I have flown. They have full instrument panels, and we learn to constantly monitor these gauges for engine performance and flight attitude.

Our airport is a vast paved field capable of launching dozens of aircraft at a time, and it is a miracle of head-turning that prevents ground and midair collisions. The danger of accidents increases, when early one evening there is a loud growl of many engines along the flight line when we start night flying activities.

I have never flown at night before, and my first night takeoff is totally bewildering. With my instructor at the controls, we zoom into a black void. It is a pitch-black night, with no moon, and stars are so scattered in the sky that I cannot tell which way is up and which is down. It takes me a while to get oriented, but I soon come out of that confused state and take the controls for all the flying except the first landing. I realize the value of instruments more than ever - it is all you have to go by when visibility drops to zero, and vertigo gives you the illusion that down is up. You could be flying inverted and not know it. There sure is a lot to learn here.

Ground school is even more intense, as navigation becomes a big part of classroom instruction. Plotting courses on charts, and planning cross-country flights is great stuff. Our first cross-country is in a group, shepherded along by an instructor, with emphasis on reading charts for landmarks such as railroads, towns, and highways. I thank my Civilian Pilot Training Program instructors for this background back in Massachusetts, and find myself very comfortable on cross-countries.

Basic Flight School piles on a great deal of military instruction. The army is intent on training its new officers in its best traditions, expecting a lowly second lieutenant to set an example of the finest military organization in the world. The upper class hits hard on this, and we endure a schedule of rigorous instruction, accompanied by strong discipline, constant braces, and working off punishment tours by performing some manual chores on the grounds.

All is not work. Even the exercise program turns out to be fun, as we see its benefits, and how it leads to better athletic performance in baseball, swimming, and other sports. Open post, our time off the base, starts Saturday noon, and once again I find my fun at the local cadet club, looking for that special petite dancer who can share the joy of jitterbugging. I find some elegant company, who arranges dinner invitations at her home and with friends. My Model A Ford is as much my ticket to social events and fun times as if it were a deluxe Pierce Arrow or Packard, which abound in Augusta, and my classmates treat me like royalty, with a personal chariot that we can all enjoy.

Our main topic of conversation besides flying is girls. On Sunday nights back at the school before lights out, the usual gossip starts about who did what with whom, and the skeptical looks that mean. "That's a crock". My dancing partner is a lovely young lady who tells me right off that she is engaged, but feels that she must do her part to make me feel at home. She takes me home to dinner and I become a friend of her family. They are as warm as I were a family member, and there are times that my friend forgets she is otherwise engaged. It is a sad goodbye in Augusta when it is time to move on to Advanced School, which takes me back to Albany. I am now 10 weeks closer to earning my commission and getting my wings.

The changes in Albany are amazing. It is the new home of Turner Field, Single Engine Advanced Flying School. While I attended Darr on the other side of town, Turner was being built and we are the second group to attend. It is a huge facility that has sprung up on swamp land east of town, and will soon become a very efficient pilot producing center. One thing that carried over from Darr is the mud. Paving is not completed, so we are constantly cleaning our shoes.

Turner is a full-fledged army post, and instruction is entirely by army officers. Single Engine means Pursuit School. We fly the famous North American AT-6, a low wing monoplane with a Pratt & Whitney 600 horsepower engine (how I love those), constant speed propeller, retractable landing gear, full instruments, and radios. Cruising speed is 150 miles per hour, and we do all the maneuvers we have done before, including several cross-countries. Unfortunately, the training command is still sticking to group cross- countries, for fear of losing some airplanes, as has happened. They know how cocky a cadet can be with 150 hours total time, and how easy it is to lose yourself in flat country with no outstanding landmarks. We go cross-country in groups, but are supposed to do our own navigation to check on the flight leader.

After five weeks, we move into upper class status, and take off for Eglin Field in Florida for three days of gunnery practice. We will shoot .30 caliber machine guns at targets mounted on floating barges that are anchored offshore in smooth water.

I have an amazing streak of good luck in this gunnery exercise. I fly in the first division, early in the morning, when there is no crosswind that would require me to crab sidewise. My machine gun is perfectly aligned with the airplane sight, and in three passes I hit the bulls eye with every shot. It is so easy for me that I think I'm pretty hot stuff. The following two days I'm not quite as good, which settles me down, but with that head start, I run up the top score for the three day event.

Back at Turner, we practice a lot of formation flying. Lt. Krakowski, my instructor, has a lot to say to cocky pilots like me. One day we land a formation of three at a nearby practice field, and he orders me to tun around the entire field, wearing my parachute, because I had come in a "little tight, mister" and almost chewed off his right elevator in formation practice. If I had said what I really thought, "Sir, I was in perfect control all the time," he probably would have had me running all night long. All I could respond was, "Yes Sir, no excuse, Sir." Excuses or casual replies are a no-no, and this close to graduation, we are very careful to make no errors.

Another new event is high-altitude flying using oxygen. This sounds quite normal, but on my first flight I feel a very uncomfortable sensation of remoteness flying solo at 20,000 feet with a huge range of visibility below. Like all new flying experiences, this strange feeling soon disappears, and 1 get to enjoy high altitude.

Graduation day for Class of 41-1, December 12, 1941, is approaching fast. I have been spending my time off with my old friends in Albany, with Margie again my steady date, and we are all speculating on where I am likely to be transferred. Perhaps I will be an instructor at Turner, which obviously, would please her and her family no end. I sense that they have some plans for me.

On December 1, word spreads like wild fire; the postings are listed on the bulletin board. On graduation, my new assignment is to the 2nd Pursuit Squadron at Selfridge Field, Michigan, where the group is flying the Bell P-39 Aircobra, Selfridge is a top-notch assignment, as it one of the three major Pursuit bases that protect the United States. On the east coast, the 1st Pursuit Squadron at Mitchell Field on Long Island protects the eastern seaboard, and in California, Hamilton Field in the San Francisco Bay area is the home of the west coast unit. Selfridge protects the industrial heartland of America and is considered a prestige unit, just right for a 'hot pilot' with all of 200 hours flying time, and top gunner in the class. It couldn't be any better.

Chapter 6
GRADUATION DAY

There's an often-repeated saying in flying, so old it has whiskers that states, "There are old pilots, and there are bold pilots, but there are no old, bold pilots."

Take it from someone who's been there; the saying is true. Sure, I've taken chances. But in military flying you often have no choice. I wish I could say that what saved my neck was talent, finely developed skill, superior flying ability, or whatever. But this is pure ego; there were many men with far greater skill and experience who did not make it home. I think it was just plain luck, fate, or whatever you want to call it, that kept me alive, and if one believes in karma, perhaps saved me for some other purpose.

* * * * *

There is no bolder pilot than this graduate of the Class of 41-1 at Turner Field, Georgia, on December 12, 1941. It is only five days after the attack on Pearl Harbor, and the nation is still in shock. The news on December 7 was so startling that none of us knew quite how to receive it. We are not certain about the future now that we are at war, but we are so full of self-confidence that we are not dismayed by this event. WC are the 'cream of the crop,' having made it through Single-Engine Pursuit School and will soon be flying the best and the hottest pursuit planes, a prospect that is so thrilling that even the thoughts of war fail to shatter our joy. Few of us are worried. Youth is indestructible.

We are on top of the world! Our class of 41-1 is the only one in the Southeast Air Corps Training Command that had no fatal accidents throughout the training program. Every Flying Cadet in the country has seen the inspiring movie "I Wanted Wings", starring Robert Taylor and Veronica Lake, and now we have our own real wings. We know we will easily defeat those buck-toothed near-sighted Japanese pilots, which is how the enemy is described in popular rumor. We are so filled with the glory and pride of accomplishment that we feel that we own the sky!

On graduation day my lovely date pins on my shiny new wings and plants a big kiss. I stand there resplendent in my shiny new uniform, with shiny gold bars of a second lieutenant, and a shiny Sam Browne belt that is the very ultimate distinctive: symbol of an army officer. As all the graduates line up and admire each other. I am awed at the immense change that has taken place among us. We are now officers and gentlemen, no longer the straggly group of new cadets that entered the service a short eight months ago. The transition that has taken place in such a brief period of training is absolutely astounding; those sows' ears had truly become silk purses! Every one of us feels that he truly graduated from the status of a 'callow youth' to a new level of manhood.

As I have grown older, I am convinced that good military training is one of the greatest developers of character in young people. Add the responsibility of command, and the experience of coping with life-threatening situations, and you have potential leaders.

Our guest speaker at the graduation ceremony is the mayor of Albany, Georgia, home of Turner Field. He speaks very pompously to an audience that is obliged to remain silent and pay total attention. He orates at great length about his envy of "young warriors who are girding their loins to do battle with the evil enemy of our country". Some of our freshly minted second lieutenants, who have an inkling of what war and casualties can mean, whisper that he is welcome to take our place. We critically, and unfairly, label his speech as an example of older men sending young men off to war, but in our joy of graduation we dismiss his words as unimportant. I am one of the graduates who is cynical about his speech, but I have yet to learn in a few months just how much I have underestimated the danger, and how damaging war can be.

Our highly respected commandant of cadets, Lt. Philip Von Weller, congratulates the Class of 41-1 in a short speech which he makes every five weeks as each Flying Cadet class graduates. He introduces his staff, and the class officers, and then gives me a great thrill by awarding me the prize for first place in gunnery, in the form of a very precious Kodak movie camera that will have a lot of use.

The trophy was won in the gunnery event at Eglin Field, where I had fired .30 caliber machine guns at floating targets. Was I good enough to take first prize? I think I was just lucky to be the first one to fly that first morning, when there was no wind to create ocean chop or air turbulence. Naturally, I think I'm pretty hot stuff, and in my eagerness for adventure, I look forward to the challenge of actual air-to-air combat.

We then march down the cavernous mess hall for our final graduation ceremonies, and enjoy a relaxed dinner while our commandant tells us stories of his cadet days. I am one of the lucky ones with my own date, Margie, a real southern charmer, who plants another large kiss on me in public, making me the most envied graduate, and we dance the evening away. This has to be the most thrilling day of my life! I am moving on to new adventures, new places, and as an officer in the United States Army Air Corps I have a status in the world of men I had never dreamed of achieving.

It is the next day, December 13, 1941. Pearl Harbor is many thousands of miles away, and we are not yet ready to accept the realities of the war that erupted six days ago. Washington may be in a furor of activity, but we can only sit and wait for orders. Several of us decide to go aloft and celebrate our new status as Officer Pilots. Our AT -6 is the finest training airplane for single engine Pursuit, and we have 65 hours logged, most of it solo. We consider ourselves pretty "hot", and now that we have our wings we want to let loose.

Three of us take off and fly formation. But unlike supervised formation flying, we now snug in so close we are practically touching wings. With one slight error in judgment, one of us will chew the tail off another. This is the bold flying that gets you into trouble. We are slightly giddy with our new status and willing to try anything. We do some rolls, loops, and anything else we can think of. After many months of highly disciplined flying we are now responsible for our own behavior, and this is not too good. I film a classmate with my new camera and later realize that his maneuvers were totally out of control. I am amazed we survive this little bit of careless indulgence. Perhaps fate has us destined to perform more important duties.

The history of military flying demonstrates that showing off causes many losses of aircraft and personnel. A victory roll at low altitude coming across the home field after a successful mission is a show-off gesture that has claimed the lives of many pilots; who forgot themselves in the elixir of victory. Military flying is dangerous enough without taking ridiculous risks that come with over-confidence. New pilots with 200 hours behind them are particularly vulnerable. That is why careful training and disciplined operation are of the highest priority.

*Cadet James Segel (top) and
Stearman PT-17 Primary Trainer*

*The Army Air Corps
recruiting poster of 1941
was an incentive to join.*

LG-4QG-74IN-T.F.X(12-14-41-10P-6")
GRADUATION DANCE OF 41-I, TURNER FIELD, GA

Graduation Dance of Cadet Class 41-1 Turner Field, Georgia December 14, 1941. Second Lt. James Segel far left.

With my instructor and Vultee BT-13 basic trainer.

Chapter 7
NEW ORDERS

I looked forward to my transfer to Selfridge Field. There I would check out in the incredible P-39, one of the newest fighters, powered with a 1200 horsepower in-line Allison engine and armed with a 20 mm cannon as well as .50 caliber machine guns. It had tricycle gear and was one of the very hottest of the hot.

But on December 13 the earlier orders sending me to the 2nd Pursuit Group to fly Aircobras were put on hold while the War Department got into high gear, facing the sudden eruption of war. All assignment orders were held up until things could be sorted out. We crowded around the bulletin boards waiting for new assignments while the powers that controlled such things debated on where to send us. Our fate was in their hands and rumors had us going in every direction. The suspense was immense.

Fate stepped in and my transfer to the 2nd Pursuit was cancelled. I later learned that the group was already on its way to the Philippines, and reports were that the P-39 did not do well in tactical operations in that theater. The P-39 had some unpleasant features of which I was not aware. Its tricycle landing gear was designed for paved runways, and the nose wheel assembly was very lightly built to reduce weight, a vital factor in fighter design. The rough dirt fields in the Pacific islands, with ruts and bumps, could put severe loads on the nose wheel, sometimes causing it to collapse. The result was a sudden crash stop with the nose of the airplane digging into the dirt runway. The heavy Allison engine was mounted behind the pilot, connected to the propeller by a long shaft running under the floor of the cockpit. A crash stop put such great stress on the engine mounts that they sometimes broke loose, with the engine smashing forward against the pilot, sandwiching him against the instrument panel, with fatal results.

Another flaw was a flight characteristic that killed new pilots who had low hours in high performance airplanes. The P-39 had a tendency to flip over in a sudden stall when making a low speed steep turn into final approach. A stall at this low altitude has no room for recovery. Result: a fatal crash.

Almost every military airplane has characteristics that some pilots fear, and the P-39 had its share. Another was the Martin B-26, comically called the "Flying Whore -- No Visible Means of Support," because of the small wing area and high wing loading that could quickly cause a stall and crash if an engine failed on takeoff.

Even the much celebrated P-38 Lockheed Lightning had its critics, and many newly hatched pilots were scared of it until factory test pilots taught them what a beautiful airplane it was. An engine failure on takeoff just after reaching flying speed caused a number of fatal crashes among new pilots and the rumor started that the P-38 was a killer airplane. Crashes always develop fear in a new pilot, but once he learns the idiosyncracies of his airplane, knows its flaws and how to cope with them, he begins to feel at home in the cockpit. Pretty soon he will be bragging that his is the greatest airplane ever built, and that he is a total master of this death-defying machine.

The P-39 had some fans, but many pilots were happy to fly other types of airplanes. Eventually, under Lend-Lease, most Aircobra production went to the Russians, who came to love them.

After a week of waiting, the new orders were posted. Fate had once again pushed a button that was a big surprise and disappointment for this would-be fighter pilot. I was assigned to the Jack Frye Multi-Engine School run by Transworld Airways at Albuquerque, New Mexico, to check out as co-pilot on B-24 bombers for the Ferrying Command. How this selection was made has always been a mystery to me, as it made no more sense than assigning a cook to dental school. I guess the names were just picked out of a hat by someone who decided that a well-trained pilot could fly anything. I had no multi-engine time and sorely missed the chance to fly fighters, which was always the ultimate in military flying, but every new airplane is an adventure to be anticipated with a thrill.

Before I boarded that slow moving Southern Railway train to New Mexico, I had to say goodbye to two very special friends. One was a beautiful southern belle named Margie, who had been my close companion during many months of cadet days in Albany. We had danced every Saturday night to records of Glen Miller and other famous bands at the Cadet Club, spent lazy Sundays at her family's spacious place on the outskirts of town, and I had become very close to her family.

Her aunt, a fun-loving, gregarious and gracious southern lady changed very quickly into a concerned and very business-like chaperone who took me aside when she heard I was leaving town, and bluntly asked me, "What are your intentions?"

I was a 22 year-old Air Force pilot shipping out, and when I pleaded "the war" she shrugged her shoulders and dismissed me out of the picture. I learned later that Margie did marry a cadet of a later class, a fine young man from my home city of Boston, a young man who had more serious intentions.

My other love was my 1931 Model A Ford sedan, a true and faithful companion for two years, at home and in my travels. We had driven from Massachusetts to Georgia with no fuss or bother, and I was always able to fix it with wire or tape when it acted up. Its engine used lots of oil, so at every flying school, I made arrangements with airplane mechanics to obtain a good supply of drained airplane oil to fill its crankcase.

Every weekend we loaded six or seven cadets and rode into town like a bunch of hungry cowboys just in off the range, "a-lookin' for a good time." My Model A was more than just my first car. It was my green Golden Chariot, giving me freedom to go wherever I chose, to wander, to dally under a shady tree with a pretty girl, to dream of new vistas. I was going to miss it, and I shed a tear when I said goodbye. For hard facts, this magnificent vehicle had cost me 40 hard-earned dollars back in 1939, and I sold it for $75.

In late December, 1941. I rode a slow train across the southern states on a trip that seemed to last forever. The big surprise was when I awakened on the fourth morning to see a sight new to me - sagebrush and limitless prairies. I had arrived in the great West. The railroad station at Albuquerque was most colorful, with Indians parading the platform and doing business as usual, offering blankets and other local artifacts for sale to the tourists. This was Indian country! I felt that I had entered a whole different world. We were checked into the Hilton Hotel, very deluxe accommodations after life in the cadet barracks, and went to work on the flight line the next day.

My introduction to the B-24 was very exciting. I had never seen one up close, and the bulging boxcar fuselage and the high thin wings were very impressive, and I wondered how long it would take to get checked out in one. In peace time, pilots were carefully trained in a new airplane, with months of instruction. One of the common complaints was that Air Corps instructors hogged most of the landings and takeoffs themselves, because there were restrictions on the number of flying hours available, and they needed to maintain their own proficiency. It took months of training before a new pilot was checked out, and he usually flew as copilot for a long time. Now that we were at war, all restrictions were gone. We had civilian instructors who had 30 days to check us out.

Airplanes were coming out of the factories faster than qualified pilots were being trained, so it was not unusual to give a new pilot a brief check one day and turn the airplane over to him the next. The result was often accidents, attributed to pilot error: but more appropriately should be called 'lack of adequate instruction.' The Jack Frye Transition School gave us a much better opportunity to learn how to fly the B-24 than many combat pilots received later in the war.

My pilot, Lieutenant Jack Griffin, had some twin-engine experience, but not much. I had flown nothing larger than single-engine trainers, and was sure that the B-24 cockpit, with its maze of controls, valves, switches, and instruments was much too complicated to master in a short time. But expert instruction made it all fall into place quickly, and in a few days I took on the dual jobs of co-pilot and assistant flight engineer.

The first take-off, with civilian instructor Simms at the controls, was mind-boggling.

We started slowly down the runway with the roaring sound of four great radial engines, and, sitting tensely in the jump seat behind the control pedestal, I wondered if our monstrous boxcar would make it into the air. We were lightly loaded, and when we reached the halfway point, Simms was horsing back on the wheel, and I was surprised to find we left the ground amazingly quickly.

The month at the four-engine school went very well. I rode right seat and had the usual gripe about never getting a chance to do my own takeoffs and landings. I was still awed at the ability of those four engines to lift that massive box of an airplane off the ground so readily, and to this day it is not my favorite airplane.

We lived well at the Hilton Hotel, being paid per-diem for temporary duty. This hotel was, very fortunately for my social life, the overnight stop for Transworld Airlines crews, and there were plenty of cute stewardesses around all the time. We were sharp new second lieutenants, and we enjoyed an active social life.

Albuquerque was a new experience for me. I had never seen such clear blue skies, or breathed such brisk mountain air, and I luxuriated in the great outdoors that surrounded us. I skied the Sandia Mountain slopes, and enjoyed an occasional roll in the snow with the right company. Ever since that month, Albuquerque has been one of my favorite places.

After our checkout in the B-24 was completed, we were ordered to the Boeing factory in Seattle, to ferry B-17's. At this early stage of the war, February, 1942, things were in a great turmoil, and it was essential to move airplanes from the factories to the staging areas quickly. We had never flown a B-17, but after four weeks in the B-24, the transition to the four-engine B-17 was easy. The new E model was just coming on line, and production was being pushed to the maximum.

I consider the Flying Fortress, as we called the B-17, a beautiful airplane, just the shape I had admired as a kid building model airplanes, with its low wing design and tall tail. Our job was to ferry these wonderful new B-17e's, the first with tail guns and bottom turrets, to MacDill Field in Florida, where the 8th Air Force was getting ready to move to England. Our Ferrying Command office was located on James Street in downtown Seattle, near the top-notch Olympic Hotel, which gave us a special rate of $2 per night, so I lived very well for the short time I was there.

On ferry flights we flew only daytime, and under Visual Flight Rules (VFR) which meant no bad weather. This policy was the most conservative way to insure that ferry missions would be completed safely. The returns to Seattle were very special. We flew United Airlines from Tampa to Chicago, and in the evening, boarded United's sleeper flight with its fold-down bunks allowing us to sleep our way to Seattle. It was great to be tucked in by a courteous stewardess, but a goodnight kiss was not part of the service.

I loved to fly the B-17, which had excellent flying characteristics and was what we call these days 'user friendly.' Since building up flying time is the goal of every pilot, I volunteered to fly co-pilot on Army Air Corps acceptance flights at the factory at Boeing Field. My pilot was an old time major whose job was to test each airplane before giving it the stamp of approval for military use. These hops were pretty routine, but the major jealously hogged all the takeoffs and landings, while I did the routine jobs of raising the gear and flaps, locking throttles, and other co-pilot duties.

On one of these hops things got exciting. My expert pilot announced that he was going to try a stall maneuver with the new Minneapolis-Honeywell electric autopilot (AP) to test its performance. He gradually reduced power, and slowly raised the nose by turning the vertical control on the AP until the airplane started to shudder, warning us of an impending stall. The B-17 was a docile flying machine that had no tricks up its sleeve, and it gave lots of warning long before it would make a complete stall, drop a wing, and go into a spin. With a stall coming on, the major did the right thing: he pushed the wheel forward to get the nose down and pick up airspeed, and recover from the stall.

Unfortunately, the new model autopilot was made of tougher stuff than he was used to, and he could not overpower it. The airplane shuddered some more, and started to fall off on one wing, a prelude to a full spin. He yelled to me to help him out, "Push the damn wheel!" I tried but even with my added muscle we could barely budge that wheel. The major was in a panic; it was one of those white-knuckle moments that every pilot has when he feels he is losing control of his airplane.

But this problem had a simple solution. The three switches on the AP that controlled elevators, rudder, and ailerons had a master switch - a bar across all three. I reached over to the control pedestal and flicked the bar down to the OFF position. The AP instantly released its control of the airplane, and with our forward pressure on the wheel, the nose of that big airplane immediately plunged down into a steep dive angle, safely recovering our flying speed.

The major also recovered, but not as quickly as the airplane. His complexion was pasty, and he suggested that I fly it back. After a few minutes, he said quite casually, "I guess we learned something new today," and, after landing, he disappeared for the rest of the day. Boeing was a busy beehive with production rising rapidly. We expected a long stay in Seattle, which would have been just great. Tired of checking in and out of the hotel for each flight, several of us moved in with families that offered rooms for rent. I shared a room with a buddy in a suburban home overlooking Lake Washington, and had great plans for some sailing and other activities when the rainy season ended. The family had two lovely daughters, and my roommate eventually married one of them.

But my stay there was not to be very long. Our commanding officer was ordered to send one pilot to join a special project in Florida, and I was selected. I wondered, why me? Could it be because he found me sitting at his desk one day using his telephone, making a date? Probably.

I received new orders instructing me to proceed immediately to Morrison Field, Florida, where the American Military Mission to China (AMMISCA) was being prepared. I knew nothing about this unit, only that I was moving on. The personnel officer at our Seattle office cut orders directing me to travel by military airplane, with enough delay time en route to allow me to visit Boston for a couple of days and show off to the family. I hitched a ride to Wright Field in Dayton, where I was temporarily put to work doing slow time on Stearmans that had just received new engines, which required three hours of air time at reduced power before approval of the work. This was very dull work and I was glad to get an assignment to ferry a civilian airplane to Morrison Field, where it would be used as a utility airplane. It was a very old Cessna that cruised at about 100 miles per hour, and I could see a long trip ahead of me. Here was a budding fighter pilot, top gunnery scorer, flying a shaky old airplane that had a very questionable engine. It was so rickety that I called it my Model A airplane, and treated it with tender loving care.

It took three days to make the trip with stops at Augusta and Albany where I had gone through cadet training, and where I visited old friends who laughed at the contraption I was ferrying to Florida, instead of some sleek fighter or powerful bomber. On arrival at Morrison, I handed over the old airplane and was greeted with the news that I had just missed the promotion list by not being there. Along with a few other latecomers, I missed a promotion to first lieutenant; and it took me many months to catch up.

Things were happening fast. It was really a lucky day for me, as I was teamed up with another late arrival, Lieutenant Curtis Caton, who became my friend and mentor, and taught me most of what I ever learned about flying.

Chapter 8
CURTIS CATON

Perhaps my middle name should be "Lucky," for the simple reason that I am still around after my tour of duty in the China-Burma-India Theater and in other high-risk ventures. It must have been luck that kept me alive, or perhaps I was fated for other things in my life.

One of my luckiest breaks was my assignment as co-pilot to Curtis Caton, who became my best friend and instructor, and saw to it that I learned everything he could teach me about flying. He must have been very good at it.

Curt was a slim, sandy haired southern gentleman, from Mobile, Alabama, 26 years old, a very quiet speaking person, with great concern for his fellow man. He resembled Jimmy Stewart, smiled a lot, and displayed a lazy, easy-going nature. This was deceiving, as he had great energy and an adventurous spirit. I came to admire something very special - his totally unflappable disposition. No matter what emergency he faced, he stayed cool, and I never heard him raise his voice to anyone.

Curt had spent several years flying for Eastern Airlines, and was one of those very unhappy copilots who was drafted by the Air Corps when it "requested" 75 captains from the major airlines for the American Military Mission to China (AMMISCA) project. The airlines were unwilling to lose their skilled captains, so they filled the request by promoting 75 of their senior copilots to the rank of captain, and releasing them to the military. They were immediately commissioned as second lieutenants.

This was a great upset for the copilots who were expecting early promotion to the status of airline captain, a highly paid position. The airlines were expanding rapidly, and there was a critical need for their skills, but now these men were in the army and felt like a group of draftees. They were older than most of us new military pilots, in their late 20's to early 30's, and most were leaving behind wives and small children. They sacrificed good airline salaries for a lieutenant's meager pay: $220 per month, plus allowances. Most expressed bitter feelings at this turn of events.

Curt's lovely wife, Audrey, joined us for a short time at West Palm Beach, Florida, and I learned that she was expecting a child that fall. I am sure that she shed many tears at the thought of her husband leaving for parts unknown. It was infinitely easier for us younger, single, eager army pilots, and I had no qualms about going overseas to new adventures.

The ex-airline pilots were very unhappy that they had been "drafted," but soon their adventurous spirit took over and they started making plans for our exciting assignment, which was taking us to India. To every one of them, flying was a way of life. Most had worked their way into flying the hard way, in the 30's, when flying was a sport for barnstormers and daredevils, and flying time was hard to get and expensive. They all had nourished dreams of flying to foreign places and sampling the wondrous mysteries of Africa, the Orient, and any other places their wings would take them. Now they had this chance, thanks to Uncle Sam, and some were expecting real adventure, flying into the wild blue, destination unknown. All had supreme confidence in their ability to fly a C-47 to any place in the world.

Curt had over 4000 hours flying time, most of it in DC-3's, as compared to my total time of about 500 hours. He had many hours of actual instrument time, whereas my flying "by the gauges" was done entirely in a Link trainer, a simulator used for teaching instrument flying. He had undergone an intensive training program required by his airline, and he had extensive knowledge of the DC-3, its flight characteristics, and mechanical systems. Best of all, he took great pride in teaching me the ropes and I overheard him commenting to other pilots that he was pleased with the way I caught on. This greatly inflated my ego.

I tried to back up this praise by learning all I could about the C-47, reading the technical manuals, and doing some basic service work on our airplane with our flight engineer. Curt gave me lots of DC-3 airline technical material to read which was a big help, as the Air Corps had very little technical information to offer, nor did they have a training manual on the C-47 airplane.

I was excited the day we were assigned our own C-47, for under the dull camouflage paint I visualized that shiny DC-3 airliner I had dreamt of flying some day. Our airplane was serial number 7797 and we were happy to find that it had very low hours compared to some of the airplanes in the project that had lots of time on them, and needed extensive overhauls. This was our own airplane, and was to be our home for a long time, our personal flying carpet, so we decided to give it a name. Our crew of four offered a variety of names, and selected "Ferdinand," for reasons I don't recall.

We had taken on two more crew members. Our flight engineer was Sergeant George Saylor, a handsome fellow who hinted to all that re resembled screen idol Robert Taylor. He loved the ladies, and always kept an eye open for female company. He also kept a close watch over Private Fred Sibold, our radio operator, a fun-loving youngster, who was fresh out of radio school. Fred had never flown before and was airsick much of the time, so we all took turns at the radio. Sibold was a skilled mechanic and was very good at scrounging, finding scarce items that no one else knew about. He showed up with such things as extra first aid kits, flares, tools, and enough canned foods to overload us.

On our first inspection of Ferdinand, Curt showed his total familiarity with the C-47. He stepped into the cockpit and proceeded to check the controls, switches, and radios to see how this military version compared with the airline DC-3's he had been flying. He was so utterly at home in that left seat that I knew we were in the hands of an expert. This contrasted greatly with some of the other pilots I had flown with on ferrying trips, who had very little experience in their airplanes, and were very jumpy when things went wrong. Curt's superior training and heavy experience gave him the confidence that he could cope with any situation, and it was a pleasure for me to share the cockpit with him. We had a long way to go, and while flying all the way to India and China across many foreign lands was a very exciting prospect for me, the real burden of arriving safely weighed heavily on the guy who sat in the left seat. He checked the airplane carefully, paying special attention to the extra tanks and fuel system inside the cabin that increased our fuel capacity from 800 to 1600 gallons, giving us up to 20 hours flying time.

We flew Ferdinand across the flat Florida landscape to shake out any bugs, and found its cruising speed was only 155 miles per hour, compared to the DC-3's 165 MPH. The extra weight of reinforced flooring and other added features cut our speed.

Curt then proceeded to check me out as carefully as he did the airplane. He taught me about all the systems, and had me fly the airplane until I felt comfortable with it. This was a far cry from other first pilots I had flown with, who did most of the flying, and never let a copilot do a takeoff or landing. Curt gave me single-engine practice, and then went into takeoffs and landings. He insisted on making three-point landings, which he felt would be important in overseas operation, and were a devil to get right. In a three- pointer, all three wheels hit the ground together, as contrasted with a wheel landing, in which the main landing gear touches down first, and the tailwheel follows as the airplane loses speed.

Eastern Airlines required its pilots to become proficient at three-point landings, which were done at a slower landing speed, and allowed a shorter landing roll, making it easier to operate into many small airports. Doing these landings was easier said than done. To make a smooth three-point landing I had to develop a feel for the stalling point, which varied with load, altitude, and wind condition. If you stalled out too soon, you fell hard from too high. If you came in a little fast and tried to get the tail down, you simply ballooned up, and then fell hard when the stall came. If you gave it a little throttle, to smooth out your landing, you only stretched out the landing roll.

It took lots of practice to master the three-point technique. Many times I goofed it and ended up bouncing down the runway like a jackrabbit, hitting tail first, then main gear, then tail again, then main gear - all a sure sign of a novice. Short field landings turned out to be very useful overseas, and we used them all the time, but in my later flying of C-47 and DC-3 airplanes in the states, I went back to doing wheel landings that were smoother and easier on the plane, pilot, and passengers.

There is a famous saying that most flying consists of long and boring hours that are occasionally interrupted by moments of panic. That's when the pilot earns his pay, and learns how to cope. Curt was well worth his pay. His calm attitude did rub off on me because he set such a good example on handling emergencies. I can recall reporting some impending hazard, and having him sit there, totally impassive, with me wondering if he had even heard me. It turned out that he had heard me, and was just digesting the information. Then he would calmly say, "I guess we better do 'thus and so'", and it was always the right decision. I learned from him to always maintain a calm appearance, to impress others that I always had a solution for any problem, even though deep down I might be pretty scared. As I gained more confidence, it came easier.

"Ferdinand" was our wonderful C-47 that took us to
China and served us well throughout my tour of duty.

Chapter 9
PREPARATION

There is no substitute for experience, and I was lucky to sit at Curt Caton's right side and absorb all I could of the technique of good piloting. My late arrival at Morrison Field caused me to miss the promotion list, but being assigned to Curt made up for it. He was my role model in the air, and I cannot imagine how I would have survived the hazards of this dangerous and complicated venture on my own, with my meager 500 hours of flying time. Many pilots with the same limited time as I had were put in charge of heavy bombers going overseas, and many of them never arrived due to poor navigation or lack of experience in handling emergency situations. The unflappable Curt gave me complete confidence in our ability to succeed in our mission, and taught me more about the C-47 than I would ever have to know.

Another expert, who was a delight to work with, was Major Tom Rafferty, our commanding officer, a most unusual and wonderful guy. Rafferty had started his air Corps career at a very young age as a mechanic, and over the years had risen in the enlisted ranks, eventually qualifying for a commission. He was an excellent pilot, and best of all, knew the military system, how to cut through the paperwork and get things done. His crew meetings were an education, for he briefed us on the coming trip and what to expect en route. He handed out supply lists that were much larger than the ones handed us by supply officers, as Tom had been overseas many times, and knew that we would have to be self-sufficient once we left the States.

He praised the skills of our first pilots, and told of reports that had filtered back of heavy bombers heading for Asia getting lost due to poor navigation, bad weather, or mechanical problems. Their crews had a low level of experience, and he wished there were enough ex-airline pilots to fly every airplane across to Asia.

He praised our airplanes, pointing that there was never a better design built than the Douglas DC-3, with its two Pratt and Whitney engines. One day I jokingly told him that I checked the serial numbers of our engines and discovered that I had personally helped build those two R-1830's the previous April at the factory. Tom was twice my age, a short wiry weathered man, with reddish hair and a great sense of humor, a regular guy we could joke with and treat as 'one of the boys.' He patted me on the back and gave me the age-old flyer's advice, "Take good care of your engines, and they'll take care of you. " It certainly worked out that way for me.

He advised us on flight technique, pointing out why we should avoid afternoon flying with its build-up of huge cumulous clouds over the mainland of Central and South America. He recommended we fly in groups of two or more airplanes for safety reasons, and to check each other's navigation.

Curt and the other pilots who were "kidnapped" from the airlines by the Air Corps, were still complaining about their bad deal, but Tom Rafferty quieted them down, when he said he had "overheard" that they could be assigned to the infantry if they didn't like their current status. After they learned more about the importance of our mission, their enthusiasm grew, and they went about the business of outfitting their airplanes.

We younger copilots had no command responsibilities. We expected our first pilots to solve all of our flying problems, and we concentrated on our job of preparing the airplanes and hunting for supplies. We had long supply lists, but we heeded Major Rafferty's advice, and kept adding things. He warned us that there were no convenient stores loaded with merchandise where we were going. That was the understatement of the year. If we had known we were flying to some of the most remote locations in the world, we would have loaded truckloads of drugstore items, clothing, cameras, and any other portable items we could carry.

We went downtown on shopping expeditions like a bunch of college boys preparing for a fraternity party. Francine L. was the young woman manager of the local drug store, and she knew all about our needs, and probably all about our mission. We bought the usual assortment of drug store items, and some suggestions of hers, having a lot of fun with the more personal items.

In those days, condoms were ordered by a whisper to a male drug clerk, but Francine was so open that we treated her as "one of the boys," and let her set up our drugstore kits. In addition to toothpaste, aspirin, shaving cream, and razors, she gave us the lowdown on the best "rubbers" to take, and even gave instructions on how to use them to some of the blushing shy guys. It turned out that she was a very "with it" girl, who loved a good time, and dated a number of departing pilots, leaving them all with fond memories of their last few nights in the U.S.

An embarrassing event took place under the wing of our airplane weeks later in Africa, when a few of us were talking about recent fun times back in Florida. Several told about taking Francine to dinner, and how a night spent with her was a delightful and memorable occasion. One of our men was silent. We knew he had been with her a great deal so we kidded him about the times he spent with her. He stuttered, coughed, and finally blurted out the startling statement, "Hell, I married the girl!" No more discussion about Francine after that.

I visited various parts of Morrison Field picking up supplies, and one day, to my dismay, came upon the ruins of the old Cessna that I had flown in from Wright Field. Someone had parked a B-24 in front of it and had then done an engine run-up. The propeller blast from the 1200 horsepower engines had picked up the little Cessna like a kite and flung it against the hangar wall with such force that all that was left was a pile of wreckage. This was not a fitting end for my little airplane that I had carefully nursed all the way to Florida. I reached down and patted a broken wing section in sympathy for the long life the Cessna had led and the many thousands of hours it had flown. It was like saying goodbye to an old friend.

To travel around the base, we used government issue (GI) bicycles that seemed to be common property. Eventually, one of them disappeared into the cabin of our airplane, hidden in the toilet, and traveled with us. Our commanding officer, Major Rafferty, acquired a motor scooter in the same way, so we didn't feel so guilty about our "moonlight acquisition." Our bike was the handiest tool we had and we guarded it carefully, until someone else "borrowed it" at our stop in Karachi, India.

We kept piling items into Ferdinand until it looked like there wasn't room for any more. Four large fuel tanks, each holding 200 gallons, already occupied most of the cabin space, so we piled things over, under, and around these. Little attention was paid to weight and balance of the airplane, and I wonder to this day how we ever got the tail up on takeoff with so much gear loaded in the tail section.

We actually did not know our final destination beyond Karachi, India, until a few days prior to our scheduled departure date. The Pentagon had issued orders stating that all troop and aircraft movements were to be classified information, so often the personnel involved did not know where they were heading. Learning of the airlift to China added to our sense of adventure. Young Air Corps pilots expected to lead a dangerous life, so we did not spend time worrying about pending events.

While all our preparation was going on, Morrison Field was going through an explosive expansion. This was my first real look at the preparations necessary to dispatch a group of military airplanes off to war. The streets of the small base were crowded with jeeps, military trucks, and civilian trucks hauling in lumber and other supplies to put up new buildings as fast as they could. The flight line was jammed with a large assortment of aircraft waiting for maintenance. The overflow of airplanes was parked all over the field, on grass areas in between the runways. I saw B-17 and B-24 heavy bombers, mediums like the Mitchell B-25, the Martin B-26, and Lockheed Hudsons, some with American markings and others with

British RAF insignia. There were small fighter bombers like the Douglas A-20, and various fighters scattered about, aimed for Caribbean bases.

Far across the field was a nondescript group of airplanes, perched with noses tilted high in the air like a group of eagles ready to take flight. These were our C-47's of the AMMISCA project, humbly placed among fierce-looking combat aircraft that sported menacing machine guns and bomb racks. We were too busy to notice the difference, knowing that our mission was of great importance.

Our crew-members moved about the area asking each other countless questions, relying on each other for valuable tips.

"We're doing a test hop tomorrow - can you lend me your local chart?" "Where is that mechanic who was supposed to replace the leaky valve?" "Where do we get parachutes? Somebody borrowed ours. "

"Isn't there any decent food on this base?" "Where's the finance office? I haven't been paid for two months." "Where the hell is that jeep? I've got a heavy date tonight. " "Where do I find a good bar with lots of cute girls?"

These were the usual questions asked by any group of red blooded warriors. We were all nervously waiting for the final check-off that would give us the okay to leave.

During the delay in preparing our airplane for the trip to India, I looked around Morrison Field for other aircraft types to fly. I was offered the co-pilot seat in a Lockheed Hudson on submarine patrol missions off the Florida coast, and thought this would be quite exciting. It was quite the opposite - very monotonous. We flew for hours, keeping our eyes peeled for periscope wakes or any other signs of these deadly undersea craft, but all we saw were the wrecks of cargo ships that had been torpedoed and were half submerged in the shallow waters.

This was my first sight of the ravages of war, and we knew there had been lives lost on these vessels. It was chilling to imagine the same attacks taking place in the frigid North Atlantic where a few minutes exposure to the icy cold water meant certain death.

I had some light moments, too. We were invited into the luxurious homes of some wealthy Palm Beach residents who arranged pleasant parties for the young flying officers. Some of these homes were on the Lake Worth waterfront, with their own docks, and whenever I saw a small sailboat tied up at a dock I wasn't shy about offering to give it a sail. That lake and the Intercoastal Waterway are a boater's paradise, and I spent some refreshing hours sailing small dinghies, reminding me of past days on the Charles River in Boston .

Chapter 10
INTO INDIA

Would our airplane fly? I calculated that with the double fuel load of 1600 gallons we grossed about 30,000 pounds. In addition, we were loading a never-ending amount of supplies, so I mentally added another 2,000 pounds. Then there was last minute stuff, and we knew we were so far over our maximum allowable gross takeoff weight of 31,000 pounds that we lost count. I visualized us staggering into the air, just clearing the trees. Curt laughed, and said to pile it in, as he had complete faith in our airplane.

So we stowed more canned foods, heavy on Spam, on top of our field rations, the First Aid kits, bedding rolls, tents, inflatable life rafts, signal flares, and the countless other items that the supply people thought necessary for over-water and jungle flights. Our medications included a 1000-tablet jar of sulfanilamide, which became the target of many thieves, being worth almost its weight in gold. We loaded a spare Very pistol flare gun, extra signal flares, our side arms, and a Thompson sub-machine gun with spare drums of .45 caliber ammunition.

There was a shortage of Colt .45 semi-automatic pistols, so I became owner of a .45 caliber six-shooter revolver that looked like it dated back to the early days of the cavalry. I joked that I had General Custer's personal weapon, and this long barreled beauty looked it. It was the kind referred to in western movies as a "hawgleg," fit for cracking walnuts, and it was so heavy and cumbersome hanging from a GI web belt that I could never wear it in the cockpit, as it would have greatly interfered with a fast exit. I was happy to trade it off later to a buddy for his standard issue 1911 Colt semi-automatic pistol, which I wore in a shoulder holster. He was most grateful for the swap, saying he always wanted a six-shooter, and he practiced quick-draw with it continuously, almost blowing off a toe.

On the afternoon of May 12, a staff sergeant drove up in his jeep and presented me with a form, saying, "Would you please sign here, sir?" It was a receipt for "One Douglas C-47 Airplane, Equipped for Overseas Flight." What if I didn't bring it back? Would I have to pay for it?

One more addition was a bulky envelope containing $5000 in small denomination bills that we picked up in the finance office. Curt signed for that. This was our emergency money, to buy fuel, food, or other necessities in the event of a critical need for cash. We never had to use these reserve funds. Later we learned that there was a big fuss about the failure of some of the crews to account for part or all of this money, as some of the funds had disappeared in unexplained ways. Various excuses were made for the cash shortage, and some headquarters brass were pretty upset over this. There were some threats made, but no one was ever charged for the loss.

Departure day was May 13, 1942. We double-checked our gear and at 0530 we started our engines for the last time in the States, heading for the Far East and what the fates had in store for us. This was to be the great adventure of my life, the first time I had ever left the States, and I was very excited. If I had been solely responsible for the airplane as first pilot, I would have had butterflies in my stomach, and probably a great worry about the future. But with Curt in the left seat, I had such confidence in his ability to handle any emergency situation that it never occurred to me to have any fear. This feeling was a great luxury denied to 95 percent of new pilots during the early days of the war. Most were given airplanes to fly without adequate training on how to handle the countless dangerous situations that always threatened. They were truly placed in harm's way, and the crews sensed the fears that clutched the pilot's gut. I was very fortunate to have such a mentor as Curt Caton.

Another C-47 took off with us, and we kept in touch, comparing navigation accuracy and fuel consumption. Our fight plan called for departure at dawn, with arrival early in the afternoon before the daily build-up of great cumulus clouds that could block our route. These towering clouds contained extremely violent turbulence and no pilot would think of flying into them. As we flew over the Caribbean headed for Puerto Rico, we could see the clouds building up to tremendous heights over the Mexican mainland to our right.

We made overnight stops at Puerto Rico and Trinidad, and then flew a long nine-hour 1300-mile hop to Belem, Brazil, on the 15th, crossing huge jungle areas that seemed to go on forever. In our practice flying across the extensive Florida Everglades, there were always towns in sight. The South American jungle was very different - it was so vast that all we could see for hours was an immense green carpet of tropical growth, and we could only imagine the wild life that existed in that awe-inspiring untouched world that unfolded beneath us, hour after hour. It was comforting to have two reliable engines moving us over an impenetrable part of the world, and we had our first experience with placing total faith in our airplane. It is hard to believe that in more modern times a very large part of these endless jungles is falling victim to the developer's bulldozer.

Belem sits on the south shore of the mouth of the great Amazon River, the largest river in the world. The bay is so large that when we left the northern shore, the opposite shore was not visible, and we kept checking our compass, as all we saw was water. It was some time before we spotted the south shore and for a while I was concerned that we were actually heading across the Atlantic.

I have a striking memory of Belem as a real frontier town - a tropical version of Dodge City of the old West. It's muddy streets were lined with ramshackle wooden buildings, one of which was our hotel for the night, the most deluxe hotel in town, but a very shabby place. The hotel introduced us to something new - primitive indoor plumbing. The toilet was nothing more than a hole in the floor, but there were convenient footholds set in the floor to avoid a disastrous slip. Signs warned, "Don't drink the water." Beer was OK.

The town was very lively, with military and commercial activity making it a real boom town, and I expected to see a sheriff, with badge and six-gun keeping the peace. The local police had it under tight control despite the many tempting places to get into trouble. People roamed the streets looking for recreation, and there was plenty available.

There were many bars and dance halls, all showing an assortment of girls for company. My eyes popped at the sight of a life style that I thought only existed in movies, but this was the real thing. Doors swung open for us as we walked the downtown area, but we kept our distance from the dark, smoky cubbyholes that sported pretty, seductive looking girls who waved and gave us the come-hither look.

We were carrying a passenger with us, a Pan American Airlines employee named Ted Orozco, who was our guide and who jokingly warned us, "Don't mess around. Look but don't touch." We didn't need the warning, as it was all quite strange to us.

After a walk through the main street, we retreated to our hotel, where the bar offered a three-piece band and some cute senoritas for dance partners. This looked like the best place to spend our brief evening. Orozco looked over the girls, found a willing dance partner, and volunteered to teach us some Latin dancing. They took the floor and showed us dance steps that I had never seen before. This was the tango, and they put on a real show, with fancy footwork and some very daring and erotic moves. I've been a fan of tango dancing ever since. We applauded loudly, and the pace picked up until it looked like a first class party was brewing, with all the ingredients of gorgeous girls, handsome young officers, hot Latin music, lots of dinero, and no house rules.

We were caught up short when someone reminded us about our early takeoff plans, and the military rule, "No drinking if flying the next day," so we just watched the action and drank cokes. It was great fun while it lasted, and vastly different from the well-behaved and stiff-mannered officers club at Morrison Field.

The next morning, our good behavior was rewarded by the absence of any hangovers. After an early takeoff we made a seven-hour 1000-mile flight over more jungle to our next stop at Natal, the most easterly point in Brazil. This was the jumping-off place for an Atlantic crossing, and a busy beehive of an airport, with airplanes landing and taking off every few minutes. It was expanding rapidly like all the other bases we had visited, to accommodate the much greater air traffic expected in the near future.

It was a major base for anti-submarine operations, as German U-boats were taking a heavy toll of cargo vessels off the coast of South America. Day after day there were reports of new sinkings, and we were asked to be on the lookout for any signs of U-boats. Our chance of sighting a U-boat was very unlikely, as we planned a late afternoon departure and would be flying all night.

Slow-flying twin-engined Navy PBY amphibians were the best submarine patrol aircraft available, with their long-range capability, and they were in constant activity. Some had spotted submarines and had learned to be very cautious about approaching them, as the PBY was cumbersome and slow, which made them sitting ducks for an accurate deck gun on a sub. But they were obliged to attack, and while some reported hits and even sinkings, some had failed to return from their missions. I take my hat off to the Navy pilots who flew these dangerous missions, for they flew an airplane totally unsuited for attack.

We topped our tanks off, loading a total of 1600 gallons that provided at least 18 hours of flying time, and were ready to go on the afternoon of May 17th. Takeoff time was scheduled so that an all night flight would bring us to the African coast in the morning. Hauling that full load of fuel, we staggered into the air at 1830 on May 17, 1942, heading for Roberts Field on the coast of Liberia, 1975 miles to the east.

Looking back to our departure, I can recall that heading into a pitch-black night, to cross a huge ocean was a frightening event for a young pilot with only about 500 flying hours. In those early days of the war, many young men faced this scary venture with even less experience than I, flying medium and heavy bombers and even some fighters across vast expanses of water. Many planes and crews were lost because of faulty navigation or emergencies for which they had no preparation. I was very lucky that some farsighted person in Washington had seen to it that the first pilots on the AMMISCA project were highly qualified civilians recruited from the airlines by the Air Transport Command. I thank my lucky stars that Curt was command pilot on our airplane, and I had complete faith in his ability to take us anywhere we were ordered to go. The ATC decision paid off handsomely, as AMMISCA never lost an airplane on the route to India.

We were assigned a navigator, fresh out of navigation school, who had never made a transoceanic flight and kept apologizing for his lack of experience. He seemed so unsure of himself, that Curt and I had a little conference and decided we'd better do our own navigating in addition to whatever help this young man could give us. We had received lots of warnings about navigational problems. First, there were no experienced navigators available. Secondly, the radio beacon transmitter at our destination, Roberts Field, was very unreliable. It was low powered and operated only in short spurts, and we could not expect to pick it up over 50 miles away. This limited operation of the beacon was intentional, making it difficult for enemy bombers to find the base, and for subs and other enemy vessels to use the homing signal to shell the field. There were no defensive fighters stationed at Roberts, so it was wide open to attack. Dakar, about 750 miles to the north, had been surrendered to the Germans by the French, and was being expanded into a German air base, which would soon go on the offensive

Weather forecasts were OK, coming from pilots' reports, but we could only guess about our winds aloft most of the way. A crosswind of 30 MPH, for example, could throw us off by several hundred miles at our slow cruising speed of less than 150 MPH, so we relied very heavily on reports from pilots who had just made the crossing. I carefully kept a running plot of our course, noting down airspeed and headings, and factoring in the estimated wind. I asked the navigator to do the same, and he was happy and relieved to find me doing my own plotting. This system is called dead-reckoning, and we both came up with the same answers.

After a few hours out, we asked him to try locating us by celestial navigation, shooting sights on stars, as we had a beautiful clear night with a heaven full of sparkle. He went to work under the clear plastic bubble called an astrodome, and was quite busy for a long time. After a while, I asked him for position checks, and he scratched his head and mumbled something about not being quite ready, and retreated to his nav station to refigure his calculations. This did not inspire much confidence in Curt or me, so we didn't pay much attention to him. There were some famous jokes going around about Atlantic crossings, like the one about the navigator reporting that his calculations showed their position in the middle of Kansas.

Curt and I took turns at the wheel because our auto-pilot had a tendency to wander off course. We took two hour shifts watching our heading, but when I was supposed to sleep I was too keyed up and spent my time checking our nav plot on the chart. Of course, it resulted in my getting very sleepy when I took the wheel after turning off the auto-pilot. On an early morning shift, I was watching the compass, and was mesmerized by the gauges, when I felt a tap on my shoulder. Curt was standing there, freshly awakened, and pointing out that I was in a 30 degree bank to the left, and about to return to South America or worse, if I didn't wake up. I had committed the worst sin, by snoozing at the wheel. Was I ever embarrassed! Between fatigue and vertigo, I was putting us in danger, and resolved to hunker down and get my rest when I was off watch.

Our flight progressed smoothly after that. Our engines purred like well-behaved Pratt & Whitneys should, and we seemed to be burning only 80 gallons per hour, giving us lots of reserve fuel. Our navigator had worked himself to a frazzle and was making some progress, but not good enough to pinpoint our position. We suggested that he take a rest, and he was most grateful for that.

As carefully as I plotted our position, the uncertain winds and the erratic low-powered direction finding (DF) transmitter at Roberts made it quite possible that we would miss our target, ending up either to the north or the south of the field, and not knowing which way to turn. Curt decided to do the old mariner's landfall trick. After 12 hours of an anticipated 14-hour flight, we took a 30-degree cut to the north, which should place us well north of Roberts when we hit the coast. We would then turn south and follow the coastline until we found Roberts. If there were a strong south wind, it would push us further north, so it would take longer to reach the field. If there were excessive drift to the south, we would not find Roberts but after 200 miles would turn the corner of the coast and land at the emergency field at Abidjan.

The plan worked like a charm. We reached the coast after a flight of 13:30 hours and swung south. In 30 minutes we picked up Robert's DF signal very faintly, and landed there in 20 minutes, with a total flying time of 14:20 hours. Three other C-47's landed that morning with no problems. They relied on the reported light winds and flew straight in, picking up the DF signal from offshore, saving a half-hour flying time.

There was nothing unique about our flight. Thousands of airplanes made similar crossings during the war years, most without incident, but this was OUR trip, and OUR experience in helping to get a war under way.

The afternoon of our arrival, after rejoicing with our buddies at our safe trips, we removed our cabin tanks, and hauled cargo north to Freetown, which was preparing its defenses against possible bombing attacks from Dakar. We then flew south, following the coast to Accra.

Accra and Lagos were sprawling seaports handling most of the commerce of West Africa. They were busy melting pots, teeming with people of all races, who were energized by a war that had become world-wide, and were scrambling to build up their businesses in a changing world. The African continent has many worlds, many ethnic groups, and is a never-ending source of new sights. Our trip through Africa reads like a desert safari, with stops at such primitive places as Oshogbo, Kano, El Fasher, and Khartoum. We spent every spare moment visiting the towns, and awed natives sometimes treated us like visitors from another planet.

We owe a great debt of gratitude to the people of Pan American World Airways, who were truly modem pioneers. The vision of Juan Trippe, the founder of Pan Am in the 1930's, was to create a network of bases to provide round-the-world air travel, and he had succeeded. His routes totaled 82,000 miles with bases in 47 countries, and most of these were of great assistance to Allied aircraft passing through foreign countries during the war. Pan Am people helped us in South America, across Africa, and through the Middle East. They did a masterful job, providing us with assistance without limit, well beyond the call of their jobs.

All across Africa, wherever we landed, we were met with smiling young men who supplied us with fuel, housing, and total hospitality. They advised us on customs of the people, briefed us on our routes, and described the hazards and how to cope with problems. Without their ready help there would have been many more lost and strayed airplanes scattered across the continent of Africa. Our own air force ground personnel were starting to spread out across foreign countries to provide this assistance, but they lacked the experience that Pan Am brought to us in those early days of 1942. I am most grateful to all these dedicated people who helped us achieve our mission goals, and I hope they received proper recognition from the United States government.

From Oshogbo to Kano in central Africa, we had our first experience with a sandstorm, sighting what looked like heavy mist off to the east. We had been warned of these by Pan Am people, and told to steer clear even if it took us way off course. Many aircraft have been lost in these terrible storms, with engines fouled up by blowing sand and forced landings in the desert. We noted the direction the storm was moving and took a wide detour, which kept us out of the worst part of the storm. We still had very limited visibility at Kano and landed with a 300 foot ceiling. We rushed around the airplane covering all the engine openings to keep out the sand, which can cut engine life in half.

Our Khartoum arrival was after dark and this was another scary event. First we had to find the field. We spotted what appeared to be a road with tiny flickering lights, but could not find the runway. Fortunately, there was a control tower and when we asked him to turn on the runway lights, the Pan Am tower operator informed us that what we saw was the one-and-only runway, and that all they had was kerosene lanterns that flickered. It was a moonless night, and until we were on final approach, we weren't even sure that we were heading for the runway. A pilot's delight is a safe landing after a hazardous flight, and we breathed a happy sigh of relief after that night landing. From then on we made it a point to time our flights to land during daylight.

In May of 1942, aircraft were being routed north to Cairo, but later flights across Africa went directly east from Khartoum to avoid the dogleg route, saving time and mileage. We were directed to Cairo, and that was a big event for us.

First, we had to get there safely. The British had been fortifying the city and surrounding areas against attack by German forces, which were very close. We were warned before arrival to follow the prescribed air route to the city very carefully, or risk an attack by Royal Air Force (RAF) Hurricane fighters watching for German bombers that had a nasty habit of masquerading as Allied transports. As we approached the inbound corridor I found an RAF fighter flying parallel to us, giving us a careful look. I slid my side window open just enough to put the muzzle of my Very flare pistol through the gap, and carefully fired the correct color rockets per instructions. The inquisitive RAF pilot waggled his wings and peeled off.

We found that Cairo airport was busier than any field we had touched down at so far. Rommel's forces were aggressively moving across the desert, moving closer to Alexandria every day, and the British were frantically building up their strength to avoid a disastrous defeat. Curt and I left Saylor and Sibold in charge and went to RAF operations, where we received warm greetings. The Operations Officer joked about the closeness of the enemy who were only "70 miles from

Alexandria, but we aren't about to let them get any closer, are we?" Everyone was at a high level of stress and the joke going around was that if you stayed calm under these conditions you must be crazy.

We arranged the guard detail for our airplane and all four of us were whisked downtown to a colorful place, for despite the emergency, we were now in what was known as the Paris of the Middle East.

We stayed two nights at the world-renown Shepheard's Hotel, stopping place for the great and famous. Lawrence of Arabia, Winston Churchill, Greta Garbo, and royalty of all nations had been guests, and it was newly invigorated, playing host to an assortment of officials and military as well as RAF and American pilots, who wanted nothing but the best. The classical look of the hotel with its period furnishings, old oak paneling, and marble columns made us feel like we were in a museum. But the bar scene in the evenings belied that, as it was crowded with uniforms of all the Allied nations, all clamoring for drinks. The noisiest groups were the young, enthusiastic airmen of the Royal Air Force, who sounded like a group of college boys preparing for the big football game. Anyone in civilian clothing was looked on with suspicion, as the hotel was rumored to be a hangout for German spies, which made it even more exciting.

The RAF pilots outnumbered us 10-to-1, and were happy to recount some hair-raising stories of their adventures. One mentioned a C-47 being shot down by an RAF fighter because he failed to give the correct signal in the entry corridor, but his mates shushed him, and insisted that the story was untrue. Most of the British were very appreciative of us Yanks coming over to assist, although a few made some sour comments, like, "It's about time you got here," and, "We've been at it for three years, while you blokes were sitting on your arsses," and, "When do the troops arrive?"

Overall, they were a great bunch to sit with and listen to. Most were very young, with barely a fuzz of a moustache, while others, slightly older, sported the great curled handlebars that we Americans admired. They were alternately cynical, having witnessed disastrous defeats and heavy losses, but moments later they would bounce back full of youthful buoyancy, expecting eventual victory. Rommel's advances placed Cairo and the Suez Canal in great danger of being overrun, and these men were the defenders. We could not find fault with their gripes and greatly admired their good spirits. These were brothers in arms, and we were glad that our country was helping them.

Cairo was thronging with troops of all of the Allied nations, great amounts of military supplies clogged the streets, and everyone was on the alert for an air attack. The British had been at war with the Axis for several years, but this was new to the Americans, and held us spellbound. I wondered how we would react if one of our cities were threatened, and I blessed the Atlantic for keeping the dangers that the British faced away from our front door.

Our airplane was to be tied up for maintenance for two days and someone suggested a visit to the pyramids and sphinx nearby. Despite the war, there was still a thriving tourist business, mostly consisting of visiting military like us, and the hotel arranged for our short safari to those great Egyptian sights.

Naturally, we chose to go by camel, so off we went to meet some mean-tempered smelly beasts that put us back 1000 years in history. We were introduced to Alzam, a smiling Egyptian guide, a very interesting character who looked like he had been taken out of an Arabian Nights movie created in Hollywood. He was a tall stocky man of impressive manner, who wore a tasseled red fez at a jaunty angle, and a loose fitting striped burnoose that looked like a nightgown. He was an old hand at dealing with tourists like us, and started out by handing each of us a fez to make us look like authentic tourists. He then showed us the proper way to mount a camel. This is a violent maneuver in which the camel kneels first while you board, then stands erect by popping his front landing gear down in a snapping motion that throws the unprepared rider back with a neck-wrenching jolt.

Camels may be called the "ship of the desert", but I would jump ship if I was faced with a long ride. Mine tried to bite me on several occasions, and had to be prodded with hard whacks by the camel boy to behave. His breath was like a decaying garbage dump, so I soon learned not to inhale when he was exhaling in my direction. He got a high grade for reliability and I got the impression that he could go on for days at his leisurely pace without let-up. I soon got used to the camel's gait, but it was hard to imagine that this awkward animal could gallop at high speed across a surface of soft sand. The camel ride was a wonderful experience, one of the many we come across in life that we enjoy one time only. This is all the more enjoyable to remember because I have a photograph of it.

Alzam was a real salesman. I think he could have sold the sphinx if it hadn't been so heavy. He suggested I have a picture taken of my pals and me on the camels, and promised me that he would send it to my family in Boston. I doubted that he could deliver it in wartime, as he had in peacetime, but he was most persuasive, and we posed for it. Much to my surprise, I received word from home several months later that they had received a splendid photo of the five of us. My father proudly took it to the Boston Globe and it was published with a caption that read, "That's Me in the Middle, Ma."

All around us the world was in turmoil, with savage fighting on many fronts, and millions yet to suffer from the stupidity of man. But my camel, whom I named Jezebel for her nasty habit of trying to bite the hand that guided her, plodded along at her slow loping pace as camels had been doing since time immemorial. We ploppety-plopped along desert roadways, amidst the smells and sounds of an ancient country that had witnessed the follies of mankind for thousands of years. Curt and I were not normally a very philosophical pair, but surrounded by this unchanging, but always changing, desert we were impressed with a sense of history. We talked about the wars, and the many civilizations, and the historical events that had taken place on this very ground. For thousands of years the Pharoahs and other leaders had ruled, fought, and died in their struggles for power. Our current struggle against evil forces, which was absorbing the resources of great nations and leaving millions of victims in its wake, appeared to be only a small ripple in the stream of centuries of strife. Some day it would also be regarded as a mere instance in time.

At that point in time, we decided to climb the huge Pyramid of Giza, which is a miracle of construction. We examined the sphinx, smelled strange aromas of food cooking at stands near its base, ate more dust, and finally slogged back to Cairo and a boisterous bar scene at Shepheard's. Whenever I visit a zoo and see a camel I smile at the memory, and am delighted to say hello to this distant cousin of my old acquaintance, Jezebel.

The sights and smells of Cairo are hard to forget. The streets were crowded with every form of vehicle; street-cars, trucks, army vehicles, open touring car taxis, bicycles, and wagons drawn by horses, camels, oxen, and donkeys. The city vibrated with the excitement and pressure of the war, and the danger of possible defeat stimulated everyone to a fever pitch. It was a cauldron of activity, and we breathed a sigh of relief when we boarded "Ferdinand," and headed down the runway on the next leg of our trip.

We received our flight clearance to leave Cairo with some very careful briefing about signals and routes to follow. We were in dangerous territory with fighters patrolling the skies in all directions, and we were warned that even the familiar profile of a C-47 meant nothing to trigger-happy pilots if we didn't show the right colored flares. I told Curt that I thought they were just trying to be officious and it was a scare tactic, but he suggested I make sure to shoot the right flares and not argue with .50 caliber machine guns. Like at Dodge City, they were ordered to shoot first and ask questions afterward.

Flying from Cairo across the mid-East we crossed huge deserts and felt great sympathy for the unfortunate men who spent their lives in what must be one of the most inhospitable parts of the world. Mile after mile of desolate lands passed under our wings with a few low hills to break up the flatness of the lonely landscape.

In my youth I saw a wonderful action movie about the French Foreign Legion, called "Beau Geste," with famous actors of yesteryear. I remember actor Ronald Colman wearing an immaculate high-necked tunic, tightly buttoned despite the intolerable torrid temperatures of the desert. It told of the terrors and hardships of life in the Legion, and its setting was the endless sand reaches of the Sahara. I recall that the movie was so real that I developed an immediate thirst, and I wondered that anyone would volunteer for desert duty. And I still wonder about those high-necked tunics.

Crossing the Syrian Desert and the Jordan Valley, we made stops at places with the odd names of Habbaniya and Basra in what is now Iraq, with a last stop at Sharjah on the coast of the Persian Gulf before reaching India. None of them resembled the lush oases that we had expected, with turbaned Arabs and mysterious veiled women. They were sun-baked villages, with people eking out a miserable existence.

The landing strip at Sharjah was alongside a beautiful sandy beach, so I took a short swim in the surprisingly clear and warm waters of the Gulf, despite warnings from some of my fun-loving friends about sea serpents, water snakes, crocodiles, and German subs lurking just under the surface. It was great and refreshing.

The military post was a British fortress, which looked exactly like the Hollywood-built set for the movie, "Beau Geste. " But this British stronghold was the real thing, a square building, of huge stone blocks many feet thick, with enormous wooden gates. Around the upper level ran a continuous wall notched every few feet, so the defense forces could safely fire their rifles, or arrows, or spears, or dump their boiling oil, whatever the weapon of the era. This isolated fort was built on top of a rise with a 360 degree view of the most bleak, barren wasteland. It was a place of refuge for generations of soldiers stationed in a desolate land, and was our safe overnight stop. The thick walls helped maintain a livable temperature, and the food was rough but hearty, consisting of bully beef and assorted strange vegetables. We were invited by the British commander to bunk in at the post, but decided to sleep in our airplane parked a mile away, after seeing the guard they lent us for the night.

Our overnight guard provided us with comic relief. He was a wizened little man of indeterminate age, standing slightly over five feet tall, looking very undernourished. He wore a ragged uniform, and carried a very ancient rifle that looked like a museum piece. He spoke no English, but made motions to prove to us that he was a warrior. He proudly showed us his prize weapon, a long knife which he brandished a few times to impress us.

On close examination we discovered that the knife was made of old discarded gasoline cans that had been hammered together to form a long sword. Our British hosts told us that the troops in this backward Arab country were required to provide their own arms.

We left our staunch hero in better shape than we found him, with some nourishing food, to his everlasting gratitude.

On May 27, we left Sharjah for the five-hour flight to Karachi, India, having been enroute for 14 days. We found Karachi to be very much like Cairo, with the hustle and bustle of wartime energy spurring everyone to hurry things up. Our Ferry Command headquarters was already established and doing business at the Karachi airport, and we had two days for orientation before moving on across India.

There was cargo to haul across India, so we were advised to unload all unnecessary gear to provide room. We left our personal duffel bags in the care of a small warehouse that was newly established for such gear, and this turned out to be a very big mistake. On our return to Karachi several weeks later, the warehouse had moved, and so had all our baggage, which included spare uniforms and all sorts of personal items, and was never seen again. We learned to never, never let our things out of our possession.

We loaded up and left Karachi on May 30, 1942, for our first crossing of India. Much of this country resembled the open desert we had crossed in the mid-east, a dry barren land, with winds sweeping up sand to create haze that made navigation difficult. Towns were the color of the surrounding area, and it was hard to believe that population of hundreds of millions were supported by the small farms, mainly located along the rivers. Like the Nile River of Egypt, India relied on its great rivers, the Bramaputra, Ganges, and other huge rivers that were fed by the melting snow packs of the mighty Himalayas that ringed the country to the north and the east. We made stops at New Delhi and Allahabad, searching diligently in the haze for their airports.

Dinjan was easy to find when we arrived on the 31st. It lay alongside the Bramaputra River in the center of the Upper Assam Valley, which is a flat plain, surrounded by high mountains and dense jungle. It was highly cultivated, having a perfect climate for growing tea and was a major revenue producing asset for the British Empire. The tea plantations stretched for miles, and the landscape was dotted with large frame structures that we learned were drying racks for the tea plants.

Our airfield was set in the center of the plantations, and more fields were under construction, much to the disgust of plantation managers. They took great pride in their production, and they hated to see their idyllic plantation life style disrupted by wartime building with its noisy bulldozers, dust, and other inconveniences. Assam was to be our home base for the next year, and I have much to write about life there. But first, I want to talk about my first impressions of the Hump, and the job we were sent to do.

Jim and "Ferdinand" arrive in India. *Time off for good behavior.*

Chapter 11
FIRST HUMP TRIP

The Himalaya mountain range has an extraordinary beauty that would delight the eye of an artist, but to the pilot it is the shroud of death. These are the highest mountains in the world and produce some of the worst weather for a pilot. The frightening name of "the Aluminum Trail" describes the mournful loss of the many hundreds of aircraft and thousands of lives that were sacrificed to its voracious appetite for our fragile machines and men.

It is June 1, 1942 and we are on our first round trip across what everyone now calls the "Hump." We just arrived at Assam yesterday, and received little briefing on finding our way, but we are lucky to have clear weather that allows us to see the awesome terrain. I had flown the Rocky Mountains many times, so snow-topped peaks were nothing new, but these seemed to go on forever. We left the Assam Valley climbing steadily, and adding heavy jackets over our tropical clothing as our cockpit got colder. The cockpit heater could not match the outside cold at our cruising altitude of 16,000 feet, and before long we are wearing gloves and breathing frosty air.

We fly the 500 miles to Kunming over frigid looking snow topped mountains reaching to the heavens in such abundance as to form a ragged field of white blooming flowers. Gales of enormous winds sweep across these crests creating clouds of snow that sometimes obscure the summits. We are careful to maintain a direct heading that allows us to clear the peaks at 16,000 feet, as our airplane is heavily loaded and unable to climb higher. To the north are peaks reaching to 27,000 feet.

Below the snow-covered peaks are immense forests of towering trees that magically change into tropical jungles at lower levels. This dense dark green wilderness completely carpets the steeply pitched mountainsides that are broken only by torrential rivers. The rivers are not huge in width, but are roaring cascades of water in deep gorges tumbling violently over boulders and waterfalls as they carry off the melt of the snows of 1000 violent blizzards. These raging waters create an almost impossible barrier to cross on foot, and would be the despair of any airman who parachuted into the jungle and tried to walk out.

The majesty of the peaks is accentuated in the late afternoon as the lowering sun creates total darkness on the east sides of the slopes. Peering into that threatening blackness on our afternoon return flight is a chilling experience.

The lonely pilot winging his way across this forlorn patch of the earth has no appreciation of the stark beauty of nature. He has other things on his mind. His ear is fine-tuned to the sound of his engines, acutely aware of the slightest murmur if they drop out of synchronization. His eyes move from engine instruments that show power settings and temperatures, to his flight instruments as he flies manually by compass and altimeter, holding course and altitude. The airplanes are equipped with auto-pilots, but most of these delicate machines have been out of order for a long time due to lack of spare parts. Pilot and copilot take their turns at the controls, and each keeps his eyes raking the skies around them for signs of other aircraft that might be unfriendly. Rarely is there another airplane in sight, not even a friendly C-47 flying a parallel course.

As shadows turn to dark, the feeling of being lost over a great black void to which there may not be an end wells up in the pilot's mind. He wishes he had started an hour earlier so that he could arrive in daylight, when finding the home base is easy. He hopes the homing beacon on the ground at Chabua is operating today and that his airborne ADF (automatic direction finder) will pick up the signal.

He alone is solely responsible for the safety of the airplane and its crew, and his decisions are critical. It is little wonder that young pilots get gray hair at an early age.

* * * * * *

Our leaders in Washington, London, and elsewhere around the world were facing monumental challenges, trying to fight Axis powers who were well prepared to wage war and were determined to rule the world.

While they were making critical decisions on how to cope with this worldwide menace, in April of 1942 a tiny fleet of 15 Douglas C-47 cargo airplanes was sent to India with the mission, code-named AMMISCA, of supplying China by air to replace the loss of the Burma Road. Other aircraft followed to total 75.

The first military flight from Chabua in the upper Assam valley to Kunming over the towering Himalaya Mountains was made by Colonel Caleb Haynes, who followed the lead of China National Airlines (CNAC), a commercial company that had been crossing the lower southerly mountains before the Japanese invasion of Burma. He described the dangers of the direct route as terrible weather conditions, unpredictable winds, extremely high peaks, and no possible rescue if forced to make a crash landing.

Our instructions to establish an airlift were somewhat overwhelming when we realized just how much we would have to haul to supply huge Chinese armies. We were struck with the total inadequacy of our effort but maintained an inspired attitude about the importance of our mission. We knew that we were the only source of supply for our own people on the other side of the mountains, and that without us they would surely be lost.

It took much effort and many gallons of fuel to bring one gallon of aviation gas over the Hump, but these meager supplies were critical to the operation of our air force in China. This "air force" was the American Volunteer Group, a civilian organization flying P-40's from Kunming and other bases in western China. I learned later how critical and important this group was to our nation.

Besides the perilous flight conditions, we faced other critical problems: shortages of replacement airplanes of later model and better equipment, unavailability of spare parts, lack of navigation aids such as homing beacons and long range radios that could transmit across the vast mountain ranges, lack of weather forecasting facilities, and the everyday threat of enemy fighter action. All these were topped off by the misery of our primitive living conditions.

We soon learned what it was like to be part of the "forgotten war". It is still amazing to me that even though authorities in Washington knew very well of our incredibly poor situation, and were ordered by the President himself to drastically increase supplies, we suffered acute shortages right into 1944, two years after the Hump operation started.

Why this situation prevailed I discuss in another chapter. As a pilot on the Hump run, I bitched and moaned the same as all the others, and cussed out the people responsible for our problems whoever they might be. My love for flying never diminished, but was sorely tempered by the dangers we faced.

Here are some specifications for number crunchers. Our C-47's had a normal service ceiling of 12,000 feet with a 26,000 pound gross weight. We flew at a minimum altitude of 16,000 feet and were usually overloaded to 30,000 pounds gross weight.

There were no "normal" flights over the Hump as each one faced threats every minute. We learned how dangerous it was to cut through a low pass between ridges that we thought would be a shortcut. We discovered that there were huge updrafts and downdrafts caused by high velocity winds streaking through these gaps that looked so safe. Caught in one of these vertical drafts you could lose or gain thousands of feet of altitude in a few seconds, and the enormous pressures could tear the wings off an airplane if the stresses were great enough.

I had one very scary experience of this kind early in the mission. Looking to keep lower than the customary 16,000-foot level, I headed for a pass between two Gibraltar-like mountains. As I neared the opening, an immense downward force gripped my airplane and caused a sudden drop of over 1000 feet. Hauling back on the wheel did little good as the downward force was too great and I was almost at stalling speed despite using full power.

The fright of seeing the mountain coming up rapidly as I sunk down was incredible. Our fate was out of my hands. I had no room to turn as I was too close to the face of the mountain, and I felt that we were being pulled by a power greater than our own. Some people pray in a situation like this, but I resorted to swearing. Maybe the cusswords worked. It occurred to me later that fate was a joker that day, and was saving me for a bigger event in the future.

As I got closer, the downdraft subsided and I was able to sneak through the pass just barely above stalling, hanging on my props, and almost brushing the snow-filled gap underneath. I never let myself get caught like that again and I passed the word around about the danger of cutting through a pass. It was vital to get this information out to everyone, as pilot-to-pilot reports were our most valuable source of information.

Some of our pilots were not as lucky. Eyewitness reports came back from one pilot who observed an airplane doing just what I tried, and not making it over the edge. There was a flurry of snow, and the airplane disappeared into the heavy snowbanks.

I can recall many trips crossing from east to west, homeward bound in beautiful clear skies, when I was filled with lonely fear. Here we were just barely maintaining flying speed, close to stalling speed, at our maximum altitude, above an impenetrable landscape, looking at terrain devoid of emergency fields, no places of refuge, no people on the ground except wild tribes of jungle dwellers.

In the late afternoon, with the sun about to disappear over the horizon, it was a mighty lonely place to be. We were far from home, halfway around the world , and all alone in that huge empty sky, in a terribly remote and dangerous place. We had no company except each other in that little airplane that normally seems so large sitting on the ground. The loneliness can become so acute that you are vulnerable to panic attacks. It is easy to slip into a well of fear. So much can go wrong with an airplane, its engines and instruments, all so critical to staying in the air. You must overcome this feeling by creating your own confidence in your mastery of flying, and in the total reliability of your aircraft.

The steady beat of the engines is reassuring, as well as knowing that this airplane has made this trip safely many times. You shake off the temporary fear that has threatened to engulf you. As pilot, you are in command and are responsible for the safety of airplane and crew, and must keep your distress under control. If you show fear, you shouldn't be in command. A healthy mental attitude is vital.

Some of our senior pilots, family men, became victims of a fear so acute that they were taken off flying status and given ground jobs. At my age of 22, with a number of Hump trips under my belt, I am still cocky enough to think that bad things happen to the other guy, not to me.

 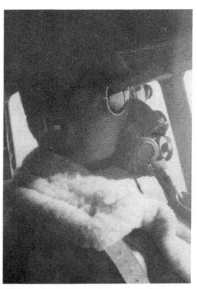

"Ferdinand's" crew from Florida to Kweilin China: Left to Right: Sgt. George Saylor, flight engineer; Pvt. Fred Sibold, radio operator; Lt. Curtis Caton, Pilot; Lt. James Segel, co-pilot

The only way to fly at 16,000 feet. On oxygen and hope the O2 tanks are full.

Stopped in Agra, site of the Taj Mahal on our way to China and several more times

Section II

INTO the LAIR of the TIGER

Air Corps joins the Flying Tigers

Chapter 12
INTO THE LAIR OF THE TIGER

It's morning in Kunming, a clear cloudless day, and the weather is crisp at this altitude of 6200 feet. It is June 30, 1942, and Curt and I are ready for the return flight to Chabua on our fourth Hump trip. Several crews stand around the operations office waiting for west- bound loads. We like flying back empty as it allows us better performance at high altitude.

The operations clerk pops out of the office, very excitedly waving some sheets of paper to impress us with the importance of the flight clearances we are about to get. At this early stage of the AMMISCA project, we don't attach much importance to clearances, as we are pretty much on our own. We can take any route we wish, and on clear days like this, we choose a northerly route, towards those very high mountains reaching to 25,000 feet, to keep our distance from the Japanese air bases to the south. In bad weather, when Japanese fighters are grounded, we plow our way straight through the heavy weather on instruments, or even take a southern loop to avoid the hazard of a strong southerly wind that could push us north into the mountains.

Something new is happening, and the clerk blurts out, "I need someone to take a load to Kweilin - - who wants to go?" This is a change of plans, and nobody answers. We know nothing about Kweilin or how to find it.

"It's easy to find, no DF (direction finder transmitter), but lots of railroad tracks to help you find it. It's got sharp pointy hills all around it that look like sugar cones. It's an easy run. You can't miss it. Who wants to go?"

We have already learned the old army adage that tells you to keep your mouth shut, and not volunteer for anything. There is total silence.

"It's a great place. Lots of girls. It's called the Paris of China." We don't believe a word of this.

"The Flying Tigers are there, and they've got great food. "This is an even worse lie; they're probably starving.

"Come on, guys, this is a very important job. They need this stuff at Kweilin real bad. They're out of .50 caliber ammo, and desperate for spare parts." Now it's getting to us. One foolish guy can't keep his mouth shut, and breaks the silence. I find my big mouth saying, "Where the hell is Kweilin?"

Uh, oh! Our friendly clerk now homes in on me. "You'll find it, no sweat. They need this stuff so bad, they'll love you for it. You'll be bringing them mail, milk (AKA beer), and lots of other stuff."

I look at Curt, who is my superior and plane commander, and ask him, "What d'ya think, Curt? Do you want to go?" Despite his lazy, relaxed manner, Curt is an adventurous guy. He has a faraway look and a half smile, and in his slow southern drawl, he says, "Sure. Why not? It's someplace new. Let's see if we can find it."

This has been an interesting situation. We are part of the Army Air Corps, and can be ordered to go anywhere. The American Volunteer Group, or Flying Tigers, is an independent mercenary air force, a civilian organization, asking us for help. No one knew if it was legal, and no one cared. As we agreed later, we were glad we spoke up, as it was a prelude to a great adventure.

In less than an hour, Ferdinand is loaded to the brim, heavy with fuel drums, .50 caliber ammunition, spare parts, mail, and food, and we take off for Kweilin, 460 miles to the east, on a heading of 88 degrees. We are flying into a combat zone, only a hundred miles from Japanese territory, so we keep our eyes peeled for anything moving. Just what we would do if spotted by a Zero I don't know, as all we have to throw at him are cusswords.

The suspense doesn't last long. We have good charts, the weather is clear, and I've become a pretty good navigator, and we hit it right on the nose. Sure enough, off in the distance, those pointed hills around Kweilin look like upside-down sugar cones scattered across the plain. I get on the radio, hoping I can reach them, and call in, "Kweilin radio, do you read?"

I'm startled to get an instant reply, "We hear you loud and clear. Who are you?" Oops! I didn't identify myself on my first call, which is standard procedure, but I'm a little leery about telling who I am this close to Japanese lines, and I didn't know if Kweilin had a radio.

"Army C-47 number 7797 about 10 miles west. We don't see the runway. Advise where you are and give landing instructions, please." The reply is prompt, "Look for the tallest hill. Our runway is just behind it. We have light winds from the north. Land to the north."

Suddenly we have company that pops up out of the blue. Two Flying Tiger P-40's are flying in formation with us, looking us over, and then they give us a big wave and peel off. This is our first view of the Tigers in flight, and I am thrilled to find them on the alert, and ready for action. They are quite spectacular with their shark's teeth insignia, and we feel very comfortable to have them as company this close to Japanese territory. Curt and I like this reception committee.

We land to the north, and wheel up to the flight line and park along a row of P-40's, all bearing the same menacing insignia. This is a forward fighter base, and it looks like these boys really mean business. A casually dressed operations man introduces himself as we climb out of the cabin, and welcomes us warmly. "We've been sweating you guys out for three days. We're just about out of .50 caliber and haven't seen a load in over two weeks. " Curt and I are soon aware of how desperately our load is needed, and we are glad we volunteered to make the trip.

We walk up a pathway on the nearest hill to a spacious cave cut in the rock, which contains their operations HQ, and are introduced around. Curt and I are in our tan uniforms, with no rank insignia showing. These men are all civilians wearing scruffy old clothes, sport shirts, and shorts, and we can't tell who's in charge or what anyone does here. They are all ages up to 40, and some wear beards or handlebar moustaches, some just look unshaven, and all appear to be undernourished. It is hard to realize that this raggedy looking, most unmilitary bunch is the deadliest group of fighting men in the world, champions of the air, who have devastated the Japanese Air Force and saved China from defeat.

These are flight leaders and pilots and operations men crowding around us, and we feel like we have discovered the "Lost Battalion." We soon understand why. They have received little mail and have little faith in the truth of broadcasts they pick up on short- wave radio. They bombard us with questions about conditions at home, anxious to know if the country is in danger, if you can buy a car, if there is a food shortage, and above all, are the people at home aware of the war they are fighting in China. They are indifferent to learn that newspapers back home have given them much publicity, complaining, "What good is it if we don't get some help from the Air Corps?"

The American Volunteer Group (AVG) is technically a Chinese military operation, staffed with civilians, that has been isolated from the rest of the world, with poor communications, and practically no support from the U.S. Air Corps. It is astounding to realize that this is the only fighting unit taking on the Japanese Air Force, and doing a magnificent job of it.

They were promised 100 P-40's, received 75, and are now down to less than 40 that are in bad condition. They are using up their supplies at a great rate, and eagerly bombard us with questions about bringing in another load of ammunition, fuel, airplane parts, and the many other things they need to keep operating. The AVG is in even worse shape than our Hump operation, and is desperate for help. We will hear these same pleas at every AVG base we visit to disperse our load.

Right now, we're in a hurry to get back to Kunming before dark. Curt asks the chief of operations, "How soon can you get us unloaded so we can head back to

Kunming?" "Not so fast," he replies, "Some of this has to go to our Hengyang and Lingling bases, and you guys have to haul it." We protest that we are under orders to return to Kunming, although, actually, we have no such orders. We are totally on our own, with only verbal instructions to go to Kweilin, and that's all. We are a little uneasy about delaying our return, so AVG Operations appeases us by agreeing to contact Kunming for permission for us to continue the mission. In the meantime, we are shown around the cave, and find they are very poorly equipped. They are working with minimum equipment: mainly some airplanes and a lot of spirit. We are about to learn just how impoverished they are.

In a short time Operations informs us that Kunming has Okayed our staying on to finish the trip. Curt and I listen to this story, and later, in private, we have a good laugh, as we don't believe any such communication took place. This is a very informal war we are fighting and these needy men don't have much patience with army regulations. Are we supposed to follow their instructions? We don't really know the answer. We are flying a U.S. Army airplane, in support of a group of mercenary pilots who work for a foreign government, and we have no military supervision or any orders. If we thought too hard about it, we would probably run for cover.

Nothing doing! We're staying! We are fascinated by this operation and thoroughly hooked into working with them, especially because they really need us. Ferdinand is the only cargo airplane available in all of China to help the AVG. We have no conflicting orders and doubt that we'll be missed for a few days, so we make the decision to stay and finish the delivery.

* * * * * *

So begins our "Temporary Duty Assignment" to the AVG, which stretches out from a few days to months. We are told later that if we hadn't agreed to stay, they probably would have kidnapped our airplane and us, so badly were we needed.

Our airplane is being unloaded and the cargo sorted out for distribution to the other bases, and we get briefed on how to find those places. They proudly tell us about their AVG operation in answer to our many questions, and the more we learn, the more pleased we are that we agreed to stay and help.

We are very concerned for the safety of Ferdinand as we look down from our high place in the mouth of the cave. There sits a neat row of fighters with our big C-47 sitting in the middle like a mother hen with her chicks. We learn that they park in a row to make it easier to service the planes with the few broken down fuel trucks available, but it makes them vulnerable to a strafing run that could wipe out the entire fleet.

Safety against a surprise raid is insured by the marvelous warning system the Chinese established for the AVG, and we learn all about this very soon. Right now, I ask for a P-40 escort airplane to accompany us, but Operations tells us, "We can't spare an airplane to lead you, but we'll send one of our pilots along to show you the way. Don't worry about Japs. Just stay on the radio, and we'll call you if there is any problem." An AVG pilot, named Charlie, climbs on board and we take off for the 120-mile flight to Lingling and Hengyang. These bases are strung out to the northeast of Kweilin and are the most easterly bases under AVG control. Charlie fills us in on some details, shouting into our ears in the noisy cockpit. "We're so close to the Jap bases they used to come over every night and bomb the hell out of the towns. That was until we showed up a few months ago. Now they try to sneak in a few Betsy (bombers) at night trying to catch us asleep. It doesn't work," he goes on. "But we're running out of everything and you guys have to give us help, or we'll have to shut down one of these bases."

Lingling and Hengyang are small bases and they look alike. Around the single runway are mud shacks that house all their facilities. Mechanics are working on airplanes under bamboo shelters, which are blended into the surroundings to offer some camouflage. At first look it appears that they have a number of airplanes scattered around the field, but a closer look reveals that these are just dummies made of bamboo covered with fabric. That's one way to build up your air force. It looks like they are a shoestring operation, with a few broken down trucks and radio equipment at the base that was once in an airplane, but was removed when the airplane got damaged beyond repair.

The squat buildings are sparsely furnished, and everything is worn out, including the personnel. They look like they haven't changed their clothes in weeks, or had a square meal in that time. We get a very warm welcome, with everybody turning out to ask us for all the things they didn't get. They are desperate for spare parts for their broken-down airplanes and vehicles, for tools, radios, and such everyday needs as canned food, magazines, newspapers, mail, beer, and booze. They look at us like we are driving Santa's sleigh. We hate to disappoint them, but make promises to do the best we can in our next run from Kunming. It sounds like we have joined the AVG, and in truth, we have.

This hard fighting group is doing an incredible job. They are like men cast away on a desert island, over 12,000 miles from home and from the main sources of supply. This is the ultimate example of a stretched out supply line that is so long that is totally unable to handle the needs of the only Allied fighting air force in China. We thought that our needs in the upper Assam Valley were neglected, but a base like Lingling is three giant steps further away from sources of supply. Curt and I marveled at the route that their supplies take - first the major task of getting materiel by ship or by air to India, and then by rail to Assam and over the Hump to Kunming, then to Kweilin, and finally to Lingling. It is a wonder that anything gets here at all. Ships are lost to submarine attacks. Commanders along the air route from the States snatch short items from the airlift loads as they cross Africa and India, and there are always losses from thievery and breakage. We agree to do what we can to help them in our own small way.

At Lingling that night, we park Ferdinand in a revetment for protection against bombing raids, and remain over night at the hostel, formerly a school, that is located a mile from the field. The revetment is a new experience for us; it is a three-sided airplane parking lot made up of dirt barriers piled high. It is no protection from a direct bomb hit, but excellent against a bomb that hits outside the enclosure.

The following day we fly to Hengyang with the balance of our load, and find the AVG crew anxious about our arrival, but disappointed by how little we have for them. This base has a small city close by, so they have a few more conveniences, but "it ain't the Ritz," they jokingly tell us. There is a river running through the town, which turns out to be the scene of some excitement in a few days, when one of our P-40's has to ditch.

Welcome sight of a Flying Tigers P-40 on our wing.

Chapter 13
THE FLYING TIGERS

The dreaded Japanese Red Dragon regiments are moving swiftly up the Burma Road, under orders to capture west China's Yunnan province, and take over the key city of Kunming. If this stronghold falls, all China is lost, for Kunming is the eastern terminal of the Hump airlift, and its surrender will shut down the only supply route remaining into that battered country.

It is April of 1942, and the Japanese have proven themselves to be invincible, moving into Burma, and taking over the major port city of Rangoon, overpowering the British, Indian, and Burmese forces opposing them. The retreating troops have fled northward into the hinterlands, first destroying any military supplies they could not take with them.

They were joined by hordes of civilian refugees traveling by truck, wagon, or on foot, fleeing a ruthless enemy that is practicing a scorched earth policy, ravaging the country. All civilians who are political leaders, or educated, or wealthy, and might be a danger in the future, were being executed along with their families. The fleeing people, troops and civilians, are unable to pass through the dense jungles, and are converging on the last escape route, the Burma Road. This is a hazardous single-lane road, carved out of steep mountainsides, that provides the only access into China.

Hard-hitting Japanese infantrymen race up the road, knifing into the crowds. People who block the way are ruthlessly cut down by the invaders, and pushed with their carts and wheelbarrows off the road into deep ravines. Chinese troops are sent down the road to stop the invaders, but are out-gunned and out-numbered, and soundly defeated in all skirmishes. The Chinese infantrymen are so poorly equipped that only one in three has a rifle, and some have only swords as weapons. Their last delaying action is to dynamite the one bridge across the fast flowing Salween River. In their haste, they are forced to ignore the safety of many refugees who are trapped on the wrong side of the river.

The Japanese are not stopped by this wrecked bridge for very long. They move their bridge building engineer battalion into the area, and immediately go to work assembling a pontoon bridge. Within two days they have replaced the destroyed bridge, and are once again ready to move troops across the river. A Japanese victory is imminent, for once the troops cross the Salween River there is no stopping them, as there are no further obstacles to a steady advance into Kunming.

At first light whistles blow and the rumble of heavy truck engines starting up echoes in the gorge, The first of the heavy vehicles moves onto the muddy road heading for the floating bridge over the Salween, and the Japanese commander breathes more easily as he begins the last stage of the advance into China.

But suddenly he hears a chilling sound, a sound that is all too familiar to him, the unique moaning sound of Allison engines powering Flying Tiger P-40 Kittyhawks. Down into the Salween Gorge comes the terrifying vision of a string of bomb-carrying fighter planes, adorned with grinning shark mouths that strike terror to the Japanese soldiers.

The four fighters are flown by Tigers with special skills, ex-marine pilots who know how to dive-bomb with precision. On their very first pass they each drop a 500-pounder around the flimsy new bridge and destroy it completely, along with many vehicles. Their mission is only partly done, for they then make vicious strafing attacks on the trucks and troops of the invasion forces, which are concentrated around the bridgehead or jammed into the tight confines of the narrow road. Panic prevails among the ground troops, who have no place to run, and the destruction of men and machines is devastating.

Running out of ammunition, Tex Hill, squadron commander, next calls in four more P-40's which are flying top cover to protect the bombers, and these go into action with more strafing, until the Japanese column is in ruins. No enemy fighters have appeared, so this top cover group is able to expend all of its ammunition far down the road to annihilate most of the troop train.

The following day the raid is repeated, but this time the target changes. The strategy calls for bombing the side-walls of the canyons through which the Road passes. This bombing is even more effective, for it causes huge landslides, covering much of the enemy troop convoys and breaking down the roadway that hangs on the edge of steep cliffs. This action continues for several days, completely destroying the roadway, and making the blockage permanent. The Japanese are unable to rebuild the road to cross the Salween River, and eventually make a permanent retreat southward to more friendly territory.

The Chinese army had been fighting for weeks to stop the invasion, and failed. The enormous impact of this tiny but spectacular action was largely overlooked by the press, which seemed more interested in the dramatic stories of airplane-versus-airplane battles taking place almost daily. Even the AVG pilots were not fully aware of its importance at the time, and considered it just routine, one of their many bombing and strafing missions.

The Salween Gorge Mission deserves a special place in history as one of the most spectacular and incredible events in World War II, yet the least publicized. A tiny force of eight Flying Tiger fighters blockaded the Burma Road access into Western China, stopped a Japanese division, and saved China from invasion. There should have been huge celebrations over this event, but hardly a word reached the press. Tex Hill, Ed Rector, and other Tiger leaders commented later that if they had not stopped the Japanese at the Salween, there was nothing to prevent the enemy from moving right into Kunming, and putting an end to China's resistance. The Japanese were forced to continue maintaining large numbers of troops and a sizeable air fleet in China, possibly saving India and Australia from invasions that could have changed the course of the war.

I consider this one of the most fascinating stories of WWII. Shutting down the Burma Road had its parallel in ancient mythology, which describes how the hero, Horatius, saved Rome by almost single-handedly holding the Etruscan invaders at the Tiber River, until his comrades could destroy the bridge.

Winston Churchill praised the Flying Tigers for this outstanding accomplishment, by paraphrasing his earlier praise of the Royal Air Force in the Battle of Britain, saying, "Never have so many owed so much to so few ..... "

* * * * * *

Pilots flying the Hump knew little about the Flying Tigers and their combat operation in China, being totally absorbed in the problems of flying the most dangerous airlift in the world. Our trip to Kweilin shifted Curt and me from our basic job of flying the Hump into the middle of one of the most fascinating air operations in the war, the American Volunteer Group (AVG).

On our first day with the Flying Tigers some of their stories trickled out. We prodded them for more information about their accomplishments, how they had taken control of the skies over western China from a much larger enemy and stopped the bombing of Chinese cities. They mentioned the Salween Gorge mission, but didn't make a big deal out of it. In following weeks we learned about their life style, their attitude, and their problems. We witnessed the adoration that the Chinese people felt for their heroes, and realized why they were heroes to the folks back in the States.

We found them to be great guys, all loyal Americans, cocky as hell, and eager to fight. The American press had called them "our gallant warriors," and the public was jubilant to hear that a group of "our own American boys" with the intriguing name of "Flying Tigers" had stopped the Japanese Air Force and was winning the air battle over China. Their victories were doubly important to the folks back home because the war was going so badly in other areas.

We saw that after months of continuous action without a letup, they were worn down, sick, underfed, and sour on the failure of the US to give them the needed support. We were amazed to learn that they had received little recognition from the US Army command, who treated them like unwanted relatives.

We learned about the unique way the AVG was organized. With President Roosevelt's approval to release military pilots from the services, a commercial enterprise was established by the Chinese government called Central Air Manufacturing Company (CAMCO). CAMCO recruiters were given permission to visit US. Army, Navy, and Marine air bases throughout the country, and advertise for pilots and crewmen to fight for China. By presidential decree, a pilot joining the American Volunteer Group would be permitted to resign his commission, and then resume it after his one-year contract with CAMCO was ended.

Many of the pilots had been flight instructors in military flying schools with many hours in the air, but tired of their monotonous routine. Others were experienced Navy carrier pilots, and some already were highly trained pursuit pilots. All shared a sense of adventure and a desire to fly high-powered pursuit planes against a real enemy. The

AVG offered them combat flying in heavily armed fighters and good pay. Their contracts called for a salary of $600 per month, with a bonus of $500 for each plane they shot down, compared to the average military pay of $220 per month they had been receiving. Ground crews were hired for $300 per month, three times their military pay.

The true story of the AVG is as exciting as any fiction, but these men were actually living it. There were 100 pilots and 100 airplanes, supported by a mere 150 ground personnel, compared to the thousands of support people that would be required in an official military operation. Their entry into the skies over Burma in late 1941 made a great change in the battle to save China. They flew Curtiss-Wright P-40b fighters that were not the latest model, and had been rejected by the British Royal Air Force in favor of a more powerful model that was more competitive with German fighters. They developed a combat technique that overcame the shortcomings of the airplane, and soon took on the mantle of knights in shining armor.

Their affect on the morale of the Chinese people was tremendous. Years of bombing and strafing of their cities by Japanese aircraft had become an accepted way of life. The picture changed when the AVG took command of the air, and the Chinese no longer feared a "bombers moon" clear night. The people idolized the Tigers, and gave them heroes' welcomes wherever they went.

The AVG first taste of combat against the Japanese Air Force took place over Rangoon at Christmas time in 1941, when they took on large fleets of Japanese bombers that expected no opposition. The enemy was shocked to find deadly resistance, for in the first three days of heavy fighting the Tigers destroyed 33 Japanese aircraft. They developed confidence in their fighting ability and the power of their airplanes, and accomplished miracles facing odds as high as 10-to-1 against Japanese aircraft that were more maneuverable and heavily gunned. In the eight months of the AVG operation they downed 299 aircraft against 12 losses of their own, and destroyed many more on the ground.

Japanese troops captured Rangoon on March 8, 1942, and started a relentless march northward up the Burma Road towards China. This forced the AVG to continually move its bases northward barely one jump ahead of the enemy, often losing airplanes on the ground and precious repair facilities. They moved into China and set up their main base at Kunming, with forward bases 450 miles east in the Kweilin area.

At about that time, American correspondents heard the full story of their deeds, and publicity came in a storm. The AVG victories were the only good news our nation was hearing in 1942, a time of military losses and great fear. At home they were hailed as heroes, and a legend was born that exists to this day. A "Flying Tiger" holds a special place of high esteem in our society.

The whole world knew that they had saved the day for China and stopped the killing of the innocents, but, amazingly, there were critics in high places in our own Army Air Corps who put roadblocks in their way. They failed to give them credit for their deeds and ignored their need for supplies. They were belittled as mercenaries and "hired guns operating outside the boundary of civilized warfare." Is there such a thing as "civilized" warfare?

Curt and I were welcomed into their group as equals, and they were very glad to have us. They desperately needed the help we and our airplane could offer, as this was the only air transport available to them. They loved to bitch, and since Curt and I were Army Air Corps, they heaped their complaints on our shoulders. They ribbed us as being part of that "really screwed up Air Corps" which had failed them badly, but there was no animosity and we quickly made friends. They knew that two lowly pilots flying a C-47 did not have any influence with top brass, but they got it off their chests. In turn, we made solemn promises to do our best to bring in more supplies.

They supplied us with charts, extra gear, and advice on flying in China. They had "Blood Chit" panels painted on the backs of our A-2 flight jackets, to identify us to friendly Chinese. Roughly translated, they read, "This American is a friend of China, helping us fight the war. Give him assistance." We learned simple sign language that went like this: Point to yourself and loudly say, "May-Ru-Gan," (Amer-i-can) over and over again.

I received a fascinating insight into the life of a most unusual person, the mercenary soldier. These were not blood-thirsty pirates, ready to plunder and run, as some of the public perceived them. They were ordinary guys like us, just out of the military service a year, who were lucky to fall under the guidance of an extraordinary leader, General Claire Chennault. Without Chennault's expert knowledge of the enemy, and his ability to command and inspire his men by his own example, the Flying Tigers might have become an unruly, out-of-control bunch of free-lance soldiers of fortune. Instead, they were a fine example of a close-knit fighting team that performed in such an outstanding way, that even after more than a half a century, their reputation remains undiminished.

In June of 1942, when we joined them, they were showing acute signs of exhaustion, caused by the constant fighting for their lives against a superior force. They displayed a happy-go-lucky attitude most of the time, but occasionally one would lose his temper about some trivial thing and show signs of extreme stress. Even to my 22-year-old youthful eyes, it was obvious that they were living under great pressure and needed time off and some good food.

Curt and I were official army, and had become accustomed to a military way of life. We found the Tiger casual lifestyle a great change and got into the swing of it very quickly. We were not exactly "spit and polish" military ourselves, but compared to the AVG, we were the best-dressed men in town. Their clothes were anything they wanted to wear, ranging from flowery shirts and shorts to coolie outfits complete with locally made straw sunshades. They had no dress code, but for a visit downtown or for official events and photographs, they would wear a Chinese Air Force uniform with leather jacket and emblems.

The Tigers usually spent their evenings in the resident hostels provided for them, formerly college dormitories, housing two to a room, and offering running water, sometimes hot enough for a shower. They were the very best accommodations available. They played never-ending games of poker, but when Curt and I showed up, they took us out "on the town," to enjoy the meager entertainment available. Liquor was in short supply, limited to what we could bring from Kunming, or the local rice wine and other suspicious looking beverages. I never saw signs of heavy drinking, as they had learned the hard way to avoid it, but I heard of heavy drinking in the early days.

The "Adam and Eve" squadron was located at Kweilin, which was our base of operations. Tex Hill, Joe Rosbert, Bob Neale, and R.T. Smith were some of the pilots and we found them great company. They had some great stories to tell us, some funny, some tragic, but all accompanied by the pilots' hands-on demonstration showing how they flew a certain mission. They certainly befriended us, giving us the lowdown on surviving in China, with warnings about what not to eat, how to cope with shortages, and keeping out of trouble in the air. By this time they were on limited diets, and it wasn't long before our own digestive systems had us mainly subsisting on fried egg sandwiches on coarse farmer bread. The "Delhi Belly" could attack you in India or in China, and the results were the same, a bad case of dysentery.

The Tigers took us on shopping trips into the local town, and we joined them in the sport of haggling with the local merchants for the few things available to purchase in this impoverished country. They taught us about Chinese currency; inflation of Chinese dollars (CN) was so large that they carried great amounts of paper money to bargain with, sometimes so much that they packed it into pillowcases. The CN had a legal rate of 20 Chinese dollars to one US dollar, but on the black market we could buy as many as 100 CN for one dollar.

The Tigers may have been casual about their clothing and most other things, but when it came to a mission, they became very business-like, for their lives were at stake. Chennault and his squadron commanders ran the show very efficiently, and made sure that everyone toed the line. Their training was directed by the "Old Man" himself, and he taught them his own hard-earned lessons. He had flown many missions against the Japanese in the late 30's when the enemy was trying out its new Zero's and other combat aircraft. Chennault and his Chinese pilots were badly handicapped, flying obsolete airplanes, which were poorly maintained and totally unreliable, making them easy targets for the superior Japanese. He learned about Japanese techniques, and how they would follow their leader closely, based on their system of discipline. If the leader was shot down, his followers might become totally disorganized, and unable to continue any offensive action, leaving them prey to a well-planned attack.

Chennault taught the Tigers well. He made sure that they understood that performance of the Jap fighters was superior in most ways to their own P-40's. The lighter Zeros could out-climb and out-maneuver them, and were superior in a dog-fight. The instruction was, "never try to turn inside a Jap, as he can beat you that way." The P-40 had its own advantages, being a heavier, stronger airplane, armored for pilot protection, and it could dive at higher speeds. They learned the hit-and-run tactic, which called for diving down on Japanese formations from a higher altitude, making as many hits as possible on that first pass, and continuing to dive at high speed to leave the area. They would then re-group well away from the enemy, climb up again, and make a second pass. His skill at training the AVG made them such a superior fighting force that fighter units around the world eventually copied his techniques.

For hit-and-run attacks to be successful it was necessary that the AVG know the location of the enemy at all times, so Chennault and the Chinese established an air raid warning net. This was a most remarkable system considering how little equipment they had. The Chinese made expert use of their very meager telephone, telegraph, and radio systems. The warning net was amazingly efficient; working well even in remote places, and AVG Ops claimed that some outlying stations were using drums to send warnings.

Some lookout posts were so close to Japanese airfields that it was possible for a message about a pending raid to arrive before the enemy aircraft even took off. A typical message would read, "Six airplanes with propellers turning at Xingpo airport". The next message would read, "Six airplanes left Xingpo at 0800 flying heading 295 degrees direction of Kweilin." Other reports would filter in giving progress and Ops would calculate the likely target and estimated time of arrival. By that time the AVG would have P-40's waiting at 16,000 feet, above the normal cruising altitude of the invaders, ready to pounce. And pounce they did, with disastrous results to the enemy. Their score of 299 airplanes destroyed was small as military numbers go, but had a great impact on the war and on fighter training methods in every theater around the world.

The AVG maintenance men were as deserving of credit as the pilots. After many months of hard work and improvising they had learned to do more with less, and were able to keep an astonishing number of airplanes flying despite their worn out condition. They worked under thatch roofed shelters alongside the runways, sometimes fabricating repair parts by hand with inadequate tools. I flew our C-47 "Ferdinand" on daily shuttle flights between fighter bases, transferring spare parts scavenged from badly damaged fighters that were cannibalized to keep the others flying. For example, I might pick up a radiator and a radio from a downed airplane in Lingling and transfer it to Hengyang. Sometimes, it took several damaged planes to make one good one, and these were the miracles that kept our fighter units in the air.

There was a joke among us that these mechanics were so good, they could take the dummy airplanes the Chinese had built out of bamboo and cloth and spread around the field as decoys, and with a few parts, could make them into real airplanes.

The Tigers had many stories to tell of their adventures, and after a few beers they would come pouring out. Bob "Moose" Moss was from Georgia and planned to visit home very soon. His victories in the air were acknowledged by medals awarded personally by the Generalissimo and the Madame for bravery, and for his daring escape on foot from behind the Japanese lines when he was forced down by a bullet in his radiator. This was a very hair-raising story, and had been widely publicized in his hometown newspapers.

He fell in love with some photos I showed him of the girls I had met in Albany, Georgia, when I was in flying school, and he planned to look them up on his return, and give them my regards. His homesick comment was, "I almost forgot what a Georgia peach looks like." He had lots of that kind of company on his return home. Sometime later I bumped into him at Calcutta where he maintained an apartment after returning to flying, this time on the Hump for China National Airline Corporation (CNAC). He escorted me around the city, showing me the sights.

Jesse Hennessey was another Tiger returning to his home just outside of Boston, with many stories to tell, and taking along some of my film, which he delivered to my family along with my greetings.

The boys who walked out of the Burma jungles or China hinterlands after they had forced landings, were members of the "Hill and Dale Club." Cliff Groh of Chicago landed his P-40 safely on a sand bar in a river, and spent 47 days walking back. He told us about the friendly Chinese he met, who treated him royally, passing him from one village to another like a celebrity, and wining and dining him at every stop. At several towns he was greeted with banners in English, hailing him as a hero. He claimed that he learned enough Chinese to talk to his laundryman back home, and could even write his name in Chinese. The "Blood Chit" he wore on his jacket describing him as a Flying Tiger was his ticket to safety and freedom.

* * * * * *

AVG personnel felt that they were being deliberately neglected by the failure of the Air Corps to provide even minimal support from the Army. They received another devastating blow to their morale from General Clayton Bissell in late June. This officer showed up in Kunming with the mission to recruit these exceptionally experienced pilots and their ground crews into the Air Corps on termination of their contract on July 4th. They were badly needed to train pilots of the newly formed China Air Task Force (CATF), which was taking over the Flying Tiger operation under command of General Chennault.

Bissell offered the AVG pilots commissions that would reinstate them to the ranks they held before joining the AVG, but he then proceeded to alienate them by making the most stupid statement possible. In a very high-handed manner, he actually threatened the AVG men. "If you don't accept my offer," he stated, "you will be drafted into the infantry on the day you arrive back in the states. You know, there is a war on!"

Bissell had managed to make one of the great military blunders of the CBI war. His threat was guaranteed to inflame the sorely tried temperaments of a group of high-strung pilots who very definitely knew there was a war on. Many of these men had every intention of joining up after they took some time off for rest, but changed their minds when Bissell insisted on immediate signing up with no time off.

This threat of the draft to a group of combat pilots who had stood the world on its ear with its string of victories, was almost laughable, and it triggered a very vicious response. They didn't know whether to laugh or swear, but they very clearly told Bissell what he could do with his offer and walked out. They told me bluntly that they were completely shocked by the audacity of this officer, and "the Air Corps can go to hell!"

"If top military brass is so stupid as to send a son-of-a-bitch like Bissell with such outrageous demands, we aren't interested in signing up with this SNAFU outfit." They were not under U.S. control and had other alternatives, among them offers to work for CNAC, the China airline operated by PanAm.

Five pilots, flight leaders who were loyal to Chennault and realized that he would be severely handicapped without their help, decided to join up, and were commissioned with the rank of Major. Many others went to CNAC, which was under contract to the U.S. Army, and were happy to fly the Hump for triple the military pay. Some of the retiring AVG were so incensed at Bissell's high-handed attitude that they taught Chinese ground crews at Kunming to sing a little ditty each time they met an airplane newly arrived over the Hump. The words, carefully learned, were, "Piss on Bissell."

In later months, when I met former AVG pilots at various airfields now flying for CNAC, they laughingly pointed out how their salaries flying commercial compared with mine. They had many other benefits, such as time off after flying 100 hours per month. They generously offered me the use of apartments that they maintained in Calcutta, with "all the fringe benefits, such as live-in maids".

* * * * * *

On July 1, two weeks after we joined the AVG, my status changed from copilot to first pilot. Curt was stricken with a severe malaria attack at our hostel in Kunming, where we were picking up another load to take to Kweilin. It happened overnight, and he was running a very high fever and was much too sick to fly. Kunming Operations checked with him about my qualifications to take the trip, as I was the only C-47 pilot in Kunming who had ever been to Kweilin. I had flown as his copilot for two months, during which time he passed a lot of his skills on to me and he had checked me out in the left seat. He was the pilot in command, and I always relied on his good judgment to bring us home in one piece. That was about to change.

I heard Curt answer the inquiry from Operations, drawling in great discomfort, "Hell, Jim knows the way better than I do. Send him." Ferdinand was already loaded for our "Express" run with P-40 drop tanks, drums of aviation fuel, mail, groceries, and other assorted cargo, so I recruited one of the fighter pilots to fly right seat, moved over into the left seat, and took off for Kweilin.

Many wartime pilots may wonder and say, "What's the big deal?" Every copilot was expected to check out as first pilot eventually, so why all the fuss? The answer is that most combat missions are flown in formation, with squadron leaders showing the way and keeping an eye on first pilots with limited experience. Flying a cargo run for the Air Transport Command is different, as you are totally on your own, doing your own navigation across strange territory, and making your own decisions, all of which take experience and skill. Curt's lessons proved to be invaluable to me, and on several occasions, when I was in a tight spot, I asked myself, "What would Curt do?" There was always a common sense answer.

The move into the left seat meant more to me than a promotion in rank, for now I was wholly responsible for the airplane and its precious cargo. Our C-47 was valuable, being the only cargo carrier in China, and our loads of .50 caliber ammunition, belly tanks, and assorted parts were badly needed. Ferdinand offered the only way to carry these and other vital items. I am reminded of the famous saying from Benjamin Franklin's Poor Richard's Almanac, " For want of a nail the shoe was lost; for want of a shoe the horse was lost; for want of a horse .... the battle was lost." On a lonely flight across the vast expanses of China, I realized that the success of the next fighter mission, and the safety of many lives might depend on my safe arrival. I had no backup, nobody to ask for advice.

When I landed at Kweilin, Operations asked, "Where's Curt?" I replied, "He has a bad case of malaria and he'll be out of commission for a week or two." They commiserated about his illness, which most of them had already suffered, and I saw a big change in their attitude when they realized that I was the skipper.

That day was a turning point for me. I had a new self-image, regarded my crew as my dependents, and could now taste what being an officer in command in the field really meant, with no one to ask for instructions. It explains how "a position of responsibility can turn a boy into a man in a hurry," a bit of wisdom that has applied to every generation. I have often noted how easy it is to find the command pilot out of crew of airmen, all dressed alike. He is the one who is not kidding around, telling jokes, laughing to offset the stress of dangerous missions. He is the busy one, with a serious face wrinkled in thought as he prepares for a new flight, or reviews the one he has just completed. He may be a lowly second lieutenant, but he stands out as the man in charge

Curt was gone for two weeks, and when he recovered, we flew together many more times, but we flew as equals and he was happy to split first pilot credit with me. He took special credit, for making me the highly qualified pilot that I had become.

A major event took place on July 4, 1942. Chennault wrote, "The AVG passed into history. " On that very important day, the American Volunteer Group was replaced by the China Air Task Force (CATF), an official military unit of the U.S. Army Air Corps under command of General Claire Chennault, newly commissioned a brigadier general in the U.S. Army. Chiang Kai-shek had insisted that Chennault was the only leader he would tolerate to lead the CATF, and he was given this command despite top-level resistance. Chennault and Chiang Kai-shek were further assured that in exchange for demobilizing the AVG, their new command, the CATF, would receive an entire new air fleet of fighters and medium bombers and the necessary backup of supplies. This was a false promise. It did not happen.

The CATF inherited only twenty-nine worn out P-40's plus a squadron of seven B-25 Mitchell bombers that were transferred in from India. This shockingly small number of airplanes was the entire US Air Force in China! It was hard to realize that many thousands of aircraft were pouring out of factories back in the States, but none coming to us. General Harold "Hap" Arnold, commander of all U. S. Air Forces, along with other. Pentagon brass, who should have celebrated the past successes of the AVG, showed bad faith in failing to keep their promises. We always wondered why this was so.

Colonel Robert L. Scott took over as CO of flight operations and found he had serious personnel problem on his hands. New CATF pilots transferring in had no combat experience, and the new Air Corps mechanics had a limited knowledge of the P-40. This left Scott in a poor position to continue aggressive action against the ever-threatening Japanese. He got an assist from 18 AVG pilots and a number of ground crew who volunteered to delay their departure and stay on for another two weeks to give the "Old Man," as Chennault was fondly called, some support during the critical transition period.

This turned out to be a fatal decision for John Petach, who was shot down during a July 10th raid on a Japanese air base, leaving behind his pregnant wife, "Red," an employee of the AVG. This was a very sad occurrence, and we all grieved with Red when she left for home without her husband. Another loss mourned that day was Arnold Shamblin, who bailed out of his disabled airplane and disappeared into a Japanese prison camp.

Curt and I were now under command of the CATF, which was a change for us. After flying Ferdinand with the AVG for several weeks, we had felt like free-lance barnstormers, with our own private airplane, making our own decisions as to where to go and what to haul. Of course we were at the beck and call of the AVG, but they never ordered us about, but always politely asked us to make certain trips. We were away from military command, and pretty much on our own.

This situation now was changed when the CATF took over, but the nature of our work remained the same. Colonel Scott assured Curt and me that we were to keep on flying the "China Express" as before, and we were happy to continue, rather than return to the routine of flying the Hump. Once again, nothing was in writing - just verbal instructions.

Curt was back from sick leave and we were busy flying General Chennault and other VIP's to Chungking and other cities, hauling cargo, and carrying parts back and forth for the maintenance crew. We picked up loads at Kunming, and delivered them to the three forward bases. We flew to Chengtu, Chihkiang, Yunnnanyi, and Chanyi, where we picked up locally made belly tanks and other items from storage areas where the Chinese had cached away vital military supplies.

We realized just how much our airplane could accomplish compared to other means of transport. There is an amazing story about moving drums of gasoline over the road from the Hump terminal at Kunming to our outer fighter bases at Kweilin, Hengyang, and Lingling. Dilapidated trucks or ox carts usually hauled the fuel drums the 500 mile trip.

We had flown this route many times, and marveled at the difficult terrain over mountains with dozens of dangerous hairpin turns. We were astonished to learn that when there was a shortage of vehicles, hundreds of coolies would use large wheelbarrows, crudely built wooden-wheeled vehicles, to haul the drums. When that simple vehicle was not available, coolies would actually carry the drums, weighing 500 pounds, on a four-man sling, a back-breaking task, often resulting in many deaths from pure exhaustion. As a last resort, they would roll the drums the entire 500 miles on these extremely bad roads, at a tremendous cost to life and limb. Labor was plentiful, and was always there to fill in when the machinery failed or just didn't exist to do the job. When a coolie dropped from exhaustion, another stepped up to take over. It took up to ten weeks by road to move a drum in these crude ways. The durability of the Chinese, and their extreme dedication to this task, was truly remarkable. By contrast, in Ferdinand, we could move 13 fifty-five gallon drums to Kweilin in three hours. We were proud to be doing such an important job with our one C-47.

I kept a diary during the time I spent in China. Here is one very special excerpt:

"July 17, 1942. En route Ling-ling to Kweilin. Weather clear. Unknown aircraft sighted. Identified as Jap Zero. Turns out to be a friendly! Finish trip okay."

That is a brief entry, but there is an exciting story here. I was a sitting duck that day, a defenseless bird unable to fight off a well-armed enemy. Off to my left I saw a speck moving fast. He turned towards me and when it got closer, I recognized that it was a blunt nosed airplane with a radial engine, and that meant it definitely was not a friendly P-40. He closed so rapidly that before I could make any change in my heading, he crossed just over my nose and I saw a large red circle insignia on the side of his airplane. It was a Japanese Zero!

"Son-uv-a-bitchl I knew I should have some machine guns!" I was in a very bad place, and frantically grabbed my microphone to yell for help. All we had on board for defense was one Thompson sub-machine gun and two .45 caliber pistols, while the Zero was loaded with heavy armament. We were at 3000 feet, much too high to escape by a dive to the deck, no clouds to dodge into, and we were really in great danger.

The Zero disappeared, and I expected heavy caliber shells to pierce our cabin any moment. Nothing happened. I strained my neck for a look and suddenly the Zero appeared again, tucked in neatly just over my left wing, flying close formation, the pilot waving madly. What in hell did he want? Was he trying to surrender to me? What a prize if I landed at a fighter base with a captured Zero! I could see my picture on the cover of Life magazine with a caption, "Unarmed Transport Captures Japanese Fighter."

My mouth must have been hanging open, in total wonder, for he slid his goggles up off his face and gave me a big grin from a very occidental face with straw-colored hair. It was Tex Hill, squadron leader. He flew along with me for a few seconds, but before I got over my shock and thought to grab my camera, he peeled off and was gone, whereby I missed one of the greatest photo opportunities I have ever had.

That evening at the hostel, he came over to chat about his big practical joke which, of course, I didn't find very funny. It seemed that the Zero had been captured after it made a forced landing when the fuel line plugged up and the engine quit. The pilot was captured by the local peasants, and he must have had a very hard time, because his remains showed considerable punishment. The airplane was picked up by the AVG mechanics and trucked to Lingling and repaired, and Tex, and a couple of other highly qualified pilots put it through its paces to test its performance against our P-40's. It eventually went to Wright Field for evaluation, but it served its very important purpose right there in China. My beef with Tex went something like this:

Me: "Tex, you scared the hell out of us."

Tex: "You've got to keep your eyes peeled for someone creeping up on you from behind."

Me, sarcastically: "We don't have rear view mirrors in a C-47 like you have in a P-40."

Tex: "Well- - -let's see what we can do about that."

Whereupon Tex went into the supply room, and came out with a pair of Navy style goggles and helmet. "Here," he said, "wear these and stick your head out the window to see if anyone's on your tail. " I was delighted to get this prize AVG item and I thanked him, neglecting to mention that sticking my head out of the sliding window at 160 MPH might be hard on my tender body. I still have those goggles, and wear them faithfully whenever I fly an open cockpit airplane, with my white scarf and all. Tex never did say he was sorry for scaring the hell out of us, but the gift made up for it.

Tex was quite a hero. He had a long string of victories, and in one famous incident knocked down a Zero right over the field in a daylight raid. The warning net had given us information about incoming aircraft so they were expected. The Tigers used their standard hit-and-run tactic, and only two out of six Zeros got away. I was there on the ground that day when Tex approached the wreckage, which crashed very close to Ops, and gave it a quick kick. Some people dispute that he ever uttered this sentence, but I was there. He said, and I remember it as yesterday, "That'll teach him to make a head-on run at a P-40 with six .50's. "

About this time I tried to make a bargain with Tex to get checked out in a P-40. I admitted that the hottest airplane I had flown was an AT -6 advanced trainer.

"Tex, how would you like to get some twin-engine time in a C-47 in exchange for my checking out in a P-40?"

"Now Jim, why would you want to do that?"

"I went through fighter training school, took first prize in gunnery, and haven't fired a gun since. You could use more fighter pilots. "

"Jim, you gotta be kidding. It's a big step from an AT-6 into a P-40, and our guys usually get 40 hours of instruction before going on their first mission. Besides, we don't have enough airplanes and you sure aren't bringing us enough gas to run a training program here. Every hour we fly is for a mission, and that's the Old Man's orders."

Tex laughed, and added, "Shucks, Jim, my guys are jealous as hell of you. You do as much flying in one day as some of us fly in a month. They'd swap jobs with you in a minute to do all that flying. Stick to it. You're doing a great job." It was true that on some days I was spending over ten hours in the air, and was way over the official 100 hours per month pilot time limit. Tex stopped me cold, and I didn't ask again.

My flying included some instrument time, which had become second nature to me, but I avoided this as much as possible. Scattered clouds were okay, but in China, flying on instruments in thick clouds or on top of a solid layer could be deadly without a radio homing station to bring you home. There were a few radio homing stations, but they were very unreliable. After you arrived over the station you still had a problem, finding a hole in the overcast to let down, as there were no instrument approach procedures. Without that hole you were in serious trouble. I almost never flew on top, but when I did I always managed to find a hole someplace, as I had enough fuel supply to keep looking. The fighter squadrons had lost some airplanes that got stuck on top when they couldn't find a hole and ran out of fuel, with pilots bailing out. We had no intention of getting into that situation. That can spoil your day.

Every time you took off you started making decisions, some good, some bad. On one occasion I was making a short trip from Lingling to Hengyang, and decided to fly directly up the valley following the road between two parallel ridges of low hills. The weather was clear, and I was just being lazy, not bothering to climb over the surrounding hills. I suddenly ran smack into a rain squall, which completely blocked my forward visibility despite windshield wipers going full blast. Looking out my side windows, I saw that I was flying lower than the hills on both sides of me and had no doubt that there was a hill dead ahead of me with my name on it. This was a very scary situation. Only one thing to do!

I went to full power and pulled back on the wheel to pop up as fast as I could, to fly up and over the squall. A C-47 does not climb very fast, and I did not take a breath until I broke out on top in the clear, a thousand feet higher. I never pulled that stunt again, always climbing to a safe altitude and staying there until I saw my destination. Our safety margins were very small, so we flew as if our lives depended on our good judgment, which they did.

Here are some more diary entries, and a very exciting air raid with a lot of action:

"July 27. Another Jing-Bau (air raid warning) at Hengyang last night. The gong sounded that we were expecting company within the hour, and everybody started moving fast. The alert crew headed for their four fighters, and I dashed into Operations and announced that I was going to save my C-47 by taking off and heading west for a couple of hours until the all clear was radioed to me. Ops turned me down cold. 'Stay on the ground, or you'll get shot at by our own guys, who won't be able to identify you. Also, ground spotters will get confused and think you're a Jap. Leave your airplane in the revetment, get your crew, and join the rest of the guys for a nice boat ride up the river.'"

A revetment was the equivalent of a slit trench that hid an airplane. Chinese labor had built these by piling up long mounds of earth in a "U" shape, and we had parked the airplane in this shelter, where it was fairly safe from anything but a direct hit.

I thought I was being kidded about a boat ride, but, sure enough, a truckload of us rode to the river, got aboard a large launch, and leisurely headed upstream a couple of miles.

We had ringside seats to watch the air action, but it was a black night and no aircraft were visible until the fighting started and tracers were flying. Fighter strategy was different at night, as it is difficult to spot a formation flying without lights. The only possible way to find the invaders was by flying lower than they and looking upwards for the flames of their engine exhausts. It took sharp eyes of our pilots, but once they sighted the intruders, it became a one-sided battle, proving the wisdom of their tactics. The enemy did drop some incendiary bombs in their haste to avoid our fighters, but it was the end for four bombers out of six, with two escaping into the night.

In a letter home that week I wrote about my reluctance to leave my airplane on the field and take the boat ride. I wrote, "I chewed most of my nails off that night worrying about Ferdinand and jumped with worry when the incendiaries lit up. I could have sworn it was my gas tanks going up in flames. I learned later that only two sticks of bombs had landed near the field, with no major damage."

All four fighters in the air called in safe, until Major Johnny Alison reported an overheating engine. A lucky bomber gunner had put a bullet into the very vulnerable radiator and he lost coolant rapidly. He later joked that Alison's Allison engine froze up, but it wasn't very funny at the time as Johnny's engine was about to quit, and he was too close to the ground to bailout. He spotted the river, and very expertly ditched in it, a tough thing to do at night. No one knew what had happened to him for several hours, and he was feared lost.

But this was a very tough pilot. He climbed out of the cockpit before the airplane sank, swam, waded, and crawled up the muddy banks until he hit dry land, grateful that he was a good swimmer. A few hours later, to our great delight,

Johnny showed up in very regal style, very much the hero, being carried on a throne-like sedan chair by a group of cheering locals. His only injury was a deep scratch on his face suffered when he hit the instrument panel during ditching.

The airplane was as tough as Johnny. It slid along the surface of the river in one piece and then settled in about 20 feet of water. Every airplane was precious to us, and we pondered how we were going to raise it. Amazingly, the local people had it up and out in three days. They used the famous native method of diving down and tying many bamboo poles under the wings and fuselage until they created enough buoyancy to bring the airplane to the surface. Years later I heard that native divers in the South Pacific used the same method to raise all types of heavy objects.

Johnny Alison was a college mate of Curt and we had a big party to celebrate his survival, and his fourth victory. Alison went on to more victories, rose to the rank of general, and in later years, achieved the high office in the state department as Assistant Secretary of State for Air. This was a true warrior, a most admirable person, and a good friend.

More diary entries describe my social life and other matters, through the eyes of a 22-year old who still had some growing up to do:

"July 4. This is the last official day for the AVG and they're making a big party, which will probably include some heavy drinking. A few of us went downtown to a safe restaurant, and I was introduced to a lovely young Chinese lady, Miss Betty Jo Ping, who is an interpreter working for the AVG. With all of them leaving for other places, I thought Betty Jo would be free to enjoy my company, and she said she would be happy to give me her telephone number, except that she had no telephone. She gave me directions to her home and we made a date, which I was not able to keep, thanks to enemy interference. (Note: War is Hell!)"

"July 11. Very hot day waiting for a load at Peishiyi. Local resident, Doreen Davis, told about living comfortably for many years at Shanghai, a modem city with department stores, air conditioning, and good food. Japanese commanders are very satisfied to live the good life in the coastal cities and leave the hinterlands to us until they are ready to make a heavy push to the west. Most of us would be very happy to move out and give it to the Japs as a gift. It certainly wouldn't lower the living standards, and it seems to be the accepted theory that after a few generations, inter-marriage would absorb the Japanese military into the local citizenry. "Sounds like a good idea to drown the whole of Japan's 75 millions in the sea of 450 Chinese millions."

"July 15. Got one of the coolie gangs down at 5:00 AM. to haul Ferdy out of a supposedly filled-in crater into which the chief taxied her last night. About 40 boys pushed us out to the accompaniment of much grunting, shouting, and blowing of whistles by the foremen. Later flew to Kunming. General Chennault, an obliging guy, took over part of the flying for me in return for which I made up some corned beef and peanut butter sandwiches with tomato juice. Best food he's had since the States, he said. I am disappointed to hear him refusing permission to a "Time" correspondent to put his picture on the cover, with a big write-up of China activities. We'd like some publicity - it might get us more airplanes. But his Tigers already had received world-wide publicity, causing criticism in Washington, so he declined."

"August 4. Brought the last group of AVG personnel to Kunming for return to the states or wherever they are going. Gave one of them, 'Red' Petach, a very swell girl who was a nurse for the AVG, two silver bracelets that she promised to send to Boston on her return. Red was in mourning for her husband, John, an AVG pilot who volunteered to stay with Chennault another month to help get the CATF started, and was shot down in July."

"August 16. Had a real heavy day today. Up at 4:00 AM, flew to Hengyang, Lingling, Chan-yi, Hengyang, back to Kweilin. Arrived after dark after flying 11 hours. Wait till the Airline Pilots Association hears about this. Then went downtown riding on the back of a motorcycle. Who says flying is dangerous?"

My diary reads, "Tuesday, August 18th (1942). A great day today —returned to Kunming from Kweilin and found 19 letters waiting for me ... five from parents, three from (sister) Irene, eleven from Dotty, Margie, Pat, and Essy. It will be a pleasure to spend the next month answering them all." Girl friends are great! Their letters were just frilly notes, but they are the lifeline that keeps an army man going, and I kept writing them all in return to show my appreciation.

My diary has many mentions of that wonderful mail from home, which is the best of all gifts for a soldier. Every letter from a 12,000-mile distance is cherished. Wherever I landed my C-47 at a China base, the first man on board would ask, "Got any mail?" If my answer was affirmative, his face would light up, and he would go to the door and shout, "Mail call!" In minutes, a crowd would show, jostling for room close to the volunteer mail clerk. Those receiving mail were sensitive enough not to brag, as many anxious men received none. Some went for months without mail because of frequent moves, and this was often cause for serious depression. It is easy to feel forgotten when you are half-way around the world and have no word from home.

Most precious to me were letters from my family, with sister Irene keeping up the good work, informing me about the family. When I received a handful of letters in one bunch, it was like manna from heaven, to be tasted slowly, one at a time. With great foresight, Irene saved all the letters that I sent home, and I find some of them are really funny. They reflected some very narrow viewpoints of a young man who had much to learn about the cultures of the world, and who thought that the only society that counted was his own.

My letters to home read like a travelogue, telling of the interesting places I visited and the customs of the people. I assured them that I was flying a safe military airline, no one was shooting at me, and we never lost an airplane. Some of those statements must have seemed odd to my family when they read of military losses all over the world, but it was the only way I could give them peace of mind.

We flew every day, but were sometimes delayed by air raid alerts. Then we would sweat it out in the Operations cave on the hillside, hoping there would not be any surprises.

"August 17, Kweilin. Jing-Bau warning sounded at 5:00 AM. No Japs showed, but had to delay takeoff to Chan-yi until Ops gave me okay to go at 11 :00 AM. Hated to wait as it was probably 100 degrees on the field by then, and the airplane was an oven." The Kweilin Operations cave was a good place to wait out a mission. It was a deep cave in one of the cone-shaped hills that surround the runway, and the temperature held about 72 degrees winter or summer, while the airplanes on the flat plain below us cooked in the summer heat. We had a clear view of the entire field and the flight line.

One late morning in June, Curt and I were in the cave preparing for a trip to Hengyang, and bitching about getting started so late, which meant we had a very hot airplane to climb into. Someone shouted, "Here they come!" We knew it wasn't a Jing-Bau as no air raid warning signal had sounded, and everyone dashed for the cave entrance. We were treated to the distinctive moaning sound of a pair of Allison engines at high power buzzing the field. Two P-40's in loose formation swept down the runway about 30 feet off the ground and then pulled up at about a 30-degree angle. The leader did a victory roll and his wing-man did the same. In a few moments they did U-turns, popped their wheels down and performed perfect fighter approaches and landings, leveling off just before their wheels touched down.

I recalled my days in advance flying school, and said to Curt, "Those guys are good.

Let's do that kind of approach in Ferdy." Curt laughed, "We can do it, but it won't be quite the same. I was just a frustrated fighter pilot, and resolved to try it out some day in our C-47.

The two Tigers climbed out of their cockpits and were greeted on the flight line by men congratulating them and giving them a back pat. They started up the walk to the cave doing the "pilot's visual demonstration" with their hands, showing how they made moves that brought down two Zeros that day. They were heading east on a strafing mission when the warning net reported four Japanese single engine airplanes heading west in the same sector. The two climbed to 16,000 feet and luckily spotted the enemy flight as it passed below. They dove at the formation out of the sun, made two successful hits, and just kept going downhill. At their high diving speed they were well away almost before the Japanese knew they were there. The Zero pilots must have been caught totally unaware until the surprise attack as they took no evasive action, and the two surviving Zeros turned in a hurry and headed back home. The two scores proved once more the value of the warning net, which was to save my neck soon after.

This was our first introduction to victory rolls after combat operation. We saw other landings that were not as happy, with parts of airplanes shot off, but the pilots surviving by good luck, or the strength of a well-built airplane.

The cave provided us with some good entertainment, from radio programs broadcast by the Japanese and from our own Armed Forces Radio. Tokyo Rose was one of our favorite entertainers, a familiar voice throughout the Pacific area, who often broadcast information about our own operation that was amazing in its accuracy. She was a native Californian of Japanese descent, who became known world-wide as a symbol of traitorous behavior, and was tried for treason after the war, receiving a long prison sentence. She broadcast Japanese intelligence releases, that were a major source of information to us, often giving us details about the war before we heard them from our own sources. She also broadcast propaganda that was supposed to discourage us, but these were so greatly exaggerated as to be laughable. They told of large numbers of Flying Tigers shot down while all Japanese aircraft returned safely to base, and we knew the truth was just the opposite.

One day we got the most flattering report from Tokyo Rose, when, in her cultured voice she reported, "We know that there are no more than 300 Flying Tiger pursuit planes in all of China, and they are being destroyed rapidly." The General loved this comment, as at that time we had only 34 P-47's. Someone suggested that we change the numbers and the colors of the propeller spinners every few days to give the impression of many more, but Chennault said that we shouldn't give the enemy enough time to read the numbers before shooting them down.

Tokyo Rose was entertaining, but we were delighted and also homesick when our cave radio picked up music programs like the Lucky Strike Hit Parade from high powered stations in the States or Europe. We listened avidly to the voice of Dinah Shore, and orchestras of Benny Goodman, Glenn Miller, and Arty Shaw playing favorites like *Tangerine, Skylark,* and *Begin the Beguine.* My diary says, "What a blessing to hear those stations. Makes me homesick, and I can imagine dancing to these wonderful tunes with Jeannie (or Margie, or Essy, or Dotty, or Pat) in my arms." Fickle!

Flying Ferdinand on hundreds of shuttle flights between bases made us feel like we were operating a trucking outfit. Many times, I envied the fighter pilots for their sporty flying and their dashing attitude, which dated back to WWI, the days of Baron von Richthofen, Captain Eddie Rickenbacher, and other airmen who fought one-to-one in the arena of the air, surviving by their skills. On the other hand, the fighter pilots envied me for the heavy flying that I was doing, compared to their few hours due to fuel shortages. Yes, I wanted to fly a fighter, but fate placed me in a very practical C-47. This airplane later received the terrible nickname of "Gooney Bird", but to me it was a beautiful aerodynamic machine that saved my ass many times.

I could even count the bullet holes I had acquired. Daily inspection showed a number of suspicious holes, and we assumed there was Jap infantry taking pot shots at us. Perhaps some Chinese farmer, frightened of any airplane, was taking aim at us as we passed overhead, and might just have made a lucky shot. The holes were all scattered around the tail, so we were thankful that they never learned how to lead a bird in flight.

I sound pretty cocky about always finding my way around China, but this was not always so. Carrying a load from Kunming to Kweilin in bad weather one day, I kept dodging around heavy clouds and found myself over strange territory when my estimated time of arrival (ETA) ran out. My copilot was another Hump pilot, Lieutenant Lusky, who was a headstrong person, several years older than me.

Lusky insisted that we were lost. "The only thing for us to do is head right back to Kunming." He was very unhappy at being assigned to me as copilot and wanted to have an equal say in performance of the flight.

"Lusky, we have flown three hours and I'm not going to waste that time and fuel by returning to Kunming. We are close to Kweilin, so calm down."

"Look," Lusky heatedly replied, "If we run out of gas and end up in a belly landing, we'll probably run into a bunch of local people who can't tell the difference between an American and a Jap! We could get killed!"

My copilot was quite frightened, and frantic to do a '180' and head back, until I reminded him in strong language that I was in charge. I wasn't very happy at being lost over central China either, so I fell back on my private solution, which was to concentrate on the thought, "What would Curt do?" I started to fly a search pattern of ten minutes each way, hoping to pick up the Kweilin homing beacon if it was operating. First I flew ten minutes more to the east, and then turned south, as we seemed to have a northward drift, judging by smoke on the ground. In about five minutes I heard the sweetest sound, the faint beep of the Kweilin beacon, which proved we had been well north. In another ten minutes we found ourselves among the friendly peaks of the Kweilin plain. What a relief! I changed copilots after that.

Curt and I joked that without us the war in China would surely be lost. This was a slight exaggeration, but we certainly played a major part in keeping the AVG and the later CATF in business. The extraordinary job that the maintenance people were doing to keep a group of worn out P-40's in flying condition was only possible when parts from grounded airplanes were swapped back and forth by our "China Express." It felt great to consider ourselves almost indispensable. We were especially welcome for the extra food and drink we tried to include with each load.

* * * * * *

July 21 was very special for me. On that day a ferocious looking shark rescued me from a bold Japanese pilot, who was trying to knock our C-47 out of the air.

I was approaching Lingling and called the tower requesting a straight-in landing. "Roger, Express. Come straight in. Hope you have some mail and beer." Then he added, "We have a report of a single bandit over you at about 20,000 feet." This was probably the occasional recon flight the enemy sent over our string of bases to count our planes.

I didn't worry about this until a second call just a few seconds later said, "Bandit diving down heading for twin-engine airplane near Lingling." That's us! We're his target!

He was a daring pilot, dropping this low near our fighter base, but I wasn't about to award him a medal for bravery. I was in trouble. My adrenalin kicked in, and I poured on full power and shoved the wheel forward, heading down to the treetops. I hoped my camouflage paint would make me less visible to this lone ranger.

By now, I was so close to Lingling that I could have seen the runway if I hadn't been down so low, dodging trees and hills in my attempt to escape. I yelled at my copilot, "Do you see the son-of-a-bitch?" and got a badly frightened look in return. Then I yelled into the mike without ceremony, "I need somebody up here to get this guy off my ass, if you want your mail and beer!"

I was almost scraping the leaves off the trees, zigging and zagging, egged on by the threat of a 20 millimeter cannon and machine guns ready to blow us out of the skies. Sweat poured off me, and Biggins, my copilot, who normally flew a P-40, was cussing his bad luck to be in an unarmed transport on his first encounter with the enemy. I heard a rattling noise in the cabin and hoped it was just some loosely tied down cargo shifting around, until my crew chief, Sergeant Saylor, ran up behind us in the cockpit, and yelled, "They're shooting at us!" I expected bullets in the cockpit any second, and zigged more wildly than before, and picked up the mike again, yelling, "Where is everybody?"

There was a short period of silence, and suddenly a voice boomed in my headset, saying, "It's OK, Jim, you can come up now. He's gone home." And just ahead of us at about 500 feet was a P-40 circling lazily around. It was Major Bob Neale, squadron commander, giving me top cover. What a beautiful sight! I fell in love with that ugly grinning shark's mouth, and never forgot it.

That evening Bob told me that the Japanese pilot was gone by the time he reached me. I never did see the intruder, who probably realized he was at great risk this close to our fighters at Lingling, and left in a hurry. I thanked Bob for the rescue, and he laughed and said in his slow, droll way, "Heck, we sure wanted that mail and that beer."

We counted about 15 bullet holes in the tail, but none vital. Some of those were already there before this incident, so I couldn't score the Jap's marksmanship. I decided that it was time to mount machine guns to fire out of our cabin windows, but the proposal got turned down. The fighter pilots laughed and said, "Leave the fighting to us," a job they did very well.

The Tiger insignia is a prominent decoration in my home. It was a menacing kiss of death for Japanese pilots, but was our good luck symbol in China. We flew close to Japanese lines most of the time, so the sight of a pair of P-40's with that glaring face keeping us company was most reassuring, and we got to love that ugly look.

Many people have inquired about the origin of that insignia. The British Royal Air Force had first used it, and General Chennault gave Tiger pilot Eric Shilling an okay to decorate his airplane with that spectacular design. The entire A VG liked it and adopted it. When the CATF took over the airplanes from the AVG in July, they continued to use that design to decorate their airplanes and to use the name of the "Flying Tigers. "

The public response to this emblem was overwhelming. It was a symbol of a victorious air fleet that was defeating the Japanese at a time when we had few victories to celebrate. Sixty years later, that famous face is showing up again on a number of P-40's that hobbyists around the world are restoring to flying condition, and it is a world-wide renowned emblem.

"Blood Chit" fastened to back of flight jacket, identifies wearer as American airman. It instructs all Chinese to give him aid and provide a safe return. Many downed fliers owe their lives to this famous patch.

Chapter 14
THE CATF TAKES OVER

"The China Air Task Force had to fight, scream, and scrape for every man, plane, spark-plug, and gallon of gas. The CATF .... was facing death from acute starvation. " General Claire Lee Chennault

We thought the cavalry was coming to the rescue when the China Air Task Force (CATF), an official Army Air Corps unit of the 10th Air Force, took over air operations from the AVG on July 4, 1942, under command of newly commissioned Brigadier General Claire Chennault. Chiang Kai-shek was reluctant to disband the AVG, which he boasted was his own personal air force that had saved China. He agreed to do so only after Generals Stilwell and Bissell made promises of new fighters as well as a bomber fleet, promises that inspired new life into the combat units and the Hump airlift operation.

They did not keep these promises, which left the new CATF as poorly equipped as the AVG had been. This was a severe blow to the morale of the men who had expected great things to happen. What did arrive was the paper brigade - the army brought in a number of personnel whose job was to establish the correct military organization required by the "book." We were swamped with paper-pushers.

A few P-40's finally arrived, and a tiny bomber unit consisting of seven B-25's was transferred from India. A few C-47's trickled in to Assam to add to our airlift, but this fleet was actually shrinking, as our losses on the Hump were greater than the number of replacements. Our pilots were well trained, and our losses were not the result of accidents, but by the death-dealing weather conditions.

Washington expected us to maintain an active combat force and an adequate airlift, but did not give us the tools to do the job. All this time we faced the frightening spectacle of a huge armada of 500 Japanese aircraft that was sworn to wipe us out.

Just how badly off were we? We were worse off than ever. Before the AVG shut down, it was able to put as many as eight P-40's in the air over Kunming at any one time, despite their age and badly worn condition. Kweilin and the other eastern fields at Lingling and Hengyang were able to fly a similar total, spread out among all the bases, and Chennault's very effective strategy was to shift these from base to base, which gave the appearance of even larger numbers. The AVG mechanics had learned all of the short cuts and managed to keep them flying by ingenious repair work.

The CATF had taken charge, and the situation was almost laughable. There were more people than ever at Kunming, to support the operation, but on some days we had only ONE FIGHTER AIRPLANE in flying condition. If the Japanese had been aware of this cutback in available aircraft they undoubtedly would have mounted powerful attacks, but by a miracle of timing, they appeared to have been scared off for a while.

Lieutenant Matty Wottow was a former flying school classmate, now stationed at Kunming, flying a P-40. He complained, "All we do is sit on the ground all day, playing cards, bored to death. We don't have a decent airplane to fly. Can you use a copilot on your C-47?"

This was a common story among the CATF fighter pilots, who had little confidence in the airworthiness of their patched-up P-40's, and considered them a danger to fly. The newly arrived air corps mechanics lacked the know-how of the AVG men, and some pilots joked that they were using baling wire and tape to hold them together. Maintenance rules often required replacement of certain defective parts with new parts from a supply depot. The rules were ridiculous, with the depot 12,000 miles away. We scavenged from other airplanes, or repaired the part.

Chennault wrote, "The CATF had to fight, scream, and scrape for every man, plane, spark plug, and gallon of gas. The CATF .... was facing death from acute starvation."

So we continued to operate as before. We pulled the spark plugs on the P-40's and my C-47, cleaned, and reused them over and over. Our engine oil was drained and filtered, and used again. Tires were so badly worn that every takeoff and landing was made with a prayer. Hydraulic fluid from damaged airplanes filled the reservoirs of the ones in use. Chinese workers made perfectly useable belly tanks out of bamboo frames covered with cloth and cemented with fish oil.

The brief lull in Japanese activity was a result of the great victories achieved in July by the group of AVG pilots and ground crews who volunteered to stay on for another 15 days to back up the "Old Man" during the difficult transition period.

On July 30 and 31 the Japanese attacked with almost 200 aircraft, aimed at final destruction of the CATF. Tex Hill, Ed Rector, Johnny Alison, and John Petach led the squadrons that savagely fought off groups of incoming Japanese bombers and fighters, and shot down over 30 of them with no more than 10 fighters available at any one time. We lost one of our own, Lieutenant Lee Minor, the first army casualty. These heavy enemy losses at the hands of the tiny CATF discouraged further raids for some time.

This was the grand finale for the AVG flying under its own banner. Now the CATF was on its own, led by a handful of former AVG pilots, newly commissioned as Air Corps majors and captains.

The slowdown in combat activity after the July raids was very welcome. Colonel Robert Scott took over command of the newly designated 23rd Fighter Group and found his hands full, training the most eligible new pilots after shipping the unqualified ones to other commands. They learned combat skills quickly under the coaching of the former AVG pilots who formed the nucleus of the Group. They adopted the Flying Tiger shark insignia which boosted their morale and instilled confidence, aware of the victories won by the Tigers in these very same airplanes.

Our forces were able to do long delayed maintenance and start to build up supplies, as our fuel stock was down to less than two days supply. In October, there was an increase in Hump tonnage that brought over more fuel. More airplanes came on line, and that fall, Chennault put the CATF back to flying aggressive missions, scheduling as many as they could fly while the fuel supply held out. Everyone put maximum effort into following his orders, for he was truly a hands-on combat leader who inspired his men. The Japanese got the message quickly that Chennault was back to work.

The CATF operated like a guerilla force, as the AVG had done so successfully. They never hit the same place twice in a row so the enemy never knew where they would strike next. There were strafing missions and bombing raids, with targets as far east as the coastal port cities, meeting very little air opposition.

Even my C-47, Ferdinand, got into combat on a bombing mission out of Kweilin one night in August, a mission I almost missed because my stomach was out of commission. Colonel Morgan, a newly arrived bomber commander, approached me at dinner as I tried to calm my grumbling stomach with a fried egg sandwich. He informed me that his B-25 was out of commission and he was borrowing my airplane for a special night mission. I objected to anyone else flying my airplane, and couldn't figure out how he planned to use it as a bomber, but could not argue very well as he outranked me by five grades. He didn't exactly pull rank; instead he praised me for being so concerned about Ferdinand, but reminded me that it was his airplane too, and promised to take good care of it.

He was a very personable officer, and jovially invited me to come along for the fun, as he called it. He said they planned to slide some 50-pound bombs out the door over Hanoi.

I was infected by his carefree manner and decided to join up, although I expected to spend part of the flight in the head. I guess I didn't really trust him although he had time in C-47's, and knew what he was doing. I spent part of the time back on the toilet and occasionally came up front to see what was happening. They found a brightly-lit city that they guessed was Hanoi, located what looked like an airfield, and dumped out twenty 50- pounders. His big problem was finding his way home again, which he managed with a lot of agonizing. I could have stayed home, but I hated to let some stranger take my airplane. Such is a pilot's pride. Besides, Ferdinand got a mission insignia, a bomb painted under the cockpit window.

On Sunday, August 4, I ferried some of the AVG to Kunming on the first leg of their trip home, and some of them swore they would never come back. 'Red' Petach, former AVG nurse and a very pregnant lady who had lost her husband, John, the previous month, was one of them, and she was extremely anxious to get home and forget all about China. I was surprised to receive a letter from her a month later, telling me she had mailed my gifts home to my family, and then complained about the boredom of state-side living. "I sure miss you wonderful guys and the exciting times, and wish I was back with you." Her heart was back in China, as was her husband's grave.

When fuel supplies ran short again, flying was cut back to defensive missions only. The CATF pilots bitched about lack of flying time, and the risk of losing flight pay. They asked if I could use another pilot on the "Express," or if they could be transferred to Hump flying. They could have flown as copilots on the Hump run, but they had no multi-engine time and little instrument training, that was needed most.

Morale of the pilots became a problem, so they were assigned various ground duties to keep them busy. An order came from New Delhi requiring inspection of cargo flights arriving at Kunming to make sure that there was no illegal cargo on board. The idle fighter pilots were given the nuisance duty of inspecting arriving airplanes. The reason behind these inspections was the misdeed of a Hump pilot, whom I shall call "Mac," who made the grave error of hauling some non-government goods to Kunming. You'll hear more about Mac and his court martial later.

A Hump pilot flying to Calcutta or other large city would spend all his ready cash on liquor and other personal items to bring to friends in Kunming. There was no limit to the appetite for anything we could buy in India and bring to China. Cigarettes, Parker 51 pens, cosmetics, and every kind of medicines available in apothecary shops in the big cities were in demand, and were frequently resold at premium prices. You could win the affection of an oriental lady with a gift of cologne, intimate apparel, or a lady's .25 caliber pocket pistol. All over the world, nylons gained the reputation as the greatest way to a lady's heart. Or her boudoir.

The CATF fighter pilots hated the job of inspector, which made them "spies for HQ," but soon found a reward for the task. Arriving crew-members would claim that all their luggage was personal, and the fighter pilot-inspector would check off the airplane as clean, usually receiving a token gift of good English gin or Scotch. Many a Hump crew member arriving at Kunming would head for the overnight hostel lugging two fully packed B-4 bags, the all-purpose air corps luggage bag, and claim that they held his shaving kit and spare sox. They would be loaded with "trade goods." HQ might pass many regulations, but nothing was going to stop this little business, so everyone shrugged it off, saying, "So what!" All over the world, pilots were carrying items across international borders, and it was a way of life.

One thing we were very much on guard against was theft from the airplanes of equipment critical to our safety. We heard reports of airplane parts, parachutes, and guns being stolen right out on the flight line. This was a pretty serious business. Any Chinese caught in the act was turned over to their local authorities, who asked a few questions and then marched the culprit out to the edge of the airport and shot him.

The CATF had other problems besides shortage of fuel and parts. They were plagued with diseases such as malaria, dengue, dysentery, and various venereal diseases, some never seen before by our medics. Another ailment was depression, which caused a major loss in efficiency among troops kept overseas for long periods. Ground personnel were not scheduled for rotation like flight personnel, and were subject to serious bouts of depression that were almost as troublesome as enemy action.

In March, 1943, the 14th Air Force came into being to replace the CATF, but the same problems still prevailed. Chennault wrote, "The CATF passed into history with its planes still grounded for lack of gas, and its personnel huddled around charcoal stoves ..... still cursing Delhi for the lack of supplies." Nothing much new there.

Over the next two years, the 14th built up very gradually until it eventually boasted a much larger fighter force, and small units of B-25 medium bombers and B-24 heavy bombers. They harassed the enemy without letup, bombing, strafing, sinking vessels in the harbors, and destroying enemy fighters in the air and on the ground. They received a compliment after the war, when Japanese General Takahashi, commander of all troops in central China, stated that 60 to 70 percent of the opposition his troops met was from the 14th Air Force, and if not for them, his troops could have gone anyplace they wanted.

Despite its slow start, and the shortage of everything from Ammunition to Dzus fasteners, the CATF and its successor, the 14th Air Force, was inspired by its leader, General Chennault, and had great success in combat. They became one of the most decorated units in the Air Force. They continued to call themselves "Flying Tigers," and kept up the reputation of the AVG, the unit that had paved the way.

In July of 1945 General Chennault was replaced, a very sad occasion for his loyal men. He had been fighting for China for eight years, and made a solemn promise that he would return to help that country.

Chapter 15
GENERAL CHENNAULT

General Chennault boarded our C-47, "Ferdinand," at Kweilin, and settled back in his favorite wicker chair for his weekly flight to Chungking to meet with Generalissimo Chiang Kai-shek. The other passenger was Colonel Doc Gentry, flight surgeon and his personal physician.

It was late morning and my gnawing stomach told me it was time to dig into the bread and cheese we had brought for our lunch. While Curt flew the airplane, I left the cockpit and went back into the cabin to see our VIP passengers.

I asked the General if he would like to take over the controls for a while, while I made some sandwiches. "No" he said, "You fellows fly the airplane - - it's my turn to make lunch." To my great surprise, he got out of his comfortable armchair and proceeded to slice the cheese and bread and prepare lunch, with some help from Doc Gentry. They weren't used to this kind of work and acted like a couple of kids on a picnic, trying to decide who would slice the cheese, and who would do the bread

How many general officers would make lunch for their crew? This was the only one I know. His concern for his men was well-known, but this was only one of many reasons why I have such great admiration for General Claire Lee Chennault.

At the Chungking airport he turned to Colonel Gentry as he was stepping into his staff car, and said, "Doc, we're staying overnight, so you take these boys downtown to Sing- Sing restaurant and get them a good dinner. Make sure they get plenty of ice cream.

Sing-Sing was the best of the approved restaurants, and we ate delicious steaks. 'Doc' would not let us order salads, and we ate only cooked vegetables. We dipped our utensils in boiling water first, and were lectured on how to safeguard our stomachs. It was good advice, but over the weeks, the Kweilin Krud caught up to us as it did to everyone stationed in China. That night was a holiday for us, and we gulped down as much ice cream as we could hold. Then with 'Doc' as our guide, we walked around the downtown area, bumping our way through the teeming crowds of chattering locals. This was the newly established capital of Nationalist China, and armed soldiers were everywhere, as though expecting a Japanese attack.

On July 4th, the China Air Task Force had become the official U.S. Army air unit in China, under command of General Chennault, now commissioned a brigadier general. Curt and I were now back working for the army after weeks of 'free-lancing' for the AVG, but our job had not changed as we were still the "China Express." We had invented that name and stuck to it. Our temporary home base was Kweilin.

Two weeks earlier, we had made our very first trip with the already legendary General Chennault. He had climbed aboard with Colonel Gentry and announced that we were going to Chungking, and asked, "Do you know how to find it?" Curt replied that we hadn't been there but he was sure we could find it, as it stood out pretty well on the fork of the Yangtze River. Curt's soft Alabama accent must have sounded very reassuring to the General, a southerner himself. He asked us how long we had been flying the airplane, and when he learned that we had brought it all the way from Florida, he grunted, and simply said, "Let's go." I plotted out the heading on our charts, and we took off. When I had a chance to look back, I saw him settled in for a nap in his wicker chair, placing total reliance on our ability to get him there safely.

This was characteristic of his style of command, which was to find the best men for the job, tell them what had to be done, then turn them loose to do it without constantly looking over their shoulder. It is difficult for a leader to keep his hands off when he is close to the action, but it certainly worked well for Chennault.

That first meeting with Chennault left us very much impressed by the stern look of his craggy face. In private, we compared his face with the Hump we had just flown, full of peaks and valleys, the result of years of flying in an open cockpit, with wind and weather etching lines in his face.

Many people saw the great character in his square-jawed determined look. I am delighted every time I read about Winston Churchill's remark after their first meeting:

"What a face! Thank God he's on our side!" The big surprise was that this hard-bitten look masked a warm-hearted, friendly person, whose high rank meant little to him except as a command tool. He would sit and chat with his men, play cards and an occasional game of softball, and get to know his men personally. He was very quiet-spoken, but when he did speak, we listened, because this was the expert, the "Old Man," whose word was gospel. General Chennault may have had critics elsewhere, but he was much loved and admired by the men of his command.

* * * * * *

Many books have been written about General Claire Lee Chennault, and I will touch only briefly on his earlier life. He was born in 1890 in Texas, and spent his boyhood as a farm boy in Louisiana, becoming an avid hunter and fisherman. He was mainly self-taught, and seemed destined to lead a quiet life as a schoolteacher, principal, and family man.

He changed his life when he joined the army, receiving a reserve commission in the infantry in 1917.

He won his wings in 1919, too late for World War I, but became an expert pilot, working his way up to the rank of captain and chief of flight training at Maxwell Field, Alabama. He became an advocate of pursuit aviation and authored a book in 1935, called "The Role of Defensive Pursuit," which claimed that fighters were capable of clearing the skies of bombers. Chennault promoted pursuit aviation, by leading a trick flying group called the "3 Men on a Flying Trapeze," which was a forerunner of the later day Blue Angels.

They gave exhibitions of precision flying aimed at stimulating interest in this form of combat at a time when heavy bombers were the main interest.

War Department experts were sold on the idea that fleets of heavily armed bombers flying in close formation could concentrate enough firepower to defend themselves against pursuit opposition. This concept had great support with European military. A famous Italian air force expert, General Giulio Douhet, promoted this theory in his 1921 book called "Command of the Air," and it became policy in the U. S. Army Air Corps between the wars. Chennault was opposed to this strategy, and was disliked by a top officer, Lieutenant Colonel Harold "Hap" Arnold, later chief of World War II air forces. At one time "Hap" was heard to ask, "Who is that damned fellow, Chennault?" Old ideas die hard in the military, and Arnold never became a supporter of Chennault even after his victorious record in China made him the foremost airman in the world.

No one disputed the Douhet theory until World War II, when large fleets of B-17 Flying Fortresses and B-24 Liberators, armed with many guns, suffered tremendous losses under savage attack by Luftwaffe fighters in raids over Germany. It was only then that Air Corps leadership saw the light and realized that bombers needed fighter protection. Priority was given to production of long range P-38, P-47 and P-51 fighter that escorted bombers on raids well into the heart of Germany, and saved many bomber crews by taking on enemy fighters.

Chennault eventually gave up his army career by retiring in 1937, supposedly due to defective hearing, and possibly due to pressure from superior officers who considered him a loose cannon with a free-speaking attitude. Top ranking generals expected their subordinate officers to follow their policies without dispute. A captain who publicly opposed his leaders' strategies to the point where he became a thorn in their side was not likely to have a very happy career in the Army.

But it did not take long for Chennault to get back into harness. In 1938 he was hired by Generalissimo Chiang Kai-shek to lead his almost non-existent Chinese Air Force, and build it up to a useful level of operation, and was given the rank of general.

Chiang was in serious trouble. China faced a major threat from the Japanese who were building up military strength to achieve their long-range goal of domination of all of Asia. Some northern cities were already invaded, and others were being repeatedly bombed without any opposition.

Chennault went to work with the poor tools at hand, to build a viable air force out of a motley group of obsolete aircraft and poorly trained pilots and ground personnel. He faced almost overwhelming obstacles. Aircraft maintenance was so poor that crashes were routine occurrences. Most of the pilots were sons of influential Chinese, and they regarded themselves as glamorous playboys. Crashing a plane and walking away from it was considered a heroic deed, and there were reports of this being done deliberately by impulsive young men who were indifferent to their true mission, and would spend their leisure time bragging about their great adventure.

Chennault gradually improved training and dredged up better airplanes. He flew missions himself, which gave him the opportunity to test his theories. He learned about enemy tactics, experience that proved invaluable in creating a powerful, hard-hitting fighting group.

Taking Chennault out of retirement gave him a new lease on life. His work dominated his life, and he found a true place in China. He became a devoted aide to Chiang Kai-shek, and was happy to work under the leadership of Madam Chiang, whose husband gave her the job of reorganizing their puny air force. This unswerving loyalty to Chiang Kai-shek brought him much criticism, for the Chinese leader had a reputation of ruthless domination of his country and had many enemies. But Chennault cared intensely for the welfare and survival of China, and this earned him great honor and respect from the Chinese people.

President Roosevelt's daring move in 1941 to provide fighter aircraft to

China and the pilots to fly them was probably the most critical event in saving that nation from an early defeat. Formation of the American Volunteer Group was a major boost for Chennault's military career. Tommy "the Cork" Corcoran, close aide to President Roosevelt, stated, "Chennault was standing on the right corner when the parade went by."

Our nation was lucky that he was there, for he made history in 1941 by developing the AVG as a first class fighting force. In July of 1942 as a newly commissioned brigadier general taking command of the China Air Task Force, he did the same job over again, working with mostly untrained pilots and a fleet of aircraft fit for the junkyard. He saw the objective clearly and stuck to the job until it got done, in spite of the many obstacles placed in his way by his own peers.

Some military experts regarded the accomplishments of the American Volunteer Group insignificant in the overall worldwide strategy, but the A VG produced some very valuable results. It gave courage to a nation that was being depressed by world-wide losses in the war, and it created new ideas in combat that were widely copied by other fighter units.

There is a maxim in the military that "Generals fight the last war" and some carry the nickname of "General Yesterday." The "safe" way to command is to follow the book and avoid any risky decisions, which can ruin a career, if wrong. History tells us that this approach has caused many costly blunders, as the old rules don't always work in new situations. New technology and tactics radically change the way wars are fought. Aggressive leaders who won't follow the old rules are resented by the 'old guard,' and Chennault ran into disfavor because his new fighter tactics, which worked exceedingly well, were not done "by the book".

History keeps repeating itself. I found a fascinating parallel in the story of General Billy Mitchell, an outspoken supporter of air power, whose superiors would not accept his new theories of air war. Mitchell had been very successful as commanding general of the Aviation Division of the Signal Corps during World War I. He foresaw the power of aviation and spoke out boldly for expansion of the air service. His hidebound superiors regarded airplanes as solely useful for observation, because this was their past experience, and they stubbornly downgraded its importance in a manner that infuriated Mitchell.

In 1921, Mitchell made a much-publicized claim that his bombers could sink a battleship, a statement that shocked both the top navy and army men. He was begrudgingly offered the captured German battleship "Ostfriesland" to test his claims, with the anticipation that he would fail dismally and put this ridiculous notion to rest. The admirals and generals were amazed and very chagrined when they saw his bombers send this battleship to the bottom. This success infuriated his superiors, who called it a streak of luck.

He became very vehement in his statements about air power, and some labeled him an outrageous fanatic. He spoke out so boldly and made so many enemies that, in 1925, he was court-martialed for insubordination, and in 1926 resigned from the service. In later years, when his theory that air power is vital to a nation's security was proven right, he received many awards, most of them posthumously.

Billy Mitchell fought a hierarchy that was lined up against him and refused to accept his view of the future of military aviation. Like him, Claire Chennault was not taken seriously in his theories of pursuit aviation. Had he stayed in the army as a captain after the war started, Chennault probably would have been sent to some Siberian-type outpost to waste away.

As the head of the Chinese Air Force, as weak as that group was, he was free to explore his theories and practice the trade he knew so well. Arrival of the American Volunteer Group was the tool he needed to prove himself as the foremost expert on fighter tactics in the world.

Chennault had faced many problems right from the start. In forming the AVG from the aircraft and personnel that Roosevelt lent to China, he discovered that many of the pilots were not as qualified in high-performance aircraft as they had claimed, so he started a special training program. Assembly of the aircraft in Rangoon was done under the threat of advancing Japanese forces that eventually entered the city, forcing the AVG to vacate in a hurry, leaving behind some precious unassembled aircraft and parts. There were so many problems at the start, that without his strong guiding hand, this project could have failed, or amounted to a mere nuisance to the Japanese. Wise organization kept it from deteriorating into a group of reckless airmen mainly intent on finding excitement. Under his leadership a powerful military force skyrocketed into view, changing the face of air combat in China. It is small wonder that we all idolized him.

All early organization took place before Pearl Harbor thrust us into the war. The project was kept secret, as we were maintaining peaceful discussions with Japan at the time. The Japanese were actually aware of most of the details, but considered it a mere pinprick, not a threat. This was a bad mistake on their part.

After the AVG took control of the air over a large part of China, their victories against an enemy that sometimes outnumbered them 10-to-1 became widely publicized. Fighter commanders world-wide heard of Chennault's success and eagerly adopted his fighter tactics.

Chennault was revered by the Chinese and became a hero of the American press, but his opinions and ability were continually ignored by top brass. Some referred to him as "that retired captain," or the "lackey of Chiang Kai-shek," and he was an outsider who was kept out of the intelligence loop. For example, he did not receive any advance information about Doolittle's April 1942 Tokyo raid, even though he could have given special aid to crew members who crashed or bailed out when they ran out of fuel.

There were other reasons for his lack of popularity in Washington. For one thing, the Pentagon regarded the Chinese Air Force a farce, something that existed mostly on paper. They had a very low opinion of the Generalissimo and of Chennault's rank of general, since he had retired as a captain. Without the pedigree of West Point or some other equal background, he was considered a maverick. He was disliked for his past tendency to speak out, and for defying established doctrine and creating his own methods of combat. And lastly, he led a group of "guns for hire," mercenaries who flew for money.

Perhaps some of the problem was jealousy on the part of desk-bound officers who resented capable leaders who achieved success in the field. I found the comment by his Chinese wife, Anna, very illuminating. She wrote that he was, "hated and feared by the Japanese, but regarded by his military superiors as a stubborn, argumentative rebel with an unfortunate genius for being right." He was a hero to the nation at a time when our war effort was in very bad shape, and we were in desperate need of heroes and success stories. To his pilots he was God.

This negative attitude of the brass helps explain why the AVG and the entire China-Burma-India Theater suffered such shortages. No one seemed to care. Chennault faced the indifference of Generals Stilwell and Bissell. Stilwell was an infantry soldier who had little faith in air combat. Bissell was a long time opponent of Chennault's theories, and had made ridiculous suggestions in the past. Among them was his idea of fighting enemy bombers by dangling heavy chains to foul up their propellers.

Chennault's memoirs, titled "Way of a Fighter," are a fascinating story of finding victory despite great obstacles. Roosevelt's instruction to build up the CBI air units were not acted on very promptly by the military, but despite the delays, Chennault proved to be a tenacious fighter who never gave up in his fight against the brass and the Japanese. He was certainly a hero in my eyes at that time, and even more so since I have reviewed the history, and discovered how many battles he had to fight behind the scenes. I am proud of the time I spent with Chennault and his men, working under his leadership.

* * * * * *

General Chennault seldom issued us a direct order, but simply asked if we would kindly fly him to Chungking, or Kunming, or wherever. He wore a tired, pre-occupied look in July and August of 1942 when we flew him to Chungking for conferences with Chiang at least once each week. Colonel "Doc" Gentry usually went along to keep an eye on the "Old Man," who was under great strain.

Despite his fatigue and stress, Chennault remained the same even-tempered person, and was most comfortable to be with. On July 19, I sent a long letter home in which I described in some detail an evening with the General at the AVG hostel in Chungking.

"It's about 9 PM and hot—much too hot to sleep. All the house-boys are out on the grass playing with 'Tige', a beautiful leopard cub, the AVG mascot, which is quite savage as they all tease it. We are listening to the very weird wail of the Chinese fiddles. We are sitting in the rather run down garden, a few of us, listening to Chennault tell some stories of his past experiences in flying .

"He remarked rather jokingly that his feelings were hurt the other day when, flying with us, he took over my seat to do some instrument flying through a light overcast, and Curt kept his hands right near the controls ready to grab them if the General messed up. He's a heck of a good guy, though, very easy to get along with, really unassuming, and most modest. Denies having earned any of the laurels placed on him in the June, 1942, Readers Digest, and refused to consider an offer by Time magazine, which has a correspondent here, to have his picture on the cover, with a write-up of his life similar to the Digest' article.

"He really shows concern for those who work for him, told me to take it easy and stand by tomorrow, saying that both Ferdy (our C-47) and I need a rest. I'll be happy to spend a few hours on the cool grass in the shade of an umbrella."

When Chennault reorganized his fighter unit as the Air Corps China Air Task Force unit, he had no more airplanes to work with, but now had new green pilots to train. He also acquired many new bosses, as just about every Air Corps general in the army outranked him. He forged ahead, creating victory in spite of obstacles.

I match Chennault's qualities of leadership with other famous men. Like Winston Churchill, he showed an indomitable spirit and refusal to accept defeat, in spite of the overwhelming odds. I also compare him with Lawrence of Arabia, in his spirit of total involvement with his men, living, fighting, and suffering with them right at the battlefront. His idea of leadership, which left his carefully selected group leaders loose to conduct their missions without his immediate supervision, was a lesson in management to me. He was a compassionate person, sentimental about his men, and very affected by the losses that occurred.

He was undoubtedly the most important American in the fight to preserve China, which kept that nation free of Japanese domination, and may have changed Asian history for the 20th century.

We flew generals Chennault and Stilwell for conferences with the Generalisimo. Left to right: Chennault, Stilwell, and Bob Scott.

Chapter 16
COLONEL ROBERT L. SCOTT

Thirty feet off the runway, a lone P-40 flashed by at full throttle. He pulled up into a neat chandelle, dropped wheels and flaps and settled in for a perfect landing, the sign of an expert fighter pilot. From the entrance to the Operations cave at Kweilin we watched him taxi in, and heard the remark, "I wonder what the One-Man Air Force shot up today."

This might have taken for a sarcastic remark, but was not intended to be that, for the pilot was Colonel Robert L. Scott, who had proven himself just that; a one-man air force. The American press gave him that tag when they learned of his solo missions into Burma looking for targets. Going on such missions without a wingman for company was not the smartest thing to do, but this was an impatient man, a true warrior who gloried in searching for trouble.

Colonel Scott stood out tall and in proper uniform among the AVG people in their motley collection of clothing, the day Curt and I arrived at the operations cave at Kweilin, and were introduced around. We were surprised to find a full colonel. One look at his stem hawk-like visage and command pilot wings caused Curt and me to look at each other with the silent question, "Who is this 'bird' colonel, and is he going to be ordering us around?"

There is a big gap between a full colonel and lowly second lieutenants and we were greatly surprised when he greeted us with a big smile, shook hands with us, and said in a very southern drawl, "Good to have you boys here. Sure can use your help." His relaxed warmth just rolled off him, and from that moment, we felt a kinship with him, and knew we were in a friendly atmosphere. This was a fighting man, and a good guy.

Colonel Scott had an impressive background in the Air Corps, serving in various units and flying all types of aircraft, but his first love was fighters. He was in his mid 30's when he helped fly a group of B-17 bombers from Florida to Karachi in 1942, with the intention of creating a bomber group to attack Japan. The plan was cancelled, and he took over the Hump operation in April.

Scott was happy in any airplane and made Hump flights himself, but placing this expert fighter pilot into a cargo plane was like putting a highly trained racehorse behind a plow. He made constant appeals to Washington for a fighter group assignment but was turned down as too old to fly fighters. He got around this by borrowing a P-40 from Chennault's American Volunteer Group, ostensibly to fly fighter escort for our transports, but found he could do more good flying into the heart of Burma looking for enemy aircraft and other targets.

Scott's P-40 was the only fighter plane in the Assam Valley, so he flew his missions solo, targeting Myitkyina and other Japanese bases, constantly placing himself in harm's way. He often returned with bullet holes in his airplane, but luckily escaped injury himself.

He flew some missions with the Flying Tigers out of Kunming and Kweilin for the special purpose of learning their fighter tactics. His "Show me, so I can learn from you" attitude and his personal charm helped smooth the way for very remarkable cooperation from the Tiger pilots, who had developed an intense dislike for almost anyone with the label of "U.S. Army Air Corps." He was credited with several confirmed kills and did major damage to many ground facilities, especially railroads which were the lifeline of Japanese forces in Burma.

Scott's affable manner and his eagerness to learn all he could of combat tactics, made him quite popular with the AVG. He was a graduate of West Point, making him a member of a very exclusive club that has been groomed for many generations to be leaders of our armed forces, but he was never heard pulling rank with subordinates or lording it over the civilian members of the AVG. He showed he had guts, and everyone appreciated his prowess except, perhaps, some of his own peers back in Washington, who resented his popularity. His independent attitude and his unwillingness to follow the book classed him as a true maverick, which was not a popular status with the Pentagon. .

Scott earned his spurs on those combat missions with the AVG, and was in high favor with Chennault and the Generalissimo, who saw a fighting man rather than a desk officer. His experience earned him the position of commanding officer of the newly formed CATF under General Chennault in July, 1942. This was his first combat command and the big thrill of his military career after years of routine assignments. He was an active combat leader, flying many dangerous missions with his men. At any time, I might see his airplane, named "Old Exterminator," at Lingling, Hengyang, or Kweilin, wherever there was action. The fighters moved around from base to base, giving the impression of many more than the 35 airplanes in our inventory, and Scott moved so fast it looked like we had several Colonel Scotts.

Tex Hill strode across the airfield at Hengyang on that famous day when some 15 Japanese invaders were shot down all around the field. Some diehard Japanese pilot had made a head-on run against Tex, who blasted him out of the sky and watched him crash right on the edge of the field. I hiked across the field with Colonel Scott following Tex Hill, who stalked up to the crashed Zero with its very dead pilot, and made highly critical remarks about the foolhardy pilot who dared face his six .50's. Scott later described Tex as the image of the "Texas gunfighter of fictional fame." To me, that description fit Scott as well, for he was a gunfighter of fame, tough on the outside, but soft at heart, and passionate in his work.

Eventually Washington got the message that Colonel Scott was a valuable person, adored as a hero by the public, and an outstanding example to the armed forces everywhere. He was ordered back to the States in 1943 with a new mission, to tour the country and sell War Bonds.

He wrote a book that year in an astoundingly short time, with the title, "God Is My Copilot." It is a wonderful story of his experiences. This was a time when the country was in serious need of heroes, and his highly publicized record with the AVG placed him high on the popularity list. His book was such a huge success that a major studio in Hollywood made a movie of it, with Scott as technical adviser.

After spending boring months on bond-selling tours, Scott was placed in command of a flight training school, a position that was far beneath his capabilities. He had flown in deadly combat, matching his skills against the enemy, and his airplane had symbols of his victories painted on the side. He received awards and public acclaim, while most of the Pentagon brass sat firmly on their backsides behind desks. The assignment to a training post appeared to be a blatant display of resentment by brass at the Pentagon over the Lindbergh quality of this aggressive flyer, who went his own very successful way.

His requests for more combat duty were ignored for some time, but eventually he pulled the right strings and was ordered back into combat in the CBI. Once again, he led fighter units, and later went on to command fighter groups in Europe where his experience was of great value.

Colonel Scott led a charmed life, and like another celebrated warrior, General Jimmy Doolittle, survived many dangerous situations with hardly a scratch. In his senior years, a retired brigadier general, he has written memoirs that read like a fictional account of a true fighting man of the air. As a West Pointer, he had many opportunities to serve in administrative positions, but he always retained a boyish enthusiasm and chose the life of a true adventurer. He was a non-conformist, somewhat like General Chennault, under whom he served, and he set his own agenda, which included some things not exactly called for in the manual of army regulations. Much military progress is made by individuals who march to that different drummer, and Scott put the tactics he learned in China to work, establishing new training programs worldwide for fighter pilots who were badly in need of these new methods of doing battle.

In his retirement years he fulfilled a promise he made in earlier days. He had flown many missions over the Great Wall of China, and had resolved that some day he would walk its entire length and visit with the people. He requested permission from the Communist government to do this, expecting to meet resistance from officials who might resent that he had worked for their enemy, Chiang Kai-shek. Instead, he was royally treated as a welcome guest who had helped free their country from the Japanese, and he walked the Wall in great style, escorted by many hosts.

I admire this man for another very special reason. He wrote very openly in a later book, titled "The Day I Owned The Skies," of how his deep despair over the loss of his wife to illness brought on a desperate bout with depression. He developed a view of a very bleak future. He had achieved all his goals and had little left to live for. Many lonely elderly people have this desperate feeling, but Scott was not a man to stay down for long. He found a solution that sets an inspiring example for others.

He started a new and exciting activity by opening an Air Force museum in his hometown of Macon, Georgia, at the Warner-Robbins Air Force Base. He had the right contacts to obtain retired aircraft and equipment, and put his energy to work creating one of the finest institutions of its kind.

His enthusiasm shows in a letter that I received from him, telling how much he loved the work. "I work here at the museum as a volunteer, for free, but feel like they pay me a million because it provides a purpose in life. I would pay them to let me work here." His age at the time, 90 years young, still working, flying, and enjoying life to the maximum, sets a wonderful example for all seniors.

Jim —
note how young
I look when
they let me
fly an F-15
on my
birthdays

Bob Scott

BRIGADIER GENERAL ROBERT L. SCOTT, JR., USAF RETIRED

 • World War II Fighter Pilot "Ace" – 22 Victories
• Author of <u>God Is My Co-Pilot</u>

R.T. Smith's famous photo taken from the cockpit of his P-40.

*In India, after our China tour, our flight surgeon gave us the OK to take
time off. We checked into the luxurious Grand Hotel in Calcutta.*

Chapter 17
LIFE IN CHINA

Our primary residence in China was "Ferdinand," our C-47 airplane, where we stored our personal gear, although we often stayed at hostels in the various towns. We took turns sleeping on board, with a Tommy gun and Colt.45 close at hand, as there was the constant threat of thieves, or worse; spies paid by the Japanese and bent on sabotage.

Every airfield had guards, but our airplane was especially well guarded, as it was a most valuable piece of equipment, the only means of air transport in all of free China at the time.

In June, July, and August, our "China Express" flew supplies and personnel into many small cities in China, and I met some highly dedicated volunteers who were giving support to that backward country. There were missionaries, teachers, doctors, and nurses, all living in very primitive conditions, but inspired to stay on despite offers to leave. We tried to supply them with items not available locally, but were mostly able to offer meager support in the form of medical supplies and precious mail.

This vast country of mystery and intrigue had always fascinated me in my youth, and I enjoyed visiting every town where we landed. Old movies had presented a mystical Orient, and I searched for that "inscrutable" hidden side of China. I was greatly disappointed to find the reality, a poverty-stricken society that had existed this way for thousands of years. All that most Chinese people could hope for was to eke out a precarious existence from day to day, which we Americans found very discomfiting. Surprisingly, they showed a remarkable sense of humor, and laughed happily and frequently. This was a great lesson for us in appreciation of our privileged status; we were blessed with so much, and we marveled at their cheerful outlook in the face of such a bleak existence.

In small cities like Chengtu and Kweilin, 'May-ru-gans', as we were called, had not yet arrived in large numbers and we were treated like strange curiosities. As we moved about the city we were accompanied by hordes of giggling, chattering people of all ages, who did not at all resemble the mysterious Oriental 'Charley Chans' of movie fame.

Shop owners welcomed us warmly, seeing us as big spenders. They were unhappy when our followers crowded into the tiny stores with us, despite the shrill warnings of the shop- keeper that he would call the police if they didn't clear out. This only brought out more laughter, which increased when we started negotiating for some souvenir item. Without an interpreter, our business was conducted by sign language. We always refused their opening prices, loudly saying, "Bu Hau," roughly translated as "too much." We waved our hands and acted very indignant at the prices, which drove the crowd to gales of merriment, and we got to enjoy hamming it up and putting on a show for the people.

I bought filigreed silver items, embroidered robes, some jade, and small embossed water pipes, paying for them all with Chinese dollars, or CN, that each cost me about two cents American. In later weeks, prices climbed considerably as the number of souvenir hunters grew. The price of a dragon-embroidered bedspread rose from $200CN equal to $4 US, to as high as $20 US, where it was no longer a bargain.

New arrivals in China could tell instantly from the smell that the Chinese had far different standards of sanitation than we had. We tried to protect ourselves from intestinal infections, but usually failed, and I suffered almost continuous stomach problems. To stay on the safe side, we ate most of our meals in the hostels, but occasionally ventured downtown to sample the night-life.

The only cities that offered recreation for Americans were Kunming, Chungking, and Kweilin. Local restaurant owners tried to get "Safe" approval to feed and entertain us, and there were a few that provided us with acceptable food. The results were poor, but we did eat out occasionally, with great care. All food had to be well cooked, and we ate no fresh vegetables or fruit. The farms all used "night soil," or human excrement, for fertilizer, and just the thought of this was enough to spoil our appetites. We never drank water unless it was well boiled, and we dipped our tableware items in boiling water to sterilize them. Even in our hostels the food was very questionable.

In the months I spent in China with the AVG and CATF, I lost 20 pounds and eventually went on a diet of fried egg sandwiches and Spam, when available. Many mornings I dreaded the thought of getting into our C-47, because my growling stomach warned me that I would be racing for the toilet frequently. When I left China in September and resumed flying the Hump out of Assam, I would load up as much food as I could scrounge in India to bring to friends in China, who were suffering from the cuisine prepared by Chinese cooks. Their eyes would light up when they saw canned juices and foods, Spam, and other basics that looked like manna from heaven, although nothing was ever as precious to them as mail from home.

Entertainment in the restaurants was pretty bad, but occasionally we would find a musician playing American tunes on a horn or piano. If we were in good spirits we might even try a sample of the local wines, but probably ended up suffering for our daring.

Kunming was the big city at the eastern end of the Hump airlift, a very old walled fortress city, where the only signs of its former elegance were two elegant memorial archways on the main street. Most of the city was made up of shabby structures that looked like they were a hundred years old, and nothing was ever rebuilt until it collapsed. The city vibrated with the hustle and bustle of an estimated three million energetic people. The streets were noisy and cluttered with people on bicycles, ox carts, and rickshaws. The main roadway through the city was so badly rutted and pitted that trucks and jeeps had to pick their way carefully to avoid damage to the vehicles. I filmed the fancy archways while perched on the front of a jeep and got very shaky results.

Vehicle drivers preferred to blow their horns rather than wear out their brakes stopping for a careless pedestrian. People were totally indifferent to others' problems, and a victim of an accident might be left unattended on the road while others just walked around him.

Funeral processions blocked traffic on the main street every day, and were noisy events with families walking alongside the hand drawn cart bearing the casket, blowing horns. Passersby usually ignored the affair. They also ignored the coolies who carried twin buckets of "whatever" hanging from a pole balanced on a shoulder, and leaving a leaking stench behind them, which I found quite nauseating.

The people entertained themselves by walking the streets in the evenings, and we sometimes joined them. They made a big parade, crowding the streets between 7:00 and 10:00 P.M., avoiding their hot homes, and finding social activity. Occasionally, an attractive, well-dressed young Chinese woman would send a coquettish look in our direction, and we'd wonder if she might be a prostitute looking for business. Most young women walked demurely with eyes cast down, as custom required.

It was said that anything you wanted to buy could be found at the Kunming Thieves Market, which was an open area off the main street. That statement was greatly exaggerated, as the market displayed a hodge-podge of hardware, cooking utensils, badly worn garments, and other unidentifiable things I could only call junk. More valuable items were kept under covers, and were carefully unwrapped only on request, as merchants do all over the world, to give the impression of special value. When displayed, these goods looked like more junk to us. The merchants sat on the ground, patiently awaiting buyers, tending cooking fires, some selling food to the public. They smoked their pipes, chatted and argued with each other, and it was a very orderly and social scene. These were second-rate vendors, compared to merchants in stores.

The cities certainly had "atmosphere." The aroma of the cooking, added to the smells of a city with no sewer system, and the odors from vegetable gardens that were fertilized by night soil was enough make me gag and promise that I would never again visit the Orient. In later years, just a photograph out of my album is enough to recall that pungent aroma and make me renew that promise.

I made friends with some young Chinese officials who were anxious to make friends with American pilots, presumably to improve their command of the English language. After we got to know each other a bit, they told me of the other type of market in the city, a real Black Market that was conducted in secret, and I heard stories about illicit business that were hard to believe. But why doubt them? The Chinese were very enterprising people, who never let an opportunity slip by, even if it meant great risk.

They warned me that it would be dangerous for me to penetrate this market even if I found a willing guide. Here were traded many stolen or smuggled items, and what made it especially dangerous for both buyer and seller was that some things traded were supplies stolen from our airplanes. Every airplane had many items of equipment that were targeted by thieves. For example, each AMMISCA C-47 airplane left the States with a container of 1000 sulfanilamide tablets, and these were reported to be worth at least two dollars a tablet on the black market. But that was small stuff. Rumors were that you could buy a Thompson sub-machine gun, Colt semi-automatic, flare pistols, rations, fire extinguishers, medical kits, and just about anything that could be spirited away,

I heard about jeeps for sale on the Black Market, and this was easy to understand because they were so easily stolen. At first we would remove the distributor cap to prevent starting the engine, but the thieves found spares and could make off with one with your back turned. A jeep could simply disappear off the street, and sometimes we would assume that another army man had borrowed it. It might never reappear and probably was sold for a fortune at some distant place. We finally learned to post a guard on every vehicle. Punishment for theft was severe; Chinese caught stealing American supplies were shot by Chinese military police within hours.

I heard that some of our own military people were charged with theft, and it was difficult to believe that any of us would sell a firearm or other precious item. On second thought, I'm sure it happened. The temptation was great, with large rewards. A Tommy gun was reputed to bring as high as $25,000 American. We soon learned to take proper care of our precious items, but they still disappeared.

On the outskirts of the city we found little villages made up of primitive houses, with dirt floors, no plumbing, and squalor everywhere. The toilet was a nearby ditch, and people squatted openly to relieve themselves. Small children wore shabby garments that all had one thing in common, a long slit in the seat that permitted them to squat without removing their pants. Tenant farmers lived in these hovels, while the land-owners lived in slightly better hovels. Many owners farmed their own property, as the plots were very small. Every hillside was terraced into farm plots, separated from neighbors by stone borders. From the air, these stacked up terraced farms made a very neat geometric appearance and showed how completely the land was used. Water for irrigation came from ponds located at the top level of the hills.

Wherever we went, even thousands of feet in the air, the odor followed us. I can almost smell it now.

With Lee, our interpreter.
Sgt. Saylor on the wing.
I lost 20 pounds in China

Taj Mahal - my favorite
sight from the air.

Chapter 18
CALCUTTA

Our more than two months in China, eating those unhealthy meals had taken its toll on our health, and our AVG messmates were much worse off after eight months of the same. We all had digestive problems, and sometimes missions were aborted due to frequent need to go to the toilet. I got kidded as having the only airplane in China that had a toilet on board, while the fighter pilots had to cuss and hold if they could.

Our favorite meal now consisted of fried egg sandwiches on course bread, but as monotonous as this may seem, it was far better than the hamburgers that we had previously eaten, made of highly questionable meat. Our chef was very unhappy when we refused to eat this favorite "Melican" delicacy. We wondered about the absence of dogs in the Chinese cities, and eventually avoided any food containing meat.

The AVG was officially out of business as of July 4th, but our job flying the "China Express" had not changed one bit. We now worked for the China Air Task Force (CATF), headed by Chennault, who was now a brigadier general in the U.S. Army. We continued to fly from Kunming to Kweilin, Hengyang, Chungking, and other places.

There was one shocking change: our fighter operation efficiency dropped almost to zero. The AVG always kept ten or twelve P-40's in readiness at Kunming, with fifteen top- notch pilots, and did a great job of keeping our skies clear of the enemy. The eastern bases, around Kweilin, had almost as many, and kept moving them around to look like more.

The newly arrived CATF mechanics had little experience in maintaining badly run-down aircraft in the field, and there were only a few former AVG experienced maintenance men there to keep the worn out P-40's running. Our fleet was reduced to as few as one or two P-40's available in flying condition on any one day, flown by pilots who had no combat experience. Had the Japanese known of this, they probably could have taken back control of the air. Chennault's handful of loyal squadron leaders, who had accepted Bissell's offer to join the Air Corps, were keeping things going by a very narrow margin.

It was time for Curt and me to fatten up. We were given the opportunity to return to India, when Al Nowack and his crew took over our job in China. As bad as Assam living conditions were, returning to India sounded like paradise to us, and we gladly made the switch. On August 24th we flew Ferdinand back to Chabua, which finally completed our fourth Hump round-trip.

We wanted some time off, but were told that no one was getting any leave time. So we checked in with the flight surgeon, who took one look at us and ordered a week of sick leave. We flew the "milk run" to Calcutta, where we would spend the week, and turned our airplane over to another crew that would take the airplane back, loaded with supplies. Almost tearfully we said goodbye to Ferdinand, our ever faithful airplane, that had carried us half way around the world and survived many adventures. We had taken very special care of #7797, and cautioned the new crew to "take good care of our baby. "

We were ready for time off, and I looked forward to celebrating my 23rd birthday on August 28th, in style, sampling the splendid life we had heard about in one of the great cities of Asia.

Calcutta in 1942 turned out to be far from the splendid city we expected. This young American found it hard to understand how such poverty and filth could exist in a country that had been under the management of the British for so many years. The British boasted that the "Sun never sets on the British flag," and India appeared to be a prime example of the immense value of colonialism to the parent country. The "Raj," as the occupation by Britain was called, had run the country for generations, and India was the gem of the worldwide British Empire, bringing huge amounts of money to the Crown from the labors of the population.

India's people were very restless under this system, and had rebelled in the past, but nothing was likely to change during wartime. India was a likely target of Japanese bombing and invasion, and only the British had the military strength to keep the country safe. A small group of militant Indian people threatened to invite Japanese occupation as an alternative to the British, but they were not much of a threat.

Calcutta teemed with uncounted millions; many made homeless by floods and famine, all looking for a better life than rural poverty. All needed shelter and food. They slept in the streets, begged for food or pennies or annas, and showed a remarkable indifference to the death and disease that were so prevalent. I walked the streets looking at the sights, and was constantly confronted by beggars, small children, and even grownups, all begging for a coin. A stunning sight was the deformed and crippled, who were everywhere. They sat or lay on the sidewalks, or hobbled pitifully across our paths. Local people told me that parents intentionally deformed their children, to make a more pitiful sight and bring in more money.

It was shocking to hear this, and then learn that Hindus were forbidden to eat meat, for they considered cattle to be sacred animals, and allowed them to roam the streets freely. Weren't the children sacred, too?

India has not changed much even to this day, though some of the more barbarous customs have been abolished. Reports from friends who have visited India in the 90's tell of countless beggars, cattle roaming the streets, and poverty-stricken people.

Under the Raj, the British had allowed the caste system to continue, and added their own, colonial style, where they lived like royalty, served by the native population. This was only one example of luxury alongside poverty. The other example was the way the upper caste Indians and royals lived in isolated splendor.

We asked for the best hotel in the city, and checked into the sumptuous surroundings of the Great Eastern Hotel, a haven of luxury. It offered comfortable suites, fine food, liquors, and great service. Everywhere there were servants, "wallahs," who bowed and scraped and did our every bidding. First they provided a hot bath, then a change into clothing that miraculously appeared freshly laundered after a few hours. Our own private wallah was assigned to us, and he remained seated in the corridor outside our door, ready to give instant service. We visited the hotel bar, a very elegant place, where the only disappointment was that when you ordered whisky you got Scotch, as bourbon or rye were almost unknown in India. So, when in Rome, you drank Scotch.

The Great Eastern was one of the finest hotels in all of India, yet prices were still incredibly low. This was 1942, before the influx of large numbers of Americans, so the British set the economic level. A lavish meal could cost three rupees, equal to one dollar US. Servants normally received tips of one or two pennies from the British. Unaware of this penny level economy, we thought nothing of peeling off a few rupees to reward a servant, and this was quite a surprise to the wallahs after the penury of their British masters. They soon became accustomed to our generosity, and refused to serve their former masters. The Brits were quite disgusted at our free spending habits.

The Great Eastern Hotel was a dignified extension of the British Empire, and the sedate atmosphere influenced our behavior a great deal. Several more crews checked in, and we all observed our best manners, avoiding the normal boisterous attitude of fighting men on leave, as we had observed at the Shepheards Hotel in Cairo. Occasionally we let loose with some noisy laughter, which created a certain coolness in the attitude of the British officers we met at the hotel, but we soon learned that our easy way with rupees was affecting them more. A high-ranking British officer, a brigadier general, drew pay about equal to that of a U. S. Army sergeant, and could not keep up with our life style. They were further offended to see that our enlisted men checked into the same hotel as the officers, and often dined with us, which was not done in their army.

After good food and some rest, our thoughts turned to a search for feminine company, a normal outlet for young energetic men. Sergeant Saylor, my crew chief, gave me a knowing wink, and said he and some friends from the other crews were going hunting. I cautioned him about the high level of venereal disease that I had heard was prevalent, and suggested he locate a "pro" station ahead of time. Saylor was several years older than I, and a very self-confident young man. He smiled knowingly, and said that he was aware of the situation. He assured me that during all the time we spent in China he had avoided any contact with Chinese girls. We had walked through special sections of town where professional prostitutes lived, and laughed at their "come hither" looks and motions, and occasional coy display of their wares, but the filth and smells of those towns were enough to discourage even the most eager American. Calcutta was different, offering many opportunities for the boys' entertainment, and they went their happy way.

The Great Eastern Hotel lobby was a beehive of social life. The atmosphere was warm and comfortable with a Victorian decor of dark wood and overstuffed sofas. It seems that every English colony had a central hotel that carried on the traditional look of the Empire, so that all Brits would feel at home. British ladies sat about chatting, doing needlework, and waiting for their men to return from the wars. These were the wives of higher- ranking officers, who could afford to live in the luxury of a first class hotel, and they were quite delighted to strike up a conversation with an American who dressed neatly and was polite.

I was overjoyed to sit and talk with a most beautiful young lady, named Celia. Her long chestnut-colored hair framed a lovely face with the peaches-and-cream complexion that abounds among young English girls who live in a country where the sun seldom shines. This girl was a "knockout," and my reaction to her was quite obvious. Of course she had a companion, a most dignified looking middle-aged lady who introduced herself as "Mrs. Brigadier Cowell," a title the British used to indicate her husband's rank in the British army. She looked dignified, but she was a real gossip, and apparently overjoyed at having an audience of young American officers.

At one point she whispered in my ear, "I see you are quite taken with our lovely Celia. Forget it. She is recently married and very lonesome for her handsome 'leftenant,' who is someplace in the jungle. It takes a while before these young girls get lonesome enough to find another man". She was right, for Celia showed herself the perfect lady. When they heard that I was suffering from stomach problems, they became instant mothers. Mrs. Brigadier Cowell suggested to Celia that some of that special personal medicine they used would probably be most helpful to me. Celia invited me to escort her to her room where she handed me a dose of the brew to calm down my growling insides, and she very pointedly displayed correct behavior by leaving the door to the room wide open to the corridor. I was most grateful for the help, but most disappointed that I had not managed to charm this elegant and beautiful young lady.

Disappointed, but not for long. Late that afternoon the hotel bar became the social center, as it filled with some of the prettiest young ladies in Asia. They were secretaries from local offices, mostly Anglo-Indian and Anglo-Burmese, some of them dark-skinned, all well dressed, and gorgeous in our eyes. They heard that Americans were staying at the hotel, and our popularity was immense, as we had a well-earned reputation for being big spenders, especially when it came to fun-and-games.

Tangere was the name of one beauty, who sat with us and charmed me with her lilting British accented voice. High school educated, she was the daughter of an English father and a Burmese-Indian mother, and she had the petite looks of a Burmese doll. We dined very well in the luxurious hotel dining room that boasted candles, wine, steaks, and a subdued air that could not have been more elegant. I found her a fascinating companion and we became quite involved in each other that weekend. Her lilting and charming voice, her sense of humor, and her gorgeous looks gave me just the lift I needed to forget the messy side of our war. We danced the evening away to the very good three-piece band, and the following morning enjoyed a lovely breakfast for two served in bed by our meal-wallah, while outside the door our room-wallah sat patiently, ready to shine shoes and perform any other errands that we requested. It was difficult to visualize the real world out there waiting for us to return. I became a very spoiled person, and found myself talking with a British accent, and just reveling in this way of enjoying a leave. Of course, this was before the onslaught of thousands of Americans changed Calcutta life to a crowded military headquarters.

Tangere educated me to some of the mysteries of the mid-east. I learned about the life of a half-caste, who is not accepted by the British, being part native, nor by the Indian people, being part Caucasion. They were very bright, and qualified to hold down good jobs, but had a natural resentment over their social status. There is a large population of Anglo-Indians, the result of generations of British occupation, and they had their own ethnic society, and lived in their own neighborhood. The war was exciting for the girls, as it brought in Americans, who were the most generous of people and oblivious to the racial divide that the British observed .

Curt bowed out of the social life and bunked with another pilot, leaving me privacy in our room. While I was doing my best that first weekend to play 'catch-up,' he spent much of his time trying to phone Mobile, Alabama, to talk to his pregnant Audrey.

Curt kept out of trouble, and that is more than could be said for Harry, another pilot on leave. Harry met Lili, an exquisite Anglo-Burmese girl, an acquaintance of Tangere, and was delighted with her company. He did not do too well a few days later when he entered into a business arrangement with her. She told him that she had an acquaintance who worked in the medical field, from whom she could purchase some very hard-to-find medications, that could sell in Kunming for an enormous profit. Harry was intrigued by his charming cohort, was putty in her hands, and handed Lili as much cash as he could borrow from friends, about 1000 Rupees, or $300 American. He waited three days for Lili's return with the goods, but she never did show up, much to Harry's chagrin. He lost the $300, lost Lili, and was razzed by his friends who pointed out that he had been saved from a life of crime. His bitter disappointment was salved when we bought him a few drinks and introduced him to another lady who saved him from celibacy. He was happy, once again.

A contrast in life styles was evident when late one night two happy pilots volunteered to escort our dates home despite their objections. Our cab driver drove into an area of the city where these lovely young ladies lived that was incredibly shabby, strewn with rubbish in the streets, and homeless people sleeping in the open. They apologetically said, "This is where we live," gave us goodnight kisses and daintily left the cab. It was a shock to find such bright young people living in what we considered a slum.

Friday, August 28th, was my 23rd birthday, and Curt and I were invited to visit the Calcutta Swim Club, an exclusive British private club, to which American officers were offered temporary memberships. We enjoyed their fine food, cocktails, and the company of young officers who were involved in fierce fighting in the Burma jungles.

Some of these young 'leftenants' had fought with Orde Wingate's Raiders, and their blood-curdling stories of fighting in the jungle were enough to cause me to bless the Air Corps. They were most appreciative of the dangers our C-47 pilots faced making drops of food to their troops fighting their way through almost impenetrable terrain. They lived off the land, and were pursued by enemies of all types - Japanese troops, Burmese traitors, headhunters, vicious animals, reptiles, and disabling diseases. We heard that the Raiders lost one-third of their 3000 men in a six-week foray aimed at cutting Japanese supply lines. This was ground fighting in some of the worst possible conditions, and we were awed by their outwardly casual attitude.

We talked later to medical people who gave us the inside story. These rugged warriors were just as vulnerable to battle fatigue and mental exhaustion as any fighting men, and many of them suffered severe after-effects. They dreaded returning to the jungle, being quite sure that they would never survive a second time. We shared lots of rounds of drinks, bragged about our different experiences, and I learned that brothers-in-arms are truly brothers no matter what their national allegiance.

I noticed that Curt always insisted on paying the check when the first round of drinks was served, and I asked him why he was so eager. His reply taught me something: "Always buy the first round, and everybody sees you're a good sport and warms up to you. They'll all end up taking turns, anyhow." Good advice.

Birthdays are regarded by some as a time to look back at lessons learned from the past, and a time to look forward to bright future events. On this 23rd birthday, I was much too occupied in my search for recreation to ponder the past, and had no desire to contemplate the future except to optimistically assume that I would survive.

Since that time, I have reflected about the past, and wondered about the remarkable way that small events direct our lives and futures. There I was, an Air Corps pilot observing my birthday in August, 1942, at the very elegant Calcutta Swim Club. What if, eighteen months before, I had not ventured into the east side of the Pratt and Whitney factory and caught a glimpse of a young Air Corps pilot climbing out of his airplane, a glimpse that was enough to move me into military flying? What if I had chosen to wait for the draft board to call me up and place me in the infantry, or driving a tank, or serving on a battleship? Every move we make has a lasting effect on our lives, and we are blessed in being unable to foresee the future. I had been leading a charmed life, and I intended that it should continue. No crystal ball wanted

We swam in the Club pool, and Curt, regaining his strength on good food and drink, took first place in swim sprints, having been a college swimming champion We were joined by Red Probst and Moose Moss, former Flying Tigers, now flying for CNAC airlines, and had a great time. Of course, this was a strictly British club, which did not admit Indian people, and was representative of a society that would soon go out of existence.

The sights and smells of Calcutta never ceased to fascinate us. In my diary for August 29, I noted that the city was very cosmopolitan, and very international, much like Cairo. It was loaded with refugees, many of them lovely Burmese women, and with big money operators, according to gossip from CNAC pilots. The city was a great place for visitors looking for a good time. Night life was abundant, transportation good, and dates plentiful. For more quiet relaxation there were some 'splendiferous' movie theaters, such as the Lighthouse, with its very large chromium bar, or the very sociable hotel lobby and bar with fine gin gimlets. The war had not blocked all public recreation, for there were horse races at the track every Saturday, and street fairs that appealed to the visitors.

From our hotel window we looked down at a noisy main street that thronged with all types of vehicles, street-cars, trucks, ox carts, and yellow cabs, all accompanied by the constant tooting of the popular India bugle horn with a giant rubber bulb to squeeze. The odors of a huge, overcrowded city without adequate sewage system, that had overpowered us at first, faded away in our minds until we no longer took notice.

Every day we were reminded of the war that was taking place not far away. Just down the highway from the hotel, right in the central part of the city, there was an open park, with a small airplane runway cut out of the greenery. Each day at noon, we were startled by a gigantic roar as two RAF Hurricane fighters took off from this narrow strip, on a daily patrol. What was even more startling was watching them land in such limited space in downtown Calcutta. These fighter pilots had developed a landing pattern that was remarkably tight, but they did it right every time.

The week in Calcutta was a grand vacation, and we overstayed it by a few days, hating to go back to work, but the day came when a new crew showed up at the hotel with formal instructions to get ourselves back to Assam. I had said a somewhat emotional goodbye to Tangere the previous evening, left her a gift, and promised to see her again on my next trip. Leaving the magic fairyland of the Great Eastern Hotel behind us, Curt, Saylor and I taxied to the airport in great style, in a bright yellow open touring car, driven by a tall, turbaned Sikh.

We climbed once more into our familiar beast of burden, with the smells of airplane oil and past cargoes that permeated the hard-used C-47. We were introduced once more to midday heat in the cockpit, switches too hot to touch, and the prospects of living once more in a crude basha, in primitive conditions. We took up a heading for the Assam valley, flying a load of Spam for anyone who wanted to eat it. Our lavish life style had spoiled us, and we would not eat Spam for awhile. But after a short time, when our local food started its mysterious effect on our tender digestive systems, Spam looked pretty good again. By that time, our stay in Calcutta felt like an unreal dream, from which we had come back to real life.

Section III

THE AIRLIFT

"It is essential that our route be kept open, no matter how difficult." President Roosevelt

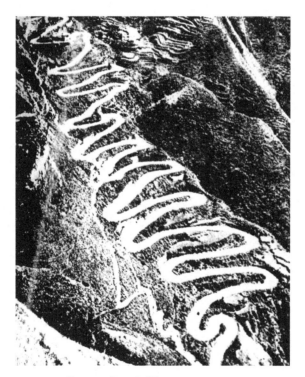

Burma Road. Photo courtesy of National Archives.

Chapter 19
RETURN TO THE HUMP IN THE AIR

In September, after our carefree vacation at Calcutta, Curt and I returned to the serious business of flying the Hump. We had built up a lot of flying hours in China, but we only had four Hump trips to our credit, well behind the rest of the original crews, and it was time to catch up. In a previous chapter, I described the awesome feeling I had at my first view of the Hump, but there is much more to tell.

Once again we took up residence at our Chabua air base, in the rain-saturated Assam Valley. The map shows the Valley to be a unique land area, a narrow finger that juts eastward from the main body of India in such a spectacular way that I always felt it was telling us in a fateful manner, "This is the path to your destiny in China. Lots of luck!"

The Naga Hills border the Valley to the south and east, and the towering Himalayas form a solid barrier to the north, with dense jungles in the foothills. The great Brahmaputra River slices through the area, carrying snowmelt from the mountains to the sea at a leisurely pace, and creating fertile farmlands in northeast India. Some ground personnel confessed they had a claustrophobic feeling after examining our maps, when they realized that the Valley was hemmed in on three sides. Flight crews generally escaped this phobia, knowing that they could fly out of the landlocked area.

I looked forward to better living conditions in Chabua after the terrible diet and other discomforts in China, but after a few weeks of grubby living and several hazardous Hump trips I regretted our decision to leave the China operation. I missed the stimulating flying that we had been doing as the "China Express," where we were an indispensable aid to General Chennault's combat units. We felt that we were saving lives every time we brought a load of supplies to one of our far-flung bases, and we enjoyed the prestige of flying generals to many different places, often receiving VIP treatment. On the Hump airlift, we faced a mind numbing routine, highly dangerous, but repetitious. However, our decision had been made and there was no going back, so we went to work.

We found that flight operations in the Assam Valley had not changed much since we first started flying there in May. Very little support had come from headquarters in New Delhi or Washington in the past three months. Our CO, Major Tom Rafferty, worked hard with Ferry Command Headquarters to improve conditions and obtain more supplies and equipment, but made slow progress.

We had a unique operation in those early days of 1942 and 1943. Our experienced pilots ran flight operations in a very informal way, with individual pilots making their own independent decisions on how to conduct each flight. These were the former airline pilots like Curtis Caton, Johnny Payne, Warren Peterson, Al Nowak, and others, whose skill in instrument flying was far superior to that of the new military pilots like myself, who were their copilots. Their thousands of hours in DC-3's earned them great respect, and they used this know-how to get through the bad weather. No one gave them orders to "fly, or else," for no one was more qualified to call the shots than they were. Senior officers often flew with them as copilots to gain experience from the experts. It would be some time before high-ranking officers would change things to a true military style operation.

We had no weather forecasting facilities, and our radios had limited range, so we relied on reports from each other, and tried to avoid extremes of turbulence and icing. If weather on the direct route was really bad, we made detours to the south where mountains were lower, to find breaks in the overcast and avoid ice. This took us close to Japanese-held bases in Burma, but we knew that enemy fighters would find it hard to locate us in that maelstrom of bad weather. Seldom did anyone turn back.

Copilots flying with these experts learned quickly. Instrument flying became second nature, and we learned how to fly the C-47 under all kinds of conditions. Eventually we all graduated into the left seat as first pilots, and discovered what it was like to carry the responsibility on our shoulders. We were proud to be known as "Hump Pilots," for that title was held in the highest esteem by all flying men who knew that we faced the most dangerous enemy of all - the destructive Hump.

There were some easy flights occasionally, that we called 'milk runs,' which were trips to pick up cargo at Calcutta, New Delhi, Karachi, and other western cities in India. These were a relief from flying the Hump, and allowed us to visit many fascinating places. I was intrigued by the sights and by the cultural extremes of the people, who ranged from the lowest untouchable caste to elegant royalty living in superb palaces. This travel was quite an education, and boosted my appreciation of our American way of life.

Hump flights were severely hampered by shortages we had not expected. A very critical item was oxygen. At first, most of us were comfortable flying as high as 16,000 feet without oxygen without ill effects, but as time went on, we had less tolerance for this. We were losing some of our robust health, and I found myself needing oxygen at 10,000 feet. There was seldom a replacement supply of oxygen at Kunming, so our return trips usually started off with only partially filled tanks. Running out of 0^2 can be deadly, as anoxia sets in and judgment is impaired. A pilot can misread his compass, forget to switch fuel tanks, develop vertigo on instruments, and commit other errors. I am sure we lost a number of airplanes because of this shortage.

Cold weather flying gear was also in short supply, and our airplane heaters were never adequate. Eventually we scrounged some fleece-lined clothing, and carried it on board for our high altitude flights. We started our flights in tropical heat wearing light clothing, in temperatures ranging up to 110 degrees. The airplanes were like ovens, with interior temperatures reaching 140 degrees, but as we climbed to altitude we cooled off. At high altitude the cockpit temperature was very low, often below freezing, and we added warm clothing, piece by piece, for the heater seldom threw off enough warmth. On the return trip, we did a striptease, peeling off cumbersome flight gear as we approached the tropical heat again.

Operations never gave direct orders to make any flight that might be especially hazardous. There would be a request for volunteers, and there was always some pilot stepping up to challenge the risk. One of them was Captain Johnny Payne, who took the initiative in making the first night flight across the Hump. His exploit made headlines in the CBI newspaper, the "ROUNDUP," published in New Delhi on September 17, 1942.

Johnny's flight, the first night crossing of the most hostile terrain in the world, was the ultimate in daring, and the newspaper described it in great detail.

"Captain Payne took off from India into a sky with the usual thunder-storms and lightning flashes.

'The moon was up, but we were on instruments most of the time due to storms. We ran into severe icing conditions over the mountains. I saw a thunderhead before us, and decided I'd bite into one to see what would happen. Ice formed over us very quickly, and we were forced to turn south and drop to a lower altitude over Burma to get rid of an inch and one-half sheet of ice over our wings.'

"Over China, Payne, who had been flying by dead-reckoning, hit the airport on the nose. Everything was pitch black except the runway faintly outlined by the dim lights of smudge pots set out by the Chinese. 'We were shooting for smudge pots 600 miles away,' he said. He jokingly called his navigation system 'Destiny.'"

The article goes on:

"The pilot made a normal landing in the darkness, and shadowy Chinese coolies worked rapidly unloading and reloading the plane, while Payne and the crew drank cups of steaming hot coffee before taking off for the return flight to India in 45 minutes, with a load of Chinese raw materials for American war industries.

"A few hours later the huge plane rumbled across the pitch black Indian field from which he had left originally between more flickering smudge pots. Payne and his crew went off to bed. 'I'm dead,' Payne said. 'It's been three hops over the Hump for me in 22 hours.'

"Payne and his crew have shown the way American pilots will be soon streaming night and day into China under the nose of the Japanese, carrying supplies to beleaguered China. The flight, which Payne described as 'rather monotonous,' will soon be routine for American pilots. "

Despite Johnny's hearty manner, we knew that it was a very scary flight that took a lot of guts, and could hardly be called monotonous or routine. It would be a long time before night flights became routine, and when they did they were accompanied by huge losses of airplanes and crews.

Every mission we flew had some unusual event with danger attached to it, and required that we improvise and make decisions. Many times the pilot would look at his copilot when things got "hairy" and ask, "What do you think?" and the responses were often, "Beats the hell out of me!" Luck was another crew member that rode with us. The rugged individualism shown by Johnny Payne was not acceptable in later days.

After the original AMMISCA pilots were rotated home in 1943, operational control changed from senior pilots to senior officers, who ran things in a military manner. By 1944, pilots were flying schedules and were given little opportunity to make their own decisions. This is how the military normally operates, but the system suffered what pilots considered a serious abuse when Colonel Tom Hardin in 1944 ordered that there would be "no weather on the Hump." It meant that all flights would go despite impossibly bad weather. The airlift was not equipped for this all-weather flying, and the result was many men condemned to death. It was an order would have been laughed at and ignored by AMMISCA pilots in an earlier day, but now the military structure had taken over, and it had to be followed, even though Hardin ignored safety in favor of results. It caused skyrocketing losses, as I relate later.

In those later days the crews had few milk run flights and few opportunities to visit the cities as I had done. One pilot related that he had crossed the Hump to Kunming 90 times, and had never visited that city, or any other city in China. Another pilot told me of a so-called recreational milk run to Calcutta. He arrived late in the day, stayed overnight at the airbase, and returned to Chabua the next morning, never getting downtown. Many milk runs were taken over by the higher ranking officers, who found lots of business to attend to in Calcutta and other larger cities. "Rank Has Its Privileges!"

By the time all these changes took place in 1944, our surviving AMMISCA pilots were back in the states with a wonderful feeling of accomplishment. We had started the Hump airlift, and now we were teaching Hump flying technique at a special training base at Reno, Nevada. We were aware that the Hump challenge was still there and would remain until the war was over.

ON THE GROUND

In September, our "palatial residence" in Chabua was the same primitive basha that we had moved into in June when we first arrived. This was quite a contrast from the luxurious Great Eastern Hotel in Calcutta where we had recently vacationed. Even the shabby hostels in Kweilin and Kunming, China, where we had lived with the Flying Tigers, were palaces compared to the bashas.

A basha was the most primitive type of barracks building, nothing more than a long narrow native-built hut with a thatched roof, sitting on a hard-packed dirt floor. The walls were made by splitting bamboo poles and weaving them into flat panels, which were then laced together. Roofing materials were layers of palm fronds. Interiors were furnished with double rows of bunks, and a shroud-like mosquito net hung over each bunk, hopefully keeping out undesirable flying bugs. Malaria was very widespread, for Burma and nearby areas were considered the most malarial part of the world. We took great precautions to avoid it, constantly taking medications, and regarding every flying insect as a mortal enemy. All types of insects and wild life were able to find their way into our bashas, and we were constantly inspected bedding, clothing, and shoes, looking for dangerous invaders.

A cement slab foundation was laid next door to provide for a shower and toilet room, so we had indoor plumbing most of the time. Water came from overhead tanks filled by local 'water wallahs,' who worked in shifts all day long at long-handled pumps to fill them. When toilets were plugged up, as often happened, we resorted to slit trench latrines out back, and at night faced the danger of meeting strange creatures on the way

These slit trench latrines and the other trenches dug for air raid emergencies were a hazard in several ways. Several men had accidents falling into the foxholes at night until safety fencing was built. Everyone was warned that in case of air raid, look before you leap - there might be a cobra or other unfriendly creature already in residence, unwilling to share his space. Another danger was that you might jump into the wrong trench during a raid, and find yourself in a latrine instead of a foxhole, with most unpleasant results. That opened the question of how choosy should you be during a raid.

An appropriate poem was circulated around Assam, its writer anonymous.

ASSAM PERIL

The dangers are all around, with deadly snakes on the ground.
Somewhere a jungle beast growls, and a savage headhunter prowls.

A thousand insects are on the wing, dread diseases do they bring. There's
a sudden fearful hush; could be a Jap coming through the brush. That's
the very frightening scene, and it's only on the way to the latrine.

Another major hazard was the poor food. In those early days, most of the food was supplied from local sources, and the cooking done by houseboys we jokingly called chefs. Whether from tainted food or unsanitary conditions, everyone acquired a dose of "Delhi Belly," our 'fun' name for dysentery. Flying long trips with a churning stomach and related problems made us bless the toilet compartments built into the C-47, for these were well used. Everyone qualified for the "Crud Ribbon," a brown ribbon with a red streak, which we considered a badge of honor. Gnawing stomach pains was another distraction that could affect judgment in our flying, and this loss of concentration undoubtedly caused accidents.

The rains came in October, and never seemed to let up. Our only paved area was the runway, and all the rest was a quagmire of mud. We slogged through ankle-deep sticky brown goo, and it followed us indoors. I bought a Raleigh bike in Calcutta just before the rainy season, and this was poor timing, as the thick muck resisted any wheels. Even jeeps and trucks with 4-wheel drive had hard going, and our vehicles were constantly breaking down.

When the rain occasionally ceased, the sun poured down unmercifully. In the late winter and spring seasons, the heat was so intense we were grateful for the pith helmets that had been issued us in the States. In that heat, tools and airplane parts got so hot that aircraft maintenance had to be done either early in the morning, or late in the day. The interior of an airplane sitting on the ground heated up like a furnace, and even touching switches to start an engine required using a rag to avoid burning fingers.

We couldn't change the weather, but we bitched loud and clear about our barracks. Basha bungalows might be very picturesque at a resort in Tahiti, but as permanent housing with lots of crawling, climbing, slithering, and flying creatures for company, they were abominable. We brought in visiting VIP's from New Delhi to experience our conditions, but they usually raced back to HQ leaving promises behind. They lived in luxury, so why should they stay around to share our intense discomfort?

Eventually our efforts brought results, and we were rewarded with better housing. A new airfield was built a few miles away, at a place called Doom-Dooma, promptly renamed "Dum-Dum," and 25 of the AMMISCA crowd, who had seniority, were transferred there on October 12th. We were housed in a spacious two-level bungalow, formerly the home of a plantation manager. It had decent plumbing, our own kitchen, and houseboys to do the cooking and chores. These were elegant quarters compared to the bashas, and we felt that we were living in luxury as we lounged in wicker chairs on our wide upper-level veranda. All we missed was a cooling rum punch and a beautiful lady at our side.

We requisitioned such scarce items as electric pumps for the water tanks, portable generators, and numerous other comfort items, and when they didn't come promptly we sent out a few "expediters." In mysterious ways these people made some wonderful acquisitions. We had such luxuries as reading lights, chests of drawers, mirrors, and even a phonograph with popular 78 rpm records like Benny Goodman and Glen Miller classics. This was like living at the Ritz, and we enjoyed the privacy of smaller rooms and screened windows. Hump trips could be very exhausting, and our new surroundings made it much easier to catch up on sack time between flights. After a good rest we could use up our excess energy playing tag football or badminton on the expanse of green lawn in front of our quarters.

There was no shortage of local help. We had "wallahs" to do everything: cook, clean, shine boots, pump water, make beds, mow lawns. They were quiet, cooperative, and enjoyed the company of friendly Americans after generations of stiff-backed British. Our generosity with money kept them ready to perform any errands requested. The cooks were a problem, as all we had available were poorly trained extra cooks from the local plantations. We named our cook Sniffy, because of his constant sniffle. He had little cooking ability and his cleanliness was in doubt, so we taught him as best as we could.

There was no recreation at first, but eventually a movie projector arrived. We would see the same film every night it was run, as it gave us something to do besides write letters, spend time in the sack, and complain about conditions. There were hazards to movie- going, as the brightly lit screen drew hoards of insects, so we bundled up in total protective clothing.

The British had learned to live in this unhealthy part of the world by building their homes bright and airy, raised up off the ground, using native materials. Some of the local planters came to visit and welcome us, and give us tips on how to cope with the local living conditions. They welcomed the presence of new people into their midst, and helped create a modest social life for those of us who enjoyed good conversation and played bridge. They hosted social mixers where they entertained us with storied about their life in India and the days of the British Raj. They were charming people, and we found the presence of their wives gave us a feeling that we still lived in civilized country.

There were no other women in residence except native plantation workers. Our only glimpse of them was on their daily parade through the tea plantations, walking very erectly while balancing baskets of tea on their heads, and usually carrying an infant in a sling against their bosoms. They looked neither to right or left, and were just part of the colorful background.

The tea plantations spread for miles, but were now broken up by various airfields that British contractors were building for our use. Scattered over the landscape were large two-story steel skeleton structures that were the drying racks for tea. Gone were the polo fields and other luxuries enjoyed by the British in pre-war days, but they still lived very well, with some assistance from us.

Chapter 20
BRITISH RAJ

"Mad dogs and Englishmen go out in the midday sun!"

These words from an old English music hall tune remind me of the British plantation `managers I met at Dum-Dum in the Assam Valley. They were representative of colonial British all over the world, people who had moved into inhospitable parts of the world and created industries such as the tea plantations. They built a society for themselves and lived well despite the terrible climate and the many natural dangers that surrounded them. We socialized with them and I found them to be charming people who lived a life-style that was quite unique to this city boy from Boston.

The British "Raj," or colonial rule of India, had existed for over 200 years, and was destined to end soon after the war. The Raj maintained tight control over the country, and were rewarded with profits from various industries that benefited from low cost labor. Some small effort was made to change the caste system among the native population, which served them.

A local plantation manager, Charles Burkhart, paid us a call ostensibly looking for bridge players, but after we chatted for a while he admitted that he would like to spend time with some youthful, high-spirited warriors, who were very much like his Royal Air Force members. His younger employees had been taken into the army, and he complained that his circle of middle-aged duffers was quite boring. He and other plantation managers became our hosts on many occasions, and became a wonderful diversion from our stressful flying.

Their stories were about a life that was foreign to ours. One very intriguing tale was why an Englishman would choose a career in far-off India. The reason was, very simply, to better himself. In England, social position largely depended on family connections and the schools a young man attended. For example, a middle class education usually kept a person in a middle class social niche for his entire life.

Employment in one of England's far-flung colonies gave a great opportunity to improve one's status, and a position as a young executive on a tea plantation was highly regarded. Applicants were carefully screened to insure that they would be permanent employees, willing to spend their lifetime in company service. The young men chosen for these positions looked forward to leading a splendid life, with social position, good income, servants, and lifetime security.

It was well worth the risks of tropical diseases and the many other discomforts to be found in India.

In peacetime, the tea plantations were normally staffed by young, unmarried, British assistant managers, each in charge of a section, living in his own bungalow, attended by a staff of servants. The general manager was a married man, living with his wife and family in a larger home, more centrally located. As senior executive, he enjoyed such luxuries as trips to the big cities, the best of food, motor cars, and even a string of polo ponies. He had the opportunity to send his children to top-notch boarding schools in England when they reached school age.

When an opening for a general manager was to occur within the next year or so, the top-ranking assistant manager was slated for promotion, and sent on a six-month furlough to England. He had much to learn at the head office about the tea business and the secrets of running a plantation.

He was given a very special personal duty to perform as well. He was instructed to find a suitable young lady, marry her, and bring his bride with him on his return to India, prepared to establish a proper household. The job of general manager had great responsibility, and it was considered bad form to have an unmarried man in charge. Younger assistants could live very well as bachelors, seeking out the company of the few available females, but the man in charge of the entire operation needed the stability of a full family life, to avoid the erratic behavior that sometimes accompanied the lonely life on a plantation.

During our social visits with planter families, playing bridge or hearing about the "good old days," we heard amusing stories about the difficulty of finding a suitable bride to bring back to India. It took the right combination, and many times the poor young woman was seduced by the thought of luxury living, but not given a complete picture of the heat, insects, wild life, and other hazards of living in India. Many marriages suffered as a result, and unhappy people often looked for escape and diversion in alcohol and occasional wild behavior.

We had found the Brits reserved at first, but they gradually warmed up to our presence. One of our hosts, Mr. Jock Bullard, gave us great personal insight into the life of the planters, with some off-color stories about unconventional activities that a bored group of Englishmen and women indulge in when isolated from home, and out of the sight of conservative society. In our presence, bridge became a major interest, and we found them very skilled at this game, and at holding a great deal of gin, often doing both at the same time. We received many invitations at first, but when Americans arrived in large numbers, the Brits were overwhelmed and had to cut back on their hospitality.

Raising children in India created problems of health and education, but another problem cropped up when the children were old enough to go "back home" to an English boarding school. This was a heart-wrenching experience for the family, for they knew that visits would be few and far between and family life would never be the same.

We absorbed some "British-isms,", and some of our personnel were heard speaking with a British accent. The Brits have created some interesting additions to the English language such as lorry, loo, and pram. Another word seldom heard in the states is "POSH" which refers to something of luxury, or first-class. It came from the abbreviation for "Port Outbound, Starboard Homebound." A ship on a southbound heading for India, traversing the Suez Canal and the Red Sea in 120 degree temperatures, found the cooler side was the port, or left side, away from the hot afternoon sun. The reverse was true when heading north, when the right, or starboard side, was the cooler. All this was long before the day of air-conditioned vessels.

The expression, "White Elephant," took on a new meaning for me when I learned that it originated in India. It was the mythical story of a Maharajah, who punished a subject by making him the gift of a white elephant, considered a sacred animal. The man could not afford the gift, as the animal required very costly special care and feeding, and the owner was eventually reduced to poverty.

The plantation managers had many complaints about their situation. They complained about the loss of their young assistants to the army, which left them handicapped in managing the large tracts of tea-producing land. The managers themselves were excused from service, being mostly older men and essential to the economy of England, as tea was a very profitable export.

They worried about their children at school in an England that was under heavy bombardment, although the schools were well away from target areas. They were unhappy about sacrificing their polo ponies, as this was a sporting activity that placed them in the same league as royalty, truly a sport of kings. They fussed that their beautifully manicured polo grounds were now runways for our aircraft, and would never be the same. They also complained that there was a shortage of help to construct these runways, buildings, and other facilities for our growing air force establishment.

Our neighbors in Assam suffered some wartime shortages, but managed very well. There was an oversupply of native help to do the laundry, the cooking, and the cleaning, all at a cost of only a few pennies a day. A young native boy was the 'punkah wallah', providing air conditioning by pulling a cord for hours swinging a woven ceiling panel. A 'dhobi wallah' would work for hours to hand-pump water into an overhead tank that provided running water for the master.

The presence of energetic young Americans gave a great boost to the British in many ways. They certainly enjoyed the ready availability of many small luxuries that had been shut off by Britain, but now came from Americans, such as household items, soft drinks, beer, and liquor. We provided equipment such as pumps, generators, and other devices that would benefit them as well as our own troops. Curt and I, and other pilots living in Dum-Dum bungalow, very obligingly scrounged up such major items as bicycles, car parts, appliances, and very vital medical supplies, on our trips to the big cities of Calcutta, Karachi, and New Delhi.

The colonial British looked forward to spending their retirement years in England, where they would lead a leisurely and companionable life and chat about the glories of days gone by. In 1980, I vacationed at the seashore resort of Southampton in southern England, and met many retirees from the colonial service at our residential hotel. I developed great rapport with several residents when they heard that I was a veteran of the China-Burma-India Theater, and had lived in India, which they regarded as the most outstanding example of British colonialism. They were happy to finally come "home," only to find that the rigors of the cold, raw climate in England were more than many could endure, after a lifetime spent in the tropics, and caused serious health problems.

Chapter 21
THE TAJ AND INDIA

Whenever I see a picture of the Taj Mahal, one of the most photographed buildings in the world, I am reminded of my first view of that fabulous building. It was from the air, and as I flew a tight circle around it, with my left wing tip pointing directly at the dome, even the cumbersome wartime scaffold surrounding the top could not distract from its true beauty.

The next day, I rode a horse-drawn gharry from our hotel to view the Taj close up, and came away with an unforgettable memory lodged in my mind, for I had just seen the most beautiful building in the world. Striking Indian ladies clad in traditional saris, bearing insignia of caste on their foreheads, strolled through the gardens, adding to the feeling that I was viewing a centuries old civilization.

The Taj Mahal has been the goal of tourists for a long time, since its existence became world known. Built in 1643 of white marble with a central dome, its history has all the ingredients of a wonderful story, including powerful royalty, lifelong romance, and an exquisite and everlasting memorial to a great love. You can't beat that for a wonderful plot. What woman would not want such a remembrance? Whether this is truly the romance of the ages I cannot say, but I found it a gorgeous building, and a moving experience. I consider it the most inspiring sight in all of India.

Its home city of Agra has become famous as a result of the Taj. Even during the war, Agra was the number one attraction in India, with the visitors wearing uniforms instead of the fashionable garments of well-to-do tourists.

Agra became a favorite stopover for our 2200-mile trips from Karachi to Assam. We would remain overnight at the small but elegant Agra Hotel, long preferred by the rich and famous, where a deluxe room cost only $3 American. Our enlisted crews stayed there also, and my crew chief, Saylor, laughed one morning at breakfast, remarking that he heard that the same toilet he used had been sat on by some of the most famous and royal asses in the world.

Despite the war, local tradesmen saw no letup in their business, for American troops are the greatest of tourists. Agra excelled in shops offering custom-made boots, suits, and uniforms made quickly and cheaply. I ordered a pair of calf-high boots of the finest leather, and watched the cobbler make an outline of my foot for a pattern. These were finished overnight, and I was pleased with their wonderful fit. However, something went wrong, as about two months later, after they sat idle for a while, I was unable to slip my foot in. They had shrunk by several sizes. Not such a great bargain, after all.

I had better luck with a custom uniform made of a very fine lightweight English worsted wool, woven with colored threads that gave it an iridescent look, rippling and changing color as I moved. It was definitely non-regulation, but quite handsome, and in India no one cared about the rules. I wore it Stateside, purely for social events, and it stood out.

Another bargain was the snake charmer outside the hotel, whose King Cobra performed to the piper's melody for a few rupees. He offered us lessons in snake charming for another few rupees, and one of our bold pilots agreed to try. He changed his mind when someone suggested that the snake might not be totally defanged, and that there just might not be a reliable antidote for cobra venom. So we moved on down the road, entranced by the shows put on for our benefit and our rupees, and looked for someone to demonstrate the famous rope trick, climbing a mysteriously suspended rope, but we never found such a person.

I was so fascinated by the Taj Mahal, that each time I left Agra I would circle the grounds once more. To this day I am still entranced by its beauty and permanence that have survived many wars and other catastrophic events, and hold its visitors in awe.

1942 India was a fascinating place to visit. It displayed so many different life styles, so many unique customs, so many ugly sights, so many beautiful objects to admire, that it would take a very long time to really learn much about the country. I visited New Delhi, where the British had created a modem, park-like city that was the seat of the government. It had modem buildings, broad avenues, and was rightly called the jewel of the empire.

Right next to it was the city of Old Delhi, where the pattern of life had not changed for many centuries. I found it crowded and colorful, with many sights and smells, and alive with the hustle and bustle of native commerce. It was a great place to find souvenirs to send back home, but I doubted that they would arrive, so I only indulged in items I could carry with me. At first glance, Old Delhi looked like a typical native city to tourists, but it was really a huge souvenir market, neatly cleaned up to suit the visitors' tastes.

The true picture of life in India was seen in the smaller towns, where people lived far differently than those in the larger cities. The first thing I learned was that the caste system was still alive and flourishing. In the States we live with the creed that "all men are created equal," and it was astounding to find that in India an ancient custom still guided the lives of most of the population. The caste system dates back 3000 years, and tradition had held it in place despite some attempts by the British to soften its harshest rules. It rigidly kept a person at the social level to which he was borne, with little or no opportunity to rise above that level. Occasionally, a man of the merchant class who achieved some level of business success, might gain a higher status, but this was a rare occurrence. At the lowest end of the social scale, the untouchables lived a hopeless life of utter squalor, and could never rise above their level.

The visits to the small villages were fascinating, but the smells were revolting. The streets were unpaved, and dust settled everywhere. The stores were little shacks or tiny shops showing items that could only be of interest to the local people. Poverty prevailed in all of India, with inadequate food, no medical care, ragged clothing, and a hopeless outlook. They lacked sanitary knowledge, and used ditches by the sides of the roads for open sewers. Filth and disease were part of their normal life. The aromas of cooking foods mingled with the stenches, and we were grateful that we had our own messes where food preparation was carefully controlled - we hoped. They bathed in a sacred river that was their source of drinking water as well as their public laundry, but it was shocking to see that the river was also used as a sewer.

I was mystified at first by the remarkable contrast between the sullen, down-trodden appearance of Indian people, and the friendly, joyous peasants I had seen in China. Rarely did I see a laughing native, appearing to be happy, and it was usually in a city after I had given a large tip of rupees to a 'wallah.' In the small Indian villages the attitude was very dismal. In Dibrugah, in Assam, I saw only sad faces, people who avoided eye contact and appeared to resent our presence.

Then I realized that they probably associated all Americans with the oppressive British colonials, who had deprived the Indian people of freedom for more than century, and derived great profits from their labor. The caste system was another depressing element in the way that it drastically limited their ability to ever achieve a better life.

The Chinese lived in similar poverty, lacking the simplest conveniences, and suffering greatly from disease and often from hunger, but they smiled and laughed readily in our presence and constantly gave us thumbs-up "Ding-hau" signals of friendship. They idealized the Flying Tigers as their rescuers from deadly Japanese bombings, and included all "Mayrugans" in their worship of these heroes. Despite the heavy hand of the tyrant, Chiang Kai-shek, they enjoyed freedoms and a vision of better things to come if left to their own fate.

This contrast in attitude drives home the importance of freedom. Many emerging young democratic nations have suffered reverses that caused their former colonial masters to say "I told you so," but, we have our own precedent in a great patriot who expressed it simply as, "Give me liberty, or give me death."

Chapter 22
ICE-HO

The steady but very loud drone of our two Pratt & Whitney R-1830 engines in perfect synchronization makes the poorly insulated cockpit of our C-47 too noisy for normal conversation. I must lean over the short distance between us and yell into the ear of my copilot to talk.

It is early morning in December, and we are over the center of the Hump, returning to Chabua in the Assam Valley after loading up at Kunming. We are flying direct, on a magnetic heading of 295 degrees, bucking moderate headwinds, estimating a three and one-half hour flight. Our fuel load on takeoff is approximately 500 gallons, enough for five hours. Our cargo is tungsten ore, fifty 100-pound bags of a precious metal that is used to make high grade steel. Tungsten is a critical war item, and China is one of the few sources in the world where it is available, so our westbound trips have a load.

Our weather is rotten, as we expected. We have absolutely no weather reporting services on the Hump, something our planners seemed to forget about, so we rely on other pilots already en route to tell us what to expect. Our radio reaches them if they are within about 40 miles from us. They report a solid overcast on the direct route, with breaks to the south over Burma, which is Japanese territory.

Our cargo is just a tiny part of the war effort, but it has loaded us to a gross airplane weight of 26,000 pounds. This weight is okay if we are flying at the normal service ceiling of 12,000 feet for a C-47, but we must hold at least 16,000 feet over most of the Hump, and that is a different matter.

Because of the high altitude, our throttles are full forward, but we are only maintaining an indicated airspeed (IAS) of 115 miles per hour. Correcting our airspeed indicator for altitude, our true airspeed is actually 155 MPH, which should get us home in three hours plus, with luck

Sometimes I am almost lulled into a sense of security by the sweet sound of those beautiful engines. Two years before, I worked at Pratt & Whitney Aircraft, and I recall how we closely inspected every part that went into these engines. They were carefully assembled by first-class teams of mechanics, who built an entire engine on one stand, with great care. At the time, plans were under way to convert to an assembly line system that would be far more efficient, but as a pilot now, I prefer the old system, where the team was directly responsible for the entire engine. I like to think that these are two of my very own engines that

I fussed about, because now our lives depend on them. I only wish that we had the more advanced R-1830's, that have two-speed superchargers, giving more power at higher altitude. We might be able to maintain 18 to 20,000 feet cruising altitude, instead of barely hanging on at 16,000.

The engines sound great, but I am tense as we punch our way through solid overcast, totally surrounded by massive clouds. We expect this weather at this time of the year, when the monsoons rage. If we have any problem at all, we will have to let down to a lower altitude to maintain flying speed, and that's not a good idea. About 1000 feet below us, at 15,000 feet, are massive mountain peaks that we picture as reaching up to grasp us in their deadly grip.

I make a 15 degree cut to the left, southward towards lower mountains, for we may have crosswinds from the south pushing us to the north where mountains reach to 20,000 feet and higher. The lack of weather reporting services makes us victims of chance, and we must always fly defensively. Sometimes we joke that most Hump clouds have hard centers. That's an old flying joke, but it is a dark thought that keeps us on our toes.

My co-pilot, Lieutenant Bob Spector, is on his second Hump flight, and has never flown in actual instrument weather before. He is nervous, his eyes darting back and forth, first to the engine instruments, which I have instructed him to monitor, and then to outside cloud conditions. I can understand his concern. Flying the Hump on instruments is not a pleasant way to spend the afternoon, and he has heard all the frightening stories about missing airplanes.

Suddenly, a loud heart-stopping crash reverberates throughout the airplane. It sounds like a large caliber bullet smashing through the fuselage next to our seats. Spector turns a very startled, scared look at me and mouths, "What in the hell is that!"

I lean over and shove his earphone off his left ear. With all the assurance of a salty Hump pilot with lots of missions under his belt, I shout in his ear, "It's only prop ice!" and I give him a half smile.

Inside, I'm not feeling so calm. When there is propeller ice, there is sure to be wing ice, and I haven't seen it yet even though I make frequent checks on the leading edges of the wings.

Ice on the props is one thing. The anti-icing system is working. It feeds anti-icing fluid to the hubs of the props and the whirling blades spread that fluid over the blades, melting and breaking off accumulated ice and preventing more. As the broken pieces fly off the blades, some of them hit the airplane outside of the cockpit, and sound like shrapnel, or worse. It is a most frightening sound, but once you get used to it, it is reassuring because you know the system is working.

Ice on the wings is another story. It is a surefire killer of airplanes, and many have been lost over the history of flying before the development of wing de-icing systems. Wing ice accumulates on the leading edges of wings and other surfaces such as rudders and elevators. It not only adds weight but it destroys the shape of the airfoil that provides the lift for an airplane. In extreme cases, the airplane is forced down to a crash ending.

There are two basic kinds of wing ice. One is rime that looks like frost and is brittle; it can be broken off by inflatable rubber de-icer boots that line the leading edges of the wings, and alternately inflate and deflate in sections, causing the ice to crack into pieces.

Watching pieces of wing ice break away because of pulsating boot action is a soul- satisfying experience for a pilot who wonders, "What if it doesn't work?"

The other type of ice is called clear ice, and this is far more deadly. It forms a glass-like layer on the wing and is hard to detect in the reduced light of heavy clouds. Once you see it, it may be too late to break off, especially since it tends to flex with the pulsating rubber boots and stubbornly resists cracking up.

I peer carefully at the wings and can now see a layer of clear ice on the edges. This is a whole new ball game and we are in deep trouble. I note our airspeed beginning to bleed off below 115 MPH indicated, and I nervously push the throttles, but they are already up against the stop, full out. I increase engine RPM to 2450, which is the maximum for continuous operation. These are well-used engines, with lots of hours, and there is always the risk of engine failure if we push them too hard for too long a time. One develops a remarkably sensitive feeling for the care of engines in this operation.

Our airspeed continues to drop. It is just above 105 MPH. This is a very dangerous situation. Thoughts fleetingly run through my mind of the C-87 fleet of five airplanes that had been added to our fleet. These are cargo versions of the huge four-engine B-24 bombers, and have supercharged engines that will take them to well over 20,000 feet at cruising speeds. We were all envious of the pilots who were flying them. With that type of airplane, we would not be in the fix we are in now.

But disaster overtook the C-87's. Three of them disappeared without any word of a crew bailing out or walking out, and we believe the cause was icing. The C-87 uses a high-performance Davis airfoil wing design, which normally makes the airplane very efficient, but it cannot carry any ice without losing a disastrous amount of lifting ability. There were no pilot reports from these airplanes, and the mountains will never tell their fate.

We have our own problems, gripped helplessly in the hand of fate, with airspeed dropping and surrounded by solid clouds

Turn on the de-icer boots! Hell! There aren't any!

Now I have a vicious thought - I would like to tear apart the supply officer someplace back in the states who overlooked our urgent request for replacement boots for the Douglas C-47s. We have consistently screamed, to anyone who would listen, for replacements. The hot, steamy tropical climate causes the original rubber de-icer boots to shred into pieces or completely disintegrate within a few months of use. A torn boot destroys lift and is worse than no boot at all, so they are removed entirely to clean up the airfoil. We are flying airplanes that are not properly equipped, in one of the most dangerous routes in the world. We are desperate for critical supplies. Even crucial items like parachutes are in short supply. What are those damn people doing back there? Who is to blame? Why are we losing men needlessly?

I get back to business. Let's get our asses back in one piece. What do we do next? The next move is to lighten the airplane. Fortunately, I am not carrying a load of 40 Chinese troops, who we sometimes haul to India for military training. We have heard of airplanes disappearing with full loads of troops. One landed safely after the pilot, Phil Owen, was in such despair that he ordered his crew to bailout. He stayed with the airplane and his passengers who were Chinese soldiers not supplied with chutes, and made a blind let- down. His luck was amazing; he let down right into the Assam valley near his airfield. Naturally, he credited himself with superior navigation, stating he knew where he was all time. He deserved credit for great bravery in staying with the airplane and passengers. His crewmen were also lucky; their parachutes opened properly, and they showed up weeks later, walking out of the jungle escorted by head-hunting tribesmen who valued the reward money more than the shrunken heads. Owen was kidded then, for trying to get rid of his crew, because they didn't shower often enough. We also joked with Owen about how his Chinese passengers felt when they saw his two crewmen disappear out the door. "Did you interview them?" we asked.

Fortunately for us, our cargo is disposable. I wave my crew chief forward and give him urgent orders: "Dump the load!" He sees two scared pilots (of course I'm scared, too) and he gets the message immediately. I send Spector along with him, and a few seconds later I hear the racket made by the slipstream when they remove the cargo door and start shoving out the 100-pound sacks of tungsten ore. It's heavy work at the high altitude, but they work with the strength of ten to unload us.

Soon we are 5000 pounds lighter and I feel better as I watch the indicated air speed creep back to 115. But we are not out of trouble because we are still in severe icing conditions. I maintain full throttle and 2450 RPM, and know that if we pick up more ice we will be right back in the same fix, for our huge load of ice is weighing us down. My eyes have been glued to the air speed indicator and other instruments, and I despair as I see our IAS start dropping again.

We are in bad shape now, about to become another statistic. I start a turn to the left to a southerly heading where the mountains are lower, and look up from the instruments momentarily. I see a small break in the clouds dead ahead. First it is a crack, and a few seconds later, it widens out to an opening, and then we fly into an area of broken clouds, still massive, but with large gaps. What a relief!

Then follows a miracle. We break out into the clear, into a huge pocket of clear air that looks like an enormous valley in the sky. Over us is a high layer of solid cloud and miles away across this opening are more ominous black clouds. But right now we are flying in the clear, and we see a green jungle valley split by a huge winding river many thousands of feet below us.

I know the air temperature down there is much warmer, well above freezing, warm enough to melt the ice, so I order the wheels down, reduce power, and start a tight circle, letting down at an ear-popping rate to get into the warmer air. I maintain a tight circle trying to stay in the center of this miraculously cloud-free valley.

This kind of a hole in the clouds is derisively called a "sucker hole." Curt took great pains to warn me about these as they can be treacherous. The sight of ground is very tempting, and it may even offer a landing spot if you are in desperate trouble. But experienced pilots know that it is like the deadly song of the mythical Siren. After you have let down below the surrounding mountains, the hole may pull the nasty trick of closing up again, enveloping you in clouds. You are then flying blind, below the level of the mountains, hoping you can climb out again without finding of those hard centered clouds. That is not a good place to be.

Our luck holds and the hole stays open. I let down to 5000 feet and joyfully watch the ice start to melt, with little rivulets of water flowing back over the top surface of the wings. We lose that deadly weight of ice, slowly at first, and then more rapidly, and in 20 minutes we are ice-free and ready to go home. I go to climb power still circling in our lovely valley of the clouds.

I feel as buoyant as the airplane, for now without a payload, without the ice, and with a light fuel load, we climb rapidly, right through the overcast to an altitude we normally cannot reach, topping out over the cloud level at 18,500 feet. We have no time to waste, as our gauges show we are very low on fuel, and our oxygen tanks, that showed almost full at 1200 pounds at Kunming, have dropped down to almost empty.

I give Spector a big smile, and pat him on the shoulder. We almost made the missing list today, but we fooled fate this time, and are now heading home.

In less than an hour we pick up the low-powered Chabua homing beacon on our radio direction finder. We hold our altitude until we are right over the field, then do a quick letdown. We land with about 30 minutes of fuel remaining.

My commanding officer is irritated at my losing my cargo; probably not so much the cargo as his having to make out a report. We are on pretty friendly terms, so I remind him that I saved my airplane as well as my ass. He laughs and says, "Welcome home." To save him time, I write up the report for him, including in it some wording he might have omitted.

All in a day's work.

Chapter 23
RICE — YOU OWE ME LUNCH

Into my office at Marina del Rey, California, one day in 1996, came a very distinguished looking gentleman, name of Aubrey Moss, for a business appointment. We were going to discuss a real estate project over lunch.

Noting that Aubrey spoke with a British accent, I inquired where he had spent the World War II war years. When he replied that he had been in Burma in 1942, my ears perked up, as I knew that we had something in common. Our conversation went something like this:

"What were you doing in Burma?" I asked.

He replied, very briefly, as though to minimize the subject, "Oh, I was with Wingate's Raiders. We fought the Japanese in the jungles, and had a very rough time of it."

"How did you manage to survive in the jungles?" I asked, leading him on.

"We started with enough supplies for about 4 weeks. When we ran out, we pretty much had to live off the land and food that was dropped to us by air. Things got pretty desperate, at times"

"Who was doing that air supply?"

"Oh, your American forces flew Dakotas over and dropped us food, mostly rice."

That was the line that I was waiting for. I proudly announced, "YOU OWE ME LUNCH!"

Aubrey had a good laugh when I told him about the rice-dropping missions I had flown, and how we searched the jungles for white parachute panels that the troops opened up on the jungle floor as targets. He had a big complaint: "Why couldn't you use double bags all the time? Some drops were in single bags that burst open on impact, and we would crawl around on the jungle floor trying to save some of the food." How about that? Someone always complains, no matter how much good you do.

Rice dropping missions were very scary. When I was asked to go on one, I thought it would be a pleasant change from a Hump trip, but this was not the case. I flew right seat, copilot, on that first mission, to learn the routine. A British navigator flew with us, guiding us far into Burma over dense jungle that seemed to stretch on without end. Just how our guide knew his way was a mystery, as we made many heading changes to avoid Japanese hot spots, and the terrain all looked the same to me. We flew at about 1,500 feet, high enough to spot the

Checking P-40 after belly landing

Our entire bomber force: B-25's at Kweilin

This P-40 pilot had little respect for the Rising Sun empire.

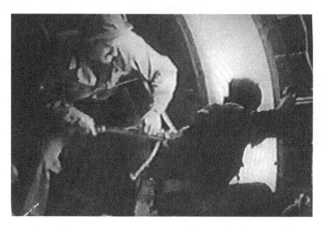

Rice drop.

panels, and low enough to make a wonderful target for Japanese troops in the jungle. We were an even better target when we dropped down to 50 feet for our drops, at a speed just above stalling, with cargo doors open and our crew ready.

We slowed down to 110 miles per hour, with flaps down for minimum flying speed. At that low altitude parachutes for the cargo were useless, even if we had them, so we hoped the goods were well packed. The drop timing was critical, so at 50 feet, the time to drop was when I saw the white panel disappear under the nose. At just that moment, I signaled the crew to shove the bags out. The cargo pushers sat on the floor and on signal shoved hard with their feet against the bags stacked up against the opening. It usually took three passes to unload the entire cargo, and I felt that by now the entire Japanese army knew we were there.

One Japanese infantryman with a rifle is not likely to be very accurate, but the concentrated fire of a group of riflemen can get lucky and knock down a sitting duck that is flying as low and slow as we were.

I flew the next mission from the left seat the following week and I ran into another hazard; the terrain. I heard of one airplane that was lost when the pilot did not have enough speed to climb over the hills after his first drop and ended up in the trees. He was lucky, as the tall trees cushioned his crash enough so that the crew was saved, although the men back in the cabin broke some bones, because they weren't strapped in. On my run, I could see that I would need to climb out quickly over the surrounding hills, or make a sharp turn to the left after the drop to fly out through a convenient slot in the hills. I chose the slot, as I doubted that I had enough airspeed to clear the hill. That was tricky, and the boys in the back didn't appreciate the steep left turn I had to make after each drop, as they slid downhill on the cabin floor towards the open door. They were not in danger of falling out of the cargo door as they wore safety harnesses.

Units of the Troop Carrier Command eventually took over the rice dropping missions, and added guns, ammunition, and all kinds of supplies for the ground troops. They claimed that their daily drop missions in C-47's were more hazardous than the Hump, with terrible flying conditions and many losses from ground fire. Flying "low and slow," the despair of any pilot, is bad enough, but adding enemy fire makes it extremely risky. These crews were in as much danger as combat pilots, and could not fight back.

After that fascinating story from Aubrey Moss, I wanted to learn more about Wingate's Raiders. Orde Wingate was a bold warrior, of the order of Lawrence of Arabia, Patton, and other famous military leaders, whose entire lives were wrapped up in combat. He was a master of aggressive tactics, and his advice on military operations was much sought after by other governments. In the '30's, as a British officer in the mid-east, he won the undying gratitude of the Israelis by leading them to victories over troops of the Arab League that greatly outnumbered them.

In Burma he became expert in the art of Long-Range Penetration, which is a fancy name for behind-the-lines attacks. His 3000 "Chindit" troops, made up of British, Indian, and Burmese soldiers, infiltrated behind the Japanese lines, destroying railroads, bridges, and supply depots, and slowed the invaders. They fought under brutal conditions, and losses were extremely severe, losing one-third of their men to enemy action, jungle hazards, disease, and starvation.

My friend, Aubrey, described the action in some detail, and I recalled the other vivid accounts of jungle fighting that I heard from the young officers in 1942 at the Calcutta Swim Club. Their memories were fresh with the horrors of the Burma campaign, and I remember how grateful I was to be flying over this, and not engaging the enemy on the ground.

Despite losing over 1000 men, Wingate's Burma campaign was so admired that other behind-the-lines campaigns followed. Merrill's Marauders mounted a similar campaign the following year, also suffering very high losses.

The Raiders and Marauders campaigns were successful in keeping the Japanese from breaking through the jungle and attacking our Assam airfields. This would have reduced our airlift to a trickle, and probably stopped our offense in China. It took heavy fighting and sacrifice of many British and Indian lives to keep the Japanese out of India.

Aubrey bought me a "nice rice lunch".

Chapter 24
GO-NO-GO

Many bad things resulted from shortages of replacement parts, and I recall some of them as vividly as if they happened this morning.

At the crack of dawn, we are sitting at the west end of the runway at Chabua, ready to take off for a flight to Kunming. Other airplanes are getting ready, finishing loading, starting engines, taxiing out, and lining up, and soon there will be a stream of aircraft taking off to cross the Hump. This everyday scene is made gloomy by the overcast condition, heavy ground fog, and the muddy area that surrounds us, clinging to our boots, and dirtying up the cockpit. We are delaying our takeoff because the ground fog completely blots out the far end of the runway.

Takeoffs later in the day avoid the fog condition that makes these dawn departures so dangerous, but then we are not able to make a round trip in one day. The daytime heat of 100 degrees or higher makes cockpits so hot that we need gloves to handle the controls. High outside air temperatures add another danger, as engines develop less power, making longer takeoff runs for our overloaded airplanes.

I notice some cows grazing in the brush close to the edge of the runway, so I wave the jeep driver sitting alongside to make a fast trip and shoo them away. Cows are sacred in India, and allowed to roam free. They also are a great hazard to an airplane on takeoff.

As I wait, I review the checklist. We did our walk-around inspection to see that rudder and elevator locks were removed, and checked the fuel tank drain valves to make sure they are safety-wired shut after draining out the residual water in the fuel.

All cockpit checks and startup were normal, and I taxied out and parked at a 45-degree angle to the runway and ran up the engines to check the magnetos. Checking each magneto separately, I see that engine RPM drop is a normal 50 to 75, well under the maximum allowable 100 RPM . Now we just sit, and wait for the fog to lift.

To go or not to go is at the pilot's discretion. It is October of 1942, and after six months in the field, we still don't have the supporting facilities normally expected in a flight operation. We have no operations office, no weather reporting services, no radio powerful enough to reach Kunming, our destination, to learn of weather or field conditions there. Back in the States we couldn't operate at all under these conditions. But this is a real do-it-yourself operation. With practically no supervision, nobody questions the pilot's decision on how to conduct the flight

Occasionally, some high ranking brass comes in from headquarters in New Delhi, makes a brief inspection, bawls us out for not wearing any rank insignia, failing to salute, or some other very petty matter. These visiting inspectors have learned to carefully avoid asking about technical and operational problems, because this opens up a Pandora's Box of complaints, sometimes with anger and vindictiveness, which they will fend off by maintaining discreet silence. Some of our pilots, who have looked death in the eye, have developed an "I don't give a damn!" attitude, and pay little attention to military courtesy in this outpost where flying is extremely hazardous. As it is, every high ranking visitor gets an earful of gripes about shortages of everything from A to Z, things that are essential for a safe operation, and they promise to take action as soon as they get back to HQ. They politely reject our offers to take them with us on a next Hump trip, usually pleading an "important meeting pending," and they retreat back to HQ. We are happy to see them go; we are much better off without this interference. We are wised up - their visits will produce no results, and we jokingly refer to ourselves as the "lost legion".

The morning sun is burning off the ground fog, and I can almost see the end of the runway, so I line up ready to go. I check my instruments, first the cylinder head temperature gauges as the engines have been running for a while. Next, I check my flight instruments, to see that the artificial horizon is working properly, and that the gyrocompass is set to match the magnetic compass, as I will need these as soon as my gear comes up.

Flight instruments are critical and must be set up before take-off There is often a layer of scud and thick haze just off the ground, which means that you might be on instruments right after take-off Pilots with minimal instrument experience can get rattled at the sudden change from visual to instrument flight, and, in some instances, have lost control and flown right back into the ground.

We do not have a special instrument flight training program, so our senior pilots give this instruction en route. These senior pilots, with thousands of hours on the airlines, know how vital this is, so we keep the new pilots in the right seat as copilots until such time as they are qualified to take over.

Our load is often 13 drums, each containing 55 gallons of high-octane aviation gas for our P-40 fighters. The drums are lashed down with tie ropes, which are adequate to hold them in place during flight, even when in severe turbulence;

however, the tie-downs are not strong enough the hold the drums in place in a crash into the brush after takeoff. A sudden stoppage will send those 500 pound drums of avgas crashing into the cockpit with devastating results. The crew gets wiped out before the fire gets to them. Our takeoffs are very critical, indeed.

We're ready to roll, and other airplanes are lining up behind me waiting their turn. I move onto the runway, line up in the takeoff direction, lock the tail wheel for directional control, and push the throttles up slowly to 46 inches of manifold pressure at 2700 RPM. As usual, with a full load we pick up speed slowly.

We are almost halfway down the runway when I realize something is wrong. I am putting forward pressure on the wheel and our tail is not coming up as it should have by now. I take a quick glance at the airspeed indicator, and am shocked to read 55 MPH instead of the expected 80.

Something is VERY wrong!

I have to make an instant decision on what to do. A million thoughts can go through ones mind in a fraction of a second but I only have one single thought - decide whether to GO or NO-GO!

The runway was recently extended to 5400 feet, and I can keep going hoping to get airborne before I run out of room. I may be able to nurse my airplane into the air, and maybe not. If I don't, I'll run off the end of the runway into brush and probably end up with a very sudden stop in a drainage ditch. If I survive, which is doubtful, I will kill that S-O-B who overloaded my airplane. But right now there is only one option, NO-GO!

I chop the throttles and hit the brakes hard at first, but when I see I have room to stop before reaching the end of the runway because of my low speed, I ease up on the brake pedals. Burned out brakes and tires are almost impossible to replace.

I taxi back with lots of guys on the ground watching me, park the airplane very quickly, and jump out of the airplane looking for the chief of the loading crew who was trying to kill me. I don't recall, but I was probably calling him some very special names, when I was almost tackled by one of the other pilots before I could commit mayhem on the poor sergeant.

"Couldn't you hear your engines?" he asked. "They were backfiring and popping like crazy. Your plugs are all fouled up and you aren't getting power!" In the cockpit, it is almost impossible to hear any misfiring at take-off power, as the overall noise drowns out any malfunctioning engine noises.

Our airplane was not overloaded; it's just the sparkplugs, loaded with oil. The engines are old, and the plugs are not changed on a regular schedule as the maintenance manual instructs, as there just aren't any plugs available. They foul up quickly when the engines idle for a protracted period of time. I was at fault also, because in my haste to get off the ground and make room for airplanes stacking up behind me, I failed to run up the engines one more time before take-off to check for RPM drop-off

The airplane is moved to maintenance for plug cleaning, and I switch to another one for the trip. I check the mags carefully, line up for takeoff, and raise my right hand with fingers crossed, waving them several times at my copilot. He catches the idea, and raises his left hand and does the same. I push the throttles forward, and we roll down the runway, making a safe takeoff. From that moment on, I never go aloft in an airplane without first crossing my fingers, once for each engine. Am I superstitious? No way.

At an evening bull session, I tell of my experience and pass the word around to re-check mags if there is a delay on the ground. Everyone says, "Oh, we always do that," but I am sure this is a good reminder.

All in a day's work.

The pilot has only a split second to make a life-or-death decision. There is no maybe here.

Chapter 25
BUDDIES
QUIET DICK COLE - TOKYO VETERAN

The carrier, the U.S.S. Hornet, swung into the wind in a heavy sea with dreary sky, and prepared to launch its aircraft. This was a strike planned at the heart of the Japanese mainland, just five months after the attack on Pearl Harbor on December 7, 1941. The Hornet had a strange group of aircraft stored on its heaving deck; instead of navy airplanes there were 16 Army B-25 Mitchell medium bombers crowded together, with a short open deck upwind for takeoff space.

It was 8:00 A.M. on April 18, and the Air Corps crews under Lieutenant Colonel 'Jimmy' Doolittle, were alerted for a takeoff many hours ahead of the originally planned time. Admiral Halsey moved the clock ahead when he learned that his fleet had been sighted by Japanese picket boats. To move any closer to Japan placed the giant carrier and its support vessels at great risk from submarine attack. The earlier takeoff meant that the B-25's had to fly a much greater distance

The carrier speed of 20 knots into a 30 knot wind added up to 50 knots airspeed for the B-25's just standing still. They needed only another 20 knots of speed down the deck to insure a safe takeoff. When Doolittle, flying the lead airplane, received the signal from the deck officer as the deck started its upward pitch, he released his brakes and pushed his throttles harder, although they were already full open, and began his takeoff roll.

This was the supreme test after many weeks of preparation. Sitting in the right seat, his copilot, Lieutenant Dick Cole, watched his right wing come perilously close to the carrier midships island as they flashed past with a clearance of only six feet, and the next moment they were over water and he was raising the landing gear. They were on their way to bomb Tokyo, followed by 15 more bombers, each making a safe takeoff. This tiny mission was one of the most daring and unique in the war, and turned out to be one of the most important.

Six months later, a new pilot, Captain Richard Cole, arrived at Assam, and was assigned to fly copilot for me on several Hump trips. Dick was a very congenial, smiling guy, who kidded me by saying "yessir" and "nosir" even though he outranked me by two grades, as I was still a second lieutenant. I asked him what he had been doing in the CBI Theater before he joined our Hump operation, and he was very vague, only saying that he had been with a B-25 bomber unit. There were only a few B-25's in our theater, and the pilots were getting very little flying time, so Dick

175

requested a transfer to our Hump unit, where he did lots of flying.

After his first flight with me, one of the other pilots asked me how I liked my new copilot, and I replied that he was a nice guy and handled the airplane well, and should check out as a first pilot as soon as he learned the territory.

"Don't you know who this guy is?" asked my friend. "He was Jimmy Doolittle's copilot on the Tokyo raid!" I had no idea that I had a celebrity copilot, as Dick never uttered a word about it. We cornered him one day and asked for details of the raid, but he just brushed it off in a very modest way, saying it was quite an ordinary event.

It was far from ordinary as General Jimmy Doolittle relates in his book, "I Could Never Be So Lucky Again." Lieutenant Ted Lawson, pilot of airplane #7, told a gripping story in his book, "Thirty Seconds Over Tokyo," which became a famous movie. Lawson was badly injured when they ditched near the shore, and lost a leg as a result.

This famous raid was our first attempt to strike at the enemy's homeland, and news of it excited every American. Colonel Doolittle (later to become a three-star General) dropped four incendiary bombs on their targets, to light fires and show the way for the following airplanes, and then headed for the China mainland. They flew their B-25 in the most careful fuel-conserving way, but knew they would have to bail out as there was no way to find a landing field in the darkness. They were in the air for 13 hours, and covered over 2200 miles before their fuel gauges read zero. They bailed out just before the B-25 crashed, and luckily landed in good shape among friendly Chinese, who provided safe passage to an American base.

It was quite a remarkable adventure, and I am still mad at Dick for not telling us all about it at the time. He, and Lieutenant Jacob 'Shorty' Manch, so-called because he measured six feet-six inches tall, another Tokyo raid veteran, made many Hump flights, and returned to the States in our first group to return home. Although a celebrity, Dick was a very modest man.

The raid did very little physical damage to Japan, but was a splendid morale booster for our country, at a time when war news was all bad. It showed the enemy that we had teeth to fight with, and pressured the Japanese to rush into the Battle of Midway, which resulted in a devastating defeat to the Japanese fleet.

The Tokyo raid received tremendous publicity. A few weeks later, another spectacular raid took place in the war against Japan that received no publicity at all. This mission had a far greater tactical value than the Tokyo raid, but it was located in such an isolated part of China that it was unknown to the press.

This was the "Battle of the Salween Gorge," a bombing mission by eight Flying Tiger P- 40's. This daring raid closed the Burma Road at the Salween River, and actually saved the nation by preventing western China from falling into the hands of the Japanese. I have described it elsewhere as one of the most dramatic and spectacular missions in the entire war.

"SIX-GUN" TEX

Some of the buddies I flew with were unique characters. For example, there was "Tex." Every air force unit has a pilot named Tex. He wears cowboy boots, and tucks his pants legs into the tops of the boots for a casual effect, and swaggers a bit. He ignores the possibility that if he has to bailout and walk home, he won't find these boots very comfortable. Our guy was 'Tex' Weston, claiming Amarillo as his home. He looked like he belonged in a western setting, with his tall lanky build, sandy hair, and always squinting look. Congenial and smiling, he was a good friend and a fine pilot, but very annoying to everyone when he practiced quick-draw, by the hour, right in our bungalow. For this he borrowed my .45.

I was issued a monster .45 caliber revolver at Morrison Field before leaving the States. There was a shortage of .45 Colt semi-automatics in the early days of the war, so my only choice was a long barreled six-shooter revolver. It was so long and heavy that it almost hit the floor hanging in its holster from a web belt, and I felt like a little kid wearing an oversize toy gun. I took some kidding about that, and offset it by claiming that it was previously owned by General Custer, and had been lent to cowboy actor Tom Mix for some of his western movies. It was the most cumbersome gun for a pilot to wear, so I usually stashed it somewhere behind me in the radio compartment. The grip was really comfortable, but the gun was a big handful, and I only wore it when I felt I might need it as a defensive threat, or to hammer some nails.

Tex loved that revolver, and kept borrowing it from me for quick-draw practice, and eventually suggested making a swap with me. I jumped at the chance to get his standard semi-automatic, had a shoulder holster custom made for it, and was happy with the swap.

Tex was also happy, until one day, while twirling his big six-gun before shoving it back into the holster, he snagged the trigger and it fired. The bullet hit the floor about one inch from his beautiful boots, and scared the hell out of his roommates.

Just imagine a report that one of us was shot "not in the line of duty", but by a crazy Texan practicing quick draw!

We nearly lost our cooking help, as the bullet went through the floor into the kitchen under our living quarters, and scared our two houseboys. They thought the Japanese were attacking, and it took a lot of reassurance and a few rupees before they were willing to come back to the kitchen and cook those awful meals.

We ganged up on Tex and ordered him out of the bungalow; not just outside, but way away to do his thing, and warned him to unload the gun to avoid killing someone.

We were military men, but our familiarity with guns was pitiful. Airplane drivers, yes, soldiers, no. Some had experience handling guns, but many of our guys were former airline pilots, with no military training. Our only practice was in shooting our .45's at the ugly vultures that perched in trees near our bungalow, but we stopped that when someone pointed out that they served the important purpose of keeping the countryside clean of dead creatures.

Each airplane carried a Thompson sub-machine gun, and occasionally someone would take one out into the jungle and play the part of the great white hunter. I think the wild life laughed at us, because with a "Tommy" gun, you had to be almost on top of the target before you could hit it, so close that it might get you first. It was a difficult firearm to use, because as you fired it, the recoil forced the muzzle up high. Practice taught you to apply some pressure to hold it down on the target, but we saw little use for this weapon, which we considered useless as an airborne defensive weapon.

We heard stories of using the Thompson to ward off attacks by enemy airplanes, but I don't believe them. Our transports were unarmed, and we constantly complained about lack of an effective weapon, but I doubt if it would have been practical. We would be no match for a Zero fighter armed with heavy-caliber machine guns and cannon. We took the Thompsons out of the airplanes before they were stolen, and kept them by our bunks in our bungalows as defense against prowling enemies, two- or four-legged.

Our best defense against enemy fighters was to avoid them, by flying a northern curve across the Hump, towards the very high mountains. We much preferred the southerly route where the mountains were lower, but this took us close to Myitkyina, a Japanese fighter base in central Burma, so it was best to stay north. It was good policy to fly close to a bank of clouds, ready to dodge into the overcast and continue on instruments if we saw an unidentified airplane; a sort of peek- a-boo routine, one wing in the cloud, one wing in the clear.

JOE WALKER'S STORY

Joe Walker became a close friend, but I had trouble understanding his southern accent when we first met. Tall, light haired, slim, and a genial joker, he came from a town called Doileen, which was not on the map, about 100 miles from New Orleans. As a northerner, I had a problem with his southern drawl, which got worse when he got excited, when he tended to stutter. After a while, I could understand him better, for he either spoke with less of a drawl, or I got used to him, and we hit it off really well, often flying together.

On one very special day, I could hardly understand a word he said. It happened when we were both making return flights to Chabua, this time in clear weather for a change, with Joe about an hour ahead of me. When I got within 25 miles of the field and was able to raise the tower on the radio, they advised that it was "safe to come in now." This was a strange message, but it was explained when I landed and heard that an air raid had taken place an hour earlier.

As soon as I stepped down from my airplane, which I parked next to Joe's, he grabbed me and started in with an almost inarticulate, stuttering story. I slowed him down, and heard all about his adventure. As he was lining up on the runway to land, a group of six twin-engine Japanese "Betty" bombers appeared over the field coming from the opposite direction, at about 1000 feet, and started to drop sticks of bombs. Their bombardiers must have been in training, because they only landed a few bombs near any strategic places, and very little damage resulted.

Our ground personnel were in a panic, and all dove for the nearest slit trenches. They had no warning, as we had no radar or any other type of warning system, and the raiders came in unannounced. This was the first bombing raid that Chabua had experienced, and no one had a plan except to jump into a hole.

Joe was so intent on landing his airplane that he failed to see the invaders until he was almost on the ground. Suddenly he saw the bombers, and said the equivalent of "Holy Moley!" when he spotted the big red circles on their sides. In a state of near panic, he pulled up his gear and flaps, hit the throttles and swerved out of the way. His airplane was light, and this was his chance to fly like a fighter pilot. We sometimes pretended we were flying fighters, and cavorted as such, but he had no guns to shoot.

He really panicked when one of the enemy airplanes turned out of formation and lined up to fire on him. He could tell, because he suddenly heard some smacking, cracking noise in his airplane, and his flight engineer, standing in back of his seat, yelled out, "They're shooting at us!"

The 'Betty" was a faster airplane, and all Joe could do was take evasive action and run. He stayed right down on the deck, doing some fancy hedge-hopping, zigging and zagging and skidding with great energy, heading in a northerly direction. After about ten minutes, which seemed like ten hours, he realized that he was still alive, and ventured a turn, finding no strange airplanes in sight. In a few minutes the tower announced that the bombers were gone, and it "looks like it's okay to come home." Joe very warily made another approach, afraid that there might be another wave of bombers, but none showed.

I had missed all the excitement. Joe grabbed me, and spewed out all this information at a machine gun rate, stutter and all, and I could barely make out what he was saying. I kept saying "What? What?" and in disgust he marched me and a few other men over to the tail of his airplane, where, sure enough, we found rows of bullet holes stitched in his rudder.

That evening, we all debated whether he was saved by superb flying, poor gunners, or a low fuel supply in the bombers. Naturally, we gave Joe credit, happy that he made it, and that no one else was attacked, and we bought him some of our precious beer. Joe announced that he wanted to fight back, and was going to join a fighter outfit, but he soon got over that idea. The China Air Task Force was so short of P-40's that the fighter jocks were sitting around all day, hoping to get a few hours of flying every month. Our C-47's were flying all the time, and we were each logging almost 100 hours a month. Joe tried to borrow a 30 caliber machine gun, as I had tried to do in China a few months earlier, but we had no way to mount the weapon.

MAC, the LOVER

A lovely Chinese lady, Chin Wei, sat at a crowded table in the Pink Lotus restaurant in Kunming, one of the two approved eating places for our troops. Lieutenant Mac MacKay sat with friends at a nearby table, talking about things pilots usually talk about - airplanes and girls. - and recognized her as the interpreter at Operations. She was surrounded by some very attentive Chinese men, and Mac's friends dared him to approach her for a chat. Mac was always ready to tackle a dare, and to his surprise, he was introduced to her brothers and other members of her family, and invited to join them.

So began an east-west romance. On every trip across the Hump, Mac hustled off to spend his nights with Chin Wei, who lived with her grandmother, and had more liberal ideas about her life style than most Chinese women her age. Mac claimed that her name, Chin Wei, translated into 'Adorable Flower,' and he became so serious about his affair that his buddies avoided the usual crude kidding that accompanies a casual romance. Chin Wei's English was impeccable, and her brothers spoke it fairly well, as their father had been a school teacher in Canton and taught the entire family.

The Japanese invasion of key Chinese cities had placed all educators and their families at high risk, so the family had purchased two trucks and made the dangerous 1000-mile pilgrimage to Kunming, which was the most westernized city in western China. Mac told us of some of the adventures that Chin Wei and her family met, such as shortages of fuel requiring them to convert to kerosene. Bandits were everywhere, so they traveled in armed convoys. Kunming was a safe city, but when they ran low on funds, their only source of income was Chin Wei's salary and a hauling business using their trucks.

That was when Mac got into the picture, giving him an opportunity to ingratiate himself with the family. Parts for the trucks were hard to find, and tires were totally unavailable, putting the trucks out of commission. Mac volunteered to locate tires in India, and on his next trip to Calcutta purchased a set of four for which he paid double, loaded them on his airplane and flew them to Assam. On his next trip, he hauled them over the Hump, and at Kunming borrowed a jeep to transport them downtown. The delivery was cut short when military police at the airport gate, alert to the widespread thievery of the precious supplies we carried over the Hump at great risk, challenged his ownership.

Mac could prove he owned the tires, but he was violating regulations. He was charged with using military transport for private business, breaking some international rules, and other official misdeeds. We kidded him a lot, telling him he was the victim of some eager military lawyers in New Delhi who had too much time on their hands and no one to practice on. But he wasn't a very happy guy when they temporarily confiscated his tires and court-martialed him for what we would call smuggling. Mac was allowed to deliver the tires because we needed trucks in Kunming, but he was punished with probation for a year, time to be served in India. During that time he flew an additional 40 Hump trips, and came very close to marrying Chin Wei, with her approving family cheering him on.

A year later, Mac turned up as one of our instructors at Reno Air Force Base, and we congratulated him on surviving the extra time on the Hump. We held a pilots' meeting where Mac brought us up to date about the quality of newly arriving pilots in India, to improve our training program Then we got personal.

"Mac, where's the blushing bride?"

"No, I didn't marry Chin Wei," he admitted abashedly, "That regulation against military personnel marrying foreign nationals is strictly enforced. It kinda broke my heart to leave her there. But we had some good times together."

Mac was somewhat moody when he talked about his lost love. He said that he had promised her he would return to China. As time went on, we noticed that Mac was paying close attention to the local girls, and soon acquired a girl friend, named Erica, a blond, Nordic type, whose looks contrasted sharply with his former Oriental beauty. We doubted that he would return to Kunming.

About flying, he said. "My extra year on the Hump wasn't much fun, but I got the DFC (Distinguished Flying Cross) and Air Medal with lots of clusters, and made captain. " He added, "I sure learned my lesson about smuggling, saved money very carefully, and now I have a good bank account. "

"From savings?" we asked. "Mostly," he replied.

THE PRESS

In 1941 and 42, the news media sent many reporters to China when they realized that Flying Tiger victories made exciting and heroic news. I often had newsmen on board when I flew for Chennault. Readers Digest portrayed the General as a world-class military leader and an air ace, and other media sought interviews and photos. He usually refused further publicity, either from a sense of modesty or, perhaps, the awareness that too much of this would inflame his superiors back at the Pentagon and at New Delhi, the very people we relied on to keep our supply lines open.

When I returned to flying the Hump in September, I carried several newsmen across to Kunming, and when they heard that I had flown for Chennault, they always asked for the "inside story on the Flying Tigers." One of my passengers was Richard Tregaskis, who later became quite famous as a foreign correspondent. He asked me many questions about the Tigers, as they were still a number one topic of interest to the public.

I had many stories to tell but was reluctant to say much. We had been told that any information about combat operations and about the Hump airlift was restricted. Much to my surprise, I found out that newspaper articles about our operation were published as early as August, 1942, in the "Herald" of Chungking, China. Another army paper, the "C.B.I. Roundup," published in New Delhi, wrote about our mission in their September, 1942, issue. Numerous Stateside papers were full of supposedly classified information. So much for security in the CBI Theater.

Tregaskis was eager for details on how we lived, our health, food, as well as information about military operations. I doubted the newsworthiness of the small details, but he reassured me of their importance. He said, "everything that goes on here is news back home, and they are hungry for it. "

"For example," he asked, "what is the 'Burma Roadster' organization?"

"Nothing but a bunch of guys who collect autographs of everyone they fly with. We paste rupee paper money and CN (Chinese currency) together into strips several feet long, loaded with hundreds of signatures. That's one of our souvenirs." And I slid mine out of my back pocket, and had him duly add his signature to it.

"But I have another story you ought to write about," I said, and fumbled in my pocket for the unique ribbon someone had dreamed up to celebrate a very special condition.

"This is the Crud Ribbon," I explained. "It celebrates the dysentery that every one of us gets at some time, and is made up of a dark brown ribbon with a red streak running through it. If you don't become a victim, you'll miss the fun of wearing one."

Tregaskis laughed. "I've been here six weeks, and I'm already qualified to wear one."

He took time later at the Kunming hostel where we stayed overnight, to tell us about conditions in the states, assuring us that no one was out of work, or going hungry. It was very reassuring to hear from this highly articulate reporter that things were under control at home, and that the home folks appreciated what we were doing.

My next meeting with Richard Tregaskis was in Boston, on Memorial Day of 1943, when we each gave a speech at the Boston Common, talking about the China-Burma-India Theater. He led a very adventurous life as a war correspondent, and claimed that the CBI was the most hazardous place of all.

Another famous newsman was Eric Sevareid , who rode the Hump and had the good luck to survive bailing out of a disabled C-46 with 20 other passengers. He wrote very eloquently of his adventure.

CAPTAIN JOHNNY PAYNE

I have to mention one of the most colorful and favorite guys in our group, Captain Johnny Payne. Johnny started flying as a kid in the barnstorming days, and his early years of struggling as a freelance pilot paid off when he obtained a steady job with Eastern Airlines. He is a good-natured big guy with a loud, outspoken manner, but he was a man who "put his money where his mouth was." He made a big fuss about being "Shanghaied" out of his airline job by the Air Corps, but he loved adventure, and changed his tune when he discovered that our mission would take us to strange, new places. His flying experience was invaluable, and we new army pilots held him somewhat in awe.

He took every copilot who flew with him under his personal wing, and taught them as much about piloting as they could absorb in the short time they flew with him.

Johnny was a volunteer with unlimited energy, always ready to tackle a new challenge. He went on the earliest rice drops, took his C-47 in and out of fields that we would bet were too small, and set the pace for others to follow. He is credited with making the first night flight over the Hump in late August, 1942, against the advice of other pilots who pointed out that the Kunming radio homing beacon had a range of less than 50 miles. He jokingly said, "Destiny will guide me."

His open manner endeared him to everyone, regardless of rank, and when he dared to land his C-47 on the polo field of the Maharajah of Cooch-Behar, he charmed that royal person, who lengthened the field to make landings easier. The Maharajah extended his hospitality to anyone who needed an overnight stop in central India, and sometimes there were several C-47's parked on the tiny field that had been home to polo ponies. Johnny became a good-will ambassador, who smoothed the way for good relationships with many an Indian VIP who had regarded Americans as noisy nuisances. A group of us probably owe him our lives, as you will see in the chapter on "Going Home." Johnny returned to Eastern Airlines after the war, retired as a senior pilot at the mandatory retirement age of 60, and spent his life deeply involved in his first love, flying.

"FALL GUY" FLEMING

Fleming was a warm, caring guy, one of the original AMMISCA group. He was an 'older man', in his mid 30's, and married with two children. And he was a very skillful but scared pilot. On his third trip across the Hump he encountered extreme turbulence, icing, periodic engine failure, and was so close to total disaster that he was convinced he would never see his family again.

He made it back, a shaken man, and was found unfit to continue flying duty. We all liked Fleming, and sympathized with his fear, which we considered acceptable for an older fellow, while most of us were cocky as hell, being ten years younger.

Fleming took over the job of operations officer, which was almost as stressful as flying.

I learned for myself just how bad it was when I took my turn as Operations Officer of the Day. I found that sweating out the return of our airplanes was just as wearing a job as flying one.

Some of our pilots became resentful of Fleming's non-flying status, however, because flying the Hump was where the real danger lay, and we were losing airplanes every week. He became the butt of some practical jokes, like telling him that new orders were placing him back on flying status, and I am sure that it hurt him greatly to be singled out. It would have been best to transfer him to another outfit, but this did not happen, as his experience was too valuable to give up.

One joke had him very upset, when someone connected up a microphone to our house radio that received news broadcasts. The Japanese had been reported cutting through the jungles near the Indian city of Imphal, and moving towards Assam. We were put on alert, ready to move out on short notice.

Fleming was in our group one evening, listening to the news, when we heard a 'flash' announcement:

"The Japanese have broken through the British lines and are moving into the Assam Valley. An evacuation order is being issued for the Chabua area!"

All of us except Fleming knew that this was a fake announcement, with one of our pilots sitting in the next room feeding in some very scary stories about airfields being overrun, airplanes caught on the ground, and personnel captured. Fleming dashed around, grabbing his personal effects, a Tommy gun, and screaming at us, to "Get going! The Japs are just a few miles away!"

We all pooh-poohed this, saying we had plenty of time, with nothing to worry about, while Fleming became greatly agitated trying to get us to dash to the field and take off When it looked like he was about to collapse from anxiety, we confessed to the dirty deed. I don't think Fleming ever forgave us for that episode.

It turned out that our fake broadcast almost came true, when the Japanese came within 35 miles of Assam before being driven back by hard-fighting British and Indian troops.

HAULING ASS

The expression to "Haul ass" means to get moving in a hurry, as if the devil is breathing down your neck with a pitchfork ready to prod you in a tender spot. But pilot Captain Matt Bogin ran into a different meaning when he was given the unusual and messy job of flying some mules into Fort Hertz early in 1943. These were pack mules, which our newly formed rescue units were using to carry medical supplies into the mountains on rescue missions, and carry out injured airmen who were unable to walk.

A report of a new crash site spotted from the air would alert the rescue units to determine if it was accessible on foot. Sometimes a native tribesman would bring word, anxious to get the reward for bringing the news, and a more lavish reward if he helped to rescue the crash victims. Para rescue teams made preparations for a rescue jump if they saw signs of injured personnel who might need immediate care.

We could save days on a rescue mission if we flew the mules to the field closest to the crash, and Bogin had the job that day of bringing three reluctant animals over the Naga Hills to Fort Hertz. He knew they would be frightened by the flying, but the native mule wallahs (handlers) assured him they were well-behaved, and would be carefully tied to prevent damage. What they did not anticipate was that one would go berserk, break his ties, and endanger everyone on board

The animals were docile enough when led up the special mule-loading ramp. Shortly after take-off things went out of control when one of them reared up wildly, broke his ties, knocked over the handlers, and plunged against the wall of the airplane. He frantically moved back and forth changing the airplane trim constantly. Bogin sent his copilot back to investigate and received the panic-stricken report that "the mule is going crazy back there, and we'll have to shoot it!"

"No guns!, yelled Bogin, who knew that a shot fired inside the airplane could do serious damage to someone or something. "Tell them to sit on it, or rope it down," he said, remembering roping contests he had seen at rodeos in his hometown of Amarillo. "Hell, I could do it myself, but I better stay here and fly the airplane," said the would-be cowboy. Meanwhile, the mule was running amok, and the handlers huddled fearfully behind cases of cargo.

Fortunately, the mule could not reach the cockpit door, as there were cases of supplies piled up in the forward part of the cabin. This gave the mule only limited space to move in, and someone got the bright idea of unfastening the cargo cases and gradually pushing them back, closer and closer to the mule until he was boxed in. Perhaps he saw the end coming, as he quieted down when he had no space to move, and stayed in that position until Bogin landed the airplane.

We praised Bogin for being an outstanding mule chauffeur, and suggested he become exclusive pilot for VIA (Very Important Animals). He declined the offer, saying he would rather carry drums of high-octane aviation gas, which he felt was safer than an explosive mule.

* * * * * *

Every pilot in our bungalow had stories to tell of his miraculous escapes from crashes, and all eventually came to believe that "I'm lucky to be here." We let off steam by making jokes out of some of the terrors we faced, to relieve the tension and try to put aside our grief over the loss of comrades.

One of our jokes was the "Pucker Factor," a name someone invented for a condition that occurs when the lower sphincter responds to a panic situation by tightening up. When your airplane is on the brink of destruction, and you are one step from doom, the extent of your panic can be measured by the length of time the pucker lasts.

This is a common condition that can happen to anyone, as for example, when your automobile hits a sudden dip in the road. In military flying, it can happen often, and last a long time, with some pilots claiming they have a permanent pucker. Flying the Hump offered enough exciting moments to really strengthen the sphincter muscles.

Other physical responses occur in an emergency. The heart may palpitate, the stomach convulse, or sweat break out, all happening when an engine sputters, or when an oil pressure gauge makes a sudden drop, or when the artificial horizon instrument tumbles over like a dead tree. The public regards a pilot as an unflappable person with steel nerves, but this is not really true. Most are just ordinary folks, subject to panicky reactions when things go drastically wrong. For this reason, pilot training concentrates on teaching emergency procedures to overcome much of the fear and prevent panic.

Airline pilots claim that their flying is 98 boredom and 2 panic, at which point they start earning their pay. On the Hump, percentages were drastically different; with 25 percent panic, and the rest of the time careful watchfulness. I don't recall ever being bored, but sometimes I dozed, with one eye open.

I was lucky that my Pratt and Whitney engines performed faithfully for me, hardly ever skipping a beat, and the Douglas C-47 airplanes never failed me. Some of the older ones creaked and groaned and sounded like they were ready to come apart, especially when flying through violent turbulence, but they held together. There were many scary moments when my pucker factor hit a high.

Some of my friends related high points in the air that gave them thrills. One told of the time he took off with his external rudder lock still in place, making his rudder useless and limiting his ability to turn the airplane. He knew that airplanes have crashed because of this forgetfulness, so he very carefully flew a wide circle, using only ailerons for very gradual turn control, and brought his airplane in for a safe landing.

That was a minor incident compared to Rivoli and his crew bailing out of an iced-up airplane that was going down in bad weather. Their adventures could have filled a book, as they related how they rounded up the spread-out crew, debated the next move, and spent a month walking out of the mountains with the help of friendly natives. But it was that first step out the door, and pulling the ripcord, that gave them the most scary moments in their lives, and a very tight pucker.

Owens' story was a winner, telling how he rode his airplane down after an engine failed, expecting to crash into a mountainside at any moment. He ordered his two crew members to bailout, but could not leave the plane himself as he carried 40 Chinese soldiers. Pucker factor was 100 while letting down lost and blind in a solid overcast. He had an incredible stroke of good luck, when he broke out of the overcast right over the Assam Valley, with the field in sight. He mourned the loss of his crew, thinking he had caused their deaths, until they came walking in weeks later.

These are just a few of the scary stories, related by survivors. There are many more that will never be told.

CROSS AT THE RED CROSS

Our China Air Task Force combat units needed gasoline more than anything else to maintain their offensive, but were handicapped by severe winter weather that cut Hump tonnage way down. This very precious commodity was carried at high risk in a C-47 in thirteen 55-gallon drums. Wasting it was a cardinal sin, and Hump pilots became very incensed when word got out that the two Red Cross female employees stationed in Kunming each had a Chevrolet sedan to help them spread their good works. There was an acute shortage of American females, and it was hinted that the good works they performed were mostly for the benefit of ranking officers and highly placed government officials of various nations. Did we believe that? You bet we did. Jealous? Yep.

An informal pilots meeting took place in Chabua, and we told our commanding officer that we were not interested in flying gas over the Hump for these two ladies, and would be very unhappy if this was allowed to continue. Military pilots do not go on strike, but we talked about injury to our morale, and our strong resentment at this situation. Our group spoke up loud and clear, and Kunming brass got the message and deprived the ladies of their vehicles, making us happy. I doubt if they missed them as their popularity depended on much more than the cars they drove. Just being a Caucasian woman in Kunming was enough to insure great demand.

In later years, a woman friend who had served as a nurse in the Pacific theater told me how popular the women were, of the wonderful life they led at major bases, and how some had returned home with considerable wealth amassed by their friendly actions and kind words.

MORE DANGEROUS THAN FLYING

Flight crews often joked that riding on the ground was more dangerous than flying.

In January, several of our men were severely injured when a British army truck they were riding in rolled over near Allahabad, with two men not expected to survive.

At chow, everyone chimed in tell his story of bad driving by hired drivers. The finger pointed to local drivers trying to show off to the Americans by fast and reckless driving. The danger was made worse by poorly maintained vehicles, overloaded and top-heavy with too many people packed in. The roads were unsafe, and no one observed common sense rules, relying instead on the horn to clear the way. Heaven help the pedestrians!

After a number of accidents, the army changed to military drivers and things improved. Jeeps were still considered almost as dangerous as a fighter airplane, as they had a tendency to roll over, often on top of the passengers, with fatal results. Pilots were often to blame for jeep accidents as they considered themselves superior drivers in any vehicle.

I told of a transportation officer in Seattle, who refused to let pilots drive a command car to Boeing Aircraft. We were very exasperated by his attitude. We must be reliable drivers; we were flying large, valuable B-17 heavy bombers on deliveries across the country. He still insisted we use an official driver. Maybe he was smarter than us.

PURPLE HEART?

Driving was dangerous, but sometimes a latrine could be worse. Some latrines had been refined and now had private booths, where one could sit with a quiet air of dignity, enjoy a smoke, read the paper, or just meditate. Lieutenant Hunter was making his usual morning call, lit his cigarette, and dropped the lighted match down the hole.

Surprise! The resultant explosion singed his eyebrows and other parts, and gave him the impression that he was in Dante's Inferno. It seems that the sanitary engineers had mixed some gasoline with the oil they normally poured in for hygienic purposes. Hunter was okay, and the "No Smoking" warning went up.

Chapter 26
RANK HAS ITS PRIVILEGES (RHIP)
SO, WHO'S THE ENEMY?

"Captain, I understand you're giving us a hard time. I want you to get your butt into your airplane and get it out of here." So said Lieutenant Colonel B. at New Delhi when he strode into airport Operations and gave me a hard look.

I was a lowly captain, near the bottom of the pecking order, but 1 was pretty cocky and ready to argue. I had flown for Chennault in China, crossed the Hump many times, and knew my place in the sun. Some of the independent attitude of the Flying Tigers must have rubbed off on me, and I was not ready to give up. I was about to get into deep trouble.

I thought I had a good reason. For months we had been sending requisitions to the depot at New Delhi begging for critical supplies, and in February, 1943, they finally notified us that there was a load ready to go. It was my turn to take a trip to the west, and I happily flew my C-47 to New Delhi to pick up these vitally needed supplies. My commanding officer at Chabua, Major Vinton Broidy, cautioned me to be sure to bring back the critical items on our list: oxygen tanks for high altitude flying, parachutes, and flight instruments such as compasses and directional gyros. I knew how desperately we needed these items, especially oxygen tanks, as I had been flying across the Hump at 16,000 to 18,000 feet, and had run out of 02 on several occasions, into life-threatening situations.

I walked into New Delhi Operations bright and early, eager to get that precious load on its way, and the operations clerk notified me that my airplane was loaded and ready to go. I very optimistically asked him where I might find the warehouses, as I carried with me an additional list of supplies that my CO asked me to locate - food for the commissary, mechanics' tools, and other short items. I was rewarded with a blank look and quickly learned that red tape had taken over. I needed special permission to just visit these facilities, with no chance of obtaining these items without more paperwork.

Then the clerk spoke up, "Sir, your takeoff time is scheduled for 8:00 A.M., and it's past that now." That left me no time left for scouting around for more supplies.

So much for that. I climbed aboard my airplane to inspect the load, expecting to find a treasure trove of supplies, and was shocked at what I found. There was absolutely nothing on board that matched our requisitions. There was not a single thing that related to flying an airplane. I was incredulous at finding a load consisting of desks, chairs, typewriters, and some boxes of uniforms, all totally useless to our Hump operation. This meant that our trip was a total failure, which I considered a disaster.

I charged back into operations, furious at the mistake. "What in the hell are your people trying to do?" I raged, although I was perfectly aware that the clerk had nothing to do with the problem. "I need airplane supplies and I'm not leaving with that load of junk!" He scurried into the back office for some help, and the lieutenant colonel then showed up and said his piece. This officer was a stout, red-faced man, who looked like he wasn't able to cope with the heat very well. I noticed he wasn't wearing wings, which meant he was a non-flying officer, so I toned down, and said, "Sir, I would like to see the Operations officer." I knew a flying officer would understand my predicament. But Colonel B. announced very curtly, "I'm in charge here, and you'll follow my orders!"

I was on shaky ground now. How does a captain argue with an officer who is two grades higher? Very carefully might be the answer. But I was feeling pretty stubborn that day, ready for an argument, because from the moment I landed at New Delhi, things had not gone well.

The trip started out well. We considered a run to New Delhi or Calcutta a vacation compared to the dangerous Hump trips. There were no mountains to worry about and we relaxed at 8000 feet where temperatures were refreshingly cool. Sometimes, we stopped overnight at Cooch Behar as guests of the Maharajah, or at the delightful city of Agra, site of the Taj Mahal, which made the trip even more attractive.

New Delhi was the headquarters for the China-Burma-India Theater, and on my first visit in June of 1942 I had discovered an amazingly beautiful city. The British built it as their capital in India, and called it their "Jewel of the Empire." So it looked, for its magnificent modern buildings, wide boulevards, and parks gave it a dream-like quality that was totally unexpected in the central Indian desert of sandy, barren lands.

We stayed at the excellent Imperial hotel, with clean sheets and immaculate service, and a good restaurant. There was an Officer's Club where one might meet some lovely women, something not available in Assam. Just a whiff of a woman's perfume was enough to remind us that there was another life besides our normal one.

Headquarters offices were air-conditioned with large evaporative coolers, which felt great when I showed up with grime and sweat on my unlaundered clothes. We envied the personnel stationed in the luxury of New Delhi, in contrast to the primitive conditions in Assam, where we lived in miserable quarters and faced serious hardship. We privately ridiculed the spit-and-polish at headquarters, with its concern about proper uniforms and military formalities, compared to our Assam life style, but we were happy to dig in and briefly enjoy the luxury. New Delhi was not yet crowded with high-ranking brass who were to follow shortly, so in June it was a good place to remain overnight.

We even found some humor in those early days, when we invited HQ staff people to come to the Assam Valley and visit us in our "rustic jungle paradise." We had no takers who were willing to give up the good life. They were all wised up and knew we were offering them an assortment of snakes, malaria, bad food, and slit trenches. We put pressure on the junior officers to help us find supplies, with the threat that we would make "an official request that you make an inspection tour of our bases at Assam," if we did not get results. This was an incentive for them to double their efforts to help us, since they were not very thrilled about leaving New Delhi to visit Assam. Yes, headquarters was a great place to be stationed and to visit, but the old adage says, "All is not gold that glitters," as I found on this later trip.

On arrival in February, I discovered that vast changes had taken place in New Delhi. I asked the driver to take us to the Imperial Hotel, and he laughed. "Sir, that hotel has been taken over by the generals, and we have strict instructions not to drop off transient officers there." "What's the next best?" The reply was most discouraging. "All the decent hotels are packed. Operations instructed me to take you to the VOQ (Visiting Officers Quarters), and you'll be lucky to find a room there." He was right. The city had been taken over by brass from many Allied nations, and space was critical. My co-pilot and I shared a room with two other transient officers, who also bitched about the crowding,

But that wasn't all. We cleaned up a bit and then piled into a cab looking for a good restaurant. This was a waste of time, for everywhere we looked, they were overcrowded, with long waiting lines. Our appearance did not help, as two grimy pilots did not make a very good appearance in contrast to high-ranking officers of all the Allied armies, dressed in immaculate uniforms with brightly polished insignia, often in the company of lovely Eurasian ladies. We sadly ended up eating poor food in the Officers Mess. A later visit to the Officers Club was no better as it was a noisy mob scene. After a beer, I gave in to fatigue and retreated to my crowded room. New Delhi had changed drastically since my visit there five months earlier.

The next morning, it became apparent that the attitude of some of its people had also changed, even more drastically. Lieutenant Colonel B. evidently had no idea of our requirements at Chabua, but worst of all, he didn't care! He was making my life miserable and I was determined to get my point across. I declared in a very positive way, "We need parts for airplanes, and you've loaded me with office supplies. We don't even have offices to put this stuff in! This junk is absolutely useless to us!"

"Captain, I have cargo to ship, and your job is to haul it. You have no time to waste. Your airplane is ready, so get going. That's an order!" He was really pulling rank, regardless of my appeal to reason.

I was hot under the collar. This trip was a foul-up of the worst kind. I was supposed to bring back a load of desperately needed life-support gear, and this son-of-a-bitch didn't care a bit that I was loaded with useless office supplies. I was furious at the supply people and even more furious at his attitude. I replied with the only fallback I had. "I have my orders to bring back certain vital supplies. My airplane may be ready, but I'm not!"

Now I was on the hot seat and that well-known stuff was about to hit the fan. I was disobeying a direct order, and this light-colonel was not going to give an inch. He was acting as though his career was at stake, and apparently thought it was more important to get another load off the runway than to fill an acute tactical need.

He bluntly stated, "I don't give a damn about your orders from somebody 1200 miles away. And I don't intend to give you one minute to look for supplies. That's not my problem. You get your ass in that airplane and leave, right now!" I could see this officer really didn't understand what we were doing in India, and was not the slightest bit concerned about our mission. I wondered why a non-flying officer was allowed to run flight operations.

I could see myself arriving at Chabua with a cargo of useless office supplies, and I had difficulty restraining my language. I expressed myself in vivid terms, something like this: "Sir, if you were flying the Hump with me, and we were about to crash because our oxygen ran out, would you be happy to know that your family would receive a nicely typed letter about your death. WE DON'T NEED DESKS AND TYPEWRITERS. WE NEED OXYGEN TANKS AND PARTS TO KEEP OUR AIRPLANES RUNNING, AND I AM HERE TO FIND THEM!" The words were not out of line, but my attitude certainly was, as I guess I raised my voice more than a little bit. I was having difficulty restraining myself. It was approaching a case of insubordination.

The colonel turned beet-red, and stomped back into his office. It was a stalemate, and I fussed and fumed and wondered what to do next. I knew how to cope with monsoon weather and severe turbulence, but dealing with this colonel and his blind stupidity was beyond my experience.

I had logged dozens of Hump trips, and faced my doom more than once. After those experiences, you cross a threshold and take on a mindset where you aren't afraid of anyone, regardless of rank. But I had not developed the diplomatic skill to handle the situation, and I sensed that if I complained any louder, it would only bring the roof down on me, and make things worse. An inner voice said to me, "this chicken-shit s-o-b knows there is a war on, and doesn't care. He isn't responsible for selecting the load on my airplane, but he is totally ignoring our urgent needs. His job to move cargo takes priority over everything else, and he hasn't got the sense to help me correct the mistake." I hoped that he would get the word from some higher-up and allow me time to do my job.

Not a chance! The outcome? A captain entered operations soon after and told me that since I had refused to take off, he had been assigned to fly my airplane to Chabua, and I could fly as his copilot and show him the way, or deadhead as a passenger. "You'd better come along," he suggested, "because Colonel B. plans to declare you AWOL (Absent Without Leave) from your outfit if that airplane leaves without you. "

That threat was just hot air, but it would be foolish for me to strand myself in New Delhi, as the airplane was returning to Assam, and I had no other way to get there. I was so angry that I told the captain to find his own way, as I preferred to ride as passenger. I had lost that battle and was now dead-heading back to Chabua in my own airplane, cussing out paper-pushers who fought the war from New Delhi. There had to be a better way to do things.

The return trip had its problems. The replacement pilot, Captain Al Pelham, had never been to the Assam area and got lost returning there just at dusk. He asked me politely to join him in the cockpit, and show him the way home. I had cooled off quite a bit, so I helped out. On my arrival, I let our CO know about my load, and he joined me in cussing out HQ personnel, again using our favorite expression, "Don't they know there's a war on? I'll bet those desks are consigned to China." Sure enough they were, probably because some clerk was just following the army regulation that provided a desk for each office in China. Of course, they never got there, as we had more important things to haul. They sat outdoors at Chabua until the natives carried them off or the climate got them. Captain

Pelham joined our Hump group shortly afterward and occasionally kidded me about the famous battle of New Delhi.

This incident in New Delhi gave me many things to think about. For one, my interest in a permanent military career went into a tailspin when I realized that I might someday be assigned to a unit commanded by someone like Colonel B. My attitude was like that of the Flying Tiger pilots who stated, months ago, that if the army was stupid enough to send a General Bissell to threaten them into joining up, they wanted no part of it. I gave Colonel B. a life-and-death problem, but instead of supporting our mission, he chose to follow routine, thereby ignoring our needs. The military gives its men no choice but to obey commands, but how smart is the commander? Is he a capable officer who will see the overall picture, or will he stubbornly insist on following procedure? There are many instances of stupid decisions that have placed men in harm's way and cost lives.

Fortunately, Colonel B. was an exception. There were very few like him, and the rumor mill usually had them sorted out, so they could be avoided. This experience gave me a greater appreciation for the officers I met who set aside the red tape and concentrated on the mission. I had learned from the American Volunteer Group how some impossible jobs get done when everyone works together and ignores the rules.

General "Hap" Arnold, commanding general of the U.S. Army Forces, made a very powerful statement about this problem when he openly announced his appreciation of subordinates who were fighters. He praised officers who "did not concentrate on the paperwork, that some officers confuse with winning a campaign." Hurray for "Hap!"

Another lesson I learned is that without rank it is hard to get things done, unless you can get the ear of the top commander. Months of flying for General Chennault showed me that a good leader is hungry for information and welcomes input from all ranks. I am sure that someone higher up would have countermanded the colonel's order and made every effort to help us, if I had been able to reach that person.

This brings up a major problem, in that the military considers it bad policy to go over the head of your immediate superior. I had no one to contact, and had to accept the situation that day. But in the back of my mind I had a strong sense of resentment that one man, or a supply officer, could be totally indifferent to our needs and cause so much of a problem. I talked it over with some other pilots at Chabua, and some of our older, wiser men agreed that we had to reach top level .

people to get results. The best way to do that was to talk to any colonel or general within reach, when we had the opportunity. We had the opportunity to do this in a perfectly acceptable way.

I discovered that the cockpit of an airplane was probably the best place for us to connect with high-ranking officers who are not usually within reach. In late February, a Colonel Gabler, head of Service and Supply, was a passenger of mine across the Hump. When I heard the key word, 'Supply", I invited this non-flying officer into the cockpit to fly our C-47 in clear weather. He was thrilled to sit at the wheel, actually flying a cargo airplane across the Hump, and have something to write home about. He was not so thrilled when I informed him that at this point over the Himalayas we were entirely out of touch with either terminal, as our airborne radios were not powerful enough to reach either Chabua or Kunming. "It gets kind of lonesome up here, Colonel, knowing we are beyond radio range. We sure do need more powerful radios." The Colonel was quite startled, and very impressed, and said he would do what he could about that situation. I never knew if he was able to help, but the idea of reaching out to high rank had taken form in my mind.

I started to look over my passengers in person, for in those days we had no printed passenger manifests. If one looked important I would invite him to come forward and take the wheel. Once in the cockpit, he became somewhat of a captive audience, and I could bend his ear without interruption. It did not take much to put a point across when, on a clear day, he was sucking oxygen out of a mask, looking out at an awesome and never-ending panorama of snow-capped mountains, and listening to me point out the hazards of the Hump route. I probably scared the hell out of some of the more faint- hearted. I might say something like, "Sir, we are having a very tough time getting replacement compasses. If this one quit we'd be in deep trouble, and it does happen." This kind of a comment caught their attention immediately, for at that moment their personal safety was at risk. Sometimes we got results quickly.

In December I met Colonel (later General) Ed Alexander, a flying officer, and now the commanding officer of our newly formed Air Transport Command (ATC) unit which was now in charge of the Hump operation,. I was checking in at Chabua operations having just returned from Kunming, and Alexander was heading east, over the Hump, and asked me for information about the weather. I filled him in on the details, and saw that this was a golden opportunity to speak up about another matter.

"Colonel, four men bailed out over the Hump last week, and they were terribly scared their chutes wouldn't open. We wonder why there's such an acute shortage of new parachutes." He said he had been hearing about these problems, and turned to ask the operations officer about this. He learned that there were no spare chutes available anywhere in the theater. This was a very concerned commander and a man of action, and within 24 hours there was a special flight rushing loads of chutes from Florida to the CBI. Shortly after, Alexander established the "Cannonball Express," which left Florida for Assam on a weekly flight, with four-engine C-54 cargo planes carrying vitally needed emergency items. These flights stopped only for fuel and crew changes, making the trip in four days.

In those early days of '42 and '43, the closer we got to the Hump, the less officious our superior officers were. They flew the Hump themselves and were totally aware of the dangers we faced. As a lowly second lieutenant pilot, I had flown several Hump trips with majors and colonels as my copilot, and was always treated as an equal. The pilot in command wears the badge of authority regardless of his rank, and I felt that I was on a par with these officers who outranked me. We might join later for dinner at the hostel in Kunming, and there would be an easy familiarity, with me asking how they "enjoyed" the flight, and some thanking me for a safe and educational trip. No one ever pulled rank, and while in flight they acknowledged my experience and would often say, "You're the boss, tell me what to do."

PROFESSIONAL SOLDIERS NEEDED

Flying Cadet training in 1942 aimed at producing good pilots, but offered cadets little background information about military organization. I had little idea of how the regular army functioned, nor how the reserve related to it. In my ignorance, all military was the same, and it was some time before I learned details about the permanent army, and about career officers who were the backbone of the armed forces, although they were largely unknown and ignored by the public in peacetime.

I learned that it took professional soldiers to run a war. Members of the regular army were our guides and mentors, with lieutenants and captains running our training schools, majors and colonels organizing our tactical units, and top brass master-minding our campaigns. I was awed at the fund of knowledge possessed by this cadre of officers, who had been highly trained, and whose entire lives were devoted to the military, of which I knew so very little.

Some regular army were young pilots who had been stuck with frustrating desk jobs in peacetime, barely able to get their minimum four hours of flying time per month to maintain their pilot ratings, while their senior officers hogged the available airplanes. Now they were moving out from behind the desks into work for which they were trained, and had plenty of flying time available, while some of the older officers were glad to do just the opposite, and take up administrative posts.

We were lucky to have such brilliant officers as George Marshall, Douglas MacArthur, "Hap" Arnold, and others like them who showed their talent in organizing and expanding the armed forces. They were the most qualified ones to run our worldwide military operations, and all were quickly boosted to rank of general. Most had attended West Point, where leaders of the future received the best military training in the world. The general public knew little about our military academies, and was quite happy to ignore the possibility of future wars, but the training went on, planning for coming events.

Graduates of the Point, wearers of the Academy ring, made up a strong fraternity, and often gave well-deserved priority to other alumni in selection of posts and making decisions. Unfortunately, this created an undercurrent of resentment among reserve officers like myself, who sometimes felt like second-class citizens. When things went wrong, a reserve officer, whose temporary commission was "for the duration, only," might be heard sarcastically blaming the West Pointers, because they were the smart professionals. Reservists jokingly referred to them as graduates of "Hudson High," and as members of the "WPPA" (West Point Protective Association), claiming they were an elite group that closed ranks, excluding outsiders. Career officers were often targets for criticism, and some of the top brass frankly admitted that there was a tendency to teach them what to think, rather than how to think. But there was no question about it: professional soldiers were the backbone of our military, and we were helpless without them.

Most reserve officers lacked the specialized training that was required for top command positions, but some did rise to the rank of Brigadier general. Jimmy Doolittle was the outstanding example who became the highest ranking reserve officer during World War II. He achieved the three-star rank of lieutenant general, as commander of the giant Eighth Air Force in Europe.

Doolittle had a unique background. Before the war he was a reserve officer, who enjoyed a career as a free-lance pilot working for oil companies, setting speed records, and participating in air races, winning many trophies. He recalled in his wonderfully written memoirs that early in the war, General Eisenhower and other top brass considered him undisciplined and poorly qualified, with his only command experience being leader of the Tokyo raiders in 1942. He learned rapidly, and his ability carried him to top rank. His memoirs show an interesting change in his outlook about the military. He applauded the discipline that one of his sons was facing as a plebe (first year) at West Point, and insisted that one had to learn to take orders before he was qualified to give them. That was a big reversal for this former free spirit, who went his own way, and often challenged authority.

Many World War II pilots hoped to obtain permanent commissions and make a career in the military. The peacetime Air Corps, with no one shooting at you, looked like a wonderful life. It offered status and security, a chance to fly all types of airplanes, and many opportunities to further your education. It sounded like an ideal profession, but I had some nagging doubts. Discipline is the keyword of military life, and I was a civilian at heart and disliked the system that required blind obedience to superior officers. I could not accept a way of life that required me to follow orders without question. This resentment had begun in cadet days, when I was hazed by upper-classmen who ordered junior cadets to perform ridiculous duties with the reason that it was "necessary to instill discipline." I consider extremes of hazing a faulty method used by people in authority, who do not know how to create discipline.

Later, I saw how much damage could result when an officer failed to understand his mission, or gave improper orders that placed his men in harm's way. Instant obedience was the military creed, but I didn't have to like it. I was leading a dangerous enough life, but I feared that some day I might have an inept commander who would place my life in even greater jeopardy. With that attitude about discipline, I was not a very good candidate for a permanent career in the military.

I did have the greatest respect for most of the commanding officers I met; they were capable, responsible front-line officers who flew the same dangerous missions that I did over the Hump or in combat. They knew the score and I found it a joy to work under such leaders.

HOW TO GET AHEAD: KNOW SOMEONE
"THERE'LL BE NO PROMOTION, THIS SIDE OF THE OCEAN"

"There'll Be No Promotion, This Side Of The Ocean," was a favorite tune sung by troops all over the world, and it was true most of the time. Promotions in the CBI were almost non-existent. I had missed the promotion list at Morrison Field and felt that I was a permanent second lieutenant. Some of the new copilots just arriving at Assam had already made captain, and I grumbled about having a copilot who was two ranks ahead of me.

Enter Colonel Walter Urbach from the Adjutant General's office in New Delhi, riding with me in November, 1942, as passenger to Kunming. He stood at the cockpit door, impressed by the array of strange instruments, and I invited him to take over the wheel for a while. He was not a pilot, and was delighted at his first "flying lesson." That night we ate dinner together at the hostel, where he could see at firsthand how we lived, and I learned that he was on an inspection trip to China. He was one of the most inquisitive persons I had ever met, asking me countless questions about our operation. When he heard that I had spent some months with General Chennault and the Flying Tigers, he quizzed me on everything I had learned about China in my short time there.

"Colonel," I said, "you sound just like an attorney on an investigation." He laughed, and confessed that in civilian life he was an attorney in Washington, with extensive background in government. He was now working for the "legal department" of the Army Air Corps, and wanted to learn everything he could.

Colonel Urbach filled me in with the overall picture around the world, how every theater was badly under-supplied for the missions they were supposed to accomplish. He cautioned me that we were part of a huge enterprise, and that things moved very slowly in a bureaucracy this large. I was familiar with the squeaky wheel principle, and talked about our supply problem, and how it had created a morale problem as well, as we felt we were being totally neglected. He listened intently to my complaints, and I hoped the word would reach New Delhi where some of the problems could be remedied.

I also slipped in my private complaint about being a lowly second lieutenant with command experience on the Hump, while copilots newly arriving from the States were already promoted to the rank of captain, solely because they were going overseas. I pointed out that our most highly experienced pilots, ex-airline pilots who were the backbone of the Hump airlift, were the forgotten men on the promotion lists, still lieutenants, and that I was lowest of the low.

Some days later he rode back across the Hump with me, asked me many more questions, and thanked me graciously for the help I had given him. He suggested that if I ever had the opportunity, I should complete my law school education, which was only half done. In parting, he said that he had made a note about morale, and he would try to do something about it.

I quickly forgot about our conversations. We were always firing complaints back to HQ, where we assumed they were dropped into the wastebasket. But Colonel Urbach came through in fine style in less than a month, for on December 6, 1942, I was promoted to first lieutenant with his signature on the orders. Most remarkably, it was just a short time later, before I had a chance to buy new silver bars, that our entire group of original China mission pilots was promoted to captain. It showed me it paid to speak out boldly to the top man.

I visited Colonel Urbach on a later trip to New Delhi, stopping at his office to say 'thank you.' Once again he helped the Hump crews. Some pilots were facing a serious problem as they could not account for all of their $5,000 "emergency fund" money issued in Florida many months before. Some people at HQ wanted to prosecute the pilots who could not account for their funds, some of which were stolen, strayed, or otherwise used. Colonel Urbach decided that they didn't have the time or the personnel to carry on an investigation, and that it would impede our mission and start a big legal fuss. It was apparent that some people at HQ got things done, and Colonel Urbach was a 'doer,' not a paper pusher.

BUZZ JOB

Our Assam Valley bases had no fighter protection against a bombing or strafing raid, and we were inviting disaster by leaving our C-47's parked in rows overnight. To eliminate this tempting target, we started dispersing the airplanes to a number of small fields scattered around the Assam valley. After his airplane was unloaded, a pilot returning from a Hump trip would then fly it empty to a nearby dispersal field and park it in a zigzag fashion to discourage a strafing attack.

We flew these short hops solo, and had fun with the empty airplane, since it gave us a chance to practice some maneuvers not normally done with the C-47. The favorite was the quick fighter approach, which meant crossing the field at about 200 feet, downwind, at a 45 degree angle to the runway, and then pulling up into a tight 225 degree left turn, dropping wheels and flaps, and landing quickly. No messing around with square patterns and long downwind legs. We were able to bring in several airplanes in just a few minutes, and amazingly, never broke one.

Another fun thing was hedge-hopping, or buzzing, flying just off the treetops, scaring the cows, although this was considered kid stuff. One day, feeling very relieved after a rough Hump trip where I ran into icing and severe turbulence, I decided to have some fun, and I buzzed our basha bungalow on the way to the dispersal field. Right after my solo takeoff I found myself heading for our bungalow compound, a group of bashas sitting right in my line of flight. I did not consciously make a decision to buzz that low. It seems that some devil inside of me just grabbed the wheel and pushed it forward enough to put me down to about 50 feet above the ground. I did not exactly run my tail wheel down the roof ridge as someone claimed, but I came pretty close.

When the pickup jeep dropped me off at Ops an hour later, I found a reception committee waiting for me. I thought I might get a few squawks about buzzing, but I got more. It was just my luck that a visiting VIP from New Delhi, a one-star general, no less, on an inspection trip, witnessed my little escapade.

We had such visitors occasionally, but paid them little attention. They never requested a formal inspection of troops, because there weren't enough troops available to inspect. They might complain to our CO about such insignificant things as our shabby uniforms, and our failure to wear any insignia of rank so they couldn't tell a private from a captain. We always invited them to take a Hump trip with us the next day, and they always declined, pleading urgent business back at HQ. This did not earn them much respect among the flight crews who were making three trips a week, "rain or shine." They ended up doing little more than fussing about our lack of spit and polish, and we were happy to see them return to New Delhi.

My dumb little joy ride was an offense that this VIP could sink his teeth into, and I heard that he practically jumped up and down in great rage that any pilot would pull such a stunt. He wanted me court-martialed. I was lucky that he had to leave before I returned, so I was spared a personal dressing down which I am sure would have been a pip.

Fortunately, several airplanes had taken off at the same time, and our CO handled it very nicely, pacifying the general by telling him that he would investigate the matter, identify the culprit, and see that he was properly disciplined.

Then the CO called me up on the carpet, and gave me hell for the stupid trick. He had to penalize me in some way to set an example, so he condemned me to fly co-pilot for a week. This covered his obligation, but was not really a penalty. All I did was stay in the right seat on the next few check rides that I was giving to some new pilots being qualified on the Hump.

I was a little more careful about buzzing after that, but it was no big deal in the CBI. On more than one occasion we had to hedge-hop as a defensive maneuver. When we received a report of unidentified aircraft in our area - and I had that experience several times in China - we got right down to treetop level, and hugged the terrain very closely, trying to stay invisible to hostile aircraft.

Chapter 27
OPERATIONS OFFICER OF THE DAY

One of the most stressful jobs a pilot can pull is Acting Operations Officer-of-the-Day (O-O-D). He takes on the complicated, heavy burden of putting the squadron to work to perform its mission. On the plus side, it can be a great learning experience, and after doing it a few times he gets good at it, and enjoys the feeling that he is performing a very vital function.

Today is your turn. You tumble out of the sack well before dawn to check the mission schedules, to make sure that the crews show up awake and alert. A feverish look may indicate malaria, which a macho pilot will deny, insisting that he is okay to fly, but you know that he may be susceptible to vertigo at high altitude. You have to find a replacement. You look for personal problems that might affect their performance. A certain amount of bitching is normal, and indicates a healthy guy just letting off steam. You get razzed about goofing off when others are flying, but they know you fly your missions the same as they do.

You talk about the weather, but all you really know is what you see over your head. We have no weather information except pilots' reports from yesterday. But yesterday's clear skies that made the Hump trip an easy run may have changed to a mass of forbidding cumulous clouds loaded with sleet, ice, and lightning, that will make today's flights a hellish run.

You check with maintenance to make sure that the airplanes on the list are ready to go. If there is any question about readiness, you have to discuss this with the crew chief and pilots, to make sure that any defects are not critical to a safe flight.

You climb aboard a few airplanes to spot check the loading. All the airplanes are overloaded, but there is a safe limit. We would like to limit the load to 5000 pounds, but we usually carry 13 drums of aviation fuel, plus miscellaneous cargo, weighing in at about 7000 pounds. You closely inspect the way the drums are tied down, as there is nothing so dangerous as a loose drum of avgas bouncing around in the cabin during severe turbulence.

Your next chore is to run your jeep down the runway to make sure there aren't any cows, goats, or other livestock wandering around. Visibility is limited by early morning mist, and the animals are hard to see even a few hundred yards away. If you find any, you select a driver to patrol the runway until takeoffs are completed. Hitting one on takeoff is a disaster, which has caused wrecks and loss of life.

At first light, you check the local weather again. The chances are that there is a mist over part of the runway and a cloud layer starting at few hundred feet. If you can't see the far end of the runway, you may delay takeoffs. Most of our pilots are highly qualified on instruments, but taking off into that stuff is extremely hazardous. It means switching to instrument flight while you are still on the runway on your takeoff run, and that's hard to do safely. You hold up takeoffs until the mist lifts enough off the ground that the airplane will be wheels-up and in a climb before entering the stuff

You already have airplanes lined up with engines running, and you drive up along the left side of each airplane and make a circular motion with your finger to remind the pilot to rev up his engines after extended idling, to clear out fouled plugs. I feel like a fussy old guy reminding them to do this, but I recall one takeoff that I had to abort when half way down the runway because of fouled plugs, and inadequate takeoff power. I managed to stop before running off the end of the runway into a ditch, which would have meant a wreck.

The mist burns off and you give the okay to go. The first airplane thunders down the runway and quickly disappears into the mist and low clouds. You hope that he has good instruments, because he is relying on his artificial horizon, gyrocompass, and airspeed indicator, and the gyro-controlled instruments are very sensitive and hard to maintain. I know the pilot personally; he is one of the AMMISCA group, with over 5,000 hours on Eastern Airlines, so I have complete confidence in his instrument ability. Some of the others have much less experience, and we are never sure how they will perform in this most exacting of maneuvers, taking off in an overloaded airplane into instrument conditions. These newer pilots have been checked out as carefully as we can manage under limited conditions, and will probably do fine, unless the unforeseen occurs.

Losing a critical instrument, or having an engine failure right after takeoff is a catastrophe in the making, requiring great skill and good luck to survive. We have lost airplanes in those crisis conditions. The first inkling we would have of the disaster was seeing a flickering flare on a distant tea plantation, indicating an airplane burning fiercely, with fire fed by full fuel tanks and a full cargo of avgas. We would send out our pitiful emergency vehicles but there would be nothing there but a burned out skeleton of an airplane. We all have nightmares about such an accident, fully aware that even in the smoothest belly landing, the drums of avgas break their ties and lunge forward into the cockpit.

If they had a choice, crews would prefer to take off later in the day in clear weather.

Then they find cabin interiors so hot that it melts their enthusiasm. Controls and switches are hot enough to burn hands, and some pilots wear gloves. The higher temperatures reduce lift, requiring a longer takeoff run, and the overloaded airplane uses up all of the runway.

It might be midday before all aircraft have departed, with delays caused by various problems, mostly mechanical. Now you can take a breather, and may even head for the basha and hit the sack for a while, resting up for your next job. This may be the hardest part of the duty, the nerve-wracking ordeal of checking the return of each of your airplanes. By late afternoon all inbound should be accounted for, but this is not the way it works.

If an airplane does not return, he may have decided to RON at Kunming, or he may have landed at another field in Assam for some special reason. The other possibility is that he may be missing on the Hump, and that is always on our minds. We ask other returned pilots for information about the missing flight, and may hear that he was still on the ground when they left, so he may be okay and planning to return the next day. If we hear that he left earlier, then we get that gnawing feeling that we may have a missing airplane. We use our very faulty telephone system to call the other local fields to locate our missing airplane. Some days the phones work, and other days they don't. If there are no positive reports, we cross our fingers and sweat out the missing airplane.

We are not even sure that he made the first half of the trip to Kunming safely, as we have no established reporting method, except by a list brought by the last flight of the day leaving China. Our operation is split up among three fields, so the list often does not reach us.

The system is totally inadequate, and is tragically hampered by our lack of high-powered radios to establish communication between the two terminal points, Assam and Kunming. Why our brass continually fails to recognize the critical need for this is something we do not understand. We have tried to establish radio contact by using our higher-powered airborne "liaison" radios, circling airplanes over Kunming at high altitude, but these proved too low-powered to reach Assam, which sits behind soaring mountains 500 miles away.

I am very aware of how bad the communication problem is. In June, Curt Caton and I left Chabua for Kunming, and did not return for almost three months, during which time we operated the "China Express." It was weeks before Operations at Chabua learned where we were. Most amazingly, we weren't even missed, so loose was the operation at that time. Our barracks mates at Chabua were just about ready to pack up our personal things and mark us off as lost, when they got our message that we were alive and well, and working for Chennault.

When an airplane disappears, we always have hope. Perhaps the crew bailed out or safely crash landed some place, and is walking out. This does happen, but rarely. A missing airplane may end up as another marker along the Aluminum Trail, perhaps to be found later by ground crews that spent many years on search missions after the war. They climbed to almost inaccessible places with the aid of natives, to find and record the wrecks and arrange a proper burial for their occupants.

The job of the O-O-D is over for the day, but a missing airplane stays on his mind. He will check back for many days to see if the missing crew has been found and will stand by with a heavy heart if the personal effects are gathered up to ship out. He pities the commanding officer, who has to write letters that give little consolation to family members, and he crosses his fingers that he will stay alive.

We all benefited hugely from taking on the job of O-O-D. Just one day on this job gives a pilot a new outlook. The most cocksure youngster undergoes a remarkable change, as he becomes a careful manager, assuming responsibility for the welfare and fate of others. I write about it many years later, remembering many details of this learning experience, and realizing how important it is to delegate heavy responsibility to young people. I conclude with a heavy heart for the many valiant men we lost.

Chapter 28
LOSSES & RESCUES

Diary ... "September 24, 1942 .... Have spent four days and seven airplanes trying to get over the Hump. Mechanical troubles and bad weather have put a crimp on most flying. Also, a 'what's the use' feeling has contributed to the lapse of activity. Only one ship has looked for Fellers to date, with no luck. It's like a needle-in-the-haystack but certainly worth the try. "

This entry shows our state of mind at the time. Airplanes disappeared without a trace, and we faced terrible weather, poor maintenance, and a feeling of despair at the lack of support. Monsoon weather was taking over, and our airplanes were tired, just as we were. Our morale was at its lowest point.

Living conditions improved a few weeks later when a number of us left the primitive bashas and moved into more comfortable quarters, a more modem bungalow at Doom- Dooma. We met local British folks, plantation managers with families, who praised our efforts and were hosts to us on many occasions, giving us a sense of solidarity and family life. This small change in our surroundings made a big improvement in our outlook.

Diary ... "Nov 26, 1942. Thanksgiving. I am shocked to hear that Curt Caton is missing on a Hump flight. Tried to get into Kunming but was not able to due to Zero-Zero weather. The field was completely socked in so all ships returned to Chabua except him. Hope he'll come walking out some day soon, but it seems pretty hopeless .... Losses are hell when they hit home."

Curt and I had a great time on vacation in Calcutta just two months previous, in September. Our interests were sometimes different, as I spent lots of time at the hotel bar making friends with lovely British and Anglo-Indian beauties, and having great success. Curt spent lots of his time trying to reach his pregnant wife, Audrey, on the phone, without success. We returned to our basha at Chabua very refreshed, expecting to fly together again, but we split up when a new batch of pilots arrived, and we needed every experienced first pilot to train the new men.

Three weeks after his reported loss, his crashed ship was found about 30 miles east of Chanyi, near Kunming, having run into a mountain. Curt was a very careful pilot, and our guess was that he had found a "sucker hole" and gotten trapped, unable to get out. The front of the ship was demolished and burned, with loss of all on board. I mourned his loss greatly. A finer friend never existed, and as my mentor, he earned my ever-lasting thanks. I have wondered many times what happened that day. Was he ill with malaria as happened to most of us, or suffering from fatigue, or did he have a lapse of judgment and fail to observe normal caution when ground control told him about zero ceiling and visibility? Did he see an opening that might offer a safe letdown? Whatever the cause, we lost a wonderful pal, pilot, and family man.

I had a very painful letter to write to his wife, Audrey, and to his parents. A year later I visited his family in Mobile. It was a most difficult time for all of us and many tears were shed. They were quite wonderful people, grieving for their lost son, and I think they were ready to adopt me to replace him.

Many years later, as I write this, and reminisce about those days and the full life I have had since then, I still mourn the loss of Curt and the thousands of other men like him whose lives were cut so short, unable to fulfill their dreams. I look at the signatures of the AMMISCA pilots on my first "Burma Roadster" bill, and wonder how many survived the war, and lived good lives after that. The veteran's lament is that war is hell, and many memories are sad.

Curt was not the only fine pilot we lost. Several of the original AMMISCA pilots with airline experience were lost, proving to us that other factors besides skill were involved in success of the missions. Poor maintenance was a common problem, as I have repeatedly told how parts shortages caused us to fly airplanes that were not air-worthy.

Luck was a factor in our flights. You might unluckily chose the wrong route, and blunder into such violent weather conditions that no amount of skill could keep you aloft. We had no weather forecasts to rely on, and pilot reports were few and far between. Our radios had such limited range, that once airborne, we lost touch with ground stations in just a few minutes, and seldom reached other aircraft. We were totally on our own, with no support system available.

When a catastrophic engine failure or other problem arose, you could elect to ride the airplane down, hoping to break out over an area that allowed a landing. Some crews took to parachutes as a better alternative than crashing blindly into a cloud-covered mountain. In the early days, we scorned the use of parachutes, when inspection of these after a few months in the tropics revealed that they would be useless. Mold caused the layers of nylon fabric to stick together, with no chance of opening properly. We had no facilities to repack a chute or hang it up to dry, and we had no new ones coming through the supply system. So the word was out - stick with the airplane, which was not a very happy prospect.

Some crews that bailed out successfully were able to find native guides who led them to safety. There were other reported bailouts where crew-members became separated, with some never found. We assumed that they had succumbed to extremes of weather, or injuries, starvation, unfriendly tribes, enemy action, or any of countless other hazards facing them in jungles or high mountain tops. Their remains join the aluminum shards of aircraft resting forever on those foreign mountains.

A few were lucky. Owens lost an engine, ordered his two crewmen to bailout, staying with the airplane and his 40 Chinese troops on board. He must have been blessed, for he broke out of the overcast right over the Assam valley and landed safely. Three weeks later we got word that his crew was okay, living with friendly natives, about 120 miles east. They returned with wild stories to tell, and Owens was a happy man. The natives were well rewarded and we soon had a group of native scouts traveling the mountains and visiting the tribes, offering substantial rewards for rescues. It paid off.

Some others of our most expert pilots were not so lucky. Dean, formerly of the AVG and more recently flying for CNAC, a highly skilled pilot, was lost. So were Fellers, and Peterson, all experts with lots of airline hours. There was no accounting for their disappearance. Just silence.

Most crashes resulted in total loss of life, but we always flew with an eye open for signals from the ground. If one was spotted, indicating that crew members were still alive after a crash or a parachute jump, a rescue crew was dispatched to reach them by air drop or ground trek. Imagine an injured airman, propped up against a tree, surrounded by a menacing jungle, wondering just how long he could last in this impossible situation, suddenly being cheerfully greeted by angels dropping out of the sky to rescue him. I thrill at the thought of what that meant to the helpless victim, and at the pride of the rescuers.

These rescuers were daring men and true heroes, who not only deserve great credit for their bravery, but for their resourcefulness in bringing the injured airmen back to civilization. They parachuted to downed airmen with food and medical supplies and stayed with them until they could be brought out of the jungle. As I flew over the uncharted mountains and thick jungles, slashed by turbulent rivers that were impossible to cross, I wondered how anyone could have the nerve to volunteer for such a dangerous duty.

Most famous of them was our flight surgeon, Colonel Don Fleckinger, commanding all of our medical facilities at Assam. This was a warm, caring doctor, a wonderful guy, who made friends with every man he met, and was immensely popular with flight crews, for good reason. We would normally expect the CO of hospital services to stay rooted to his desk, to better manage his complicated job of providing health care under very difficult conditions.

This was not the style of Colonel Fleckinger, a man with an adventurous spirit. He is called the "Father of the Pararescue Service," which he organized in 1943. In August of that year, 21 persons bailed out of a disabled C-46 in a remote area, where the only means of getting help to the survivors was by parachute drop. Accompanied by two medical corpsmen volunteers, Fleckinger personally made the jump and spent a month caring for the injured until they were brought to safety. This famous rescue stimulated the establishment of a special corps for parachute rescue work. Eric Sevareid, well known news commentator, was one of the men who bailed out and was rescued. He wrote about the men who risked their lives to save his. "Gallant is a precious word; they deserve it."

The rescue missions set broken bones and did other emergency services, and then accompanied the injured on long treks to safety. There were no helicopters available so all recovery was done on foot, often with the help of local tribesmen recruited by the lure of gifts of shiny trinkets, knives, and other highly valued objects. The natives were taught that helping a downed airman was far better than chopping off his head for a trophy A single reward for saving a flyer could make them rich for life.

We looked for some humor in every situation, and there is a funny story that I call "Hauling Ass," that I have related elsewhere. It tells about hauling pack mules by air to help bring rescued airmen out of the jungle.

Rescue missions did more than save lives. Morale among Hump crews was lifted immeasurably when the Pararescue units proved they could perform life-saving missions, and crews realized that rescue from a downed airplane was possible.

There is no final closure for many of the airplanes lost on the Hump. Some aircraft have been found by recovery expeditions that were sent into the wilds of the Himalayas and Tibet searching for crash sites, and some remains were identified. But many remain lost. William Gadoury of the Central Identification Laboratory of Hawaii (CILHI) advised me as recently as July, 2001, that these searches will continue for many years to come "to resolve the fates of some of the brave airmen who flew the Hump but did not return.

Chapter 29
FORT HERTZ

Twelve hundred Burmese refugees shiver in great fear, sitting on a large open field in the most northern tip of Burma near the village of Fort Hertz. The area is surrounded in almost every direction by the vast Himalaya mountain ranges, whose slopes are covered by dense forests, and whose peaks are so high they are snow-covered year round.

Japanese troops are moving swiftly up the road from the south and refugees have been fleeing into Fort Hertz barely ahead of their relentless advance. These are hardened troops, following a policy of scorched earth, under harsh orders to kill all adult males, bum all the villages, and lay waste to the farms and flocks. They are rooting out any remaining Burmese soldiers hiding in the forests. The Burmese refugees are the innocents, caught in a pincer of war. They are afraid of the approaching enemy, but they sit stoically awaiting the rescue that has been promised, although it may have been just a rumor.

Word suddenly comes that the feared invaders are less than 200 kilometers to the south, a distance they can cover in as little as five hours by fast moving trucks. Families gather closer in terror, with children hushed by the tension in their parents. There is no place to hide, for the mountains are impassable, and only the most hardy could survive in that hostile countryside. These are family groups with many children and elderly, and some fear that this is their final day.

Suddenly a rumbling sound penetrates the valley, and the people shake in fear that it might be the leading trucks filled with menacing soldiers arriving to start a wholesale slaughter of the helpless. The roar increases in volume and comes from the sky; faces look up fearfully as two aircraft appear overhead. The refugees know what terrible destruction an airplane can inflict with powerful machine guns strafing masses of people out in the open, for they have witnessed the horror of broken and bleeding bodies in their flight. The Japanese make no distinction between military and civilian targets in their victory march into Burma.

One of the airplanes comes thundering at a low level over the field and the refugees huddle and scream in terror, expecting to hear the deadly chatter of machine guns shooting at helpless victims. Instead, the airplane pulls up and flies a tight circle, extends his landing gear, and carefully lands on the short field that has been hurriedly cleared of the very frightened people. The other airplane also lands expertly with little room to spare, on the field that is only 1500 feet long, and taxies up to the mass of waiting people.

These are C-47's of the Air Transport Command doing a special air rescue mission instead of a Hump flight that day. The large cargo doors swing open, boarding ladders are set in place, and people are hustled on board as fast as they can climb the steps.

I fly the third airplane to land on that postage stamp size field, and it is very close quarters. I station my crew chief at the door with a Tommy gun to maintain order if there is rioting for space, but just the opposite takes place. The refugees climb into the airplanes with no sign of panic and a minimum of confusion, and seat themselves on every square inch of floor they can find. The able ones carefully make space for the elderly, and many strangers hold children when the parents are unable to do so.

The appearance of the refugees is shocking. They are all underfed, and their clothing is mostly rags, with many going barefoot. All their worldly possessions are carried in little sacks, and their food consists of small packages of rice. I know that food and badly needed medical help are waiting for them at our Chabua base, but right now, our urgent problem is to get everyone on board and safely away.

It is with fingers crossed that I push the throttles forward to maximum power on that takeoff run. The high elevation, the short field, and an overload make it a sticky takeoff, but my airplane behaves in noble fashion. We gradually gain altitude by circling and we cross the Naga Hills to the west, making fast time to Chabua. We carefully unload our precious cargo, as they look in bewilderment at the hubbub of a rescue operation going full speed. Trucks are waiting to take them to food and shelter at refugee camps established by the British, where they will be safe at last.

I am surprised when one of my passengers expresses his gratitude in English, with a British accent. This Burmese man, dressed in tom rags, was a professor at a college in Rangoon, and he and his wife have been in flight for months, hoping that the Japanese advance would be stopped. He describes their tortuous trip, their many close calls when they pretended to be destitute peasants to escape the wrath of the execution squads. They have seen ruthless murders and beheadings of people simply because they were judged to be of an elite class. He points out that many of our passengers are educators, business people, and government officials, who are principal targets of the invaders, and he sadly tells of many who have not escaped, whose fate is unknown. All are dressed as peasants, partly for disguise, but mostly because they have long ago worn their garments to shreds. He is one of several rescued people who, as poor as they are, offer us small pieces of jewelry or other trinkets in gratitude. Of course, we take nothing, for these people are carrying all their worldly possessions in their tiny bundles.

I fly two trips into Fort Hertz that day, and carry out about 140 people. We have six airplanes at work and we bring out every refugee from that valley of death. Our rescue crews are very happy about that mission, for we are saving people from a terrible fate. We feel even prouder when we hear from the last plane out that there isn't a soul left behind. When the Japanese arrive, they find an empty town.

The C-47's outdo themselves by carrying massive numbers of people on each trip, and some pilots claim to have set a record. On one trip, I count heads as we unload and am still counting at 70. The Burmese are small people but I never understand how we packed so many into a C-47.

Fort Hertz Rescue: Twelve-hundred terror-stricken Burmese refugees saved from Japanese troops. We made two trips that day. On one flight we counted over seventy refugees in my 23-passenger plane.

Chapter 30
TROOP CARRIER UNITS

Some of the dirtiest flying jobs in the CBI Theater faced the Troop Carrier and Combat Carrier Command units that reached India in 1944. Their missions were extremely hazardous, flying supplies to the British ground troops in Burma that were fighting tough Japanese jungle fighters. The dangers they faced made every mission a nightmare, and there was never such thing as an easy day's work for these daring pilots.

They made airdrops of food, munitions, and other supplies from the open cargo doors of their C-47 aircraft, into drop zones that were identified by panels on the ground. Delivery was extremely risky, for they flew low and slow over the jungle, sometimes high enough to do parachute drops, and sometimes as low as 50 feet, much too low for parachutes.

I had flown rice drop missions a year earlier, spending minutes that seemed like hours trying to find Wingate's Raiders. We knew the hazards of ground fire and we quaked in our seats as we flew very slowly, just barely above the trees, targeting the ground panels. We had no way to fight back, and our airplanes had no protective armament to stop rifle bullets. Now the Japanese were smarter, concentrating their rifle fire on the front end of our cargo ships. Pilots just had to grit their teeth and fly the pattern, for they knew that the ground troops might starve without the supply drops.

The "Biscuit Bombers," as they were called, faced risks that started right at takeoff, for they began their missions just before dawn, in the black of night, when a heavy mist shrouded the runway. A faltering engine might mean that the airplane never made it into the air, but ended up in a crash off the end of the runway.

Heavy ground fog often hid the jungle below, making checkpoints impossible to find until it burned off As the Japanese became more aggressive and aircraft were lost to heavy ground fire, the missions were changed to night drops. This gave navigators nightmares as all the jungle looked alike from the air and many missions were never completed. Radio beacons were set up to guide the ships in, but some drops were made by guesswork, with Japanese soldiers finding the packages.

Once the drop zone was located, the pilot lined up as best as he could, but from the cockpit he was unable to see if he was actually hitting the target. The cargo might land just yards out of reach of the ground troops, or might fall into enemy hands. This was a very frantic time, with the pilots yelling for information on where the drops were landing, the cabin crew shouting instructions to the pilot to move to the right or the left on the next pass, and all accompanied by the howling noise of the slipstream whistling through the open door.

Hitting the target was only one of the problems. The airplane was forced to fly very slowly, barely above stalling speed at about 110 mph. Enemy troops were often close by, and at such a low speed and altitude, the C-47 was a true sitting duck for ground fire. One rifleman aiming at an airplane is not a great menace, but ten or twenty riflemen, just shooting at random, are bound to have some luck hitting the airplane, with perhaps a stray shot hitting a pilot There was no seat armor to protect the pilots.

The system for dumping the load quickly had been worked out by trial and error. Cabin crews lined up the cargo on the cabin floor, just inside the gaping open door on the left side of the airplane. The crew sat on the floor, wearing safety harness to keep them from sliding out of the door if the airplane rolled suddenly to the left. When the pilot flashed the "Abandon Airplane" red light signal, the cabin 'pushers' shoved hard with their legs, forcing the cargo bags and boxes out the door as fast as they could. This crude delivery method was the best you could do from a C-47 with a side door, and it meant that several passes were needed to empty the airplane.

A ground soldier described how he got fed and supplied by air on a typical three-pass mission: "First they would push out feed for the mules, then ammunition on the second drop, and finally, food for us on the third." As the pilot circled for each drop, the crew worked feverishly to bring more cargo back to the exit ready for the next signal. Time was of the essence, as the less time spent over the target, the better. Every second of delay meant that Japanese riflemen might be moving closer for a better shot.

Drop zones were often situated in valleys surrounded by high hills or towering trees. The pilot lowered his wheels and flaps, and slowed down to descend into this low area, but after the drop was made, he had to pick up speed and climb rapidly to avoid mushing into the surrounding hills. A C-47 does not respond rapidly, and many a crew-member held his breath as the airplane sluggishly climbed an imaginary stairway, struggling up into clear airspace above the obstacles. Some did not make it, and ended up in the trees, with a few lucky crew still alive, able to climb out of the wreck and rescue themselves

More hazards were waiting after the drop was finished and the airplane headed for home. Enemy fighters were on the prowl waiting for the low-lying mist to clear so they could find the troublesome cargo planes that were supplying the British troops. By 1944 we had P-51, P-38, and British Beaufighters to keep the Zeros away, but there were no guarantees of safety in this tumultuous war. Drop missions were so dangerous that crews were sometimes grounded for reason of extreme stress.

Occasionally the Troop Carrier aircraft were ordered to move some cargo over the Hump to Kunming, and the crews were introduced to a different kind of flying - the high altitude kind, that our Hump pilots had been facing for two years. Any ideas the Troop Carrier pilots had that Hump pilots were softies was dispelled when they faced the monster Himalayas that reared up to challenge them.

Air drops were a vital part of the campaign to free Burma. British General Orde Wingate's "Raiders" went into the jungle in 1943 with one month's supply of food carried by mules. They overstayed their plan, and our emergency air drops helped them survive. They lost 1000 men of their 3000 man brigade, but this was considered a successful mission as a test of "Long Range Penetration" techniques, with troops working behind Japanese lines to cut their supply routes.

A similar mission invaded Burma in early 1944, when "Merrill's Marauders," under General Frank Merrill, followed Wingate's lead with 2700 American troops, the first American ground troops employed in the Theater. They also used mules to carry in their supplies, and then relied totally on the Troop Carrier C-47's for re-supply.

In 1944, another invasion entered Burma totally by air. This was a full-blown campaign that relied totally on the ability of Troop Carrier units to bring in the ground troops and all their equipment. C-47's towed gliders packed with men and supplies that landed at clearings in central Burma. This was a giant invasion, which unloaded thousands of Allied troops, over 1000 mules and ponies, and a half-million pounds of supplies. Airborne Engineers came in by glider bringing bulldozers, and went to work building airstrips, where C-47's landed with more heavy loads, and evacuated wounded.

Bringing in troops by air avoided the long exhausting marches through the jungles that had caused so many casualties in the other invasions. Aircraft brought in bigger guns and fresh troops as needed. The Troop Carrier Command continued to supply the ground troops during the entire operation, and was their vital lifeline. This air operation played a major role in defeating the Japanese in Burma.

Chapter 31
SHORT CIRCUITS

There is nothing quite so frustrating in an airplane as realizing that you are out of touch with the rest of the world. You repeatedly make calls to a ground station or to another airplane, and get nothing but static in reply. Your radio does not pack the power to reach anyone

It was even worse, totally terrifying to fly into unexpected weather conditions without adequate communications equipment, and we faced this every day, everywhere. We flew through violent Hump weather without ground contact. Flying across the flat plains of India could also be hazardous when a sudden blinding dust storm or a deluge of rain during the monsoon season left a pilot helplessly lost over terrain that had no identifying features. I experienced both types of storms, and found my radios almost useless in these conditions.

On a trip to Agra, I was making my final approach to the airport through a moderate shower when I was assaulted by the most violent torrent of rain I had ever met. The downpour was so heavy that my windshield wipers could not cope and visibility was zero. I called the tower repeatedly asking for an alternative landing field but had no reply. I pulled up my gear and flaps and did a missed approach maneuver on instruments, then waited a half-hour until the storm moved on and I could land safely. The tower never did come on the air, as heavy humidity had short-circuited their equipment.

Approaching Allahabad one day I found myself flying into one of those violent wind storms that created a maelstrom of dust in just a few minutes, reducing visibility to a few hundred feet. The dust storm stretched for miles, completely surrounding the city and airport, and the tower did not answer my continuous calls. I wondered what to do next.

Suddenly, I heard sweet words from another pilot answering my calls. "Army 7797, this is CNAC 405 about 10 miles north of Allahabad. These dust storms move pretty fast, and we're holding in the clear here until the field opens. Estimate 15 or 20 minutes. We're at 4000 feet Join up with us at 5000 and we'll sweat it out together." That was China National Airlines, operated by PanAm, a highly experienced group of pilots. Can you imagine a friendlier sound than that re-assuring voice!

We needed reliable transmitters at the airports that could give us weather and field conditions when we were 50 miles out, but most of the equipment had a range of only 15 miles. Some of our ships had stumbled blindly into air raids at Chabua, without any warning from the ground that the enemy was there. The tower operator yelled that a raid was in progress, but never reached the incoming airplanes before he jumped down and headed for a slit trench.

We needed better radios on board that would let pilots talk to each other, and pass along information about icing or severe turbulence. There is nothing so heart-warming as an in-flight report from another pilot about conditions you are about to encounter. It's like hearing from your brother, and we looked out for each other. Our on-board command sets with a 15-mile range did not let us talk to each other very well.

We needed high power equipment that would let Assam and Kunming talk to each other. They are 500 miles apart, with high mountains in between. Our former airline pilots told how everyone talked to each other in airline operation, and could not accept that after many months we still could not talk back and forth across the Hump.

Pilot Tom Shook offered to help. "I've got ham radio gear at home, and if I could get it shipped here, along with rigs I could borrow from other hams, we could have a net working here in a couple of weeks." Having dabbled in ham radio myself, I believed that ham ingenuity might work wonders. But the military system forbade this, and repeated their empty promises that, "Equipment is on the way."

AACS (Army Airways Communication Service) arrived in India in August 1943, a whole year behind schedule. This was supposed to solve communications and navigation problems, but it turned out that they failed to bring the equipment with them. All they had was telephones for local use. It took another year before the radios arrived, so slowly did the supply people move. What made this delay so surprising was the experience General "Hap" Arnold had in August of 1942 when his VIP airplane got lost crossing the Hump, and he feared that he was about to become a prisoner of the Japanese. After that episode, I would have expected him to give a priority to "nav" radio for Hump pilots, but it didn't happen.

Top brass made promises of equipment, but the right hand and the left hand were not working together. There was great conflict in policy. For two years, policy said "NO" to high powered radios, reasoning that the enemy might home in on our fields for bombing missions. This was an outrageous case of "General Yesterday" running the show. It was far more important to bring our planes home safely than worry about enemy bombers, which could not possibly fly in bad weather. The result of this unbelievable policy, which was established by someone sitting safely behind a desk in Washington, was that we groped our way home, sometimes making fatal mistakes.

Occasionally we would hear from high-powered radio transmitter located south of us. The voices spoke broken English or Japanese, and we knew they were the call of the sirens, Japanese beacons trying to lure us into trouble. Their radios were better than ours.

The ultimate goal was to install radio ranges similar to those located at every major airport in the continental United States. These would allow us to make precision let- downs to airports at Chabua and Kunming, which were located in dangerous mountainous regions with fast changing weather conditions. Colonel Tom Rafferty, our first CO at Assam, placed an urgent order for this equipment in mid-1942. They were delivered in mid 1945 (yes, that's three years later), but the war was over before installation was completed. Need I say more?

Chapter 32
CNAC

China National Airline Corporation (CNAC), was the civilian airline that first flew the Hump, and deserves the credit for pioneering our airlift. Like all the early airlines, their history is quite fascinating

Juan Trippe, head of Pan American Airlines, had a dream as far back as 1930 of creating a globe-girdling airline providing air travel to all major parts of the world. He teamed up with the Chinese government to create CNAC, the first organized airline in all of Asia, and installed the new airline as his link with PanAm in that part of the world.

CNAC started in 1930 flying single-engine amphibians, and suffering the growing pains of a fledgling airline trying to operate in a backward country that was torn by constant civil strife. Facilities were primitive, but there was a great need, and the airline grew to become a major transportation factor in China, connecting all the larger cities. The Japanese take-over forced it out of business in the coastal areas, and it concentrated on supporting Chinese forces in the interior.

The places they flew into were backward and not very supportive of an airline, making the operation highly hazardous. The pilots were the best, highly proficient at flying into unknown and remote fields, and were often called on to rescue people trapped in troubled areas, at great risk to themselves.

CNAC was the supply line for the American Volunteer Group before the Army Air Corps arrived to set up an airlift. In 1941, CNAC airplanes were flying from India to China by way of the low altitude route across Myitkyina in central Burma. Later that year the Japanese moved into Burma and forced CNAC to use the same high Hump route that our military airlift flew starting in 1942.

CNAC contracted its services to the Army, and, not hampered by a military bureaucracy, was able to operate more efficiently than the military services, based on the number of aircraft each service flew. They operated for the entire duration of the war, moving more than 100,000 tons of cargo, almost 20 percent of the total tonnage carried across the Hump, with a small number of aircraft.

Their fleet was nothing to brag about in 1941. The company had to scrounge for aircraft and supplies just as the Air Force did. Short on dollars, the airline purchased older Douglas DC-2 and DC-3 airplanes that had many thousands of hours, and needed much maintenance to keep them flying. Their mechanics became expert at improvising and repairing items that the military would normally discard as unusable. Eventually the airline received a number of C-47 aircraft under Lend-Lease to keep it operating. Lend- Lease was a program that allocated supplies to governments that defended the interests of the United States, and the Chinese government was a major recipient of this aid, with CNAC benefiting hugely.

Many CNAC pilots were friends of mine, formerly Flying Tiger pilots who joined the airline when the AVG went out of business in July, 1942, and we often met in Kunming. They were very grateful for the help we had given them during difficult times in Kweilin, when we helped keep their P-40's in the air, and made their lives a little more tolerable. We joked about the "good old days" in Kweilin and Hengyang, which were only a few months previous.

They worked hard on their risky runs, but spent their time off in very comfortable apartments in Calcutta, maintained by some exotic girl friends. Their salaries were three to four times our military pay, ranging up to $1000 per month, and they could afford to live in luxury. I was offered the use of their apartments on my rare trips to Calcutta, which included the company of their various girl friends, and the temptation was great, but I thought it best to stay at the hotel with my crew.

As all pilots do, they told hair-raising tales of exploits by their pilots that truly matched those of our military pilots. They lost 20 crews in the Hump operation, but the military did not give them any awards or the full credit due them for establishing the lifeline to China and paving the way for the military airlift. I have read many of their stories, and give a salute to these brothers-in-flight, who taught us much and shared our dangers.

Chapter 33
BLESS THE DC-3

Today many people consider the DC-3 airplane as obsolete as a buggy whip, but in my mind it almost ranks with the cotton gin or steam engine as the forerunner of a new technology. It took air travel out of the rough-and-ready stage and created the modem system that dominates travel.

The first Douglas Aircraft model, labeled the DC-I, was the twin-engine competitor to the Boeing 247, and it was followed shortly by the DC-2, sporting 800 horsepower engines. It sat 15 passengers in comfort, cruised at 135 miles per hour, and was considered the state of the art. The next in the series, the DC-3, was larger, seating 21 passengers, was powered with Pratt and Whitney engines developing 1200 horsepower, and cruised at 165 MPH. It could cross the country in the record time of 17 hours, and was the pride of the airlines.

To a teenaged would-be pilot, the captain of the airliner was an exalted person. I had no idea that I would be pilot of one of these ships of the sky when, as a kid visiting the East Boston Airport in the depression years of the 1930's, I gawked at the splendid shiny airliners that were the ultimate in travel. To actually fly one of these queens of the air was a dream that seemed as unattainable as flying to the moon. As events turned out, the war placed many young dreamers in the cockpit of a DC-3/C-47 with inadequate training, but the trusty and forgiving bird often forgave our mistakes and brought us home safely.

One pilot with a flair for poetry, described the C-47 as "an airplane of refinement and gentle manners," that offered luxury travel to the discriminating traveler. This luxury included flying as a passenger in the DC-3 model that converted to a sleeper plane. In early 1942, I was ferrying new Boeing B-17E's from Seattle to Florida. On the return trips, we boarded a United Airlines sleeper plane at Chicago, and after a good dinner, were tucked into the convertible bunks by lovely stewardesses. Early the next morning, our magic carpet landed at Seattle after a good night's rest, ready for work.

Douglas built over 4,000 of the military cargo version of the DC-3, called the C-47, equipped with wide doors and heavy floors. They were truly the workhorses of all Allied forces. Wherever in the world there were cargoes or people to be moved, you would likely see the C-47, affectionately called the "Gooney Bird", doing the moving. They crossed oceans, carried loads of all kinds, ranging from generals and ambassadors to toilet paper, dropped supplies and paratroopers, and hauled gliders. Many a military pilot smuggled his girl friend aboard to join the exclusive "Mile-High Club" that involved the closest kind of intimacy at an altitude above 5,000 feet.

The Hump was more of a challenge than the C-47 was designed to tackle, but that incredible airplane made thousands of crossings. We usually flew at 16,000 feet, which was well above the airplane's maximum design altitude of 12,000 feet. To add to the danger, we were always overloaded, sometimes by as much as 100 percent of normal cargo capacity. Pratt and Whitney made a model of the R-1830 engine that came equipped with two-speed blowers that could increase our service altitude, but these were never provided for our Hump operation. We staggered along with full throttle, indicating an airspeed of only 115 MPH, and prayed our engines would keep running.

In bad weather, loss of an engine meant a downward ride into a mountainside, unless you were lucky enough to break out of the overcast into the clear as you gradually descended. Many pilots ordered crews to dump their cargoes in desperation, to maintain altitude as long as possible. In clear weather, unable to fly across the north-south running mountain ranges on one engine, some crews survived an engine failure by following one of the deep rivers that slashed a turbulent path through the Himalayas in a southerly direction, until they found a clear spot to crash land.

Finding a suitable place to land was a desperate hope, but the wonderful design of the C-47 made it possible to do a safe belly landing on a smooth field The wheels extended several inches below the engine housings even when fully retracted. Landing on the belly ruined the propellers and damaged the bottom of the fuselage, but many C-47's that crash landed in friendly territory flew again after these damages were repaired.

After a successful crash landing on the Hump, the crews faced rescue problems that could involve many weeks of walking out provided that they had guides to help them. The Japanese and the British both bribed native tribes to bring in prisoners, and if you were lucky, the tribal people you met on a walk-out were friendly headhunters.

My personal experience in flying thousands of hours with Pratt and Whitney engines was superb, as I never experienced an engine failure. A pilot listens as his engines speak to him. If they are out synch with each other he hears and feels the vibrations, and quickly adjusts the RPM control to smooth them out. If there is the slightest stutter, he can feel it. His roving eyes constantly check engine gauges for signs of malfunction, as he knows his life depends on those power plants.

I attribute my great record with these engines to good luck, and I confess, somewhat superstitiously, to the good relationship I developed with the Pratt and Whitney company when I worked there on engine assembly in 1941. We built engines with tender, loving care, with each part carefully inspected and each bolt accurately tightened to the proper torque. I like to imagine that they returned the favor to me by straining themselves to continue running even when tired, worn out, and undernourished with defective fuel.

I have flown with engines that leaked oil, ran extra hot at times, and were hard starting, but never, never said a cussword to those wonderful P&W'S. I just spoke to them as I would to a cherished pet, and they kept running for me. Only once did I have a serious problem, and that was caused by fouled up spark plugs when we had no replacements.

I would like to award my Pratt and Whitney engines a special Distinguished Flying Cross for faithful service.

The entire airplane is a model of durability. If you had an extra 1000 pounds of cargo to load at the last minute before takeoff, you just found room and loaded it, as overloading was standard practice. The old airplane may groan and shudder at the extra weight it carries, and its wings might flutter in a scary fashion when you hit turbulence, but it will keep flying.

A C-47 pilot described his wartime flying experiences very graphically, "in a rattling, groaning, leaking C-47, with wings flexing and twisting, engines running hot, running rough, but an honest, faithful machine that flew and flew and flew, always bringing me home again."

There is no set life span, as there are DC-3's in use today over 60 years old, with as much as 80,000 hours total time. Many aviation experts consider that the creation of the DC-3 was the greatest event in modern aviation. That beautiful airplane was the most important stepping stone in establishing a giant new industry that brought air travel into the reach and desire of the general public. All the marvelous air transports built since then have followed in its footsteps.

Chapter 34
C-87 OPERATIONS

My friends, Bob Cook and Marv Siegel were very much envied at being selected to fly the new C-87 airplane. This was the cargo version of the B-24 bomber and with four turbo-supercharged engines it could fly comfortably at 20,000 feet, and carry four times the load of our C-47's. This would be the ideal airplane for the Hump, and we expected that eventually there would be a large fleet of them.

Six were sent to Chabua early in 1943, and I expected to be assigned to fly one, as I had about 175 hours of four-engine time. My name was passed over, as were all the original AMMISCA pilots, since we had completed close to our 50-trip limit, and would be returning home soon. We all wanted to fly the big birds, but as events turned out, we later considered ourselves lucky that we didn't.

That first group of C-87's ended up in tragedy, as all six were lost within a few months, three in accidents that we understood, with the other three disappearing without a trace. We were shocked at the loss of the crews, and were very disturbed at the failure of these new airplanes to perform as expected. We pondered the mystery of the three that were lost, but had no pilots' reports to provide the answers. We strongly suspected icing as the cause, as the C-87 was vulnerable to ice, and we knew that icing conditions existed in the extremely hazardous monsoon weather.

Consolidated Aircraft was very proud of the B-24/C-87 model with its thin laminar-flow wing. Wind tunnel tests had proven it more efficient than other airfoil shapes, and it gave the C-87 a larger load capacity and more speed than the B-17. It was the favorite of top brass and government officials for personal travel, and was considered the state-of-the- art. It had a major drawback in that this highly efficient airfoil suffered a drastic loss of lift if it picked up just a small amount of ice. This made the C-87 very vulnerable to the ever-present bad weather on the Hump. We did not know about this when the new airplanes first arrived, and had to learn it the hard way. There was no positive way for us to verify this as the reason for the losses, but when more of these aircraft were sent to the CBI, the pilots were very careful to avoid icing conditions if at all possible, by taking long detours or climbing high over threatening cloud formations.

Sometimes we make foolish decisions and are saved by good luck, and May of 1943 was my lucky month. My 50 Hump missions and my time flying for Chennault added up to more than 1000 flying hours, and I was on the first list of pilots returning to the States. We were allowed two weeks off for R&R (Rest and Recreation), to spend anywhere we preferred before leaving. Some of the returnees rented houseboats at Kashmir and bragged later about the good food, the luxury, the beautiful sari-clad girls, and the very special pleasures they enjoyed.

I was keen on making more movies with my little 8mm Kodak camera, my gunnery prize, which I had used with tender care, keeping the exposed film in a moisture-resistant box, for later development in the States. I was especially interested in filming the new C-87, which we considered the ultimate in efficiency and safety for carrying cargo across the Hump. Cook and Siegel invited me to ride the jump seat on their next Hump trip, which they obligingly planned to fly north of the direct route if the weather was clear. This would allow me to film a close view of what I thought was K-2, one of the highest peaks of the Himalayas. It was the wrong mountain, but high enough to tower over us even when we flew at 20,000 feet. The turbo-superchargers on those four Wright engines gave us so much greater altitude than our C-47's could reach that we thought we could fly over everything.

I filmed great footage of the slow-moving Indian crews packing cargo into the great ship, and then filmed the take-off sequence from the jump seat. We flew a northerly course, but heavy haze around the mountain reduced visibility, and blocked a good view of a spectacularly high mountain.

When we landed at Kunming, I filmed the Chinese coolies unloading the ship with great speed and energy, in a fraction of the time it took to load the airplane. The local temperature may have made the difference, as Assam was over 100 degrees, while Kunming was a brisk 60 degrees at its high elevation.

I laughed when I heard the Chinese crew sing a tune as they worked, as it sounded suspiciously like the old "Piss on Bissell" tune taught them many months before by the Flying Tigers. I laughed a lot on that trip because I was a happy guy; after all, I was already on orders to return to the states, and getting bombarded with requests to make telephone calls to families when I got back.

I spent the evening with Cook and Siegel and at dinner I introduced them to some former Flying Tiger pilots who were now working for CNAC. These boys bragged about their pay, and suggested I quit the Air Corps and join them.

"Hardly likely," I said jokingly, "don't you guys know there's a war on?"

The next day I planned to return with my friends on the C-87, but Kunming Operations needed someone to fill in for a C-47 copilot who was grounded with an acute case of "Delhi Belly," as we called dysentery. This was a priority, and as a spare pilot without a plane, I could hardly refuse. "Sure," I said, "but I want to get paid for overtime." This would be an extra half-mission.

The weather turned overcast, and we flew mostly instruments back. I flew right seat with a pilot who had only recently checked out and he was very uneasy facing this bad weather. He was happy to have this old hand aboard instead of his totally green copilot, while I cussed silently at this high-risk way to return to Assam. I always scoffed at superstition, but felt uneasy flying this way on my very last trip across the Hump. We had no problem on the flight, but I kept thinking that I could have ridden in style on the C-87, probably high above all this crud.

On my return, I went looking for Cook and Siegel, since I had promised to get their Stateside phone numbers and call their families on my return. I was shocked to hear that they had not returned from Kunming, although they had left just before me. That night they were listed as missing, and I was very upset at the loss of such good friends. That was nothing compared to the long agonizing period for their families, hoping they might walk out. We never heard a word from them, nor found any trace of their airplane. We can only guess that their airplane joined the rest of the "Aluminum Trail" that stretches 500 miles across the forlorn wastes of the highest peaks in the world. Was it ice? They had made a number of trips, and knew their airplane well, but perhaps they were not fully aware that dangerous icing conditions existed at the higher altitudes this airplane could fly. They were among the first group of C-87's that joined us, and eventually all six were gone.

I have mused about my luck ever since that day, and I have repeated for many years, "I'm just glad to be here." Someone else's dysentery that put me in the cockpit of the C-47 was my good fortune. I also wonder how different it might have been if we had radios powerful enough to permit pilots to report icing conditions and other problems.

I have also wondered many times at the protective shell you must develop in wartime to accept the loss of your friends, and still maintain your drive. One of the requirements is that you have a feeling of youthful confidence that says, "It only happens to the other guy, not me." Once you lose that, it's time to go home.

A year later, the families of Lieutenant Robert Cook and Lieutenant Marvin Siegel accepted my invitation to visit our Hump pilot group at the Reno Air Force Base, where they attended a very special commemorative service for these two wonderful young men, lost in the prime of their lives. Many tears were shed that day including my own, as I spoke to the families and to the Air Base audience about all the gallant young men sacrificed to the Gods of War.

There is a sad postscript to this story. As of July, 2001, Lieutenant Marvin Siegel and his crew are still reported by the armed forces Central Identification Laboratory as "Bodies Not Recovered."

Section IV

WHAT WENT WRONG

*Obstacles almost defeated us; killer weather,
monstrous mountains, shortages of supplies,
dissension among our generals.*

Chapter 35
SHORTAGES AND TURF WARS

Every military campaign has its "Monday Morning Quarterbacks," who sit on the sidelines and criticize the action. I am one of them, but I took part in the events, which gives me special privileges.

I was an angry pilot flying in China and over the Hump in 1942-43. Every soldier frets about useless rules, poor efficiency, and the unfairness inherent in a huge bureaucracy that overlooks individuals. But my anger came from our being sent to the farthest corner of the world to do an extremely difficult job, without adequate support. Not only were we were in grave danger of failing our mission, but it was fearful to think that the risks we took did not justify an all-out effort to provide proper backup. It was mainly the tenacity of Chennault that kept the air war going in China, and the energy of our Hump crews that kept materiel moving, despite our shortages.

The Hump pilot's mind focused on just a few things: the take-off, the flight, the weather en-route, and a safe arrival. He led a simple life, and was not aware of the reasons why he lacked essential equipment. He knew that his radio would not reach the ground stations, and there was no instrument approach procedure at Kunming, nor any weather forecasting, But he flew across that dangerous terrain, hoping that Kunming was open and that he would find a hole in the clouds. After landing, he breathed a sigh of relief, happy to have made a good trip, and headed for a place to unwind. It was a very bad feeling when one day he realized that no one back at HQ seemed to give a damn about him.

In those early days, we bitched loudly about every failure of the army to provide for us as we were constantly in danger. Now, as a mature historian, I look at the overall picture more calmly, but still find reasons to criticize the system that controlled us.

Let the reader be prepared for a big serving-up of history, and then judge if the criticism is justified.

* * * * * *

The project started when, early in December of 1941, just a few weeks after the start of the war, President Roosevelt gave orders to provide transport planes to haul supplies to China. This soon developed into an urgent problem, as

Roosevelt advised General "Hap" Arnold on May 6, 1942, in a message marked "Secret." It read:

"I gather that the air ferry route to China is seriously in danger. The only way we can get certain supplies into China is by air. I want you to explore every possibility, both as to airplanes and routes. It is essential that our route be kept open, no matter how difficult. "

Nothing could be more explicit. Yet our original small fleet of cargo planes fell far short of the president's intent, and replacements for the aircraft we lost on the Hump were almost non-existent. To make things worse, the cargo fleet was deteriorating rapidly due to hard usage, and we lacked spare parts. We took badly damaged airplanes apart to keep the others flying, but despite heroic measures by the ground crews, no airplane was totally complete. Lend-Lease was sending airplanes to foreign governments to build their strength for activities in the future, but in our theater, we had an immediate, urgent need, just to stay alive, and no one seemed to be listening to our pleas. We soon realized that we were at the bottom of the priority list.

The underlying cause of our problem was very evident: the worldwide shortage of arms, with demand far exceeding the supply. But in reviewing the history of the CBI, other, more subtle causes crop up.

One major factor was the inability of our commanding generals to work together. This condition is confirmed in the personal memoirs of Generals Arnold, Stilwell, and Chennault, in which they freely admitted that there was considerable friction among them. This failure to cooperate with each other may have contributed greatly to their inability to provide us with the tools to do the job.

Our combat units were in the same situation - almost totally neglected. The China Air Task Force inherited 38 P-40's that remained of the original 100 sent to the AVG. They were in such desperate shape they were ready for the scrap heap, and in the States they would have been quickly junked. This pathetic handful of tired old fighters was all that kept the Japanese Air Force from freely attacking cities and military bases in China. When one limped in from a mission so badly damaged that it was permanently grounded, the mechanics were delighted that they now had another airplane to cannibalize for parts. Colonel Robert Scott, commanding the CATF, reported in July of 1942, that his airplane, named "Old Exterminator," was so damaged that it was dismantled and its parts spread out among 18 other P-40's in the group.

The CATF did a remarkable job with these decrepit aircraft, but their ability to fly aggressive missions was very limited In mid-1942, the President suggested to "Hap" Arnold that he order a bombing of the power plant at Shanghai, which was an important target. The plan was officially put" on hold", as our fighters could not reach the target. Actually, it was somewhat of a bad joke, for the true reply was "bomb with what?" We had no bombers in China at that time.

Some other shortages that existed early in 1942 were not corrected for several years, despite the urgency. Here are more examples:

Our two permanent Hump bases, at Assam in India, and at Kunming in China, operated cargo flights for the entire duration of the war, starting early in 1942. These were the most important bases in the CBI, critical to our operation, but for years they lacked proper communications equipment, weather reporting, and other services, leaving us to work on the proverbial shoestring. Flights leaving Assam were out of touch with the ground stations within minutes after takeoff, and we had little idea of weather conditions we would find en route or at the destination.

We were so badly pressed for C-47's that we put some old airline DC-3's into Hump service. These were passenger airplanes that had flown many thousands of hours for various airlines, and were intended for use over the lowlands of India. They were given the military designation of C-53, and had narrow doors and floors that were not reinforced to support heavy cargoes. When I flew one on a Hump trip, I listened nervously to the creaks and groans of a true veteran, and wondered if it could still take the battering that we gave it. My only consolation was that it had flown many years, was still holding up, and probably good for more mileage. That's the best attitude a pilot can adopt when he's flying an old clunker - that it's good for a few more flights.

Even minor failures could kill you. I had a number of close calls that I blamed directly on lack of parts or ground equipment. On one flight my copilot startled me, yelling, "Hey, the damn compass isn't working!" The magnetic compass was spinning uselessly. Fortunately, I was returning to Chabua and already had the Brahmaputra River in sight in the distance, and knew my way home. Had I been on instruments, I would have been hopelessly lost, unable to determine my direction. We replaced the compass with one salvaged from a wrecked airplane. After working on it, it still read 15 degrees off normal, but we placarded it with a note of warning for the next pilot who used this airplane. Military regulations normally call for scrapping a defective compass, but this was all we had.

Another time I nearly lost my airplane and my life flying an airplane that had no de-icer boots, when I encountered icing weather. These are long inflatable rubber tubes installed on the leading edges of the wings and horizontal stabilizers that are used to crack ice that forms in certain weather conditions. The original boots had rotted away in the tropical climate, and there were no replacements. This was a continuing and extremely critical shortage that was to blame for many losses. We had no cure, for the monsoon weather created icing conditions, and there was little chance that pilots encountering ice would be able to radio the word along to other pilots.

The CBI, 12,000 miles from home, was truly the low man on the totem pole, and the last to obtain help. We were amazed to learn from visiting technical representatives from Douglas Aircraft and Pratt & Whitney Corporation that many items that we desperately needed were readily available and piling up in warehouses in the States waiting for requisitions. But no one seemed to know how to shake loose these vital supplies and get them to the CBI.

We besieged CBI headquarters in New Delhi with requisitions, and would ask in desperation, "What-in-hell are you guys doing back there, while we're busting our asses on the Hump?" The answers were always the same: "The parts are on the way." We became so frustrated that we developed a hatred for the unknown people who were falling down on the job.

On my rare flights into New Delhi I observed headquarters people living a life style that only increased my irritation at their failure to help us. The contrast between their comfortable life and our primitive jungle conditions and dangerous duties was almost obscene. It was very easy to build up anger and I had a problem restraining myself from speaking out about their indifferent attitude to our needs. They claimed they knew all about our struggles, but few had ever been to Assam, and even fewer over the Hump. I insisted that the staff people should visit us and fly with us to get a true taste of our life. You guessed it: there were no takers.

I am reluctant to place blame on people who can't answer back. Then I look at snapshots and movies I took of friends cut off in their youthful prime of life, lost on the Hump, and I wonder how many of them would be here now if some of our top-ranking officers had done a better job.

Losses were so high in fighter and cargo operations that we cynically started the rumor that pretty soon we would run out of airplanes, pack up our toothbrushes, and go home. Of course, being young, gutsy, optimistic pilots, we knew the cavalry would come to the rescue eventually. We didn't waste too much time brooding over what was missing, but put our energies to work solving our daily problems.

* * * * * *

We always assumed that our top brass were fighters also, fighting hard to get us the supplies we needed to operate. In Washington, Chief-of-Staff General George C. Marshall later stated that, "Asiatic operations were carried out at the end of the most precarious supply line in history." Washington was well aware of our problems, but failed miserably to remedy them.

We badly needed a "squeaky wheel" at high places to give us a boost. A VIP lobby went to Washington from China to give us some help, and showed just how inadequate our own leaders were. Mme Chiang Kai-shek, wife of the Generalissimo, and her brother, T. V. Soong, appeared to be more influential than our own generals. As ambassadors from China, they spent much time in Washington in 1941 and 1942, convincing President Roosevelt and other top government officials of the acute need of assistance for their floundering country. They had been making friends with government officials for years, and now this effort was paying off.

Both were well educated, at Wellesley and Harvard, and the highly articulate Mme. Chiang was able to completely charm the top echelons of Congress and White House advisers, while her brother entertained with lavish dinners in royal fashion. She made nationwide tours and was able to convince the American public that her country was the sole bastion of democracy in Asia. She created a feeling of sympathy and intimacy with China's problems. The Madame had some critics, people who knew what a powerful person she was, and some called her the "Dragon Lady." She was the power behind Chiang Kai-shek's throne, commander of the Chinese Air Force, and the 'godmother' to the American Volunteer Group, which she helped create.

This was a brilliant lady, shrewdly aware of world affairs, yet she exuded an aura of sweetness and naiveté that thoroughly captivated Henry Luce and other powerful Americans. Luce, publisher of Time and Life magazines, ran numerous articles favorable to China, and was influential in promoting Lend-lease and financial aid for Chiang.

President Roosevelt was too smart to be fooled by their claims that China was the one country in Asia flying the banner of true democracy, but he regarded this a matter of political necessity. He believed that without China in the war we might lose heavily, by freeing Japanese troops to move to the Pacific, and by our loss of a mainland base to attack Japan.

He listened to the Madame and went into action, ordering the Pentagon to supply more fighters for Chennault's AVG, and more cargo aircraft to expand the airlift. Despite the backing of the President, his generals once again failed to come through. The big question to be answered is —Why? Was it a true shortage, or inefficiency, or what?

CAST OF CHARACTERS

The leading characters in the CBI campaign make a fascinating study of powerful people exerting their influence, each one with a different agenda. The cast of characters starts with President Roosevelt, and includes Winston Churchill, and Generals Marshall, Arnold, Stilwell, Bissell, Chennault, and Generalissimo Chiang Kai-shek

At the head of the list is PRESIDENT ROOSEVELT, a brilliant tactician, who kept his head when a worldwide war exploded around him. He was surrounded by urgent problems every moment, and listened carefully to experts offering him advice. In the matter of support for China, he stubbornly disregarded powerful arguments from the generals who questioned his judgment, and stated that "wars are too important to be left in the hands of the military." He listened to his personal advisers, notably Harry Hopkins, and made the fateful decision to support Chiang. A bold and imaginative president, Roosevelt saw the United States taking a major role in world affairs in the future, and he wanted a close rapport with China and its huge population in post-war days. For the present, he needed China's support.

Roosevelt knew that China was far from being a democracy, but he was truly unaware of how backward and miserable the conditions were for its 450 million population. He had received most of his information about the country from Madame Chiang, who was quite misleading. China Watchers, old China hands who had lived in the country for many years, sent reports to the Department of State detailing the true conditions, but much of that information did not reach the President. Roosevelt was further influenced by the China Lobby, a powerful Washington group that received heavy support from Harry Hopkins and other prestigious Americans. They lobbied strongly to help Chiang, and Roosevelt agreed with their suggestions, expanding all types of aid.

The first time that Roosevelt personally met Chiang was at the Cairo conference in the fall of 1943. There he discovered how cold-hearted the China leader was. He found that Chiang had no sympathy whatsoever for the abject misery of his own people. FDR later admitted that all he knew about the Generalissimo was what Madame Chiang told him. Yet he continued to support China, and again, as he had done in April 1943, at the Trident conference, gave direct orders to increase supplies for the CBI. He would have been very disturbed to learn that his orders were not followed.

* * * * * *

WINSTON CHURCHILL was Roosevelt's political companion, adviser, and close friend, who rose to great heights as leader of war-torn Britain. His strong leadership and great optimism in the face of many defeats gave courage to his countrymen in their most critical period. He was a charismatic leader, attracting worldwide attention in the way he dressed, flashed his "V for Victory" sign everywhere, and he was tolerated for his indulgence in huge cigars and strong drink. His people adored him, and adopted his optimism.

Churchill was a sophisticated statesman who coldly analyzed the world situation. A huge German war machine was savagely battering his tiny country, and he urged FDR to devote all Allied materiel and manpower to fight the Axis armies in Europe and Africa.

The war in Asia was secondary to him. He considered Chiang Kai-shek to be a despot like Hitler and distrusted him, and doubted that China could be a factor in the war. He believed that the huge project under way to build a road from Ledo in India to China was a great waste of effort. He wanted to bypass Burma, as it had no tactical value.

Roosevelt disagreed with Churchill on the matter of China, wanting to attack Japan from many directions. The recapture of Burma was another one of his goals. Churchill regarded Roosevelt as somewhat naive about the benefit of aiding China, and made some pungent comments on this. He wrote in his memoirs, "I never succeeded in deflecting the Americans from their purpose .... Their national psychology is such that the bigger the idea, the more wholeheartedly and obstinately do they throw themselves into making it a success." He eventually gave in to FDR's plans to give major aid to China and to attack the Japanese in Burma, in order to obtain support in other areas.

* * * * * *

Chief-of-Staff GENERAL GEORGE C. MARSHALL, the brilliant tactician and manager of a million details, was kept informed by his old friend, General Stilwell, of the true state of the war in China. Stilwell was appointed chief-of-staff to Chiang Kai-shek, and supposedly given control over the Chinese armies. He reported that Chiang was reluctant to send Chinese troops to fight the Japanese in Burma, and was saving supplies and men for his ultimate battle with the Chinese Communists. Stillwell's reports convinced Marshall that the Generalissimo was not to be trusted.

Marshall's distrust of Chiang rubbed off on General Chennault as well, leaving the latter without support in the Pentagon for an expanded air operation. General Marshall claimed that he was harassed by "Localitis," with every theater commander around the world clamoring for more support. The European and Pacific Theaters ranked highest, which left the CBI in last place. Stateside production of aircraft was increasing dramatically, but so were worldwide needs, and the CBI Theater never did catch up.

* * * * * *

Next I come to GENERAL HAROLD "HAP" ARNOLD, commanding general of U.S. Army Air Forces around the globe. Arnold claimed that the demands for aircraft from all theaters caused "Theater-it is," which was his name for the same problem that afflicted General Marshall. This remained one of his chief plagues throughout the war, leaving him in a constant quandary about how to allocate his meager forces that everyone wanted.

The Hump operation received so few airplanes each month that our cargo fleet was actually shrinking due to losses, and the China combat forces received no aircraft at all. That sounded like one helluva way to fight a war. It does not appear that Arnold was paying much attention to FDR's orders.

He did become very aware of Hump hazards on his visit in 1943, when he got lost on the way to Kunming in his personal VIP airplane, a well-equipped B-17 with a highly qualified crew. This is an amusing story, and should have impressed him with our need for navigational aids.

He crossed the Hump at night with an expected arrival time of 9:30 P.M. at Kunming, but his navigator failed to find that base, and they flew further east for

239

over two hours. He claimed that a strong tailwind had placed them over Japanese territory, at least 300 miles east of their destination. This was not Japanese territory, for they were well short of our base at Kweilin, located another 150 miles further east. Arnold wrote of their concern that they might run out of gas, and have to bailout and walk through the jungle in low shoes and light clothing. This was another error, as there was no jungle. In his memoirs, he mused about the incredible situation it would be for him, Commanding General of the United States Army Air Forces, and Clayton Bissell, Commanding General of the 10th Air Force, and all his staff, to be taken prisoners. He neglected to admit that he was scared, but I am sure everyone on board was praying.

Fortunately, they carried a full load of fuel, and when the navigator finally found their position, they landed at Kunming over four hours overdue, finding a very anxious crowd waiting. From then on, all his flying to Chungking and other China bases was in a C-47 flown by experienced China pilots. One would expect that Arnold's narrow escape would have convinced him that we needed more adequate navigation aids, but it did not.

Arnold knew about our very successful combat operations. In his memoirs he acknowledged Chennault's record with the Flying Tigers and the China Air Task Force and commended his "uncanny talent for handling airplanes against the Japanese." He praised Chennault's initiative and drive that got things done, and recognized his strong position with the Chinese.

But then he went on a negative tack, giving many reasons why we could not expand our combat operations, and did not need more airplanes on the Hump. He pointed out that the railroads leading to Assam were overloaded and could not carry more cargo, so we could not obtain more gasoline to carry over the Hump. He felt that we needed more fields in China to handle more traffic. He criticized Chennault and Chiang for their "we'll get it done in spite of hell or high water" way to solve logistical problems, and their failure to recognize the supply problems.

General Arnold's reasoning was a great disappointment to the resourceful people in China, who had a history of finding ways to overcome difficult situations. Their requests for increases in supplies were blocked by Arnold's chief of logistics, General Clayton Bissell, a detail man who was called an "old woman" by Chiang's staff. Bissell went by the book, and had no faith in the ability of the Chinese to find a way. This was typical of the safe, conservative viewpoint that often squelches military success, and could have only one outcome. The Pentagon people had the key to the supply room and refused to unlock the door.

GENERAL JOSEPH "VINEGAR JOE" STILLWELL climbed on board our C-47 one day at Chungking to ride with us to Kweilin. He nodded to us pilots, and seated himself very rigidly, looking nervous at the prospect of flying. I was very impressed by this charismatic officer. A general with a nickname like that had to be a real soldier. He had a great reputation as a wonderful leader of men, and a true field officer cut from the same cloth as Chennault. He spoke Chinese fluently, and seemed a good choice as Chief of Staff to Chiang Kai-shek, in command of all Chinese ground forces.

He was easily recognized by his broad-brimmed campaign hat and his lean wiry build His men admired him for spending his time with them in the field, enduring the same hardships. His famous jungle walk in 1942 proved his mettle, when he personally led his troops out of the Burmese jungle after turning down an offer of escape by air. Enemy forces harassed his troops, but he insisted on staying with them, facing treacherous terrain and dangerous wild life, until they reached safety. This 'soldier's soldier' earned the undying gratitude of his men, but top brass criticized him for taking such high personal risk, instead of remaining in a safe place to maintain command over all of his far-flung Chinese troops. That was just not his style.

Stilwell and Chennault had such common goals that they should have worked well together, but, strangely enough, they became known as the "Feuding Generals" to later day historians. When it came to air power, "Vinegar Joe" was way out of date, another "General Yesterday." His method of fighting was "on the ground with a bayonet," following the age-old maxim that no battle is won until ground troops take possession of the land. This is sound doctrine, but Stilwell gave absolutely no credit to air power at all, and ignored the spectacular successes of Chennault's fighters, thereby causing a great rift in their relations.

Amazingly, he failed to give credit to the AVG for its extraordinary action in May of '42, when a mere handful of fighter-bombers succeeded in permanently blocking the Japanese advance up the Burma Road. Stilwell's Chinese troops had fought fiercely for many weeks, but failed to stop the enemy thrust toward Kunming. The AVG had accomplished it in two days, by destroying the Salween River bridge crossing, and blocking the road with landslides.

Stilwell ignored the reality that Chennault's fighters had taken command of the skies over Burma and western China, and had stopped the bombings that often paralyzed his Chinese armies. He insisted that the bulk of our air cargo be supplies for his ground troops, but he never acknowledged that the P-40's provided safety to our unarmed transports. He had a direct pipeline to General Marshall in Washington and could have used his influence to obtain more support, but he appeared indifferent to our pleas for more combat and cargo aircraft.

Stilwell suffered a stunning defeat at the top-level TRIDENT conference in Washington in April of 1943. He presented a plan for his Chinese troops to fight an all-out ground war in Burma, which required massive amounts of hard- to-get war supplies. Roosevelt rejected this plan in favor of a far simpler strategy; to build up an air offensive around Chennault's air force, the CATF, which had an excellent track record despite its small size. Once again, the President gave a direct order to expand the airlift and send more fighters and bombers to the CBI, and left it to his military staff to carry out this instruction. Once again, it did not happen.

Stilwell resented Roosevelt's turn-down of his proposal, and continued to have major problems with Chiang, whose armies he led. He had complained a year earlier about the problems of working with Chiang and his subordinates, and there was continuous friction between them. An exchange of radiograms between Stilwell and Chief of Staff General Marshall showed how intensely "Vinegar Joe" disliked Chiang and his staff and the friction between them. His descriptions of Chiang and his staff were extremely critical, very graphic, often in rough language. An amazing message Stilwell sent to Marshall in April, 1942, illustrated the problems:

"Operations around Toungoo hampered by breakdowns in transport, delays in supply, rotten communications, sabotage by natives, and politics in the army. These troubles fade into insignificance compared to the incompetence, lethargy, and disregard of orders amounting to disobedience on part of division and army commanders. Unfortunately my powers stop short of shooting. A fine opportunity for good slap at the Japs has been ruined by the craven obstruction of above mentioned commanders ... Under existing conditions cannot continue to command Fifth and Sixth armies without being stooge for Chinese who can bypass me for anything they want to do, and then blame me for the result. "

Chiang Kai-shek was in charge, and Stilwell was expendable. Eventually, the friction grew so great that Stilwell was replaced.

GENERAL CLAYTON BISSELL, commander of the 10th Air Force, was another officer who resented Chennault, and let his resentment show. When Chennault vaulted from the insignificant position of general in the Chinese Air Force to brigadier general in the U. S. Army Air Corps, the Pentagon promoted Bissell to the same one-star rank. His date of rank was just one day ahead of Chennault, which technically meant that Bissell outranked Chennault. This insured that control over the China Air Task Force remained in Washington and not in Chungking.

Bissell made no bones about his opinion that Chennault was not qualified to head any military forces whatsoever, despite the successes of the Flying Tigers. He held the AVG in disdain because it was a mercenary force working for pay, which was way beyond the understanding of the military mind. That was another example of a "General Yesterday" who could not deviate from established doctrine. I think his attitude was a major cause of our failure to obtain needed support.

He made a massive blunder in June of 1942, when he warned the Flying Tigers that they had to "Join the Army Air Corps or end up toting a rifle in the infantry." This threat totally alienated the American Volunteer Group, which was going out of existence on July 4th. Most of them had planned to join the Air Corps, but Bissell's amazing arrogance and hard-nosed orders to "join up, or else" were regarded by AVG men as the ultimate in insulting treatment. They disgustedly walked out of the meeting, after telling him very graphically what he could do with his proposal.

He outraged the very men he needed, and left them with a bad taste for that "stupid army that treats us like a bunch of schoolboys. Why did they send such an S.O.B.? They can go to hell!" These men were tired and war-weary, a fact which Bissell overlooked. He refused to allow them a leave of absence if they joined up. They were bitter at the failure of the armed services to recognize their accomplishments. They mourned the losses of some of their comrades, and were themselves survivors by the merest of margins.

They had trouble believing that this man was totally sane, or had any idea what was going on in China. They were so incensed that they taught some of the Chinese aircraft service men in Kunming a refrain to sing to the crews and passengers of each transport as it arrived, "Piss on Bissell, piss on Bissell. "

There was a rumor among many of the AVG personnel that Bissell's insult was deliberate, and that he intended to drive away the experienced people he was sent to recruit, in order to reduce Chennault's chances of success. This was not taken seriously at the time, but remained in our minds when he and Stilwell failed to provide the aircraft they had promised to the new CATF.

Only seven AVG pilots, mostly flight leaders, accepted Bissell's offer, wanting to give badly needed support to the "Old Man", Chennault. After Bissell's failure to recruit the entire group, he retreated to New Delhi, and we heard nothing further from him, but we sorely missed the expert pilots who left for other jobs.

* * * * * *

"Here comes the GENERALISSIMO and his wife," whispered our Operations clerk at Kunming one day. And there was Chiang Kai-shek, followed by a military aide, and by his very demure looking Madame holding a bright yellow parasol. I was one of a group of Hump pilots that was asked to line up outside Operations at Kunming to greet the "Gissmo." He was to present us with Chinese Air Force medals for "Valiant Service and Bravery in Flying the Dangerous Himalaya Mountains to Bring Essential Supplies to the Chinese Nation."

The Generalissimo was the key man in China, and the Madame, his wife, was equally important, considered to be more than just the "power behind the throne." Their surprise visit to our Operations shack in Kunming gave us a revealing glimpse of the two.

The Generalissimo and his wife proceeded smilingly down the line of 15 pilots, giving out the medals that were handed to him by his aide, but his smile suddenly vanished when he reached for another medal and was met with a flustered look. There weren't enough to go around.

Chiang looked at his aide fiercely, and some sharp words followed in Chinese, and it was an awkward moment. Then the Madame took over and showed her ability to manage delicate situations. She moved out from under her colorful parasol and, in flawless English, graciously apologized for the shortage and promised that we would all receive our medals. She gave each of us a big smile and a handshake, showed tremendous charm and adroitness in saying just the right thing. However, all I have is a handshake and the memory of that smile, as I'm still waiting for my medal, over 50 years later.

The Generalissimo was a short, undistinguished looking man, who held the fate of China in his hands for many years, and has been both praised and damned. A close look at his history tells of a poor boy, attending military schools in Japan, and working his way up in politics to achieve leadership over all of China. He was a disciple of Sun Tzu, a celebrated general of the 5th century B.C., who wrote a famous manual on methods of conducting warfare that is still studied by military leaders over 2500 years later. Sun Tzu stressed the importance of gathering intelligence by espionage and ruthless interrogation of prisoners, then preparing elaborately for battle. All military action is delayed until a quick decisive strike insures victory.

Chiang followed these principles in both political and military dealings. He was a ruthless leader with a very dark past, and had a well-known reputation for putting opposition political leaders to death by torture, and using every means to maintain power. He solidified his leadership position by his marriage to a Soong daughter, a member of the most prominent and wealthy family in China. The Soong family's climb to wealth and power, and Chiang's struggle to dominate China, are spectacular stories that read more interestingly than fiction.

China experts accused Chiang of fighting a "three-cornered war," facing both the Japanese invasion and the internal threat by Chinese Communist leader Chou En-lai to unseat him as national leader. It was rumored that Chiang was secretly hoarding half of the materiel that we brought over the Hump at great risk, for later use in his fight against the Communists. Some of this distrust rubbed off on American personnel, and there were reports of personal belongings of the Generalissimo and the Madame being sabotaged while in transit from India to China.

I heard rumors that accused Chiang of actually conducting business with the Japanese, but I considered these to be just wartime gossip at the time. Intelligence reports released later disclosed that his field generals were indeed doing just that, dealing with the enemy. Other reports told of the ruthless ways in which Chiang used his troops, sometimes sending them into hopeless battles just to show his power, knowing full well that they would be destroyed by a far more powerful enemy.

Roosevelt, the master tactician, knew about Chiang's other agenda aimed at fighting Chou En-lai, but he insisted that we needed Chiang and his huge armies to actively oppose the Japanese. To guaranty Chiang's allegiance, he sent him a message on December 29, 1941, with a prestigious proposal, an offer of command of all Allied forces operating in the Chinese Theater.

Chiang's reply was a classic example of political double-talk. First he went into great detail to explain why he was not qualified to accept this offer, but then quickly reversed himself and accepted it, thus assuming power over most of the military in Asia. The Madame had done her part by convincing FDR to become the guardian angel for China.

Chiang kept one bargain he had made with FDR, which was to make temporary peace with Chou En-lai to fight the common enemy, the Japanese. Yet he outraged his Allies by a very high-handed tactic. He repeatedly threatened to make peace with the Japanese if he did not receive the arms he requested. World leaders and our top brass acknowledged him as supreme commander of all forces in China, but they did not trust him.

* * * * * *

As a survivor of the CBI operation, I am bitter over the dissension that threatened to lose our theater to the enemy. Chennault's victories were a key factor in keeping China in the war, yet Generals Marshall, Arnold, Stilwell, and Bissell all showed such antagonism towards Chennault and neglect of our needs, that it is a wonder we survived in those early days.

Our failures and the shortcoming of our commanders create questions that have been on my mind for many years:

1 - Why did the generals in Washington fail to heed the repeated orders of the President to support air operations? Was there prejudice against Chennault?

2 - Why did our commanders in New Delhi fail to use their influence in Washington to obtain aid? Was it incompetence?

3 - Was Stilwell's disappointment at the rejection of his plans for a massive ground campaign in Burma the reason for his failure to support Chennault's air assaults?

4 - Why did Chennault's victories and his popularity with the American public offend the high brass? Why did they call his victories "accidental", and refuse to give him credit at the time for the astounding successes of his tiny air force?

5 - Why did the Air Corps ignore Chennault's successful fighter tactics, and his insistence that fighters could win battles against bombers, much to their later regret?

6 - And lastly, am I ignoring the possibility that everyone worked in good faith, and there just wasn't enough to go around?

Chapter 36
TREACHERY

In 1959, some incredible stories were revealed to the American public about commanders of Chiang Kai-shek's armies doing business with the enemy. This startling information was published by the Office of the Chief of Military History, Department of the Army*, and spoke of the Chinese dealing with Japanese generals in 1943 and 1944.

The military publication stated that in the winter of 1943-44:

"Intelligence reports were received at U.S. headquarters to the effect that the Generalissimo's attitude toward the east China campaign reflected an understanding between him and the Japanese under which they would leave him undisturbed in southwest China, if he in turn would not interfere while they took the airfields that presented so obvious a menace to the Japanese homeland."

These serious charges against Chiang were not proven. However, senior Japanese officers were queried about this in 1951, and admitted that they had close contact with Chinese commanders in east China, who claimed to be acting independently of Chiang.

The Japanese informed the Chinese generals that they were planning a drive against the important airbases at Kweilin and Hengyang, but would not threaten the cities of Kunming and Chungking, further west. They did as predicted, overrunning the eastern airfields in November of 1944, but never approaching Kunming and Chungking. This appears to have been a deliberately planned trade-off.

These dealings with the enemy would be labeled acts of treason in any country. In China, they would mean the death penalty, but this never happened. Chiang was undoubtedly aware of these transactions, as he maintained a spy network in every part of China. All signs are that the offending generals were acting with the knowledge and permission of Chiang. The "Gissmo" kept his hands off, and even refused to send troops to the Kweilin area to reinforce the armies that were under attack, and eventually defeated.

*1959 Military Publication. Reprinted 1999, "UNITED STATES ARMY IN WORLD WAR II"
China-Burma-India Theater
**TIME RUNS OUT IN CBI", Pages 8-13, by Charles F. Romanus and Riley Sunderland.
Library of Congress - Ca. Car No: 59-600003

Another shocking report was that some of the medical supplies from the Red Cross and International Relief, which we brought over the Hump to Kunming, were being trucked to Shanghai and other coastal cities that were under control of the Japanese army**. What a chilling thought! We were risking our lives to haul this vital cargo, and it was ending up in enemy hands. If our Hump crews had known of the situation, there would have been a major upset in our airlift operation, for we were putting our lives on the line every day.

We witnessed the perilous condition of the Chinese population, and knew that their armies were suffering heavy losses. It would be hard to believe that the main interest of their despotic leader was preservation of his empire with little regard for the people. We heard rumors that the Chinese were putting part of our Hump loads into storage for later use against the Chinese Communist forces, but we paid them little attention, as every military organization is a rumor mill. As good soldiers should do, we followed orders, hopeful that the job was worthwhile and that our efforts were appreciated. The unfavorable reports never reached the American public. If they had, there would have been a tremendous backlash.

Other reports told of a sizeable commercial trade going on between occupied and unoccupied China. Homegrown products such as rice, leather, lumber, and tea were transported from Free China to Japanese controlled coastal cities. Much of this activity was easily kept out of sight of westerners, hidden by a political situation that was in much turmoil.

Chiang Kai-shek committed the ultimate in diplomatic insult by his threats to make peace with Japan if we did not meet his demands. It showed him to be a world-class manipulator and bargainer. This was a classical example of the honor system: "The United States had the honor, and Chiang had the system." There was fraud and deceptive behavior by Chiang, who received Lend-Lease aid in money and materiel amounting to many billions of dollars, yet he shamelessly pressured Washington for more.

Investigations were started in Washington about the half-billion in actual Lend-Lease dollars we gave directly to Chiang and the Soongs for purchase of war materiel, but these inquiries were hushed up through the influence of the China Lobby, that influential group of pro-Chinese Americans. There were suggestions that large amounts of Lend-Lease money ended up in Soong family coffers, but these claims were never proven. There were rumors that the Chinese were selling shiploads and truckloads of Lend-Lease supplies that never reached their own front-line troops, but these were not verified either.

From many banking and financial quarters, the word spread that the Soong family had become the richest in the world. With all that smoke, there had to be some fire, and it appeared that our foreign aid to China was really a foreign raid on the U.S. treasury. President Harry Truman disclosed, after his re-election in 1948, that the total aid to China amounted to $3.8 billions, of which at least one billion ended up in bank accounts and investments of Generalissimo Chiang and his Madame's Soong family.

FDR and his advisors were sold on assisting China by the greatest salesperson of the century - Mme. Chiang Kai-shek, nee Mai-ling Soong. Sometimes called the "Empress of China" and even "Snow White" by an admiring American public, and an "Avenging Angel" by Wendell Willkie, she was far more than just the power behind the throne. She was every bit as powerful as her husband in her own way, and knew exactly how to create a legion of admirers. Truly acting like an "Empress," she insisted on being treated in a regal manner, in the way she was housed and catered to when she visited Washington. She went so far as to actually demand special courtesies from President Roosevelt and Prime Minister Churchill. When FDR invited her and Churchill to luncheon at the White House for major policy discussions, she declined the invitation in a royal fashion, and insisted that they join her at her hotel suite, which they did not do.

The Madame could also be a subtle person, and use a softer approach than her husband, when she cajoled Congress and other leaders for support. Her speeches were elegant masterpieces of persuasion, and her pleas to rescue the starving millions from the clutches of a cruel oppressor brought tears to the eyes of the American public. The United China Relief raised huge amounts of dollars from all kinds of charities and even from school children, but there were grave questions about where the money went.

Beware the femme fatale! Behind her exquisite looks Madame was a totally ruthless, power-seeking person, who occasionally bared her fangs by accusing us of breaking promises we had made to her. These were most outrageous statements from a leader whose government existed only by the generosity of our nation, and she showed incredible arrogance. It was small wonder that some insiders referred to her as the "Dragon Lady. "

Even Eleanor Roosevelt, who had welcomed her like a daughter, was dismayed when she dropped her guard and showed her tyrannical side. Mrs. Roosevelt commented that Mai-ling Soong (Madame Chiang) talked fluently about democracy, but did not know how to live it.

One of the Madame's most influential supporters was Henry Luce, publisher of Time and Life magazines, who promoted aid for China in a never -ending campaign. He was born in China, the son of missionaries, and had a life-long infatuation with all things Chinese. Time magazine pictured the Chiang Kai-sheks on its cover as the "Man of the Year" in 1938, and the Madame's picture appeared on other magazine covers.

I had met the Madame briefly on official business at Kunming, but we knew her better in a very unique way. She was the "Dragon Lady" in Milton Caniff's comic strip called "Terry and the Pirates," which every pilot read eagerly during the war years. Young pilot Terry was a member of a volunteer group patterned after the AVG, and the glamorous Lady saved his neck many times when he got into trouble.

This was pure fiction, for in real life, the very opposite was true. We were the ones who saved the power of the Dragon Lady and her dictator husband by our support. The British were far more cynical and critical of Chiang Kai-shek and the Soong family, and jokingly referred to him as "General Cash My-check." Historians agree that Chiang's sole objective was to retain his power over all of China. For this he needed United States aid to defeat both the Japanese forces and his Communist opposition. There is little indication that Chiang had any compassion for his suffering Chinese population.

With one war over, Chiang Kai-shek's empire in mainland China was shattered by his defeat to the Communist forces that set up a new Chinese government. Chiang fled to the offshore island of Formosa, taking much treasure with him. He boldly announced to the islanders that he had freed them from the Japanese, but they did not believe him or welcome him. He was accustomed to this type of opposition, and took over the island by sheer force, using the same violent tactics he had used many years before to take over mainland China. He massacred all Formosan opposition, at a cost of up to 30,000 lives, and established a new empire, living there with his family happily ever after. To our lasting shame, this takeover was part of our peace agreement, and was done with United States aid.

Chapter 37
WHITE ELEPHANT - OR NOT?

Some readers may want to pelt me with overripe tomatoes for suggesting that the China- Burma-India campaign may have been a mistake, as I question the reasons for our being there. But it's worth the risk, as it might open up new thinking about whether aid to China was essential.

The mind-boggling thought occurred to me one day that the CBI was our great White Elephant. I was recalling the mythical India story about the maharajah, who was displeased with one of his subjects, and made him a gift of a sacred White Elephant. This animal required very expensive special care, which the owner could not afford. He could not employ it as a work animal to pay for its keep, as it was sacred, nor could he sell it or even give it away, as it was a royal gift. The gift was truly a punishment, for it reduced him and his family to poverty. From this story comes the popular expression, "White Elephant," for something you cannot use, but cannot get rid of easily.

Perhaps President Roosevelt was handed a similar burden when he accepted the responsibility of supporting China. Chiang Kai-shek was in serious trouble, and so was an anxious Winston Churchill, whose colonies of Burma and India were under fire.

Both requested aid from Roosevelt, who had proudly declared the United States to be the "Arsenal of Democracy." Madame Chiang also exerted her influence on FDR, and traveled across the country, arousing sympathy among the American public over the plight of her people.

FDR was supported by highly respected advisors in approving Lend-Lease aid to China early in 1941. He was convinced that our support was essential, and he overrode the objections of top-level generals who opposed this. They claimed that China had little tactical value, and that our efforts were better spent elsewhere. But once the campaign was started it took on a momentum of its own, as do most military projects, regardless of how questionable they are, and there was no going back.

From then on, the only complaints heard were from the troops, men like myself, at the bottom rung of the ladder, who were ordered to risk our lives for a cause that many of us felt was useless or hopeless. We received such poor support that we were convinced that our mission had little value, and that we were the "Lost Battalion. "

Were we really needed in the CBI, or was it all an ill-conceived idea, a monstrous White Elephant? I reviewed the history very carefully, realizing that I was highly prejudiced, but found strong reasons to question our involvement in the CBI.

ARGUMENTS 'FOR' and 'AGAINST

1 - FOR: President Roosevelt reasoned that aid to China would keep a million Japanese troops and a large air force tied up in fighting on the mainland of Asia. This would keep them out of the Pacific, where we were in serious trouble, and reduce the threat of invasion of India and Australia.

AGAINST: If the Japanese army occupied all of China, they would still require a large army just to police the vast territory, which included China, Burma, and the Malay Peninsula. China, alone, was a major headache to control, as there were many regional warlords with private armies, who were experienced in fighting guerrilla wars. They could keep the Japanese military very busy.

2 - FOR: We would push the Japanese out of Burma and reopen the Burma Road supply line.

AGAINST: Winston Churchill was very reluctant to fight a major war against the Japanese in Burma. He stated in his memoirs that malarial Northern Burma was "the most forbidding fighting country imaginable." He told President Roosevelt that he was "not prepared to undertake something foolish purely to placate the Chinese." He requested enough aid to just contain the Japanese in Burma, realizing that a major campaign to remove them would require an enormous expenditure in manpower and materiel, which were needed elsewhere. Roosevelt prevailed, and decided to push the enemy entirely out of Burma, despite the serious problems of supply, the poor cooperation of Chiang Kai-shek, and the extremely dangerous jungle-wise Japanese troops.

Churchill proved correct in several ways. The Burma campaign proved to be one of the longest and most vicious in the war, lasting almost four years. British and Indian units lost many lives fighting a fierce enemy, and faced dangerous jungles, disease, and critical supply problems. American troops also participated, with Merrill's Marauders and other special fighting forces. The jungle fighting was so deadly that it was considered better to be killed outright than be wounded, lost in the jungle, or captured and suffer as a prisoner. Burma was eventually won back after years of fierce fighting, late in the war, helped by our airlift making huge airdrops.

The unique twist is that after retaking Burma, the Road was no longer used again as a major supply route to China, having been largely replaced by the Hump airlift. Another irony is that the British lost their colony of Burma three years later, when it won its independence.

The battle for Burma is truly a tragic story. I consider that campaign a futile and costly military exercise that should never have taken place. Brave men were sacrificed to recapture a country that had no strategic value.

In writing these words, I have thought many times of the famous Tennyson poem, "The Charge of the Light Brigade." *"Theirs not to reason why. Theirs but to do and die, Into the valley of death Rode the six hundred."* These famous lines were written to commemorate a disastrous loss of lives caused by an alleged massive blunder by the commanding officer. The history of wars discloses many such blunders.

3 - FOR: FDR's other fear was that without our aid to China and India, Japanese troops would be able to cross India and the Middle East and connect up with Axis troops in the Mediterranean area in what he described as a huge pincer movement.

AGAINST: British forces were able to protect India very well, with jungle troops aided by air-drops of food and supplies. The Himalaya Mountains blocked invasion of India from China. For Japan to stretch its armies across the entire mid-east was a task of such gigantic proportions that it defied reason.

4 - FOR: Provide air bases for bombing of Japan by our B-29 long range heavy bombers.

AGAINST: China was thought to be a logical jumping-off place for bombing raids against the Japanese homeland, but this was never done successfully. Our B-29 forces operating out of India and Chengdu, China, faced such extreme difficulties that the campaign was deemed a failure, as I describe later. The units were shifted to Pacific Island bases, from which they successfully bombed Japan.

5 - FOR: Secure certain basic war materials available in China

AGAINST: A limited supply of tungsten ore and hog bristles was exported from China, but these were not so vital as to justify fighting a war.

SUMMARY

Just what did the CBI campaign accomplish? There is no doubt that our involvement was a blessing for the desperate Chinese people who were besieged by Japan. Ruthless bombing of their cities ceased, saving many lives.

There were also very disappointing results. In 1944, Japanese leaders realized that China was about to become a giant air base from which the new B-29 heavy bombers could attack the Japanese mainland, and they took aggressive steps to halt this. They swept westward across China, capturing the important airbases at Kweilin and Hengyang.

We hauled large amounts of supplies over the Hump for the Chinese regiments defending this great area, but much of it never reached the troops as there was no transport system to do the job. Supplies leaked away as Chiang's "special forces" secretly stored much of this materiel for a future campaign against the Communists. Reliable sources reported that as early as 1944, Chiang's Nationalist forces were already using these supplies to fight the Chinese Communists. This was a frustrating outcome of the heroic airlift.

In late 1944, the fast advancing Japanese forces so badly defeated the Chinese armies in central China that Chiang's armies just evaporated. The Chinese vastly outnumbered the Japanese, but when good leadership disappeared, the troops simply abandoned their units and dispersed into the countryside, taking with them any portable supplies.

These Japanese victories in China in 1944 were quite remarkable, as they were suffering defeat everywhere else. They were losing in Burma and the Pacific, and their homelands were battered by devastating B-29 raids. Eventually, fresh Chinese troops coming north from Burma pushed the enemy back to the coast, and total victory soon followed.

Chiang continued to demand war supplies even though victory was imminent. Defeat of Japan in August, 1945, was the end of our war, but was the beginning of a massive civil war within China. The United States knew that Chiang would be battling the Communists for a long time, and refused to be a party to this new war. They stopped supplying Lend-Lease materiel, but this did not hamper Chiang, who had already accumulated vast stockpiles of arms. Chiang was eventually defeated soundly, despite his careful preparations.

The British and French regained control of their colonial empires of India, Burma, and Malaysia, but soon lost these when the colonies declared independence.

In China, the war against Japan dragged on for many years. It was the great American spirit that was enraged by the Pearl Harbor attack, our superior industrial strength, and bloody Pacific battles, and finally, the atom bombs, that brought this terrible conflict in Asia to an end.

This brings us back to the question of the need for the CBI campaign. Some historians argue that Roosevelt made the right decision, as the United States investment of men and materiel was "relatively small" but effective in keeping Japan tied up in a defensive war.

I was part of that "small investment," one of those men at high risk. We may have been mere statistics to the war department, but we were living people, and some of us died to protect Asian countries. Once started, the CBI campaign was taken for granted as an essential military operation. But its questionable results indicate that it may have been a terrible waste, costing us dearly.

Generalisimo and Madam Chiang Kai-shek with General Stilwell.

Chapter 38
LATER STORIES OF THE CBI IN 1944-45

"Never in the field of human conflict, was so much owed by so many to so few." Winston Churchill's famous statement gave praise to the Royal Air Force fighter pilots, who valiantly fought the overwhelming German Luftwaffe in the Battle of Britain. He repeated this solemn praise to honor the American airmen who fought in the China- Burma-India Theater.

* * * * * *

My overseas tour of duty ended in May of 1943, but my new assignment to the Reno Operational Training Unit (OTU) kept me closely involved with the CBI, for we were training crews to fly the Hump. Many important events took place in the CBI Theater in 1944-45 involving the airlift to China and the 14th Air Force under Chennault, and I am narrating them briefly. I also include the very dramatic story of the 20th Bomber Command under General Curtis LeMay, which flew B-29's from India and China.

After our very slow start, the Hump operation was built up in 1944 to an airlift of major size, with as many as 500 aircraft. In December of 1942, we carried less than 1,000 tons over the Hump. Chiang Kai-shek demanded an immediate build-up of tonnage, but this took place gradually. In December of 1943 the airlift exceeded 6,000 tons, and by 1945 it was carrying over 40,000 tons per month. In the peak month of July, 1945, it reached 70,000 tons.

The C-47 fleet started the airlift, but the major workhorse became the much larger C-46 Curtiss-Wright Commando, which was the largest twin-engine transport in the world at the time. It could carry a payload of 23 drums of fuel compared to 13 in a C-47, and do it higher and faster. The Hump fleet continued to grow with the addition of various four- engine aircraft, including the C-87 cargo carrier and its twin C-109 tanker, and the very much-desired C-54 cargo and passenger aircraft. Combat Cargo units, flying C-47's, were dispatched to supply the troops battling in Burma. All this activity resulted in a dizzying amount of air traffic across the mountains. There are many stories to recount of this gallant operation that supplied China with vital aid.

At the Reno OTU, our cadre of former Hump pilots taught the intricacies of all-weather flying and turned out highly qualified C-46 pilots destined for the

CBI. Despite this concentrated instruction, bad weather still played havoc with Hump pilots, causing many casualties, though the C-46 was better suited to the job and could carry ice more easily.

Military necessity placed the C-46 in service before it was de-bugged, and its defects showed up under hard use. One major problem was the tendency of carburetors to ice up quickly under certain conditions. In the dry climate of Reno this was not apparent, but in monsoon weather over the Hump it was disastrous, causing many engine failures, sometimes with both engines quitting at the same time, and crews bailing out. There was an improvement when pilots were better briefed on use of carburetor de-icing systems and heat controls, but the loss rate was still high. The war machine was like a hungry animal that devoured aircraft and crews, eating the very hand that fed it.

Colonel Thomas Hardin was the hard-driving commanding officer of the Air Transport Command's Hump airlift, whose job was to improve efficiency and increase tonnage. He visited the Chabua area during the fall monsoon season of 1944, a period of very bad weather, and demanded to know why so many aircraft in flyable condition were sitting on the ground When advised that the weather was too severe for safe operation, he issued an order to the effect that, "There is no weather on the Hump!" From that time on, flying was to continue despite what Operations considered un-flyable conditions. Hardin intended to overcome all obstacles to achieve his tonnage goals, regardless of the risks involved.

The risks were very high, indeed, because Hardin lacked the supporting facilities to back up his demand. He ordered pilots to fly a hazardous route without any weather forecasting, and he ordered them to fly to a destination where weather was often at minimum instrument conditions, without benefit of proper instrument approach procedures. Kunming weather could change quickly from good to zero-zero conditions, but ground radio stations did not have the range to warn inbound pilots of this. After reaching Kunming, if they did not have enough fuel to make a return flight, they made desperate attempts to land, often crashing.

Our original AMMISCA pilots had made their own decisions on when to fly. They were highly experienced, with airline background, and when they decided the weather was too severe for safe operation, the Hump airlift shut down. Sometimes a high-ranking officer would question their decisions, but "desk pilots" were not inclined to interfere, as they lacked the know-how our pilots possessed. As these experienced pilots were rotated back to the States, new military pilots were flying the route, directed by officers, like Hardin, who had quotas to meet.

Hardin gave a deaf ear to the argument that sometimes Hump weather was an impossible barrier. He was an experienced pilot who braved the Hump despite extremely bad conditions, and he expected his men to do the same.

Before long, he issued a more frightening order; to begin operating at night, around the clock. If there was anything scarier than flying on instruments in bad weather across the Himalayas, it was flying at night on instruments across that savage land. You flew into a black void with poor knowledge of weather conditions ahead, and poor communications to ground stations, and that took a great deal of pure guts. It was one of the worst flying jobs in the world and some of the pilots couldn't stand the strain and just quit, taking on ground jobs. Others, conversely, took pride in their ability to cope with the frightening conditions. Some pilots flew so many trips across the Hump at night that they never did see what it looked like during the day.

Tonnage did increase, and top brass congratulated Colonel Hardin on his success. However, his success had a terribly high price. The all-weather flying policy caused heavy losses of aircraft and created that awesome name for the route, the "Aluminum Trail." Hardin became the person most hated by flight crews in the CBI.

Things came to a head on January 6th and 7th of 1945, when a spell of extremely bad weather hit Kunming and vicinity and caused a disaster of major size. Dozens of aircraft were en route from India when ceiling and visibility unexpectedly dropped down close to zero at every field in China within reach. Airplanes with sufficient fuel returned across the Hump to Chabua, but the ones low on fuel were forced to attempt instrument letdowns using the very limited radio beacons available. A few were lucky to break out of the overcast before hitting the ground, but some did not. The results were tragic.

The bad landing conditions were only part of the problem. The situation was made incredibly worse by violent winds blowing from the south at velocities of up to 100 miles per hour. Pilots taking the southern route towards Myitkyina were not affected as much as the ones going straight across the Hump, who were unaware of the winds. Many were blindly pushed far to the north into the high mountain ranges. Surviving pilots reported hearing many frantic calls of "Mayday" from pilots who were totally lost, running low on fuel, preparing to bailout into the freezing unknown of the high Himalayas. The outcome of this

"Storm From Hell" was a terrible loss of over 50 aircraft and crews that either crashed in the Kunming area attempting blind letdowns or flew into the northern mountains. Few bailouts were rescued

To cap this tragic episode, more disasters occurred when pilots who survived the eastbound flight to China were told to return to India without laying over. Operations gave orders that they were to return to Chabua immediately, once again battling the same terrible weather. The reason for sending these crews out again into such dangerous conditions was not clear, but one thing was certain: more crews were sacrificed in the almost unflyable weather that had already claimed many lives.

Military commanders always face bitter decisions trying to accomplish their goals, and they expect losses on dangerous missions. But Hardin's hard-headed approach was ridiculous under the conditions that existed on the Hump. He disregarded the cardinal rule: that a commander is obligated to provide the best equipment and operating facilities for his men. Without these he was inviting disaster, and that is what happened.

I wonder how our early Hump pilots would have handled such a situation, and the answer is fairly obvious. Those airline pilots, with far more experience than their military bosses, would have refused to make such foolhardy flights. Strict orders to fly into the maelstrom would undoubtedly have resulted in their reporting a rash of mechanical problems, serious enough to keep them grounded until the weather let up. Unfortunately, in 1945 the pilots were less experienced in flying than our 1942 experts, and they were military officers, trained to obey commands. "Ours is not to reason why, into the valley of death, etc."

This loss rate was unacceptable and unnecessary. If the American public had heard of this horrendous snafu, there is no doubt that heads would have rolled. Even the Pentagon brass shuddered when they learned of the incredible airlift losses, which were far greater than combat losses in the theater. There was a great hue and cry in Washington, and it was decided that the present policy had to change.

A statement emerged from HQ that "an hour lost could be made up, but a life lost could never be replaced." This was such a disgustingly bland statement that I am sure it came from a public relations office. I am also sure that the crews that survived these disastrous events made some unprintable comments about Hardin and his policies.

Hardin's instructions were cancelled, and Operations was once again given the option to cancel flights when weather became too severe. Many flying personnel found it outrageous that Hardin continued to command the Hump operation, and they were further angered when he was rewarded with a promotion to brigadier general, There were bitter comments about career officers sometimes going to extreme measures to achieve a promotion, even if it means placing their men in jeopardy.

* * * * * *

The China Air Task Force, our combat unit, did not build up very rapidly. The Pentagon failed to keep its promise to provide a new combat fleet, but, in spite of this failure, General Chennault continued to demonstrate that a tight, well-managed organization could be extremely effective in attack and defense, even with a fleet of worn-out airplanes .

His force of 40 fighters and seven medium bombers faced an enemy air force of 350 to 400 airplanes, along a 2,000-mile front, but despite this overwhelming ratio, it did the job of a much larger air force. The Japanese met fierce opposition whenever they threatened to move into western China, and were forced to maintain a large air force.

Chennault's policy was that a strong offense was the best defense. His tiny CATF was a major hindrance to a Japanese take-over of all of China, and a major factor in Roosevelt's global strategy. The CATF made bombing attacks against such far-flung targets as the harbors at Hong Kong and Canton, and strafing attacks on targets in Burma. Their only restraint was the shortage of fuel and repair parts. They flew bold and strategically important missions, as had the original Flying Tigers.

In March, 1943, the CATF became the Fourteenth Air Force, commanded by Chennault, now a major general. It was not until the following year that his fleet expanded with the addition of very small numbers of B-25, B-24, P-40, P-38, and P-51 aircraft. Despite the huge production of aircraft in the States, the China-Burma-India Theater still had the lowest priority. A small number of the highly regarded North American P-51 Mustangs arrived in China in late 1943, but they turned out to be worn out cast-offs of Stateside training schools, in poor shape after many hours of hard use. I suspect that someone in Washington must have said, "I know what to do with those worn-out P-51's—let's send them to Chennault in China. They're better than his P-40'S."

In the first year of its existence, the tiny Fourteenth Air Force performed so many missions and was credited with so many victories that it became one of the most decorated air units in the world. It boasted over 300,000 tons of enemy shipping sunk, and provided valuable support for Chinese ground forces. It was greatly inspired by its predecessor, the Flying Tigers, and continued to wear the fierce Tiger face on its fighter aircraft, a symbol of victory that put fear into enemy pilots.

* * * * * *

The B-29 operation in China makes another extraordinary tale, well worth recounting. Called the "Superfortress," this airplane was the special project of General "Hap" Arnold, who saw that strategic bombing that destroyed enemy factories was the most effective way to defeat the enemy. He nursed the development of the Very Heavy Bomber (VHB) early in the war. The high allied command selected Japan as the best target of this new long-range weapon, as the European theater was already well supplied with B-17 and B- 24 bomb groups.

Our great production capacity provided large numbers of B-29's. Many were sent to bases at Kharagpur in western India in 1944 to conduct a bombing campaign against Japanese factories on their homeland islands, and on the coast of China. The B-29 was truly a long-range bomber, and destined to be the pride of our air fleet, but even its great range did not allow it to reach Japan from India. It was an 18-hour round trip from India to Singapore and other coastal targets, and that required a full fuel load and a very limited bomb load. To reach Japan, it was necessary to refuel in China. The flat plains around Chengtu, China, were selected as the refueling station, and a huge build-up of airfields resulted, with heavy runways over 7,000 feet long built to accommodate a fleet of over 200 of the great bombers.

As many as 30,000 coolies were at work at any one time, laboring with hand tools to build the runways, breaking large rocks into smaller ones and packing them down. It took 250 men just to haul a massive stone roller to flatten the runway surface. It didn't pay to stumble on this job. There was no way to quickly stop this juggernaut, and it was reported that it rolled over an occasional worker who fell.

The work progressed very slowly, much to the disgust of the Air Corps commanders who had ordered that these new airfields be completed on schedule.

Any expert on China could have predicted that this was not going to happen.

The next major hurdle was getting fuel into storage tanks at the Chengtu bases. Our Hump airlift was fully occupied keeping Chennault's fighting forces in the air and supplying Stilwell's ground forces, and could not supply the immense amount of fuel guzzled by a huge fleet of hundreds of B-29's. The B-29's were put to work as tankers, hauling fuel from the home base in India, across the Hump to Chengtu, draining their tanks to add to the stockpile, leaving only enough to get home. It took up to seven refueling trips to store enough fuel to supply one mission against Japan.

A single mission consumed great amounts of fuel. One B-29 would burn 300 gallons in a single hour at minimum cruise power, and on a six-hour mission would use up to 2,500 gallons, equal to 50 drums. Multiply that by 100 airplanes, and they were using 5,000 drums. This astronomical amount made it obvious why the Hump airlift could not provide enough fuel, and why it was necessary for the B-29's to supply their own. A fleet of B-24 bombers was converted to tankers called C-109's, and put to work hauling fuel to Chengtu.

Describing the route a gallon of gasoline took to arrive in China was a supply officer's nightmare. A drum of gas loaded on a ship at Houston, Texas, traveled on a dangerous 12,000-mile sea voyage to Karachi, India. It went by rail 1,500 miles across India to Calcutta, and then to the B-29 bases at Kharagpur, to fill the huge tanks of the B-29 "tankers."

Many other problems haunted the B-29 offensive. The B-29 was a very complicated airplane with many mechanical glitches. It had been rushed into production without adequate testing, and had thousands of bugs that needed correcting. Engines were a major problem, with the new R-3350 Wright engines suffering from inadequate cooling in the high temperatures in India. As a pilot, I shuddered when I heard the stories of engines overheating on climb-out due to poor airflow, causing detonation, swallowing valves, freezing up. There were incidents of frozen-up engines twisting so violently in their mounts as to rip themselves off the wings. Over 3000 repair orders were issued to correct these defects, totally overloading maintenance officers, who never did catch up, even by the end of the war.

Added to that were the hellish flying conditions on the Hump run to Chengtu, with a number of B-29's crashing en route. There were four bases spread out in the Chengtu area, but many aircraft heading for these bases became lost over China in bad weather. In June, 1944, 150 aircraft were dispatched to Chengtu to refuel for a mission, but only 68 arrived, with others turning back Other causes of mission failures were poorly trained pilots and crews, and poor maintenance.

There was the problem of overloading. The B-29 could carry huge loads, but it was decided to overload them by as much as 40,000 pounds over the rated maximum takeoff weight of 124,000 pounds. Daytime temperatures at lowland India airfields topped 110 degrees, which reduced engine power on takeoff. If one of those four great engines quit, or even sputtered, a crash could result, with little chance of survival. There were many takeoff crashes, and many lives lost in these accidents.

Things were not going well when General Curtis LeMay took over the operation in August of 1944 to try to correct the problems. He was a brilliant, young, hard-charging career officer, who had achieved great success in Europe with the Eighth Air Force, and he tried many changes to put the B-29 operation on a sound footing.

Bombing missions continued to be a dismal story, with bad weather and poor radar technique causing bombardiers to miss targets, sometimes by as much as 20 miles. On a November 11, 1944, mission of 96 aircraft, only 29 found the target. On November 21, 61 arrived over the target out of 109, and bomb aiming was poor.

Missions ended with aircraft forced down all over China, some lucky to find an emergency field, but others landing in rice paddies. Causes were engine fires or other mechanical problems, poor navigation, and fuel exhaustion. There were few losses from enemy action.

LeMay realized that high altitude bombing from 25,000 feet was useless, and ordered that raids be made from levels as low as 8000 feet. Crew members composed a little ditty:

Put your oxy mask away, Curt LeMay is here to stay.

The most moving and eloquent story came from a former flight engineer officer on a B- 29, who described to me how the loss of many crews affected him. He related how he walked into a B-29 crew barrack in India one day, and found it totally silent, a very weird feeling. He faced the terrible reality that all the personnel in that building were dead. All of the losses were in accidents, none in combat! What a shock!

There were so many problems in operating from China, that the high command was very glad to transfer the India unit to the newly conquered Mariana Islands, where they joined the Pacific B-29 group. The island airfields were close enough to Japan to allow direct bombing raids, with adequate fuel supplied from huge tanker ships anchored offshore. LeMay breathed a sigh of relief at this move, and stated that, "China had proved to be a horrible, almost impossible, logistical situation, and we knew it."

* * * * * *

Chennault and Stilwell were pleased to see the B-29's leave China, as there had been constant disagreement about use of the airlift. The B-29 commanders wanted the Hump airlift to haul fuel for the bombers. Chennault insisted that he needed the airlift to support his fighters and medium bombers, claiming that it was his small offensive air force that kept the Japanese from rolling into western China. Stilwell wanted all Hump cargo to be arms to support his Chinese ground troops that were aggressively pushing the enemy southward back through Burma.

There was such poor cooperation between these leaders that Stilwell was eventually relieved at the urging of Chiang Kai-shek. Shortly after that, the top brass ordered Chennault replaced.

The ending of the war with Japan in August of 1945 marked the renewal of the old conflict that raged between Chiang Kai-shek's Nationalist government and the Communist forces. The northern forces ousted Chiang, but he found refuge on Taiwan, where he built up a new dominion.

Another highlight that was much celebrated was the completion of the Ledo Road, extending from India to Kunming. This road, renamed the Stilwell Road, took years to build under the most difficult construction conditions, and saw its first truckload of supplies pass through in January of 1945. By this time the airlift was moving such large tonnage, that the Road was considered a case of "too little, too late. "

Chapter 39
MEDALS AND SAVING LIVES
FIGHT OR RESCUE ?

"How many Japs did you shoot down?" I was asked many times, when people learned that 1 was attached to the famous Flying Tigers. My medals and ribbons gave the impression that I was a combat hero, and people expected thrilling answers.

"None," I answered. "I flew cargo missions in C-47's." This reply always disappointed the questioner, who would likely respond with a polite, "Oh, I see."

I was disappointed for a long time, as well. Many times in the China-Burma-India Theater, I wished that I were flying a P-40 on combat missions. In my mind, there could be no greater thrill than that of flying a high- powered, heavily armed fighter plane on a mission far into enemy territory to do heavy damage, and shoot down a few planes along the way. I regarded the Flying Tigers as true knights of the air, and as I watched them take off on a mission, or fly circles around me in greeting, I was quite frustrated to be flying a stodgy, slow C-47 transport plane.

I was young and fearless, and wanted to be the hunter instead of the hunted. I felt that flying cargo was a tame occupation for an exuberant pilot, and during my time in China I made several requests for a transfer to fighters. Fighter commander Colonel Scott was very diplomatic in turning me down. "We don't have airplanes or gas to train people, so I'm turning down any pilots who don't have P-40 time. Besides, you're more important to us doing something no one else can do - bringing in supplies in your C-47 that keep us in the air. Keep up the good work." This assurance of my importance was a big boost to my ego. Another consolation was that I flew a lot of hours while the fighter jocks spent their days on the ground, playing cards and grumbling about their lack of flying time.

The common belief is that flying cargo was a safe, easy job, but that impression is wrong. Whether I was flying for Chennault in China, or doing my 50 Hump missions, the work was dangerous and exciting enough to keep my adrenalin flowing.

The threat from Japanese fighters was always present. On the Hump, our ceiling limit of 16,000 feet in a loaded C-47 required us to fly across the southern spur of the Himalayas, which took us close to enemy territory. We were very vulnerable to enemy action, and just sighting an unidentified airplane in the distance would cause a tingle of impending danger. Suppose it was a Japanese Zero, and I was his target for today! How would I protect myself? We carried pistols, and we might have a Tommy gun on board, but these were useless weapons against a heavily armed fighter.

Someone suggested mounting mock wooden guns on the side of the fuselage and out of the tail of our C-47's to scare away a potential attacker, but experienced combat pilots laughed at this idea. They pointed out that even real guns would not stop an aggressive enemy, let alone broom handles, and nothing could protect us from his heavy machine guns and cannon except smart flying. Our best defense was to fly in cloud cover, on instruments, even though we faced the danger of selecting a cloud that had a hard center.

More men and aircraft were lost on the Hump airlift than were lost in combat. In less than four years, we lost over 500 airplanes, most of them from the Air Transport Command, and others from troop carrier, B-29 supply aircraft, and China Airlines commercial operations. We had many enemies; the fiercest one was not Japanese fighters, but the monstrous Hump and its companion, the treacherous weather. The danger was so great that trips across the Hump were considered equal to combat missions. Pilots completing 25 trips were awarded an Air Medal, and a Distinguished Flying Cross was awarded for 50 trips. My medals are kept in a special place, and remind me of the friends who did not return home.

Today, I am glad that I never made the transfer to fighters, and never fired a gun at an enemy airplane. In air war, the aim is to destroy another fighting machine, a bomber or fighter plane. Opposing flyers play a deadly game of tag, and often have great respect for their opponents. The distance between them may make the battle somewhat impersonal, but a 'victory' means a 'kill.' At one time, I was quite ready to kill some other brave young man, a warrior similar to me, who was following orders and putting his life on the line for his country, just as I was doing for mine. The young Japanese pilot that I tried to kill might be a friend today, a fine citizen, loyal to his family and his country.

History tells us of the insanity and the futility of wars, which are fought by innocent people, who are pawns of ruthless political or military warlords with a lust for power. Soldiers are the cannon fodder being sacrificed to the greed of leaders, who themselves remain safely distant from the killing grounds. Japanese military rulers followed the age-old practice of tyrants, teaching their men to hate the enemy blindly, and to treat them ruthlessly. They were taught that to sacrifice their lives rather than surrender was the supreme sign of allegiance to their emperor.

My normal instinct was to hate the enemy, for we were sure that they were terrible people, committing horrifying acts. We were proud to be the warriors wearing the white hats, while our enemies were the bad guys, in the black hats. But did they not feel the same about us?

Wars make it perfectly acceptable to take the life of another person, and I sympathize with the fighting man whose job is to kill the enemy. I have met many, who in later years find the memory of those trying times very sad. A friend related a very poignant story to me about his anti-aircraft unit shooting down a German fighter that had been strafing Allied troops. The anti-aircraft gunners were very proud of their success in knocking down this enemy airplane, and went to visit the wreck which had crashed close by. They were shocked to discover the body of a very young German pilot, about 18 years of age. He wore a blue knitted scarf that looked like a loving mother had made it, and his wallet contained photographs of his family. When they realized the utter tragedy of the situation, the gunners silently walked from the scene, unable to voice their sadness. My friend will never totally erase the memory of that young man, the enemy, from mind.

At this point in my life, I despair at the concept of war, a "terrible and atrocious thing," a failure of humanity. I am pleased that I spent most of my time saving lives instead of destroying them.

BRAVERY

What is bravery? What is a hero? A single courageous act that saves many lives at great personal risk may be considered a heroic action.

Another definition of bravery is the act of doing what has to be done despite great fears for personal safety. Every soldier preparing for battle deserves this praise, as he sweats out the mission under great tension, aware of the dangers, knowing he may not survive.

As a former Air Force pilot, I believe that pilots start out with a different attitude. My enjoyment of flying, followed by extensive flight training and a gunnery award convinced me that I was about to become the greatest combat pilot in history. I was king of the air, able to master a great flying machine, and able to go anywhere in the world in perfect safety. An adventurous but safe flight halfway around the world bolstered this feeling. My first trip across the Hump was in beautiful clear weather, with blue sky and white-topped peaks, all looking like a picture postcard. I was convinced that this job would be a snap. I was invulnerable, and it was easy to be brave and content

Later, I had a change of heart when I came under enemy attack, and almost lost out in battles with the weather and terrain. Frightening experiences and the loss of companions who were far more qualified than I made me cautious. The sight of a heavy cloud layer in my path made me aware of great dangers that lay ahead. I tensed up and became acutely aware of the slightest change in my situation. Common sense became the rule, rather than over-confidence. Fear became a companion and I became an "old pilot," rather than a bold one. Was I brave? I don't know.

A VITAL JOB

Fate had assigned me to the Ferrying Command, which later merged into the Air Transport Command. The ATC established a world-wide military airline, and the pilots flying for that Command have been the most qualified and envied in the Air Force. ATC flying was regarded as the safest of all military flying jobs, but our operations over the Hump proved that wrong.

The Air Transport Command required piloting that was far different from combat flying. Combat units usually flew in formation, under the guidance of experienced flight leaders, who shepherded the new men through dangerous missions. Flying for ATC was vastly different, with each pilot a self-reliant aircraft commander. He personally approved his routes and his flight plan, supervised his loading, and signed off for the airplane. Once off the ground he monitored the navigation, weather, communications, and airplane performance. He flew a lone mission, and was totally responsible for the safety of his airplane, cargo, and passengers.

I was proud every time I took off on a mission, proud that my ability was found adequate for the job. Flying the "China Express" for General Chennault was especially gratifying, for I could see immediate benefits from delivering precious cargoes to air bases that were on the brink of extinction from lack of supplies. I carried wing tanks and .50 caliber ammunition that were often rushed from my airplane and loaded into waiting fighters. They would take off within minutes to intercept incoming bombers. My loads included food and mail that gave an immediate lift to anxious men who were starving for news from home. I remember the proud feeling that I enjoyed, as if I was Santa with presents.

Flying for the ATC was an education, a way to travel and see much of the world. If I were to paint a picture of my travels, it would be a huge collage of people and places of immense variety and contrast. It would show poverty-stricken African villagers living in filth and disease, and also portray people in large cities enjoying elegance in the finest hotels. It would contrast the rag-tag barefoot Chinese coolie soldiers, carrying outdated rifles and existing on handfuls of rice, with the highly trained and well-equipped military units of India.

I would paint a picture of crippled, lice-ridden Indian children begging for pennies, thronging in the broiling sun around the gate of a royal Indian palace whose residents lived in utmost luxury. I would picture the tens of thousands of Chinese peasants toiling in the sun under straw hats, building airfields for heavy bombers, and contrast this with the ornate lifestyle of aristocratic British in their private clubs.

That was the cross-section of the diverse world that I saw, which, unfortunately, hasn't changed very much. It was a fine education, and a great adventure. That I would gladly repeat.

TRY IT AGAIN?

Would I want to fly the Hump again? No way! One tour overseas was enough. We arrived home in the States and kissed the ground, vowing we would never, never leave again.

After many years, as I recall those times, I wonder if I would have the courage to face that kind of challenge once more. My adrenalin flows again as I recall the keyed up excitement and fear, the extreme concentration of senses and skills that came to a peak when I was faced with danger that threatened my airplane and our lives. I remember the exultant feeling of achievement at the end of a hazardous mission. Could I perform again under that pressure? Would I like another try at it? Perhaps.

I recently heard a former Special Forces veteran of Vietnam admit that he misses the excitement, and would be thrilled to be inserted behind enemy lines on a dangerous mission one more time. This may be pure bravado; it's easy to contemplate the risks when you are comfortably seated at home, where your greatest danger may be a bad golf game next weekend.

Many men look for risky venture to spice up their lives. Competitive games and sports such as sailboat racing and scuba diving are enough for me. Some find that high adventure such as mountain climbing, solo sailing great distances, or airplane racing have replaced the thrill of hunting for big game. There are some men who hunt a different kind of game, mercenary soldiers who hire themselves out to fight. They are rare, and must have an excess of adrenalin.

Perhaps the new threat of terrorism that is startling the world will provide more danger and adventure for all of us than we can possibly want.

Section V

MILITARY LIFE

"There's something about a soldier!"

Chapter 40
HOME IS THE WARRIOR

Leaving the battlefield to return home is the biggest event in the life of every military man, something he dreams about ever since he started his tour of duty. His longing for familiar faces and places, and his daydreams about the sweet comforts and carefree life he once took for granted, are an ever-present background to his life in the service. When the mind-boggling fears and pressures he faces in combat operations become overwhelming, the soldier falls back on his images of home. A Betty Grable pin-up takes second place to the memory of the local ice cream parlor or the neighborhood movie house.

Our return to the States was even more special, as we were the much envied first group to be rotated home from the China-Burma-India Theater. We were part of the original AMMISCA group, each with at least 50 round trips across the Hump. My logbook amazed me, showing over 1000-hours of flying time in the 12-month period, much of it from those long days flying the "Chinese Express". Later in the war, many pilots flew more than 50 trips, but we didn't argue when orders came through telling us our tour was over and to get moving towards home.

Twenty of us climbed into a C-47 for the trip, and found the trip home as hazardous as another Hump flight. We flew a direct route, crossing the heart of Africa, and headed for Accra, the jumping off point for the Atlantic crossing.

Our Air Transport Command airplane was a beloved C-47, and as we crossed the jungles of western Africa we snoozed and played some poker and talked about the first and the second things we would do on our return home. We were greatly relaxed, aware of how lucky we were to be heading home. Then I noticed everyone peering out the window, and a discussion started about why were flying at a low altitude of a few hundred feet, under a low ceiling of solid clouds. I noticed one of our pilots, Johnny Payne, standing in the cockpit doorway, watching the action in the cockpit.

As pilots, we probably totaled over 100,000 hours flying time among us, and we were terrible back-seat drivers. To this day I am apprehensive about sitting in the cabin while someone else drives the airplane, and in those days it was worse, as we had no idea of the qualifications of the young pilot who held our safety in his hands.

We seemed to be letting down even more until we were almost brushing the treetops. This is a very unhealthy thing to do when a hill might loom up dead ahead with nowhere to go but up into the overcast.

"Hey, Johnny, what in hell is that guy trying to do? You're closest. See what's going on." You don't normally second-guess the man flying the airplane if you can avoid it, but big Johnny, with his loud voice and bluff manner was already at work. He asked the pilot what he was doing down so low, and discovered that we had a very uneasy sweating pilot, who gave a very confused reply about being forced under the overcast, and asked what Johnny suggested doing. Johnny had a suggestion, all right. He tapped the co-pilot on the shoulder and told him to "move it", and then scrambled into the right seat and took over. We were right on the treetops, and Johnny immediately started to climb.

We all breathed a sigh of relief shortly after that when we climbed through the thin cloud layer and ended on top at about 1500 feet. Dead ahead was a ridge of low hills that extended up into the overcast with their tops showing at our height. They would have been our final resting place if Johnny had not taken over. We expected this of Johnny, a hero in his own right with several high-risk missions in the past, a number of laughable escapades, and 10,000 hours flying time. Of course, we razzed him over this event, claiming he just wanted to get more time, but we knew that he had saved our necks.

Reaching Accra in one piece, we got a big lift when we learned that we would be crossing the Atlantic in a big PanAm Clipper flying boat instead of a noisy, cold, miserable C-87 converted bomber. The Clipper was pure luxury, with a real bunk, and a hot meal, and we slept our way across at 120 miles per hour, with not a care in the world. At that time, I decided that flying for a living might not be such a bad job.

Arriving at Florida, we went through the long-anticipated ceremony of kissing the ground, then looked for telephones for our joyful calls home, and followed up with huge hot fudge sundaes. It was May of 1943, and everywhere we went we were regarded with awe as the first returnees from the mysterious China-Burma-India Theater.

* * * * * *

My two-week leave at home in Boston was a time for rejoicing. In spring of 1943 the war was going badly in most parts of the world, and news was depressing. But the family, friends, and neighbors all turned out to greet me, making it a joyous time. It took a while for me to unwind, but then I spent hours telling about my adventures. My parents found it hard to grasp that I had been through so much, but it was enough for them just to have me safely home again.

I was a very different person from the one who left Boston in May of 1941, two years earlier. From my first day back, I had a new appreciation of home, family, and our American way of life. It was springtime, and my home city of Boston had never looked so good. It had changed for me from a fussy, dirty old city that I had come to dislike, and I could "smell the roses." I could see how our wonderful country and our freedoms compared with the way of life for the countless millions who eked out wretched existences in other parts of the world. In most places I had visited, people suffered hunger, unchecked diseases, oppression by dictators, and had little hope for their future. In our country we were truly blessed.

I walked the crooked streets of downtown Boston, visiting the wonderful historical sites that I had not really appreciated in my youth. The old buildings were like old friends, as were the Common, and the Public Gardens where the famous swan boats were stored up for the duration. The rough cobble-stoned streets around the Faneuil Hall Market felt smooth underfoot to me, and everyone turned to smile at this young captain who wore bright ribbons and pilot wings. Few men had returned home and I was constantly stopped for hellos and greetings, and countless inquiries. It was a heady feeling to be regarded as a minor celebrity in my home city, and I felt like a good-will ambassador.

Every so often my thoughts drifted, for at that very moment 12,000 miles away, some pilot might be struggling to keep his C-47 aloft in icing weather, wondering if he would make it safely back. Good fortune had smiled on me and brought me safely home, and for the time I tried not to think about those who had not made it.

A visit to the Post Exchange at Army Headquarters on Commonwealth Avenue turned out to be a new adventure. A young woman introduced herself as a public relations person, and asked about my campaign ribbons. When I explained them, she said very excitedly, "Wow! Do we need you, captain!" I was hustled into the office of the colonel commanding the First Army Headquarters, who asked me many questions, and suggested that the young woman interview me for a story. The war news was bad, and the military services were in desperate need of something good to talk about. My description of our Hump operation seemed to fill the bill.

The colonel then requested a favor; that I become part of the annual Memorial Day celebration held at the Boston Common on May 30, and give a short speech. This was a command request and I readily agreed, although I wasn't sure just what kind of a speech to make. I would have to think about that.

Then he questioned me about my uniform. "Captain, is that uniform regulation?" This was a good question, for what I wore that day was definitely non-reg in the states. It was that Agra-made outfit of fine wool worsted, woven with multicolored threads, which gave it an iridescent color-changing look as the fabric rippled. Several other pilots had uniforms made of this distinctive British cloth, and even though it was non-reg it looked great, and in India no one really cared.

I told the colonel truthfully, that it was "fairly standard" in India, and he took my word for it. He then asked me to stay around to meet some of his staff and when some of them also asked about the uniform, I decided to switch to regulation garb from then on, saving my fashionable outfit for special social events.

I got a big charge out of the Memorial Day event, where I gave a speech from the bandstand. Way back in 1928, Charles Lindbergh had appeared on the same bandstand, during his big tour of the country, and I had begged for a chance to see him. My mother had finally given in, and we rode the elevated train into downtown Boston and fought through the crowd on the Common trying to get close. We didn't get very close, but I got temporarily lost, which was quite exciting for an eight-year old.

Fifteen years later, in 1943, I was temporarily lost also, but this time it was about what my speech should say. It was thrilling to face that huge, war-inspired audience from the bandstand on the beautiful Boston Common, where Lindbergh and other famous people had been making speeches for generations. I was sure I would freeze up, but that problem dissipated when the speaker ahead of me gave a brief talk about our brave boys overseas. He was a city councilman, and his speech was about coping at home with the frustrations of war time. I thought about telling what it was really like to be in a combat area, but then realized that no one wanted to hear bad news. I soon sorted out a proper set of subjects.

The mayor introduced me to a big round of applause, as "Captain Segel, a local Boston boy, just back from China, where he flew with the Flying Tigers." I had some difficulty explaining my precise connection with that great group, but no one seemed to care. All they wanted to hear was, "How are our boys doing?"

I saw worried faces, concerned for the safety of their loved ones who were fighting a terrible war, and reading bad news every day in the newspapers. They were very anxious to hear from someone who had been overseas, and needed to hear that Uncle Sam was taking good care of their boys. It would be an encouraging talk, aimed at giving them a lift with no mention of dangers, fears, losses, or shortages.

I told about the aid to China's people that the Hump operation was providing, and described the mysterious Orient and the tropical climate. I joked about our bungalows looking like part of a tropical paradise but being very primitive, and I stretched a point saying that we were well fed. Once I started to talk about General Chennault and the Flying Tigers, I could have gone on for hours, as they were true heroes, and the audience was totally rapt in my description of their war. Then it was time to change the subject.

I told of military life, and how our men all shared one feeling in common - they were all homesick and anxiously waiting for word from home. I appealed to the audience to stay in close touch by writing constantly, and to send only the good news. I described how excitedly we awaited mail call, with news from home the most marvelous tonic, to relieve our sense of separation, loneliness and fear. I told about the thrill I got from every letter I received, and how I read and reread them. I ended by asking everyone to promise that when they returned home that very day they would start writing letters, and not stop until their heroes came marching home. For a touch of humor, I suggested that, "you girls save the 'Dear John' letters until Johnny gets home. We don't want to upset a man who sleeps with your picture under his pillow, and dreams about you."

The press then took over and the local papers interviewed me. Bill Casey of the Boston Globe wrote great articles about flying the Hump, with one of them published in Colliers weekly magazine. My parents were very proud to see my name in print.

A number of Boston people phoned my home to inquire if I knew their sons, who were somewhere in the China-Burma-India Theater. One touched a very special place in my heart, as I knew a fighter pilot at Kunming who had been killed in a non-flying accident. His fiancee came to visit and wanted to know the details, and I must confess that I changed the story enough so that he came through a real hero.

I received other phone calls of a personal nature, from former girl friends, suggesting that this might be the right time to resume relationships. There were some brief encounters, but somehow the excitement of homecoming, and the anticipation of new things to happen, cooled off my interest in acquiring a steady girl friend. An old Irving Berlin song from World War I starts with the line, "How ya gonna keep them down on the farm, after they've seen Paree?" It surely applied to me. I pleaded that I would soon be moving on, and could not possibly plan ahead. My leave stretched out to four weeks, and I went back to work with a great sense of confidence that I could do anything. After a year overseas facing many dangers, nothing was going to faze me, and I looked forward to an interesting assignment.

* * * * * *

Interesting jobs did not turn up. The Air Transport Command was not ready for returnees yet, and sent us to bases where our skills as highly qualified instrument pilots were frittered away on miscellaneous flying jobs. They were comfortable posts, and I enjoyed their luxury for a while. My first stateside assignment in June, 1943, was to Dover Air Force Base, at Wilmington, Delaware, a pleasant, old-established base that made Chabua seem like a bad dream out of the past. It gave me a taste of what the military was like during peace-time, with its well maintained buildings, neat lawns, comfortable homes for top ranking officers, and excellent recreational facilities for all personnel. It conformed to military ritual, with a showy parade every Saturday morning for families and the public. At one of these, I, along with my flying mates, was presented with the Distinguished Flying Cross, in a very formal fashion. We had a grand celebration at the Officers Club that evening. Most of the base personnel regarded us with some awe, as we were the first returnees they had seen, and our decorations were most impressive.

Dover had comfortable Bachelor Officers Quarters (BOQ), but Joe Walker and I looked at all the lovely young ladies who gave us the "come hither" look and decided to move downtown. We rented an apartment that soon became the center of intensive social activity, much of it defying description, and we worked very hard to make this a great antidote for our uncomfortable year in the CBI.

We were assigned to ferrying and other flying work, and for a while, I was official pilot of the daily shuttle to Long Island, which hauled ferry pilots to various aircraft factories such as Grumman and Republic. At every opportunity I visited these factories and was astounded at the large number of aircraft in production and rolling out the doors every day. I remembered how we meticulously and lovingly built each engine at the Pratt and Whitney factory, and could see that vast changes had taken place in production techniques in the past two years.

I flew a very comfortable Lockheed Lodestar for this work, and also checked out in a marvelous old airplane, a Boeing 247, formerly of United Airlines. This old relic deserves special mention, as it was one of the very first airliners, carrying 15 passengers, and was in use long before the DC-3. This one was truly a rare bird, with over 40,000-hours, and many thousands yet to go, provided someone didn't nose it over, as it had a tendency to be nose heavy. One very special feature was the electrically retracted landing gear. The electric motor had burned out long ago, with no replacements available, so it was the co-pilot's job to manually retract the gear with the emergency system. A long pump-like handle stood to the right of the copilot, and it took 40 strokes with lots of muscle, to raise the gear, after which the copilot rested. I flew the right seat half of the time, and found that it was very exhausting work. We made life easier by leaving the wheels down for the short hops and raised them only for the long hauls. We called it the "Toonerville Trolley," like the comic of the same name, and it was fun for a while.

The airplane was interesting, but the passengers were even more so. They were members of the WASPS, or Women's Auxiliary Service Pilots, a very gutsy group of ladies, who were under contract to ferry military aircraft. These women were forerunners of a growing womens' movement. They defied convention and moved into what had been the strictly male business of flying, and carved their own niche in the history of aviation.

There were about 1000 of them across the country, and they earned the respect of the military the hard way. They qualified in fighters, bombers, and other types, and had an excellent record ferrying these diversified aircraft. WASPS were more meticulous than most male ferry pilots in reading the technical manuals, and finding out more about the airplanes they were assigned to fly. Many male pilots with inflated egos felt they could "fly anything with wings," without proper checkouts. This casual indifference about doing their homework often had fatal results. I was often guilty of that attitude, and I recall that I flew many different types of aircraft without really knowing anything about their special flight characteristics, or such technical details as how to lower the gear in an emergency, or even switch fuel tanks if one went dry. The WASPS took their jobs very seriously, and the result was an outstanding safety record. We tried to joke with them, and even did a bit of flirting, but these women were hell-bent on their mission, and had nothing but airplanes on their minds.

After one month of flying the shuttle to Long Island, I was getting restless, and wanted to move on to something more interesting. I flew an assortment of airplanes, but knew that I was overqualified for this work. A major change came when our entire group of Hump veterans was ordered to the Reno Air Force Base at Reno, Nevada, where a C-46 Operational Training Unit (OTU) was being formed. This was the work we were cut out for, and it turned out to be a most valuable contribution to the Air Corps.

I found a rare car to buy, a low mileage 1936 Plymouth sedan that had been stored on blocks when gasoline became scarce. It only cost me $300, but there were some special strings attached. It belonged to a young lady who I wined and dined freely, and I used my charm to persuade her that selling me this car was the patriotic thing to do. This dashing hero of the skies must have gotten somewhat carried away, for the next thing I knew, the young lady decided to accompany me on the drive to Reno, but on a "purely platonic basis." I did not believe that for one minute, and was certain that a week with her would have serious results. I begged off, suggesting that she come out and visit me later by Greyhound. Happily, she never showed.

I headed across the country for Reno, under conditions that were far different from my earlier trip to Georgia to become a Flying Cadet. Two years had elapsed since my fledgling days, and I was a captain now, a different person, heading for new challenges. Although I was back in the States, my war was far from over.

Back home with close friends. Jake Sartz, Jim Segel, Dick Cole, Paul Conroy. Dick was especially famous, having flown as co-pilot for Col. Jimmy Doolittle on the Tokyo Raid of April, 1942, bailed out over China and walked out.

Chapter 41
RENO OPERATIONS

The manifold pressure on the right engine is dropping rapidly, showing engine failure, and the big C-46 airplane is pulling to the right. The pilot cranks in left rudder trim, pushes forward on the yoke, and checks his airspeed to make sure that he was well above 120 miles-per-hour. "Your heading should be 185°," warns the copilot. A quick glance at his compass shows the pilot that his heading is 220°, and that the airplane is slowly turning right. The gyro-compass tells him nothing as it suddenly becomes inoperative. This is an emergency, and beads of sweat are forming on the pilot's face as he fights panic, and tries to maintain altitude and airspeed, and get back on course.

His copilot is no help. In fact, he is the cause of the problems, putting the pilot through his final instrument check ride under the hood He had cut power to the right engine, placed a cover over the gyro-compass, called out a new heading, and carefully watched the pilot's reactions. There is a saying that, "if they ain't sweatin', they ain't learnin." In a matter of weeks, the pilot will be flying the Hump run, and might be facing emergencies like these, or worse.

At the Reno Operational Training Unit (OTU) we established a demanding training program aimed at creating top qualified instrument pilots, ready to fly C-46 aircraft on the dangerous Hump airlift. We Hump veterans were the best people to train these men and pass along the priceless skills we had learned the hard way. We were proud that we were turning out exceptional graduates.

* * * * * *

The drive to Reno was a long one, but it was a pure delight, taking me to places in the country I had never seen. It was July of 1943, and everywhere I went I was treated with great hospitality. I was asked many questions about my experiences and about the war in the China-Burma-India Theater, which was like the other side of the moon to most people. News reports told of tragic losses taking place every day, and it was the duty of the returnees to help build morale as best as we could. I described how their men in uniform got the greatest lift from mail from home, with cheerful news, and how we read and reread those precious letters.

The "Biggest Little City In The World" turned out to be a compact city of about 40,000 people, in a bowl surrounded by high pine-covered mountains, beautiful in summer, and snow-covered and picturesque in winter. Small ranches lay on the outskirts of the city, and the feeling of western hospitality was everywhere. "I'm going to like this place."

The Reno Air Base, destined to be my home for two years, was a great disappointment at first look. It was located eight miles north of town, in Lemmon Valley, a barren windswept prairie that looked like the Sahara Desert, where little moved except large balls of tumbleweed, chased by vagrant breezes. The drone of large engines echoed across the valley to indicate that there was an airport there. The air base was a group of one story, dull brown buildings that seemed to grow out of the land, so dreary and depressing looking that I likened it to the Upper Assam Valley bases. They looked like temporary buildings, built to last a short time, and did not compare to my previous station at the elegant Dover Air Force Base. But once I checked into the Bachelor Officers Quarters and saw the friendly faces of other Hump veterans, things lightened up. Good friends made up for the dismal surroundings.

The Reno base was located on the edge of the high Sierra Mountains, making it an ideal place to teach high altitude instrument flying. On the Hump, we had a constant training problem, as newly arriving pilots had little or no instrument experience. At Reno, our cadre of instructors planned to make history by turning out pilots who were instrument qualified on the C-46, ready for Hump operation. We did just that.

I went right to work, and was introduced for the first time to the Curtiss-Wright C-46 "Commando" airplane, that was to become a big part of my life. It was a new cargo aircraft type, just coming into service as the step-up from the C-47, and was destined to be the backbone of the Hump fleet. It seemed just right for the job, and we had great hopes for its success as a superior cargo carrier. We did not know that we would also have a heap of trouble with this new untested model.

It was the largest twin-engine transport in the world, and it looked massive. Its bulging appearance made it natural to name it "Dumbo," after the famous flying elephant. It could carry a load more than double that of the workhorse C-47, and was powered with two Pratt and Whitney R-2800 engines, putting out 2000 horsepower each. We were pleased that the engines were supercharged with two-speed blowers for high altitude performance, which allowed it to cruise with full load at 20,000 feet. Sitting on the ground, the cockpit placed you very high, and I assumed that it would be a difficult airplane to land, but this was not so. We soon became accustomed to the height and were able to grease the airplane in for smooth landings. Since none of us had ever flown the C-46 before, we had to check out on the airplane and become experts very quickly. It took us four days to check out, get some instrument time under the hood, qualify as instructors, and start our instruction work.

Our students were experienced pilots with considerable flying time in the Ferry Command, but since most ferry flights were conducted in daytime in clear weather, they had very little actual instrument time. We gave them the same training we had been giving new copilots on the Hump. First came transition training to create competent airplane drivers, and then came a heavy load of instrument instruction. We were anxious to turn out the very best all-weather pilots, for this skill was essential to survival. The need for this was proven more fully the following year when Hump operations went on a 24-hour, all-weather schedule, and night flying became standard.

Instrument instruction was done under the hood, a canvas tent that covered the pilot's side of the cockpit interior preventing him from seeing out. He had to rely solely on his instruments, and the instructor gave him difficult situations to overcome, such as loss of an engine, loss of instruments, unusual attitudes, and other problems. We drilled and drilled on this, and we knew we were getting through to the student when we saw him perspiring heavily even though cockpit temperature was down in the 50's.

When winter weather moved in, our clear blue Nevada skies changed to solid overcasts and low ceilings, and we were in our element. Instruction got tougher as we could now give the student pilots a taste of actual instrument conditions. As the "1000-hour guys from the Hump," we got lots of respect, and we never got tired of telling our students horror stories about flying the route, which inspired them to take our instruction very seriously. We taught them exactly what to expect and how to cope with the perils we knew they would face, such as icing, extreme turbulence, and short field landings. We talked about non-flying problems also, and they thought we were exaggerating when we warned them of the snafu living conditions, the bugs, snakes, and slit trenches.

Our insistence on perfecting their instrument technique really paid off. Our course was a rousing success, as reported by former students who returned to Reno as instructors after their Hump missions were completed. They had doubted that conditions could be as bad as we told them, but after a few trips they believed us. Every one of them praised us for the way we taught them to deal with the horrendous conditions. One of my most gratifying moments came when I read a letter in the

Hump Pilots Association quarterly newsletter stating the writer's appreciation for the "Instruction I received at Reno, which saved my life many times."

But it didn't come easy at first In the early days, there was no training format established, and the instructors did pretty much as they pleased until one of them, formerly with United Airlines, suggested we use their Airline Pilot Training Manual. This became our guide until we established our own training guide and program

I came to regard myself as a pretty hot item in the cockpit, until one fine day I suffered my first and only accident in six years of military flying. It came as a big surprise, and fortunately, all that got hurt was a good airplane and my ego, which suffered a real blow.

A new student was flying the airplane from the left seat, and a second student sat in the jump seat just behind the control pedestal waiting for his turn. I was in the right seat, putting the student through touch-and-go landings before starting some intensive instrument practice.

He had just touched down on the second of the three required landings, and I told him "once more around" for a third takeoff. He advanced the throttles to take-off power, and after we left the ground and had adequate flying speed, I raised the gear handle. The landing gear came up okay, but then, to my utter amazement, we settled into the ground with full power on, and made a disastrous belly landing. The propellers ground into the runway stopping the engines, and we slid along on our belly with a terrible grinding noise and came to a sudden stop. I shooed the other men out of the airplane on the double as there was danger of fire from leaking fuel, but I sat there completely disgusted and totally baffled by this accident, the first time I ever banged up an airplane.

I was dumfounded. I had flown dangerous missions, landed airplanes where there were no suitable runways, onto fields pockmarked with bomb craters, into fields so short I never thought I could get out, and had endured all kinds of risks. But now I had wrecked an airplane for the very first time, on my home runway of all places, in front of a number of other pilots and people who expected better performance from me. I was more than unhappy; I was absolutely mortified.

* * * * * *

I was foolish to just sit there, with the danger of fire or explosion, but I can remember being so mad that I kept saying, "Let it burn!" I finally cooled off and started thinking rationally, and made my way out, happy to be in one piece.

I was told later that I greeted the fire trucks and other emergency vehicles with a somewhat lopsided grin, telling them to "save the parts." But I wasn't a very happy survivor that day, as I absolutely could not understand why it happened.

A week later, we had an inquiry board, which was made up mainly of old friends who I had been flying with for a long time. They razzed me, certain that I had screwed up in some way. All the evidence pointed to this, but I repeated my story countless times, claiming that we had flying speed to spare and everything else was "Go!" But I could not explain why we bellied in.

Then came the solution, which cleared up the cause of the accident. The other student pilot was sitting in the jump seat, waiting his turn. When he was questioned about what he saw, we were shocked to hear that he had raised the flap handle right after I raised the gear for the go-around take-off. He said that he thought he could pitch in and help after watching me raise the flaps after each landing, so he proceeded to do this on our third go-around without permission, and certainly not knowing the technique. Wing flaps, that are installed in the trailing edges of the wings, are lowered for landing to provide more wing lift and a slower landing speed. We use full flaps to land at the slowest speed.

In a touch-and-go landing, followed by immediate takeoff, it is critical that you "milk" the flaps up slowly when the airplane is airborne once again during the take-off. If you retract, or "dump" them quickly, the wings suddenly lose some of their lift, and you sink towards the ground. It is very important to never, never dump the flaps close to the ground, but that is exactly what happened here, causing us to belly in. The observer's action was totally unauthorized, as he is not supposed to do anything but watch, unless specifically ordered.

The inquiry board, all pilots themselves, hesitated to place any blame on me, because I was totally unaware of this improper action. But in the final analysis, it was my airplane, my students, and my training mission, and I was responsible. As the navy puts it, "if it happens on your watch, you are to blame." I was charged with all of the blame, which was really an empty charge. A memo went to all instructors and students telling observers to "Keep hands off all controls."

How about the airplane? It was determined to be repairable, but there was such an acute shortage of parts that the maintenance officer elected to dismantle it for spares.

He said he would send me a bill when he found out how much it cost the Air Corps.

* * * * * *

That old saying I mentioned earlier about keeping your mouth shut and not volunteering for anything is still considered good advice in the army. But there is another famous truism that says, "Nothing ventured, nothing gained." When Curt Caton and I volunteered to go to Kweilin in June, 1942, we discovered a world of new experiences, started the "China Express," and were introduced to a different type of warfare. We were glad we went.

An opportunity arose at Reno to take on a new job. I went off flying status for a month due to a mild recurrence of malaria, and had lots of idle time. I became temporary commanding officer of headquarters squadron, but this was mainly paperwork, so I volunteered to take on the job of Flying Safety Officer (FSO), also a temporary assignment When my attention became focussed on our poor safety record, I agreed to stay on permanently, as it presented a real challenge. I think: this was a wise decision, as our accident rate dropped to almost zero, and I was able to accomplish a great deal to improve the airplane.

The Air Force Office of Flying Safety was a new function, with no guidelines for the job. Our previous Flying Safety Officer had no curriculum to follow, and assumed he had to act as a policeman, disciplining pilots and ground personnel who goofed up. Flying low over Lake Tahoe was not allowed, but many pilots gave it a try, with no harm done. However, when a pilot committed the major sin of buzzing down South Virginia Avenue, the main street of Reno, at a very low altitude, the FSO was asked to issue an official reprimand, he hated to do this, as it made him a disciplinarian, while he just wanted to be a regular guy. The unpopular job was ruining his status, and cutting back on his flying hours, which he was anxious to build up, with an eye to a post-war airline job. He asked to be relieved, and the CO asked me if I would "volunteer," since I had little to do except hold down a desk.

The job of FSO was not considered important, and my fellow pilots belittled the job, and assumed that I was going to be a tyrant. I assured them that I had no such intention, and instead asked for suggestions on what we could do to improve our safety record. We had lots of airplane problems, and occasional accidents. I opened up a 'Complaint Box,' and suggestions on remedies came pouring in.

For example, the Operations Officer suggested that I spend my time giving check rides. The Training Officer suggested that I spend my time giving classroom lectures. I agreed to all this, but my real target was to reduce our potential for accidents.

Some of the problems were simple ones to fix, and just took initiative. One that we could fix right away was damage to wing tips while taxiing on our crowded ramp. The C-46 wingspan is 108 feet, and it is difficult to gauge wing-tip distances from the cockpit. A small wing tip damage was costly in time out for the airplane and in repair hours. I requested the use of wing walkers for tight taxiing conditions, who could signal the pilot if there wasn't enough clearance. I ran into strong objections from the head of maintenance, who objected to using overworked linemen to help. "Stupid pilots! If they don't know how long their wings are, I wonder how they reach the latrine with their peckers," was his crude comment. He was a friend of mine, but I had to be a diplomat to win the point. He gave in when I asked him how many man-hours were saved by their not having to replace and repair wing tip sections.

The FSO job was as big as I wanted it to be. It included such chores as driving the runways and taxiways looking for potholes; making sure there was enough oxygen on board for the entire crew on hi-altitude flights; listening to complaints from all sources. Control tower operators got special attention, as they had received little training. The classes on safe flight procedures were a big challenge as just telling a crew to "Fly Safely" was a useless instruction. An FSO from another base described his lecture to me, which made sense. "One breakdown in the airplane, such as loss of a vital instrument or even an engine failure can be overcome. A second breakdown brings you to the extreme danger point. A third strike and you might be out. The time to turn back is before you reach that point." The lecture was about attitude in the cockpit, and how to avoid panic.

I was impressed and I borrowed the lesson.

I added to it by devising tests based on "What if (such-and-such) happens?" Starting out with the pilot's biggest fear, engine failure on takeoff, we tried to cover every emergency we could think of the students thought up some new ones I hadn't even considered, like finding a skunk on board, or having a bird hit the windshield. Everyone had to think hard about the procedures to follow in these emergencies, which made this drill a potential lifesaver. It was the same technique we used in the air giving flight instruction, where we chopped an engine, covered several instruments, and then put the airplane into a stall position

I found that the position of FSO was not a popular one with department heads, who regarded it as another inspector looking over their shoulder to find flaws. At first, I was not very considerate, and would bluntly tell them when I found something wrong. Their resentment became apparent, and I had to change tactics.

I promised that I would make all reports directly and confidentially to them.

To further good relations, I asked them how I could be of assistance, and got an immediate response. For example, the head of maintenance complained of pilots abusing the airplanes. "Get on the instructors' butts and tell them to stop burning out brakes. They think they're driving a car!" Of course, the chief pilot responded to this complaint with his own, about defects repeatedly written up by instructors, such as malfunctioning instruments, that were not being repaired. I found myself often a go-between, and had to exercise some diplomacy to smooth things over. The best results came from meetings between department heads, which resolved tension. I am sure every business has similar problems.

I started a monthly Flying Safety bulletin, to which each department head contributed items. Our resident artist used comic illustrations to show safety tips, and these were very popular, even with non-flying personnel, who were able to laugh at the mistakes that flying personnel made.

The minor problems we were trying to correct were nothing compared to a tragic event that occurred when an explosion blew a wing off in the traffic pattern almost directly over the field. In the furor that followed this tragedy, I learned that similar accidents were occurring at other bases around the world, blamed on leaky fuel tanks in the wings. Curtiss-Wright was working desperately on this, having decided that defective fuel booster pumps located in the wings were causing sparks that ignited the fuel vapors. Our "Before landing" checklist said, "Booster pumps - ON," which was a safety measure to insure adequate fuel flow.

Factory modifications would eventually solve the problem, but in the meantime, we changed our checklists to read, "DO NOT TURN ON BOOST PUMPS BEFORE LANDING." All we could do was keep our fingers crossed and hope that we wouldn't have a repeat of this disaster.

Another fatal accident occurred when a flight engineer removed the aluminum cover of the circuit breaker box in the belly of the airplane while in flight. He was checking a failed circuit, and in the tight working space, he accidentally touched a corner of the box lid to a live electrical contact in the box and a hydraulic line just outside it. The resultant short circuit burned a hole in the hydraulic line, causing hydraulic fluid to spurt out under high pressure. The spark ignited the fluid. The crew chief yelled "Fire!" then grabbed a chute, and safely bailed out. The other crew members did not react as fast, and the raging fire destroyed the airplane before they could bail out.

I went on the search for the crashed airplane, high in the Sierra Nevada

Mountains. We were unable to locate the wreck from the ground until a local mountain resident offered to guide us. He was a wrinkled, wizened old man, who looked to us youngsters that he might be as ancient as 80, and we doubted his ability to lead us through those mountains. To our great surprise, he turned out to be a veritable human mountain goat, who very sure-footedly climbed those steep slopes, leaving us far behind. Occasionally, he would stop and wait for us with a disgusted look on his face, watching us huff and puff trying to catch up to him. Then he would lope off on another spurt that showed us what poor shape we were in. If we hadn't had the sad duty to examine the wreckage and remove the remains of the crews, we would have laughed at our failure to measure up to the old man.

Concurrent with the crash in the mountains, I was assigned another duty: "Accident Investigation Officer (AIO), in addition to your other duties." That was my first taste of handling a very unpleasant job, and I hated it, but Colonel Sanderson, base commander, told me bluntly that "someone has to do it." It helped to have a strong stomach, as you may be dealing with some gory situations.

Accident investigation requires technical knowledge and pilot know-how, and I dug in with the help of our engineering officer and the Curtiss-Wright factory representative. We might not be able to change airplane design, but we could offer detailed reports that would help factory people understand the problems.

As AIO. I was entitled to an office, an assistant, and even a part time secretary. I also discovered that the Table of Organization, the standard manual of job assignments, called for the rank of major, and I not-so-subtly mentioned this to our CO. Several months later, after our accident rate dropped to zero, and our monthly safety bulletin attracted lots of attention, I got the gold leaf. That was a great day, as I was now a staff officer. The promotion had some adverse effects also, as I was no longer an instructor-check pilot and just 'one of the boys.' I tried to keep the same relationship with the other pilots, but there was a subtle change in their attitude.

The new rank changed my feeling about my job. I now wore two hats: one of an administrative officer and the other as a pilot. I became a very impatient pilot, anxious to avoid any more accidents in our operation. We considered the C-46 a great airplane, but it had mechanical problems that plagued us. I wanted to spend time with factory people, but my only connection was the Curtiss-Wright representative who frequently visited our base. He supplied information about what was going on elsewhere, and I learned that everyone else was having the same technical problems. I wanted to visit the factory, but until I could accomplish that, I concentrated on improving the operation of the airplane from the pilots' standpoint, and worked on engineering problems that we could handle at the local level.

Crosswind takeoffs and landings were a major problem in the C-46, which otherwise had excellent flight characteristics. At low to medium speed, in a tail-down attitude, the huge fuselage blocked the rudder, causing almost complete loss of rudder control. This made it difficult to hold straight in crosswinds, when it could weathercock into the wind and swerve off the runway with disastrous results. Reports filtered in that a large number of C-46's were being wrecked in India, running off the runways into muddy fields. In some cases they could be saved, but in the worst cases, they ended up in ditches with landing gear struts driven up into the wings, puncturing the wing tanks, causing fires and loss of life. I learned that this was a major cause of C-46 accidents throughout the world.

A pilot normally tries to correct a swerve by using opposite brake and more power on the upwind engine. This is a poor solution, when operating off short runways. Brakes slow down the takeoff run. Applying power to an engine lengthens the landing run. We had no other solution until one fell into our laps.

One of our pilots casually mentioned one day, that he had no such trouble. He said he could steer the airplane by simply turning the wheel in the direction of the swerve. "Gosh, I thought everyone knew this," he said. Well, everyone did not know this, and it seemed so simple that we doubted the accuracy of his claim.

It was accurate. I tried it, and was able to steer the airplane with ailerons only when the tail was down by simply rolling the wheel in the opposite direction to where I wanted to go. For example, when a crosswind from the right would cause the airplane to veer to the right, turning the wheel to the right would lower the left aileron and create considerable drag on the left side. This would swing the airplane back to the left. This little technique gave us directional control at low to moderate speed, and solved a very vexing problem.

I immediately passed the word along to other units using the C-46 and some responded that "we knew this all along." Perhaps they did, or did not care to admit their ignorance, as we did. We sent an advisory to the CBI Theater C-46 units recommending that they adopt this safety technique, which we had "developed after extensive research and testing, and considered to be a valuable pilot aid." We added it to our training curriculum, and I believe that in India, where everyone operated off narrow runways in crosswinds, it probably saved more airplanes than any other single flying tip.

There are always questions and disputes about flying technique. We had an excellent safety record at Reno, but we were always open to advice from the experts. Some aircraft factories sent test pilots to air bases to demonstrate their aircraft to new military pilots just out of flying school.

We all knew about Tony Levier, famous Lockheed test pilot, who traveled the world giving demonstrations in the P-38. When that airplane was first introduced, many pilots were afraid of it, having heard stories about how easy it was to lose control if an engine failed on takeoff, often resulting in a fatal crash. Tony gave some remarkable demonstrations, giving the P-38 pilots a new lease on life. He would shut off an engine on takeoff right after wheels up, feather the prop to reduce wind resistance to a minimum, then climb up to altitude, perform acrobatics such as rolls, loops, and Immelmanns. Then he would make a perfect approach and landing, all on one engine. His standard joke was that the P-38 only needed one engine, and that the other one was just a spare. His work had wonderful results; word circulated around the world in no time that the P-38 was a wonderful flying machine, and the pilots fell in love with it They fought for assignment to P-38 squadrons, and it became one of the success stories of the Air Corps.

I asked for and got an expert test pilot from Curtiss-Wright to visit us. We were told that Al DeGarmo was another Tony Levier, and could show us everything we would ever want to know about the C-46. We looked forward to this meeting with a "Hot Pilot", who we expected would have the skills of Tony, the fame of Charles Lindbergh, and the glamour of Robert Taylor, all rolled into one.

I met Al DeGarmo at the hotel to escort him to the field, and I had to re-adjust my thinking. Al resembled a movie character all right, but hardly the hero type. He looked like he would fill the role of a stagecoach driver for a western movie, a pot bellied, tobacco-chewing guy, more at home behind a team of horses than in an airplane.

Al was one of the old barnstormers, who learned to fly long before the war. He had flown vintage World War I surplus Jennys powered with oil splattering OX-5 engines, worked the air shows, flown the mail, run a flying school, and done just about everything to keep flying in the lean and hungry pre-war years.

We couldn't imagine how this man, who resembled an over-age ranch hand and acted like one most of the time, had graduated to the very important job of chief production test pilot for Curtiss-Wright. Did he really know some things about the C-46 that were going to impress us, and greatly improve our regard for this troubled airplane?

You bet he did, and he sure impressed us.

We had great concern about the C-46 single engine capability. Al started right off to put our fears to rest. He would cut an engine after take-off, climb to a comfortable altitude, and do stalls all on one engine. He would make near-stalling turns into the dead engine, which is considered a very dangerous maneuver, and hang the airplane on its prop in a near vertical attitude. His crowning maneuver was to cut power back to idle on both engines at 5000 feet above the field, and then do a perfect dead-stick landing, hitting the runway at exactly the right spot. This precision flying demo was what we needed, and even our most experienced instructors were impressed by the old man at the wheel. He pushed the airplane to its limits, and showed us that this was a safe and versatile airplane, and we need not fear it. He made us love that airplane.

We considered Al's visit a sensational success, and wined and dined him royally. Then he would let loose, spinning yarns of the old days that would first make our hair curl, and then we'd go into gales of laughter. He described flying the old Jennys with OX-5 engines that would have valves freeze up in flight unless lubricated. He told us how he would get out on the wing and crawl forward with an oil can to squirt oil into the engine rocker arms. Do you believe that story? We were ready to believe anything this incredible skyhawk told us. His background in flying was so broad and exciting that he had a new story for us every time we met.

When Al had to move on, we hated to see him go, and gave him a great send-off dinner party. We sent some very nice letters to the factory commending him for this service, and we should have sent him a medal for being a very special guy.

Al made a suggestion before he left on how to keep our instruction at top level. As FSO, I recommended that we name our three most experienced instructors "Assistant Chief Pilot," and assign them the job of checking our instructors. This new level of responsibility insured that our instructors were kept at the best level, and it dropped our accident rate from pilot error down to almost zero.

Chapter 42
THE C-46

Our Reno OTU training program was getting better all the time, but I wanted to find out what could be done at the factory level to build a better airplane. A new airplane usually undergoes many tests under all kinds of conditions before the military will approve it, but in wartime things are vastly different. The rush is on, and often the airplane goes into the field without 'de-bugging' to correct its flaws. There is a big risk that problems will crop up in the field, and accidents will happen, but urgent needs take priority. That is the history of every new airplane designed and put into service during the war.

Every new airplane has design flaws, and correcting them is expensive, both in lives and dollars. In recent years, a new state-of-the-art fighter plane went into limited production, at a cost of hundreds of millions of dollars. The designers committed a major error. It was designed as a two-seater, with the crewman sitting to the right of the pilot instead of to his rear. This seating arrangement blocked the pilot's view to the right, an obvious error that should have been caught in the initial design stage. Perhaps the designers never asked an experienced fighter pilot for his opinion. The error became apparent in the field, and the airplane was not produced in quantity.

We did not have the luxury of time to make changes in the C-46. We filed many formal requests for modifications in electrical, hydraulic and other systems. We received few responses and assumed that new C-46's were coming out of the factory without these important changes. I had a young man's impatience to get changes made immediately , and it seemed to take forever. All the bugs and bad design features were coming to roost on the poor guys in the CBI, who did not have the facilities to make modifications in the war zone. It was vitally important to make as many changes as possible before the airplanes left the factory.

Perhaps the factory people did not realize how urgent these matters were, and I itched for the chance to tell them directly. I put in a request to visit the factory, and soon received permission to do this and confer with the design staff. I traveled to the Curtiss- Wright plant at Buffalo, New York, in January of 1944, taking with me a long list of the problems.

I arrived in Buffalo by commercial airline, on the tail of what had been a howling blizzard. I saw more snow than I had ever seen in my early years in Boston. Snow-banks along the streets were piled so high that stores and houses were hidden. Curtiss-Wright sent a courtesy car to pick me up at my hotel and the driver jokingly said it was "only a mild snowstorm, because we can drive after the plows go through. A real storm is when you can't leave the house for a week." I wondered how the factory managed to do production test flying on icy runways with 20-foot high snow-banks.

The Curtiss-Wright executives were in top form, greeting me like a visiting general, even though I had come alone, in mid-winter, with a long laundry list of glitches. They escorted me on a tour of the huge main plant, and I was very impressed by the hustle and bustle of high-level production. They were working hard to fill their world-wide orders, despite major shortages of materials. This made some of the items on my list seem less important, until I reminded myself that even some of these small faults might be causing fatal crashes, or at the very least, enough grief to put airplanes out of commission.

Very few changes could be made quickly, but I gave Curtiss-Wright credit for their earnest efforts to do the job as fast as they could. A few items received fast action, one of them being the cockpit seat adjustment. There was some humor in solving this problem.

Pilot and copilot seats were adjustable, riding back and forth on tracks. Rudder pedals were also adjustable, theoretically allowing any size pilot to get comfortable. However, short men of 5'6" or 5'7", like me, found that even with full adjustment we could not reach the pedals without an extra back cushion. This was not a good arrangement, because it left your feet dangling off the edge of the seat, causing fatigue.

When we came to that item on my list, the chief of engineering brought the head of cockpit design into the picture. As soon as he strode into the office, I could see the cause of the problem, and almost started to laugh. He was a foot taller than me, at least 6'7" tall, and I was pretty certain that he had overlooked the fact that some very short people fly airplanes. I recall giving him a big smile and a warm greeting, and then bluntly saying to this man who towered over me, "Some of us short people have trouble reaching the rudder pedals." This was not very diplomatic of me, and he got visibly embarrassed and soon left to go back to the drawing board Within two weeks we had a change-order instructing us to extend the tracks six inches forward. At Reno, where some of our pilots were even shorter than I, we had been doing that for months.

Another simple glitch that indicated inadequate flight-testing at night involved the retractable landing lights. When these were turned on, they swung up to the fully extended position, which was a good angle for the landing approach, lighting up the runway very well. However, once the airplane was on the ground in the three-point position, the lights pointed up into the sky at a such a high angle that they were useless for taxiing, and we had suffered several ground collisions. The factory executive I discussed this with acted like he never heard of the problem, and I asked him if they ever operated their airplanes at night. There was no positive response.

I told him we had been re-working the systems at Reno, adding another switch that separately controlled the retracting motors on the lights. This allowed the pilot to lower the lights after landing to the correct angle for taxiing. I emphasized the problem with a story of my almost running over some ground crew men one dark night on the Reno parking ramp. He took notes, and promised immediate action on the production line. They quickly resolved the problem by simply leaving one light stay high for landing approach, while setting the other light low for taxiing.

The most important problem under discussion was the leaky tanks, and I was shown the new assembly system that provided leak-proof tanks and non-sparking electric fuel pumps. The dark side of this modification was that there was no way to modify aircraft in the field, and we had to keep our fingers crossed, hoping that there would be no more wing explosions.

We discussed numerous other matters, and I wonder what they thought of this not-too- tactful 24-year-old Air Force major who was trying to tell them how to run their business. But I was not worried as much about hurting feelings as I was about the safety of the thousands of flights, carrying tens of thousands of people in C-46 aircraft all around the world, that might depend on how well I got these points across.

I learned a great deal from that visit. I saw how going through channels might take many months for the word to get to its intended destination, but a face-to-face discussion with the man in charge can work wonders, and get action right away. I left Buffalo with high hopes that we would see results quickly, and I was determined to keep up the pressure in my own private way. I followed up the visit with courtesy letters to the Curtiss-Wright executives I had met, and they reassured me that they were going ahead full speed.

* * * * * *

My next major project involved writing a C-46 flight manual for pilots. The Air Force published many "Technical Orders," written by technical people in engineering language, telling pilots how to operate the systems, but they neglected to instruct pilots about operating techniques. There was an acute need for a manual that would describe the peculiarities of an airplane and help the pilot fly it more safely and efficiently.

I received orders in July of 1944, to join a group at the new Air Force Office of Flying Safety at Winston-Salem, North Carolina, where pilot training manuals for all aircraft types were being prepared. I was very pleased at this honor, as the various units around the entire world were asked to submit the names of their most qualified pilots to create these very important manuals. My commanding officer jokingly commented that with our training program going well and no accidents to investigate, I should go back to work.

Pilot training manuals for active aircraft was an idea that was long overdue, and I wondered why it had taken years for the Air Force to wake up to the need. My Flying Safety Office in Reno had been publishing this information in bits and pieces, and I couldn't imagine any greater need than pilot manuals for these complex machines that would kill you if handled improperly. The manuals were to be written in pilots' language, and give practical information on flight characteristics, emergency procedures, and a thousand and one other things that a pilot should know, and often learned the hard way. They would be a blessing to all new pilots being checked out in very demanding aircraft.

At Winston-Salem, a professional writer was assigned to me, formerly a newspaperman with the New York Times, holding the lowly rank of corporal. Corporal Hal Green was 15 years older than I, and I came to regard him as my writing mentor, who taught me many skills of writing. We became good friends, and worked closely as a team, spending days going through technical orders and factory information. We then proceeded to write the manual, writing it with some humor, and including personal observations from experienced pilots. Our artists did some excellent illustrations and included cartoons showing airplanes hurting when mistakes were made. I had found this light-hearted approach very effective in our monthly FSO bulletin at Reno.

I brought the first draft to Reno for our chief pilots to review and suggest changes, and then returned to Winston-Salem for final approval. While waiting, I reviewed some 90 reports on C-46 accidents, most of them occurring overseas. I was appalled at the number of takeoff and landing accidents that occurred when a crosswind forced the airplane off the runway into a muddy bog. This emphasized how important it was for us to give a lot of crosswind instruction to our pilots. In the States, all major airports had a choice of runways to use, and the pilot could usually find one that headed him into the prevailing wind. In overseas operations, he was likely to have only one runway, with the wind often from the wrong direction. In the manual, I went into detail about the crosswind technique, about rolling the control wheel into the wind to correct for side thrust. At Reno, I held meetings with instructors, telling them about the accident statistics, and pointing out the importance of this instruction.

Accident files disclosed another alarming problem: aircraft running out of fuel on long delivery flights over the Pacific. Despite a full load of fuel and extra tanks installed, there were instances of aircraft en route to Pacific islands not making the distance.

Cruise Control was just being introduced into the Air Corps, and it was apparent that we needed to take some action in C-46 instruction. Pilots were accustomed to easy-to- remember engine power settings of "20.30," which meant 2000 RPM and 30 inches of manifold pressure. This was acceptable for stateside flying, but used excessive fuel on long over-water trips. It was essential that crews practice fuel economy, as they might face strong headwinds, navigational errors, engine failures, and other hazards that would cause them to run out of fuel. Air Transport Command Headquarters had developed cruise control charts for the C-46, but they were not distributed or explained to flight personnel. We included these in the manual, and soon after my report to Reno on this, classes were set up to teach the subject.

I considered myself quite expert in a C-46, but realized there was much more for me to learn about long range technique. I learned that it was perfectly safe to operate our engines as low as 1600 RPM without exceeding engine limits, and that it was essential to maintain an air speed high enough to keep the airplane on its aerodynamic 'step' at all times. I learned that we could increase the range of the airplane by as much as 20% by careful cruise management.

The "How To" manual turned out to be very successful, and became the C-46 'bible' at every base operating the airplane. The Office of Flying Safety published manuals for every airplane type in active service, and they went far toward improving safety records.

Winston-Salem had its fun times, too. There were two utility airplanes stationed there that got little use, as there were few rated pilots on hand, and I was happy to exercise one every weekend. One was a twin Cessna C-78, that we fondly called a "Double-breasted Cub," which I flew to Boston on weekends to obtain my required flying time for the month, and to visit my family.

I learned a lesson about safety on one of those trips. Flying into Boston one night, under instrument conditions (IFR), the tower reported "intermittent low ceilings," which meant that the weather forecaster did not know how much ceiling height to expect. The instrument approach chart for Boston allowed a minimum altitude of 500 feet. If you didn't break out of the cloud cover at this altitude, you were to pull up and go to an alternate airport. As I was letting down, I was still on instruments at 500 feet, in broken clouds.

The letdown was going so smoothly that I pressed on, expecting to break out into the clear at any moment, but did not break out until I was below 400 feet. I reported this to the tower operator, and he, in turn, reported the surprising information that "The airlines cancelled all their flights into Boston. How come the military is flying?" That was a good question, and definitely a bit of a rebuke. I was surprised at my own lack of caution. The lesson learned was that it is easy for an eager pilot to risk his neck for a family visit, or for a date with a girl friend

The other utility airplane was the famous Norduyne Norseman, a heavy, single-engine cargo plane designed for hauling supplies in the far north. This delightful but noisy "truck" trimmed out so easily that it practically flew itself, and with a cruising speed of 120 miles per hour, navigation was easy. I flew Corporal Green to New York to visit his family on my way to Boston, and gave him flying lessons on the way, which he found quite thrilling. After takeoff, he would take over, climb to cruising altitude, and fly for the rest of the trip, except for the landing at La Guardia Airport. Giving instruction broke the monotony of flying long distances at two miles per minute.

The personnel at the Winston-Salem Office of Flying Safety were a puzzle to me. This was my first experience at a top-level Air Force Headquarters facility, which exercised worldwide authority over Air Force operations. Most of the people had never been overseas and had little awareness of what life was like in a combat zone. They worked 'by the book' in a world that was comfortable and orderly. Their lack of combat zone experience created misunderstanding between us.

For example, when I commented to responsible officers on the dangerous lack of navigational facilities in the CBI, the glib response was, "Why don't they just requisition what they need?" They had no concept of the hardships faced in overseas theaters; they could not believe that we had waited over a year for such basic items as spark plugs. Overseas service was a threat to them, and many were concerned about keeping their jobs in the "seat of power" and avoiding an overseas assignment.

I talked about this with another overseas veteran, a Major Hal Grinstead, who had flown B-25 medium bombers in Africa, and was writing the B-25 manual.

He admitted that he was very frustrated at having to deal with the "paper-pushers at HQ," who, he claimed, were "not living in the real world of war." If there is a lesson to be learned from all this, it is that we need men who have been bloodied in the field before they are allowed to take responsible positions at HQ.

I have a further comment on working at headquarters. It is thrilling to be located where power rests, whether in military or civilian life. In recent years, I visited senators and representatives in Washington on behalf of a national charity, and worked with bright young staff people. They were very stimulated to be working in the center of political, economic, and military power of the entire world.

Working where big decisions are made is a powerful magnet that draws people to work inside Washington today. Some find the atmosphere so dynamic that there is a saying that "The world ends at the Beltway," the highway that encircles the heart of the city. After working in high-level government offices, many fall victim to what is popularly called "Potomac Fever," and are very reluctant to move back to the ordinary life of their home-towns. A humorous cartoon map was posted in one office that showed this attitude, with Washington, D.C., as the center of the universe, with all other countries and cities mere dots on the map. I think that in wartime, Washington brass thinks this way.

Here are two of my favorite airplanes, a C-47 in the background and a C-46 towering over me. They are not flashy like fighters, or menacing like bombers. They carried people and cargoes and saved lives. They served me well and safely for thousands of hours in the air.

Chapter 43
LEGAL EAGLE

As an Air Corps officer rises in the ranks, his duties involve more than flying aircraft. A favorite expression heard in every service is, "In addition to your other duties, you are hereby ordered to ... supervise the motor pool," (or the swimming pool, or any of a hundred other duties your commanding officer finds appropriate).

I was handed an extra duty in July of 1944 when 1 was taken off flying status due to a recurrence of malaria. "In addition to your other duties, you are appointed temporary commanding officer of Headquarters Squadron." HQ Squadron was a catch-all unit, that included most of the base functions that were not related to flying, such as personnel, the mess halls, motor pool, security, building maintenance, and so forth. I now had one foot in flying as Flying Safety Officer, and the other in countless non-flying jobs. Each department was run by a junior officer or a non-commissioned officer, who reported to me and brought their problems to my office.

I totally lacked know-how for this work, and relied heavily on Master Sergeant McLure, an old hand, who seemed to know every detail of my job. Every morning he gave me a gloomy rundown of everything that was going wrong, and then placed a large number of reports on my desk to be signed. I was swamped by these, and in my ignorance, might have sold the airbase to the enemy. I also had the 'spit-and-polish' duty of leading the Saturday morning review of troops, a standard parade function on all bases. My fellow pilots kidded me about this status symbol going to my head, so I threatened to get even by having the slot machines in the O-Club fixed to payoff only ten cents on the dollar. Even Harold's Club did better than that.

Other duties cropped up during my two months as acting Commanding Officer of HQ Squadron. The base commander called me into a private meeting one day, to meet a visiting captain, an intelligence officer from Washington. He was on a secret mission, looking for possible saboteurs who were damaging aircraft. He had received a confidential report about finding loose tools in both engine compartments of one of our airplanes, that could cause damage in flight. I pointed out that this could happen easily, like a surgeon forgetting to remove a sponge, but the intelligence officer did not find that likely. I could not see any motivation to sabotage a training airplane in Nevada, as compared to my experiences in China, where guards had shot several trespassers they suspected of trying to sabotage our very precious C-47.

The intelligence officer pointed out that tools left in one engine nacelle could be accidental, but two made it suspicious. He theorized that perhaps a mechanic was angry about a failed promotion, or resented a superior officer, and decided to do damage. He asked that our local under-cover intelligence operative, who was, much to my surprise, on our roster as a Corporal Smith, be given special emergency leave to travel to other bases and check the history of some of our line mechanics. Master Sergeant McLure was indignant when I arbitrarily ordered him to provide special leave for Corporal Smith without an appropriate reason, and, of course, I could not disclose the reason. McLure actually ran the squadron, and acted like I was infringing on his authority, which I probably was.

The search failed to turn up any likely suspects and the investigation was dropped, as we had no proof of a deliberate attempt to damage an airplane. What I found interesting was that there existed a secret intelligence network within the framework of our hard-working base. There is a popular joke about the expression "Military Intelligence" being an oxymoron, but I think there is a very active intelligence business in the military doing an effective job.

Administrative work was pretty dull compared to flying, but my interest perked up when I became involved in the court-martial trial of one of our airmen and had a taste of military law in action.

Corporal Rosti was in serious trouble, facing a court-martial for several offenses. He was in training as a crew chief on a C-46, and orders came through sending his group to India in two days. Regulations said that on receiving orders for overseas duty, enlisted men with families living in town could have overnight leave to make final farewells, but unmarried men were confined to the base.

Rosti was unmarried, but had a local girlfriend. He wanted one more evening with her, so he 'borrowed' a pass from another man in his barracks using a little bribery. Arriving in downtown Reno he found that the light-of-his-life had already given up on him, and was out with another airman. He proceeded to drown his sorrows at a local bar.

Hours later, staggering down the street, with no hat, and shirt hanging out, he ran afoul of one our officers, Captain Murrow, a normally timid supply officer, who very bravely reprimanded him for being drunk and out of uniform, and ordered him back to the base.

Rosti was in an alcoholic fog by then, and being a big strong man, he grabbed Murrow by his lapels, shook him up, and threatened bodily harm. "You son-of-a-bitch! Get out of my way!" Fortunately for the captain, two husky Military Police showed up and placed Rosti under arrest.

Next came a court-martial on charges of assault on an officer, drunkenness, and going Absent Without Leave (AWOL). The prosecuting officer, a Colonel Jason, arrived in town to convene the trial, and asked for a defense attorney to be appointed.

As CO of HQ Squadron, it was my job to find a defense attorney, but we had no legal officer on the base. "We had better import someone from McClellan Field," I suggested, that being a large air base near Sacramento. No one was available, and we were desperate. I casually mentioned that the only person I had found with any legal background was myself, with two years of law school, which would hardly qualify me, but Colonel Jason jumped on that and assigned me the job of defense attorney.

I protested that I was quite ignorant about the procedure, so Colonel Jason gave me a quick, 30-minute course on court-martials, and commented., "You'll just have to do the best you can. You know, major, there's a war on." I laughed inwardly at this comment, which I had heard so many times, coming from a lawyer who had never been overseas.

My job was to protect Rosti from improper procedure, but I also wanted to free him for duty overseas. On questioning him, I saw that there might be sympathy for a man caught in these circumstances. His defense was his great stress after receiving orders for overseas duty without any way to say a personal goodbye to his fiancee. 1 would plead that this was a momentous event in this young man's life, with the likelihood that he might never see his true love again.

During the trial, I pointed out the defendant's good character and excellent work reports, and a past record with no blemishes. He was formerly a middleweight boxer, and had a slightly flattened nose and the craggy looks that went with that trade, but he had a reputation as a good guy, despite his rugged appearance. Furthermore, he was a trained flight engineer, a key member of a C-46 crew ready to ship out.

I started my summary with high hopes. I pointed out how the system was grossly unfair in restricting unmarried enlisted men to the base, while officers had no such restrictions. I was pleased to note some nods of agreement among the jury members, so I emphasized how every one of us would hate to receive orders for overseas shipment without a chance to say goodbye to loved ones. I felt I was making a strong case for leniency.

Then the court asked the defendant questions to confirm that the facts I presented were correct. Everything was going well until the presiding judge casually asked, "Tell me, corporal, what is the name of your young lady, and where does she live?"

Rosti hesitated and gulped. He stammered out, "She lives in Reno, and ... " He turned red. He clammed up. And I was ready to hide my head from embarrassment. He did not remember her name!

I was shocked. I had made a massive blunder. I had failed to get this information in advance. I then tried to coach him, by saying, "Isn't her name Mary ...?" No response. He was tongue-tied. And even if he had taken me up on that suggestion, the moment was lost. It was obvious to the court that the young lady in question was not really his fiancee or anything close to it.

The sentence was passed; the maximum penalty of six months in the stockade. But the matter was not over yet. I made an appeal to the judge asking for a suspended sentence based on military requirements. There was no good reason to confine him to the base stockade, where he would spend the next six months picking up cigarette butts, when we were so short of crew members overseas. The judge said, "Major, we leave it to the discretion of the base commander to decide how this man shall serve his sentence." I was proud of the result after all, for in 24 hours Rosti was demoted to private, and was on his way to Assam, India. He was quite grateful at the time, but I often wondered if he might have preferred the stockade to the conditions he endured in the Assam Valley.

The C-46 looked good in the air and it carried a big load for that time.

Chapter 44
MARRIAGE

The Operational Training Unit at Reno was a very successful operation, and gratifying to me. Our experience on the Hump showed us that we must establish a rigorous training program to help our students cope with the severe challenges they would face. We made sure that when our pilots left Reno for overseas they were highly qualified for all-weather flying. We were starting to like the C-46, agreeing that "When they get the bugs out, that's going to be a good airplane." It was destined to be our major cargo airplane, and we worked hard to make it better.

After two years at Reno I requested a transfer to another base, for personal reasons that are still not quite clear to me. Here is what happened:

I shared the Bachelor Officers Quarters with other unmarried Hump veterans. We were a close knit group, spending most evenings at the Officers Club. Several evenings a week we went into Reno, eight miles away, usually to the lounge at the El Cortez Hotel. This was an active place, with entertainment and a dance band, and a good spot to meet the ladies. Reno was the divorce center of the country, and many ladies on a six-week visit pending their final divorce papers were looking for male companionship.

It was August of 1943, and I had been in Reno for two months. Joe Walker and I were leaning on the El Cortez bar one Saturday evening, sipping beer, talking flying, listening to the band, and eyeing the crowd for two suitable dance partners. The atmosphere was lighthearted and pleasant, and we were relaxing after a week of grueling flying, giving final check rides to the next group of pilots heading for India. Doing risky training maneuvers in a large airplane was intensive work and a great responsibility, but we worked these pilots hard. We knew that their lives and the lives of many others depended on how well we taught them.

Now it was fun time. I always enjoyed that special relaxed feeling that comes over me after I land an airplane, shut down the engines, and know my mission is completed. I have often taken a deep breath now that the bird is safe on the ground, and I leave the airplane feeling that a tremendous burden is lifted from my shoulders. Then we head for a place to unwind, and we felt right at home at the El Cortez, joining our friends.

Joe's eagle eye, honed by squinting across miles of open sky for other flying objects, spotted two likely targets. "Hey, those two coming in the door look pretty great. Let's go!" They did stand out in the crowd, cute as buttons. Without further conversation, Joe and I moved into position, like a two-plane element, splitting formation at the last minute, to cover both sides of the target. A speedy approach was essential, before other aggressors could make a move.

Joe and I thought that we were quite irresistible in our bright and shining armor (our uniforms), wearing our glorious badges of sainthood over our hearts (pilot's wings and rows of fruit salad), and we had acquired many gold stars in our campaigns (with the fairer sex). Unfortunately, in this crowded place everyone else was similarly dressed, so we didn't exactly stand out. The two young ladies were not especially overwhelmed by us, as they were real beauties, able to pick and choose. They had lots of choices, and they wanted to avoid drunks and other unpleasant people.

But possession is nine-tenths of the law, and Joe and I were there and in possession. We passed the inspection, probably helped by our captain's bars and the ribbons that showed we had done some good, and the four of us moved onto the dance floor. After a brief chat, Marie, my tall dance partner, looked across the floor at Joe and commented to me, "You should be dancing with my sister. She's too small for your tall friend." It was apparent that Joe's six-foot plus did not go well with the sister, who measured only up to his shoulder, and Marie urged me to change partners.

"Besides," she confided, "I'm only here for a short visit, but my sister lives here. I live in Walla Walla, and have a husband who is overseas, but she's single." I absorbed all this information quickly, and in proper military manner, took immediate action, right on the dance floor. Joe very affably agreed to switch partners and I stared into the blue eyes of this blond miniature Nordic beauty named Viola, and felt my heart go "bump."

We danced silently to slow ballads, speeded up for faster tunes, and I stopped all cutting in by the curt remark that, "This lady is taken." No one argued with the brusque captain, and my response turned out to be a prophecy: she was taken. Sometimes events take place in just a few moments that we later realize are pivotal. Meeting Viola, called Vi for short, was one of them.

A wonderful two-year romance started that night. I was working hard as an instructor, and later, as Flying Safety Officer, a responsible job that I found very absorbing. Vi was my delightful companion, who made my time-off a joy. Her sense of humor and her enjoyment of all that life had to offer were just what I needed to offset the work that I took so seriously. We spent much time together, dating exclusively with each other, and sharing romantic times at Lake Tahoe resorts.

She was a daring person, but sometimes her adventurous spirit went a little too far. She enjoyed motorcycles, and urged me to get one. I told her of the many servicemen who had been killed or seriously injured on these machines. Our base personnel had so many disastrous accidents that motorcycling was declared "off limits." Anyone riding one was subject to severe penalty, and any injuries incurred were "not in the line of duty," and medical costs would not be paid for by military funds.

Vi loved skiing, but was a novice who did not see the danger in tackling slopes beyond her ability. We should have outlawed that sport also, as many base personnel were disabled by ski injuries, but they were not fatal accidents. Vi learned the hard way one day on the local Mt. Rose slope, when she followed me up the tow rope to the intermediate level without my knowing that she had left the bunny slope. When I spotted her high up, it was too late do anything but shout "Be careful!" Down she went, unable to check her speed, until she took a serious tumble. Fortunately, her safety release bindings worked and her skis came off. The fall left her a little dazed, and she was more careful after that.

Many of our friends were newlyweds, and I was constantly asked when I was going to pop the question. They praised the delights of married life, and the glint grew bright in Vi's eyes. But this stupid hero of the skies would not make a commitment, as I did not yet realize that to truly enjoy my life, I had to share it.

Things came to a head when I was sent to the East Coast for several weeks on the assignment to write the C-46 training manual. Before leaving, I very stupidly suggested that perhaps Vi should not sit around waiting for my return, but go out with other people. This suggestion was a shock to her, and created an argument, but I shrugged it off as her reaction to my plan to be gone for several weeks. On my return, she received me very coldly with the announcement that she had met some very nice men, and had no intention of anything more serious with me than an occasional dinner. Our romance had broken apart, although we still cared for each other.

On one occasion, she accused me of improper behavior towards a fellow pilot, who she had dated occasionally. He demanded a passionate goodnight kiss on her doorstep and she resisted, ripping a button off his jacket in the ensuing wrestling match. She showed me her token button, and was probably trying to arouse my jealousy, but all I would say was, "Tsk, tsk. You shouldn't allow that to happen," or some other stupid remark.

As matters turned out, that captain, one of our C-46 instructors, had never been overseas, and his name turned up on the next schedule for transfer to India. Vi never believed that I had not engineered that transfer, even when I pointed out that experienced pilots were in big demand in India, and that even though I was now a major, I had little control over transfers. 1 think she enjoyed the thought that I was jealous enough to do the deed. In truth, I was happy to see him go.

My friends thought that I was quite stupid and urged us to get back together again. I guess that I just wasn't sold on giving up my freedom and I chickened out, and looked for a way to preserve my single life. What a coward! What do cowards do? This hero of the skies, possessor of several medals of valor, ran away from the problem.

A position opened for a Flying Safety Officer at the Stockton Air Force Base. This small base, in central California, was being expanded to handle Air Evacuation C-47 ambulance-type aircraft, and was building up its staff. I requested a transfer, which my commanding officer approved on condition that I leave a qualified man in my place. My capable assistant, Lieutenant Bob White, was delighted to take over the Reno office, which meant a promotion for him, and I moved to Stockton, where I set up the Flying Safety office.

A month passed. I did not call Vi, nor did I receive word from her. One day, I flew the 200 miles to Reno over a stormy Donner Summit, while giving an instrument check ride to a new pilot. I visited Bob White at my old office to see how he was getting along on his new job, and how his wife, Lucy, and their new baby were doing.

After business talk, Bob said, "By the way, I came across a news item in the Reno Gazette announcing the engagement of Viola Harding to someone named Jones." Bob looked at me with a very sour expression, and added his personal comment, "You just didn't know a good thing when it was right under your nose." He added, "there was a photo of her, and she sure looked great."

All four of us had vacationed at Lake Tahoe together and become a close foursome. We had jokingly suggested that he and his wife name their baby "Tahoe" as they traced the conception back to a weekend spent there. Lucy and everyone else who knew Vi and me as a couple, were disgusted with me.

I had little comment to make to Bob, but that evening, back at Stockton, I found myself very disturbed by the news. I didn't know why, although I am sure that everyone in the world could have told me. I decided to call Vi to offer her my congratulations, but I guess that any student of psychology would say that what I really wanted was to hear the sound of her voice. That was a fateful telephone call that went something like this:

Jim: "Hi, Vi, this is Jim. I guess congratulations are called for. I hear you're engaged."

Vi: "I know who this is. Thank you very much."

Jim: "Tell me, who's the lucky man?"

Vi: "It's no one you know. Furthermore, he's a civilian, and you can't send him overseas." (Where did she ever get that idea?)

Jim: "Well, uh ... the most important thing is, do you love him?"

Vi: "He's a very nice man."

Jim: "That's not what I asked. Do you really love him?"

Vi: "I told you, he's a very nice man; and furthermore, he's here!"

This brief telephone call started out very calmly, but as I spoke to her, tension was building up in me. The sound of her voice was very disturbing, and I was getting frustrated and angry. I don't know exactly what happened, but at that moment something snapped, or I was struck by lightning. I lost control of myself, and completely forgot the ancient military advice about never volunteering for anything, which had gotten me into trouble before. I volunteered!

I shouted into the phone, "I'm coming to Reno tomorrow and we are getting married right away!" Was I out of my mind?

There was total silence ... I could hear the wheels turning. What a preposterous idea!

Jim: "WELL?"

Time is going by.

A small voice replied. "I can't marry you tomorrow. I'm just getting over the flu. But I should be all better the next day!"

Once more lightning hit me. She is saying "yes!" I had expected a flat "no," or at least a big argument. I was thrilled. I took a deep breath, and asked, "Are you sure?"

Vi: "I'm sure. Where have you been, you big dummy?"

The remainder of our conversation is a secret in my memory.

After a while, I called Major Al Kaplan, friend and flight surgeon at Reno. His wife, Dorothy, answered the phone and was very excited at the news. Then she sarcastically remarked, "It's about time, you oaf. We knew you would marry her, if you ever came to your senses."

Dorothy made up for her insult by arranging everything - the base chaplain to do the ceremony, and all the fixings for a wedding on their patio. I had to borrow Al's uniform, for in my haste I forgot to pack my blouse and pinks. I would have preferred a more formal affair with crossed sabers and stuff, but no one seemed to know where to find sabers, and the bride said that all she wanted was me.

I never did learn anything about the mysterious Mr. Jones, who he was, or how he handled the loss. Some secrets a wife will never disclose.

We honeymooned at Lake Tahoe, where we played like kids, swam, walked, and talked, and planned. Vi was like a little girl rather than a mature married woman of 21, her hair in braids, her heart full of love, and I was so proud to be married to her. I was ashamed of my stupidity that had kept us apart, and had almost lost me this wonderful girl. Our marvelous marriage lasted 50 years, produced two daughters and grandchildren. I lost her to Alzheimer's Disease, but never really lost her, for she is always there in the recesses of my heart.

Chapter 45
STOCKTON

Stockton Air Force Base was home to a fleet of C-47 Air Evacuation ambulance airplanes. Each was fitted with 12 litters, in which we carried wounded and sick to military hospitals across the country. My job as Flying Safety Officer was to maintain a perfect safety record. Our pilots were the best, many Hump veterans, many with airline experience, and we made sure that passengers had a smooth ride.

Our airplanes flew empty to Fairfield-Suisun Air Base, located 50 miles north of Stockton, where C-54 four-engine transports were bringing in wounded from the Pacific war zone. After an overnight stay, the patients were loaded aboard our C-47's and flown to Army hospitals nearest to their hometowns. Flying was done in the daytime only, and in clear weather most of the time. Air Evacuation airplanes were given full VIP (Very Important Person) treatment when they landed at a military airfield. The pilot would radio his expected arrival time (ETA) to the tower well before arriving. The tower would alert the entire area, clear the landing pattern, and suspend all other flight operations.

Fire trucks and ambulances would be stationed along the runway, and after the plane touched down, escort it to the parking ramp.

Careful selection of pilots and excellent operating conditions gave us an accident-free operation. Our pilots sometimes claimed to be bored by the routine, but deep down they really loved the work. We saw how the despair in the faces of our wounded passengers changed to hope and happiness when they arrived at their home towns. We were rewarded again when we saw the glow in the faces of family members at the sight of a loved one arriving on our magic carpet.

CHICKEN REVOLT

We witnessed some very touching sights at family reunions, delivering wounded soldiers to their hometowns. On our return to our base at Stockton we looked for a humorous side to life, and occasionally, an event took place that gave us a laugh. The "Chicken Revolt" was one of these. It is a true story about a group of disturbed chickens in the San Joaquin Valley of California that revolted against the United States government. It put everyone in a 'fowl' mood at first, but ended up happily for all concerned.

On a dark and stormy night, I was giving a night instrument check ride to one of our pilots close to our air base. The tower called me and asked for my exact location.

"Army 6349 to Stockton Tower. We are five miles southwest of the field at 1500 feet."

"We have received a complaint from a resident in that area about airplanes flying right over his roof top, and scaring the dickens out of his chickens."

"Tower from 6349. I think someone is joking. We have not flown below 1500 feet except for our practice approaches."

"Well, I don't know sir, but the Officer of the Day has instructed me to order all aircraft out of that vicinity."

We landed without a further thought about the incident, but the next day at Operations I learned that a very irate farmer was threatening to sue the government. He claimed that his chickens were so disturbed by our low flying airplanes that they had stopped laying eggs, and this was costing him a lot of money.

Colonel Ifflick, deputy commanding officer, was a former city planner, and he took public relations very seriously. He suggested we discontinue our night flying, to avoid disturbing the local people. When I objected to this, he suggested I should go make peace with the complainer. "You look like a farm boy who knows how to talk to chicken farmers." Usually, when people complained about low-flying airplanes, we were able to eliminate complaints by politely reminding them that friendly aircraft overhead were far better than enemy ones. In this case, the colonel wanted to be sure that he had a complaint-free record.

"Sir," I said, "I'm a city boy, and all I know about chickens is to eat them. But one of our pilots is a real farm boy from the mid-west who would be the ideal public relations person for this job. He's been overseas on the Hump, has lots of ribbons, and best of all, can talk about chickens from personal experience."

"Send him, by all means."

Captain Bill Pickens thought I was kidding him when I asked him to go. "What am I supposed to do, major?" he asked, "Sing the chickens to sleep?"

"No, just make a nice pleasant visit, invite them into the club Saturday night for dinner, and show them how nice we are."

Bill survived the ordeal very nicely. He came back with a new attitude about chicken farms, telling me he had always hated the farm life, but had really enjoyed this visit. He talked with these folks about his hometown and his folks' farm, and was graciously accepted by the family. He was so enthusiastic about going back to visit that I assumed he had made some good friends with the Dalkin family. Indeed he had.

"Mr. and Mrs. Dalkin can't make it for dinner here Saturday, as they have a church affair. But, their daughter, Nell is coming. She's a senior at College of the Pacific here in Stockton. And she's a real knockout," he confided to me. He made no mention of the disturbed chickens but said he planned to have dinner with the Dalkins on Sunday.

We started seeing a great deal of Miss Nell Dalkin at our base, closely attended by Captain Pickens. She was a bright, bubbly young lady who charmed us all. Our relations with chicken farmers improved greatly, when four months later, Bill Pickens and Nell Dalkin joined hands in holy matrimony. I thought I should have been best man, having started it all by flying at 1500 feet over their farm. When I met farmer Dalkin we had a good laugh about that, and we had no further complaints from him or the chickens. Promoting a marriage was pushing public relations work pretty far, but it was a pleasant way to accomplish the mission.

* * * * * *

Life at Stockton was quite blissful for the many newlyweds like us, except for the shortage of living space in that crowded military town. Many of us lived out of suitcases in cramped motel rooms, and ate all our meals out. The motels were just a few minutes from the base, and often we would run home to pick up the wives for a quick lunch at a nearby coffee shop. Some overstayed their lunch hour, and blushed when kidded about having a "nooner" for lunch. After some months Vi and I found a rundown bungalow, at a ridiculously high rent. It had trashy furniture and the plumbing was a joke, but it was heaven to us.

Our social life was busy, and we soon learned that many of the wives developed a new interest in life: pregnancy. Vi announced her entry into that club in the fall of 1945. Military doctors were not handling pregnancies at the time, so everyone went to a local civilian doctor, who had more business than he could handle. He was a most affable man, and charged everyone the same fee for pre-natal care and delivery - $100 total. Few of the babies were born in Stockton, as the end of the war sent many of the personnel back to their hometowns. Our first child, Sharon, was born in Boston in July of the following year.

The war in the Pacific was over in August, and we wondered - what next? Vi told of an incident on V-J Day that showed how some of the wives were going to miss their easy- going life style. They were secure in the knowledge that their husbands were no longer subject to combat duties. The housing shortage made living conditions far from luxurious, but being young and hopeful, they looked for better days. The base had a comfortable club, a pool, and the girls were happily involved in discussing their pregnancies. On VJ Day, several were playing bridge in the Officers Club, when the radio announcer blurted out that the Japanese had surrendered. Amidst the excitement, and all the chatter that followed, Vi heard one loud voice saying, "I bid two clubs. "

The end of the war did not reduce the activity of our Air Evacuation fleet. It actually increased, as loaded transports arrived daily from the Pacific, turning their wounded passengers over to us to carry to hospitals near their homes. There were calls for more flights, and our crews returned to Stockton immediately after a delivery, ready to go again. When the fall season turned into rainy winter weather, our field was often fogged in by low-hanging 'tule' fogs. To assist our pilots in their approaches, I copied the system I had seen recently at Los Angeles airport, and set up approach lights to our main northwest runway. These helped to line up the final approach, and our aircraft were often able to avoid going to an alternate field.

I received new orders. The European Wing of the Air Transport Command needed a Flying Safety Officer, with headquarters in Paris. This sounded like a great assignment, as Paris in peacetime could be a wonderful place. I visualized an interesting life in Europe, and opportunities to travel and expand our lives greatly. It could mean a promotion for me. I was very excited about this when I broke the news at home, but Vi did not share my joy, as she had other things on her mind. My joy was bluntly cut off when I received word that dependents could not go due to lack of housing facilities. Now I had a problem, as I had to either accept the assignment or resign from the Air Force, as remaining in Stockton was not an option. That was a difficult decision to make, for the attraction of Europe and a larger command responsibility conflicted with reluctance to leave my expectant wife.

I talked it over with friends, and found that most were planning to leave the service, to return to the airlines or seek new careers in civilian life. Five or six years of war were enough, and they craved a return to a normal life style. The services were being reduced to skeleton size, and the peacetime army was revealing itself as largely busy with paperwork. I realized how bad it had become when one day I was sitting in my office, my feet up on the desk, with my greatest problem deciding what to do for lunch. The door swung open and in walked my base commander. I dropped my feet to the floor and popped out of my chair, and he sarcastically asked, "Is that all you have to do, major?" I leveled with him, a friend and former airline pilot who was planning to return to United Airlines, "Fortunately, sir, everything is going so well my duties are small." At lunch, he talked about airline flying and urged me to take the civilian flight test for an Airline Transport Rating (ATR), which I did the following week, along with several other pilots, passing with no problem.

With the war over, the thrill of doing the patriotic thing, fighting to save my country and defeat the "bad guys" was gone. Senior officers told me that there would be many changes in the services in the future, and suggested that I should not count on a career in the Air Force. I finally took the plunge and decided to resign from the service. Vi was overjoyed with my choice, for all she wanted was a lovely cottage with a white picket fence in a quiet suburb. For me, it was time to take on the challenge of post-war civilian life, and look for that airline job or other suitable position.

I left the service in March of 1946, returning to Boston with high hopes that I would be instantly hired by a major airline. My hopes were shattered when I found that the airlines and other aviation business were flooded with applicants for a very few openings. One result of this oversupply of applicants was a lowering of the starting pay for a pilot to $190 a month. Other industries were expanding rapidly, and within a week I was employed in engineering sales in the electronics field that paid very well, and was the beginning of a long career in marketing. Vi and I found an apartment in Boston on the Fenway, close to famous Fenway Park, home of the Boston Red Sox, and became real baseball fans by listening to the shouting and the radio broadcasts, to the accompaniment of the gurgling of our newborn daughter, Sharon. The next two years passed quickly, with a very satisfying job, and purchase of that cottage with the picket fence in the city of Waltham, Massachusetts.

Chapter 46
AIR NATIONAL GUARD

My Air Corps uniform was taking up space in the closet, and I finally decided to put it on again, by joining the Massachusetts Air National Guard at Logan Airport where the 101st Fighter Squadron was being rejuvenated. This famous unit boasted a history dating back to 1922, when it flew JN-4D Jennies of World War I vintage. It was now flying Republic P-47 fighters, tired veterans of stateside flying schools, and we had to search for pilots to fly them.

I joined in April of 1947 as commanding officer of the 202nd Air Service Group, and immediately found myself immersed in paperwork, and the multiple problems of bringing an old group back to life. We had little funding, poor equipment, and only a limited notion of how to function. I had been in this start-up situation before, and knew that with hard work and patience it would become an effective unit. As usual, my key man was a sergeant in the permanent party, who handled much of the detail work.

The Air Force issued a 1947 directive stating the goals of the Air National Guard. We were to establish our own training agenda, and maintain a level of military readiness. This was a vague instruction, and in this early post-war period, there were many questions about the function of the Guard, and how it should respond to both state and federal agencies. In later years, the National Guard has proven to be one of the outstanding backbones of our armed services, and the air units a major part of our air forces.

I never did check out in a "Jug," but got my flying time in the C-47 assigned to us. I found flying in my home area of New England a true delight. The green countryside and the twisting coastline had a special appeal for me, and I have always ranked the Northeast as one of the most beautiful parts of our country.

A two-week maneuver at Otis Air Force Base, on Cape Cod, proved to be great fun, but disclosed serious shortages and general confusion in our operation. I was confident that eventually the glitches would be corrected, as there was a huge assortment of supplies someplace, ready to be found and put to use.

A change in my business dictated a move to the West Coast in 1948, and in May of that year, with great regret, I officially resigned from the Massachusetts Air National Guard and returned to my Air Force Reserve status.

Chapter 47
CASH-AND-CARRY AIRLINES

"So you want to go flying again," I said to myself one beautiful Southern California morning in 1951. Living close to Van Nuys Airport, in the San Fernando Valley, gave me the urge to get back into the air after a non-flying spell of three years. A Piper Cub was not quite what I had in mind, so I applied for an opening in the California Air National Guard located at the airport.

The Air Guard at Van Nuys had an opening in their Table of Organization for the job of Air Inspector, for which I was qualified, so I went before their evaluation board. The position called for the rank of major, but the board consisted of three captains who were all hungry for the same job. Much to my regret, they turned down my application with the excuse that I was not qualified in their Douglas A-26 attack bombers. I left the interview greatly disappointed, and looked longingly at the airplanes and the fine facilities they occupied, so very close to my home.

This feeling of loss did not last very long. Within a few months, the Korean conflict erupted, and the Van Nuys Air Guard members were unhappy to find themselves called up and heading overseas. These were all family men who did not relish going back to war, flying tired aircraft under extremely difficult conditions.

One offshoot of the Korean War was a great expansion of commercial flying. Charter airlines were springing up to handle the big demand for low-priced coast-to-coast air travel, with several non-scheduled airlines offered trips for $99. I heard there was an acute shortage of qualified pilots to fly for them and drove over to Burbank Airport to check this out.

Burbank Air Terminal was a beehive of activity. Crowds of servicemen jostled their way up to ticket counters, anxious to find a flight home, where they would spend their leave time before heading overseas. The small airport building was bursting at the seams, with fledgling non-scheduled airlines occupying every inch of space, hanging handmade signs on doors to identify themselves.

I walked into the tiny office of one that I will call "Cash & Carry Airlines," that operated three DC-3's, and they welcomed me with open arms when I showed my Airline Transport Rating license. This was quite a change from a few years previous when pilots were getting starvation wages; now these airlines were competing for pilots and paying very well.

Flying for a 'non-sked' was not exactly the kind of airline flying I had dreamed about when I was in the service. Every Air Transport Command pilot wanted to fly for a major airline after discharge. I had thought it would be a snap for me to find a job with American, United, TWA, or Pan Am, with my background in the ATC and my Airline Transport Rating. American Overseas Airlines, a new outfit starting to operate DC-4's on overseas runs, did have an opening, but their salary of $190 a month was unacceptable for a family man, and for flying long hops over oceans. I received an offer to manage a small airport at Revere, but here again, the pay was very low. It seems that anything connected with flying did not pay a living wage, so I dropped the idea.

Now the tables had turned, and "Cash & Carry Airlines" was offering good pay and weekend work. The chief pilot arranged a check ride, and while I was thrilled to be back in the air, I was quite nervous. It was three years since I had flown a C-47, so I expected my first landing to be a rough one. I was so out of practice that I was only guessing my height above the ground when I flared out on final approach, but much to my surprise, I greased it in with a perfect wheel landing. The check pilot was impressed, and in a great hurry, so all he required was two takeoffs and landings, and answers to a few basic questions. Then he said, "You're hired," and I was now on their payroll, flying week-ends from coast to coast. This schedule was very convenient, as I had just started a new business as a manufacturer's representative, and could use the extra income during the startup period. I was surprised at how easy it was to lose my touch, and it took a while to become comfortable in the cockpit. I deliberately flew by the instruments even in clear weather, for practice, and relied on the cooperation of the other pilots to bring me up to good proficiency.

'Non-sked' airlines led a hectic existence, operating like the tramp steamers of old, moving from port to port, as cargoes became available. The Civil Aeronautics Authority (CAA) had very few inspectors and exercised little control over the operations of these new outfits. They went wherever the money took them, and were often negligent in adhering to safety rules. I soon learned that Cash & Carry was a cash-poor outfit, operating on a shoestring.

We flew coast-to-coast with four pilots, because we were flying well over the maximum of eight hours per twenty-four allowed by the CAA I was the fourth pilot of the four on board, but we rotated into the left seat position, so each got his share of takeoffs, landings, and instrument time. The other three pilots were very sharp, having just finished a tour of duty in the Air Transport Command flying the Berlin airlift. The most senior one, 'Captain' Arnold, was designated chief pilot. They were expert instrument pilots, and criticized this "old man" who was now over 30, compared to their average age of 26, but they helped bring me up to date on procedures.

Our first trip was an eye-opener to me. We left Burbank: early Friday for Phoenix with an empty airplane. On arrival, we taxied up to the commercial fuel pump, and waited while our captain went into a conference with the ticket agent who drove out to the airplane to meet us. The agent opened his briefcase on the hood of his car and took out a large bundle of cash, which he handed over. This was the passenger fare money less his agent's commission. We were now able to fill our fuel tanks, paying with cash we had just received, and then taxied to the terminal, where we loaded 21 servicemen passengers. Each was allowed 50 pounds of baggage, but when I hefted some of those duffel bags, I knew we were going to be at least 1000 pounds over our allowable baggage weight.

I soon discovered that we were also overweight on fuel. We filed a flight plan with Kansas City as our destination, showing a fuel load of 600 gallons. When my turn came to fly, I checked the fuel gauges and realized that we had taken off with 800 gallons, which made us another 1600 pounds overweight. The reason for the extra fuel became clear when we approached Kansas City; and the captain called in a change of flight plan extending this leg to St. Louis. This change allowed us to eliminate the Kansas City stop, with its delay, landing fees, and extra fuel consumption. Our next leg took us directly to Washington, D.C.

This overloading was a violation of regulations, and I remarked on it to the chief pilot. He replied, "I think you're mistaken, but why don't you just fly the airplane, and let me take care of the details." The CAA had its hands full with more important matters than policing the operation of all the small charter airlines, so this kind of rule-breaking was widespread.

We flew a triangle, with Washington or New York as the eastern terminal, then to Seattle, and back home to Burbank Sunday evening. We were usually fully loaded, with agents at the terminals finding passengers almost on the spot. We spent the first night in a hotel, but on the second night the off-duty crew slept stretched out in the cockpit walkway, getting stepped on by other crew members.

The other pilots were just young kids to me, and they loved to tell me stories of the Berlin airlift, another high-pressure operation like the Hump, but not as dangerous. Their airlift system was worked out so carefully that the airplanes and crews were in perpetual flight, hauling coal and other commodities to keep Berlin functioning. The pilots suffered pilot fatigue early from this monotonous routine, but were buoyed up with the thought that they were building up hours for a future airline job. This was an old story to me, but I did not want to discourage them. I have often wondered how many of them achieved their goal, or settled for a career on the ground as I had.

My income for flying 7000 miles on a three-day weekend was about $500, based on seven cents per mile, and it came in very handy. Flying two weekends a month was no great strain on me, and I kept this up for six months, until the charter business slowed down. C&C folded up along with most of the non-scheduled airlines, and I gave up commercial flying for good.

As haphazard as their operations were, the charter companies had an excellent safety record. They had a shaky financial history, and many of them merged into larger companies or ended up in bankruptcy. These fledgling companies did a great service to the public, as their competition forced the scheduled airlines to bring fares down to a level that the general public could afford. This eventually proved beneficial to the scheduled airlines, and it was a major factor in creating the great airline industry we know today.

Chapter 48
LIFE'S HUMPS

I found that there are many Humps to cross in life besides the Himalaya Mountains. Sickness, loss of loved ones, and our own mortality are among the disasters that we must face with courage, and I think my time spent flying the Hump was training me for the- extreme stresses of later catastrophic events.

Alzheimer's Disease was the tragedy that pointed its angry finger at my family when my wife, Viola, fell victim in her early 50's. She was diagnosed with this terrible ailment at a time when its existence was virtually unknown to the public. The frustration of watching her gradually lose her memory and her ability to function was agonizing for me and the rest of the family, and we were powerless to stop its progress. It was 1978 and there little information or assistance available on how to cope with the problems of Alzheimer's. Medical advice was to "just take her home and care for her." Day after day I watched her carefully to try to maintain her health as best as I could, and I learned about the problems of care giving from that bitter experience.

The primary caregiver, usually the spouse, was in urgent need of assistance. Some were under such stress from their burden that suicides and desertions were taking place. We searched for outside help and advice, but it appeared that the caregivers had to find their own solutions. I was ready to grasp at any help I could find, as I had become very depressed over Vi's declining condition. She was under nursing care in our home, as she was no longer able to care for herself, and I continued to work.

A small ad in the Los Angeles Times led me to the meeting of a group of caregivers like myself, who were gathering under the auspices of the Andrus Older Adult Center of the University of Southern California to discuss their problems. At the meeting, I heard stories of great despair, of surrender to the problems of care giving, appeals for help, and talk of suicide. We listened to the story of a wife abused by a husband whose dementia made him believe that his spouse was his enemy. We discussed the tragedy of a despondent man who had taken the lives of his wife and himself because he could not stand the strain. I learned of the "sandwich generation," young people bearing the double burden of raising children and caring for an ill parent, often with inadequate funds. I left that first meeting feeling ashamed of my own concerns, which were small compared to what some others were facing.

As we left. I suggested to the meeting director, Karen Riever, that perhaps we should organize into a more formal group to obtain official recognition and aid from public agencies. We needed to learn more about the disease, and hopefully supply information and assistance to families. We had many coffee-and-cake meetings to mull over a plan to do this. We asked many agencies for help and found we were in competition with numerous other disease organizations looking for financial help, publicity, and political support.

We just had to succeed in our quest, as there was no alternative! We organized the California Alzheimer's Disease Association, and shortly afterwards joined up with two similar groups in Chicago and New York to form the national Alzheimer's Association. This has grown from the original three chapters to over two hundred, and is the recognized source for information and help throughout the world. As a charter member and organizer, I am very proud of the assistance we have given to victims, families, and especially to the primary caregivers. There are 4 million victims in this country, which means that at least 20 million people, family and friends, are affected in some way.

I was the primary caregiver for Viola for 20 years until I lost my wonderful wife. The cost of 24-hour nursing care was high, but I continued working at my yacht sales business as an alternative to remaining at home. As first president of the chapter, I made many speeches asking the public to support our activities and to keep an eye open for ways to assist friends who were caregivers, and needed their help. Many caregivers become victims of stress-related diseases such as heart attacks, strokes, and deep depression, but now there are many programs to provide assistance.

Many people have called for help in the 20 years of our Association's existence, and we refer them to local chapters and support groups, of which there-are now thousands across the country. They can discuss their problems with other people who have experience, and receive one-on-one counseling from professionals. Callers often ask how to face their loneliness when the ill spouse is placed in a nursing home. So many face this unexpected turn in their lives that we have come to regard loneliness as another disease. Most spouses wish to return to a normal social life, but often experience guilt at the thought of the institutionalized spouse. We recommend an active life style to counteract this stressful situation.

No cure for Alzheimer's has been discovered yet. Our Association works at a two-pronged attack on this disease: supporting research to solve the riddle of the disease, and providing services to families coping with the disease. To quote our founding national president, Jerry Stone, "There are no hopeless situations, just people without hope." Our programs give hope to everyone.

Jim and Vi

41563794R00186

Made in the USA
Middletown, DE
07 April 2019